The Poetic Achievement of EZRA POUND

MICHAEL ALEXANDER

The Poetic Achievement
of EZRA POUND

UNIVERSITY OF CALIFORNIA PRESS
Berkeley and Los Angeles

University of California Press
Berkeley and Los Angeles

© Michael Alexander 1979

ISBN 0-520-03739-1
Library of Congress Catalog Card Number: 78-59449

Printed in Great Britain

For EILEEN

Contents

I ask a wreath which will not crush my head.

Homage to Sextus Propertius

Preface

The incomplete appreciation of Ezra Pound's poetry among informed readers of poetry in English has always seemed to me something of an anomaly, even allowing for the political controversies which in part explain that incompleteness. Having enjoyed and admired this poetry, and having been stimulated and sustained in reading it over twenty years, I offer this re-reading in the hope that it may be of some help to such readers, if only in dispelling the notion that all Pound's poetry is inaccessibly difficult. My intention is to present, in a manageable volume, an introductory critical survey of Pound's verse as a whole, including the translations. This purpose has meant that I have been less concerned explicitly to relate his poetry to his critical ideas. Nor have I been able to take formal stock here of the growing body of criticism and scholarship on Pound, much as I have learned from it.[1]* Further growth in Pound studies can be expected as his papers at Yale are investigated. I hope, however, that an approach such as this may be opportune at this time in helping to sort out just how much, and exactly what, of his poetry, may form a permanent 'adjunct to the Muses' diadem'.[2]

I assume that the reader will have available the *Collected Shorter Poems* (or the collected *Personae* of 1926) and the complete *Cantos*; though most of the poems discussed appear also in selected editions.[3] I also assume that the reader may be more familiar with the earlier work; but very little is taken for granted in the way of prior knowledge of the *Cantos*. I offer a general introduction to and assessment of the *Cantos*, without pretending to do justice to their contents. Any fullness of commentary on these contents is beyond the scope of this study, though the critical questions raised by the limitless reference of the poem are not neglected. The Select Bibliography and Notes indicate where further help may be sought.

After two introductory chapters, the plan of the book follows Pound's order of publication. The first chapter briefly summarizes Pound's career and the state of his critical reputation at the time of his death. The second offers appreciations and readings of poems from successive stages of his writing, with a view to suggesting, at a simple level, the ways in which Pound's poems work—a primary emphasis. This second chapter, and the modest suggestions it puts forward, are intended for

* Superior figures refer to the Notes at p. 229.

the reader who knows some of Pound's poems but is chary of specialized critical exegesis. The chapter can be skipped by those resistant to lengthy readings of poems, and by those familiar with Pound. The remainder of the book pursues a chronological if selective course through Pound's published verse, including his translations. The *Cantos* take the lion's share of attention, but I also found myself pleasantly detained by *Lustra* and *Cathay*. Space is allotted to Pound's poetry according to what I judge to be its usefulness as a foundation to an uninitiated British reader, and this may not coincide with the current reputation of its various phases. Thus, attention is paid to undervalued shorter poems at the expense of *Mauberley*, partly on grounds of accessibility. Likewise the reader is accompanied slowly up to the *Pisan Cantos*, whereafter he is left to shift more for himself.

I may add that in essaying an introduction to poetry which I deeply admire, I have not avoided critical judgement. An attitude of passive respect before so large a Poetical Works would be uncongenial to the spirit of their author and of little service to his reader. In the controversies surrounding one whom T. S. Eliot called a superior artist[4] I have felt constrained to offer no hostages, and to make my critical preferences and reasons plain.

Intending an appreciation of the whole of Pound's poetry, I have not been able to provide as much as might have been desirable in the way of explication and annotation. I therefore acknowledge with a double gratitude the help I have received from the writers on Pound mentioned in the Notes and Select Bibliography. I am deeply obliged to the poet himself and his circle for their great courtesy and hospitality. More private thanks go to William Cookson, who printed some of this book in *Agenda*; to colleagues such as Martin Gray and Robert Rehder for encouragement and advice; to Alasdair Macrae and Arthur Cooper, who read chapters in typescript; to the patient secretaries of the University of Stirling; to my editors, Giles de la Mare and Catharine Carver; and to my wife Eileen, the true repository of the variorum versions of this Penelopean piece of writing, and its dedicatee.

Stirling   M.J.A.
February 1978

1. Introductory

Ezra Pound died in Venice on All Saints' Day 1972 at the beginning of his eighty-eighth year, leaving as his chief testament his prodigious *Cantos*, begun in London over fifty-five years before. The vitality of Pound's contribution to the arts before the Great War, and the re-direction he gave to poetry during his years in Kensington, are acknow-ledged. His own poetry, however, has received less unanimous recognition, and is commonly not much considered, in Britain at least. It seems that the active English poetic tradition has still to come to terms with Pound's poetic output as a whole. While in America scholars are establishing the detailed references of the remoter Cantos, in Britain a wider apprecia-tion even of his more accessible poetry has not yet arrived.

There has certainly been a growing number of studies of Pound in recent years, of biography, literary history and scholarly exegesis as well as of criticism.[1] Yet in Britain it was clear that postwar controversy was abating only when such full-length studies as George Dekker's *Sailing After Knowledge* (1963) and Donald Davie's *Ezra Pound: Poet as Sculptor* (1964) took the natural ground of criticism that the qualities and merits of his poetry were things to be discussed and, so far as possible, demonstrated, rather than assumed. Despite all the further work of Kenner, Davie and others, however, no real idea of the nature of Pound's effort as a whole, and especially of the *Cantos*, has won acceptance in Britain, outside a restricted if enthusiastic following. This was clear from the British literary press at the time of the poet's death, as in the memorial pieces of Connolly, Alvarez and Davie—all admiring, though well this side of idolatry—and a *Times* obituary which was uneasily divided, as this sentence suggests: 'Of all American poets, perhaps only Whitman was so silly, so noble, so eloquent, so touchingly self-convinced and redundant, and, alas, so great.'[2]

Pound wrote several epitaphs for himself, of which *Hugh Selwyn Mauberley* is the most elaborate. It was 'a farewell to London',[3] published in 1920, the twelfth and last year of his siege. Beginning as a kind of *Times Literary Supplement* obituary upon himself, or a parody of himself in the person of its aesthetic hero, it grew into a satire on the War and on postwar London's literary values, and was later to be hailed by Eliot as 'a great poem'.[4] Pound's resilience in his second exile was touched by the chagrin which had attended his leaving America thirteen years before, and was to visit him again in his last years, receiving open expression at Pisa:

> As a lone ant from a broken ant-hill
> from the wreckage of Europe, ego scriptor.

(Canto 76)

Among the ironies of *Mauberley* one can hear a note of speculation about the author's own ultimate rank among the poets, for example in the conclusion to 'The Age Demanded':

> Non-esteem of self-styled 'his betters'
> Leading, as he well knew,
> To his final
> Exclusion from the world of letters.

The last line of the opening epitaph is the summing-up of a judge, albeit an imaginary English judge:

> ... the case presents
> No adjunct to the Muses' diadem.

One could do worse than to take that last line—ironic as it is—as a starting point for a study such as this.

Before reopening that 'case', the relations of Ezra Pound and the British literary world can be very briefly sketched. The years of Pound's conquest (or corruption) of several cadres of the poetic avant-garde were, from the Muses' point of view, wonderfully fruitful, and he is secure in his fame as the counsellor of Yeats, the discoverer of Eliot and the impresario of Joyce, not to mention instigations less notable only than these. Recalling the glorious days of the *English Review*, Ford wrote of Pound, 'In a very short time he had taken charge of me, the review and finally of London.'[5] *Most important influence since Wordsworth* was the *Observer*'s caption to its memorial piece;[6] yet the influence's own poetry did not take root here. It is easy to forget, now that Eliot is taught in every British school, how protracted has been resistance to the modern.

In the U.S. Army's Detention Training Center at Pisa in 1945, Pound's thoughts returned to London and to his old friends there: Yeats, Ford, Eliot, Lewis, Orage, Major Douglas. . . . But in the years between, Pound's ardour for artistic perfection, mediated with an amused minimum of urbanity, had found few echoes in the British bosom.

In the Twenties, Eliot stood by *Mauberley*; but both he and Yeats had reservations about the *Cantos*, and others had less reason to suspend judgement. Selections duly appeared in anthologies, but in the Thirties modern poetry took a very different direction, particularly in England, where Auden led English poetry away from ambitious new forms and from the impersonal, the encyclopaedic, the mythic or the sublime. Pound had been in Italy since 1924, and impressed by Mussolini. For the British, Pound was henceforward a peripheral and eccentric figure, at best a Browning, more often a cross between Landor and Carlyle. Then, unable to return to the U.S.A., he made the disastrous wartime broadcasts on Rome Radio which deeply alienated Allied opinion.[7] Charged with treason in 1945, he was declared of unsound mind and unfit to stand trial, and his detention for twelve years in St. Elizabeth's mental hospital, Washington, completed his removal from the consciousness of a London mystified by Eliot's plays and moved by Dylan Thomas. Some attention was paid when the *Pisan Cantos* were published in 1949. But the values espoused by Philip Larkin and English poets in the later Fifties were scarcely Poundian. Indifference and bafflement are today more common than hostility, though for some Pound was simply a Fascist and an anti-Semite, not a poet at all. Academic appreciation has made progress with the studies that followed in the wake of Hugh Kenner.[8] More generally, an opening-up of British poetry to America, to verse in translation, and to its own history in this century make it easier for us to see Pound's poetry. Yet to be ushered into posterity as the greatest literary influence since Wordsworth suggests that Pound's chief interest is to literary historians. Though Pound is said to have altered the course of poetry in this century, most, even among the interested parties, still do not know quite what to make of him.

If Pound's poetry is the chosen subject, it must be at the expense of his other activities. His apostolic contributions to letters and to the arts, through criticism, through encouragement, through the works of others, are part of the record, and so find no room here. Nor, except inadequately and as ancillaries, have I been able to pay attention to his biography, politics and economics, though these enter the discussion of the *Cantos*. The anti-Semitic and Fascist sympathies expressed in the middle Cantos cannot be overlooked; these delusions had a destructive effect on the poetry. Pound's treatment at Pisa, the treason charge, the twelve years of 'mental care' and the legal disabilities and press-ganging which he suffered for the fifteen years that remained to him, were, however, nemesis enough. The strife stirred up has deflected readers from poetry which rewards attention in ways that no other poetry of our time can do.

The poetic output of Ezra Pound is very large. Between 1907 and 1920 he published several small volumes, now collected.[9] During the War he began on 'that great forty-year epic' which he had proposed to himself before 1908 and which was to occupy him to the end.[10] The earlier verse is marked by a change from 'romance' to a concern with contemporary manners which culminates in the two sequences, *Homage to Sextus Propertius* and *Mauberley*. The *Cantos* themselves divide into the first thirty (chiefly about the Renaissance); the Cantos of the Thirties (Italian, American and Chinese history); the *Pisan Cantos*, partly autobiographical; and the three last volumes, *Rock-Drill*, *Thrones* and *Drafts and Fragments*. There are also translations and imitations, most of which are stations on the main line of progress, for example *Cathay* and *Propertius*. The *Cantos* themselves contain translations, for example from Homer in Canto 1 and from Cavalcanti in Canto 36. It is often remarked that Pound's poems are translations and his translations are original poems. But most of the later translations appeared outside the *Cantos*, notably *The Classic Anthology Defined by Confucius*, and his version of Sophocles' *Women of Trachis*. Such was the sequence of Ezra Pound's poetic output, revolving from 'romance' to politics and back again to a splintered realization of 'romance'.

A single approach to such a gargantuan body of work cannot be entirely satisfactory. But Pound's true achievement will benefit from an attempt to define it and to discriminate within it; and such an attempt may also help to make Pound's work more accessible to a famished British tradition in need of 'scaled invention' and 'true artistry', of a larger world of ideas and objective reference, and of a more profound self-dedication in her poets. America too, though she has recently paid Pound a more honourable and extensive attention, may need to see him more critically.[11]

As for the Muses, it might be said without anticipating too far, that though one cannot without preamble claim for Pound a major work of unflawed greatness, yet he repeatedly achieved the rarest standards of poetic excellence and invention. Indeed his imaginative writing is so frequently touched with greatness that only Yeats and Eliot seem of a clearly superior order of magnitude among contemporaries. 'Greatness' —even if, as Pound noted, it is a Victorian word—is not an easy one to do without. But poetic courage and largeness, sustained creative enterprise, integrity in his art, the intense reflection of the light vouchsafed, these are not qualities lightly to be despised.

Pound's original sensibility and poetic character preserved a remarkable constancy throughout his career, in spite of the equally constant developments of technique, and in spite also of his changes of fortune, of manner and of subject-matter. The next chapter investigates Pound's sensibility by looking at the kind of poetry he wrote. What sort of poetic achievement did he intend? A look at representative poems from different stages of his career may suggest some indications. Thereafter this exploration while remaining selective can become more chronological.

2. Examples

'MAKE IT NEW, day by day make it new', was one of Pound's mottoes, taken from a Shang emperor's bath tub.[1] Each of his poems will have to make it new with its new reader, with or without the notes offered by educational suppliers. Pound hated annotation, but his text now attracts an annotation as thick as Milton's. As the poet's father, Homer Pound, is said to have remarked to Max Beerbohm: 'There just ain't nothing that boy don't know.'[2] This notorious allusiveness is perhaps the chief obstacle to his being more widely read. I hope to show, however, that it is a misconception that he is a poet available only to the learned, and in this belief shall approach a handful of representative poems, with a paragraph of general preface.

Pound was himself a learned man, though a virtuoso rather than an exact scholar; he did not work in a field. He was, however, very widely, intensely and curiously read in literature and history. 'Curiosity' is perhaps the key word. He was an enthusiastic popularizer as well as a savant, and is held in some suspicion by specialists in each of the ten languages that he translated from. Pound was a passionate amateur of literature, a dilettante in scholarship, in old senses of these words, although lacking in the indolence associated with them, and dedicated to the profession of poetry. This pattern used to be common among men of letters—Ford was an example—and even among dons in the days when the Arts at university meant 'humaner letters' and literature meant poetry. An acquaintance with the quotable in European poetry and cultural history could then more confidently have been relied on among the educated than it can in a graduate seminar. Pound's obscurity is thus partly due to changes in what is thought to be worth knowing; he was not, for the lettered reader of his young day, a particularly arcane poet. It must be granted, however, that in old age the poet's allusive obliqueness developed into an elliptical and idiosyncratic manner of reference. Yet, when all the missing information has been supplied, the essence of his poetry remains visionary, mythical or archetypal, and for an appreciation of this kind of poetry, popular in the last century, not so very much learning is initially required, though some literary education is certainly presupposed.

Pound had Donne's 'hydroptic, immoderate desire of human learning and languages',[3] and his version of history is heterodox, but an under-

standing of his poetic truth relies more on a lively capacity for aesthetic
experience and a gift for imaginative affinities than on breadth or depth
of learning—he relies rather on quickness, and a willingness to learn.
Pound communicates a Rabelaisian enjoyment of literacy and a passionate
care for the evolution and direction of Western culture: in this crucial
sense he is certainly a poet for the educated reader. The emphasis in
this chapter will, however, be on the primary question of how the poems
work for the responsive reader rather than on what that reader needs to
know before he approaches them.

The poems taken to introduce Pound are 'The Tree', 'Meditatio',
'Fan-Piece', 'Poem by the Bridge at Ten-Shin', the last section of
Propertius, and Cantos 13 and 81—a choice leaning, admittedly, towards
brevity and simplicity. The reading of these samples should produce
some usable general ideas about the characteristic modes of Pound's
poetry.

'The Tree' has stood first in the many collections of his poems that
Pound published after 1908:

> I stood still and was a tree amid the wood,
> Knowing the truth of things unseen before;
> Of Daphne and the laurel bow
> And that god-feasting couple old
> That grew elm-oak amid the wold.
> 'Twas not until the gods had been
> Kindly entreated, and been brought within
> Unto the hearth of their heart's home
> That they might do this wonder thing;
> Nathless I have been a tree amid the wood
> And many a new thing understood
> That was rank folly to my head before.

As an overture, 'The Tree' does not have the enchantment of

> The woods of Arcady are dead,
> And over is their antique joy. . .

nor the insinuation of

> Let us go then, you and I,
> When the evening is spread out against the sky
> Like a patient etherised upon a table.

Pound was not to find his voice as quickly as did Yeats or Eliot; in old
age he dismissed the poems of this period as 'stale creampuffs'.[4]

The language of 'The Tree' is indeed dusty, the mode a little musty, yet it is a charming poem. It is a slight enough gesture, but well made, and an appropriate gesture to welcome guests to Pound's world.

The magic in which it deals is familiar enough: the imaginative identification with a natural thing leads to illumination, an illumination expressed in fantasy. One tree perceived by the rapt poet 'is' a girl, another pair of trees has grown together, and the dreamer now under- stands the stories of metamorphosis in Ovid.[5] This is a primitive version of Marvell's thesis in 'The Garden', that

> Apollo hunted Daphne so
> Only that she might laurel grow.

Laurel is the emblem of poetry, so that the myths, according to Marvell, are only the inventions of poets. Pound, on the other hand, claims that whereas in Ovid's story Philemon and Baucis earned their immortality together by their kindness to the weary travellers who were Mercury and Jove in disguise, his own vision of natural forms was granted by virtue only of his poet's act of 'becoming' a tree. Pound distinguishes and confronts these two kinds of transformation: by changing himself into a tree, the poet is enabled to see the gods changing human life into the perpetual forms of organic life. Such metamorphosis of perceived natural objects is Pound's usual way into poetry. His imagination was extraordinarily volatile; but equally his capacity to distinguish imagina- tive modes was extremely acute. The coda of the poem is a staged gesture from Browning; but the dramatic persona who speaks the beginning is near to its maker's 'heart's home'. It is by an act as conscious as that of Milton's 'Lycidas' or Marvell's 'The Garden', that Daphne makes her famous bow here; she is never to be far away from Pound's imagina- tion.

But I begin with 'The Tree' not merely to show the iconoclast of *Blast* propitiating nymphs at his début; it is rather that the author of this gentle conceit, this Pre-Raphaelite treatment of an Ovidian allusion, seems—unlike, say, William Allingham—to be in good earnest. Pound asserts that he has seen nymphs; he takes the *Metamorphoses* seriously enough to wish to explain how his experience differs from Ovid's. Sensing the vital, almost sexual, sympathy between divine, human and natural forms, he makes himself the intent indicator of this sympathy, a pointer. Animism and pantheism, of almost precisely this sort, had been in the air for fifty years. Victorians believed in fairies, Edwardians in fauns—Forster and Lawrence, for example, saw caperings among the flora, Forster with a *frisson*, Lawrence without anxiety as to whether it was 'rank folly' to anyone's head.

'Rank folly' betrays the date of 'The Tree' as clearly as a growth-ring. The diction is archaic, though not consistently so; if words are old-fashioned, their combinations are picturesque, as in 'god-feasting' and 'elm-oak'. Equally, the movement of the iambics is often predictable, though the emphases created in the first line are dramatic. Indeed, the rhythmic and syntactic confidence with which these conventional materials are handled raises them into something very definite. Once detected, the thought of the poem interests any reader who considers the significance (as well as the pronunciation) of its pivot, the word 'Nathless'. Olde English of this sort may conceal the poem's charm, as well as what may be called its thought. Yet the poem runs from beginning to end as a single utterance, a complete gesture.

'Meditatio', from *Blast* (1914), shows us the seer in a less rapt attitude. *Lustra* sparkles with epigrams, some out of the stable of Martial, others, like this one, more light-hearted:

When I carefully consider the curious habits of dogs
I am compelled to conclude
That man is the superior animal.

When I consider the curious habits of man
I confess, my friend, I am puzzled.

It is risky to expose such trifles singly to the neutral eye of criticism, for it is in constellation that they kindle their proper mood. This example does not have the asperity of Pound's classical epigrams—it is too high-spirited. Its representative value lies in that, although different in style and intention, it resembles 'The Tree' in resting upon a comparison of the seen with the imagined. The process of comparison is here made with an elaborate judiciousness that is itself the main source of comedy. The fun that Pound gets out of his mandarin speaker almost obscures the Gallic point of the joke—if indeed the point is not that the sceptical speaker, holding the 'dogs' in his forceps, admits himself to be a member, however cultivated, of the species that prefers to consider its own curious sexual habits moral rather than animal. The enjoyment of a manner for its own sake—of *blague*—affords most of the pleasure to be derived from such meditations. The alliteration creates the contrasts which fill the sketch with suggestion and vocal emphasis: the precise Jamesian first sentence balanced by deprecatory resignation in the other; the Latin collapsing into the Englishness of 'dogs' and 'puzzled'. Pound here assumes a reader with enough nous to pick up all the implications of the comparison himself, without even such stage directions as 'Nathless'.

The other epigram is of the romantic variety in which Pound had from the beginning shown his affinity with classical lyric poets. 'Fan-

Piece, for her Imperial Lord' is one of the Chinese fragments which Pound produced before reading Fenollosa and writing *Cathay*. This miniature again relies upon implication for its effect, dropped into the pool of the reader's mind, the details left to unfold by themselves. To 'explain' such a poem is, in the Chinese phrase, drawing legs on a snake. But the legs pencilled in will drop off, and when such poems are encountered again their leglessness may awaken more hospitable feelings.

The title informs us that this is a poem inscribed on her fan by a girl who has lost the favour of the Emperor. In Chinese (Pound is adapting from Giles[6]) this forms part of a large class of occasional epigraph verse, written literally *on* a thousand personal things, where fitness and elegance are all that might be looked for.

> O fan of white silk,
> 　　clear as frost on the grass-blade,
> You also are laid aside.

The starting point of the poem is that the girl and the fan are both eventually to be 'laid aside'. Any decent translation must convey this *tu quoque*, this resemblance, with its emotional potential. But the precise realization of this potential depends upon what becomes the second line of Pound's version—the middle term of the syllogism. 'Clear as frost on the grass-blade' is an example of Pound's idea that 'the natural object is always the *adequate* symbol'.[7] The 'clearness' of the silk (and the blamelessness of the girl) intervene between the apostrophe to the fan and what is to be said to it. Both frost and grass-blade are of course many things besides 'clear', and here lies the secret: fresh, delicate, minute, pristine, lowly, common, natural, short-lived. This family of properties—and the microscopic attentiveness that they invite—is transferred both to the silk fan and to the discarded imperial concubine in her 'silks and fine array' who now writes on her fan this verse. Like the grass, the silk and the girl are both wild and cultivated.

The initial point of resemblance, that both fan and girl are pretty things to be discarded at will, becomes, through association with the frosted grass-blade, the natural centre of more wide-ranging affinities. By flighting his triple juxtaposition so precisely, by timing the cadence of this fleeting thought, Pound creates a tension, a field, which elicits a considerable radiation of feeling. In this appeal to the reader's sensibility, however, there is richness but not, strictly speaking, any ambiguity. Not that the many suggestions latent in such a poem, its auguries of innocence and experience, can be exhausted.

A further aspect of 'Fan-Piece' might be mentioned, its lack of self-pity: the girl is saluting a companion in misfortune. 'For her Imperial

Lord' may make her verse a memento of his inconstancy, even of his
mortality. But what she says acquiesces with dignity in 'the common
fate of all things rare'.

This romantic epigram or cameo, thus crudely enlarged, is helpful in
identifying Pound's sensibility; not for its construction nor as a sample
of his attunement to another cultural mode, but because it is a beautiful
and touching poem. It is slight and simple, but so is Sappho's poem about
the topmost apple on the tree. It was Milton who said that poetry is
'simple, sensuous and passionate'.[8] In the reaction of his generation
against the Palgravian taste for lyric gems plus rhetorical water, Pound
helped Eliot to popularize the idea that poetry, like the novel, should
offer a more adult response to sides of life beyond the compass of the
purely lyric mode, something more robust, intelligent, complex and
critical of society and self. That was sixty years ago, but the subsequent
academic establishment of this view led to the triumph of the 'teachable'
poem—perforce a 'complex' one—and the neglect of all songs, even
Shakespeare's.

Pound, then, is not to blame for the impoverishment of the lyric
strain in modern poetry. 'Fan-Piece' does not tell the reader what to
feel and how to feel it, but it remains a lyric poem intended to move,
though the degree of its eloquence depends upon percipience as well as
susceptibility. Pound here demands an intelligent imagination. Blake
gazed at the world in a grain of sand, Pound allows us to catch the
transcendent in the trivial.

Some readers are left cold by any essay in a foreign cultural mode.
'What have the ephemeral feelings of a discarded concubine, expressed
in the conventional emblemisms of a closed courtly society, to do with
me or the Spirit of the Age?' To the demand for 'relevance' one can
reply that the freshness and precision of Pound's second line show that
the use of natural analogies to express universal human situations
remains a living convention. As for courtliness, the poem shows that
indirect and oblique means can express deep feeling. Such a transposition
of this characteristic and attractive human gesture into another human
voice, in another time and another language, enlarges our sympathies.

'Fan-Piece' suggests Pound's liking for cultural conventions that
express emotion indirectly by the presentation of objects in relation
with each other, by implication rather than by exclamation. For the
effect of the poem is more emotional than aesthetic. Precious as such a
poem has been made by 'the weight of the gold removed', it lives only in
so far as it moves the reader.

'Poem by the Bridge at Ten-Shin', from *Cathay* (1915), is translated
from Li Po, most famous of Chinese poets, via the notes of the American

scholar Fenollosa. I approach it here simply as an anonymous poem, postponing for the moment the issues raised by Pound's policies as a translator.

> March has come to the bridge head,
> Peach boughs and apricot boughs hang over a thousand gates,
> At morning there are flowers to cut the heart,
> And evening drives them on the eastward-flowing waters.
> Petals are on the gone waters and on the going,
> > And on the back-swirling eddies,
> But to-day's men are not the men of the old days,
> Though they hang in the same way over the bridge-rail.
>
> The sea's colour moves at the dawn
> And the princes still stand in rows, about the throne,
> And the moon falls over the portals of Sei-go-yo,
> And clings to the walls and the gate-top.
> With head gear glittering against the cloud and sun,
> The lords go forth from the court, and into far borders.
> They ride upon dragon-like horses,
> Upon horses with head-trappings of yellow metal,
> And the streets make way for their passage.
> > Haughty their passing,
> Haughty their steps as they go in to great banquets,
> To high halls and curious food,
> To the perfumed air and girls dancing,
> To clear flutes and clear singing;
> To the dance of the seventy couples;
> To the mad chase through the gardens.
> Night and day are given over to pleasure
> And they think it will last a thousand autumns,
> > Unwearying autumns.
> For them the yellow dogs howl portents in vain,
> And what are they compared to the lady Riokushu,
> > That was cause of hate!
> Who among them is a man like Han-rei
> > Who departed alone with his mistress,
> With her hair unbound, and he his own skiffsman!

Quite apart from the views he later formed of the ideogram, Pound took readily to Chinese poetry for other reasons, chief of which was perhaps that he found in it an habitual and instinctive use of the natural world as an expressive analogy for the human. Such a use may be universal, but the unallegorical directness of the old Chinese conventions caught Pound's imagination. This poem turns upon the contrast between the beauty of nature, which passes and returns, and the glories of the court, which are artificially kept up:

> At morning there are flowers to cut the heart,
> And evening drives them on the eastward-flowing waters.

But,

> Night and day are given over to pleasure
> And they think it will last a thousand autumns,
> Unwearying autumns.

The parallels and contrasts are established in the opening lines:

> Peach boughs and apricot boughs hang over a thousand gates
>
> .   .   .   .   .
>
> But to-day's men are not the men of the old days,
> Though they hang in the same way over the bridge-rail.

Ideally, no doubt, the imperial court itself should reflect the glories of nature:

> The sea's colour moves at the dawn
> And the princes still stand in rows, about the throne. . . .

But the splendour of the court is, as the development of the poem makes increasingly clear, an empty show. The climax is a satisfying double comparison: the pursuit of pleasure is measured against the real power of the lady Riokushu's beauty, and the deportment of the lords going in to dinner with the decisive action of Han-rei. The public import of the poem is transmitted through these contemptuous comparisons as plainly as in Lear's 'Take physic, pomp!' or Pound's own 'Pull down thy vanity!'[9] Yet the poem as a whole is full and balanced; it has not the one-sidedness of our own Augustan satire, where the positives often emerge only by implication. The celebration of natural beauty and order in the opening of the poem, which gives an edge to the poet's scorn for spineless luxury at the close, is equally as controlled and passionate.

Formally, this balance must of course derive from the original, but the translator has actually realized the balance of feelings; the opening is as evocative and poignant as the close is indignant. One has only to read aloud these opening and closing lines to realize their dynamism as speech, whether ample and regretful or laconic and scornful. A detailed analysis of the stratagems adopted by Pound to control the rhythm and the tone would be out of place, but the reality is there for any reader; and these long lines, with their weary, widely spaced emphases, develop considerable rhetorical and emotive power. The indications of tone almost amount to stage directions, however undeveloped the histrionic impulse of the reader. By making the words get up off the page like this, a translator is abolishing the gulfs of incomprehension that divide cultures and make most translations so unreal, and all Chinese poems look inscrutably and tonelessly alike.

This feat is not mere ventriloquism, as talk of Pound's technique may suggest. He does not simply rehearse, in an English free from solecism, the dictionary meaning of the poet's words; he positively inhabits the poet's mind. The *Cantos* make clear that Pound does indeed share the values of this poem whole-heartedly. Thirty years later in Canto 81, 'Pull down thy vanity' is a sermon preached on this theme: 'Learn of the green world what can be thy place'.[10] He opposes natural beauty, growth, splendour and feeling to artificial hedonism, grandeur and aestheticism; he has an old American preference for the natural and the unpretentious, and honours the uncalculated act—'character isolated by a deed'. The crisp flourish of the last lines creates that magnanimous quality he throws up again and again in his Provençal imitations and in the *Cantos*. Curiously, the diction and syntax of the last two lines are, under the microscope, mannered, involved, full of a translator's hybrid idioms and idiosyncrasies. The repetition of 'who' risks clumsiness; 'departed' is *outré*; 'skiffsman', on its own, as Saxonico-vigorous as anything in Landor's prose. However, a poem's last words cannot be thus isolated, and we have learned to trust this voice earlier.

The flourish of the ending is present throughout the poem, most obviously in the arabesques of the hanging half-lines improvised outside the frame of the original Chinese stanzas, still visible beneath the freedom of the verse.

'And on the back-swirling eddies' notably has the effect of a last-minute observation, an improvisation which only brings out the symmetry of the much-interlaced stanza, where 'boughs' balance 'boughs', 'men' 'men', 'morning' 'evening' and 'hang' 'hang'. Here 'going' complements 'gone', and the third term of the formula breaks the symmetry. This same life shows in 'cut' and 'drives'—words with the smack of a personal idiom. The idiom, as the last couplet of the stanza reveals on inspection, is Pound's synthetic rural American dialect—not yet at its Uncle Remus richest, but already drawling out 'hang' to recall to us the more natural hang of the peach and apricot boughs. Pound observed that Pope's version of the *Iliad* 'has at least the merit of translating Homer into *something*';[11] here he has done Li Po's poem into a recognizable something.

The sentiments are, by and large, the sentiments of Li Po, but the voice is the voice of Ezra.

To see what a translator gains by decision and vigour, one may consider that the success of the final rhetorical question is not seriously affected by our utter ignorance of the lady Riokushu and of Han-rei. The meaning is unmistakable, because the poem has created a world of coherent values and the context makes clear what the function of these names is to be. Pope wrote in *The Dunciad*:

> Proceed, great days! till Learning fly the shore,
> Till Birch shall blush with noble blood no more,
> Till Thames see Eton's sons for ever play,
> Till Westminster's whole year be holiday;
> Till Isis' Elders reel, their Pupils' sport;
> And Alma Mater lye dissolv'd in Port!

(III, 329–34)[12]

Peculiarly rich though these references may be for the English, a literate student of English as a foreign language could scarcely miss the drift of them. Li Po's poem may contain as dense a cluster of literary and social references as these lines of Pope, but the translator has rendered superfluous the prior possession of the items of cultural information. It is a contention of this study that many of Pound's references in his own poetry have this kind of self-evident exemplary function.

As a translation, 'By the Bridge' is no evidence of Pound's ability to construct a longer poem. However, the long lines, which are not at all Chinese, are an invention of Pound's. They have a confident rhythm, the effect of which is not unlike that of the Psalms, syntactically patterned verse paraphrased for recitation. The measure is not based on feet but on the line itself as a unit of sense, reinforced by a parallelism of syntax, of phrasing or of sound within the lines. There are three or four heavy stresses within the long line, but it is the equivalence, or notional equivalence, of the lines themselves which creates the feeling of antiphon and response, of Biblical repetition and variation upon a theme. Now that the reaction against things Victorian has run its course, the words 'incantation' and 'mood' will not suggest a mindless wallowing, except to a criticism actually suspicious of the musical power of poetry. The plainchant lines of *Cathay* allow attention both to their sense and to their appeal to the senses.

In 'Poem by the Bridge' the natural detail of the opening is at once fresh and refined. The credit of this is Li Po's; but Pound's receptivity is equal to the task and his powers of realization show in his finding a verse form that without the economy of the original is able to create its feeling, and also in his images, which have a rare sharpness. The positive first line opens into a delighted recognition of profusion in the second; then the fullness of the poet's response is checked by his acceptance of natural process. The whole quatrain creates a spring of piercing clarity and completeness. This is neither descriptive poetry nor on the other hand the 'poetry of objects', for the emotions and attitudes of a speaker are firmly intimated. The classic simplicities of Li Po—the qualities he shares with a simile in Homer—are more easily retained in translation than his freshness to the senses; yet Pound achieves an aesthetic, and not merely a representational, impression. This puts him into a very small class of translators.

Dr. Syntax may hold that the translator's duty is to be accurate (i.e. to the sense) and that he should leave originality to the original poem. It can be argued that Pound is putting his rhythmic invention and his photosensitivity at the service of the exotic glamour of Chinese imagery in order to produce elegant pastiche. But this translation, without reference to its great original—as for most of us it must for ever remain—contains all that is needed to confute such a view.

'By the Bridge' certainly makes use of exotic imagery, but the glamour is found in the middle section of satire against the court; hedonism and the search for curious sensation are rebuked by the ordered beauty of nature and by the authentic splendour of Riokushu and Han-rei. A decadent refinement of sensation is scarcely the tenor of a poem governed by a range of feelings which holds the moral above the picturesque, and finds their relation by the criterion of what is active and natural.

The charge of pastiche can only be answered by an appeal to the reader's experience of the poem. Does it work as a poem in its own right, hanging together by its own laws, or does it stand only by virtue of certain notions we have about China and by the reflected glory of Li Po? Does the poem read as a dramatic utterance, fully integrated and artistically independent, like Yeats's version of Swift's epitaph or Ben Jonson's 'To Celia'?

The chief evidence for the poem's naturalization in English lies in its harmonics; its every detail and implication seem all of a piece. 'Eastward-flowing', for example, had a similar effect to the epithet φυσίζοος, 'life-giving', in Book III of the *Iliad*, the epithet admired by Ruskin for its application to the earth, where, unknown to her, Helen's brothers lay dead: 'dead in the *life-giving* earth of their own Lacedaemon'.[13] Here the petals are borne away after their one day's life towards the next day's sunrise. What one finds at its most developed in Shakespeare is true also of this poem, that every verbal suggestion, whether physical, moral, or metaphysical, however slight, seems to grow naturally from a preexistent unity and, when pursued to its ramifications in the reader's experience, leads back into the world of the poem. In other words, the poem is an organic thing coherent in its smallest manifestations. 'Back-swirling', though at first a visible characteristic of running water and then a suggestive completion of the past–present–future formula announced by 'gone' and 'going', is ultimately a complement to 'eastward-flowing'. The petals will return next year, but 'to-day's men are not the men of the old days'; the generations of men, in this respect, are not like the generations of leaves. 'The sea's colour moves at the dawn' (a most Poundian line) has all the precision, reticence and subtlety of what it describes, and seems to invest itself with the same objective status. The 'throne' in the next line should echo the sense as well as the sound of the 'dawn': the Son of Heaven should ideally fulfil the mandate of heaven. But whereas the dawn does not deteriorate, the princes merely 'glitter' in the emperor's light. Each word amplifies the comparison of human and natural forms that the translator has realized as the fulcrum of this poem. The great force of the last couplet relies on the splendid profusion created by the natural complex of petals and eastward-flowing waters at the beginning. The 'hair unbound' of the woman and the heroic self-reliance of Han-rei have the prodigal energy of the water and of March. The harmonics of the poem are too vigorously realized for it to be dismissed as pastiche. Of the poems looked at, this translation is, interestingly, the least dependent upon literary ideas.

Of all Pound's unorthodox transactions with other literatures it is the *Homage to Sextus Propertius* (dated 1917) which most irritated the stipendiary guides to Parnassus. The odium is undeserved, because it proceeds from misunderstanding. Pound's *Propertius* is not a translation in the narrow sense of that word but a homage paid by one man to another; Pound is saluting a kindred spirit. Finding in some of the love elegies of the Roman poet an unsuspected irony and an exaltation of private over public life—a poetic priority that he felt the need of in 1917— Pound selected these elements in Propertius and drafted them into an act of homage.

The result is a revaluation of Propertius and at the same time a personal manifesto. It is not intended as a literal translation, and the ironies at the expense of Virgil, Empire and poetic pomp are not ironies at the expense of Propertius.

In the opening of section xii of the *Homage*, Propertius addresses his friend and fellow poet, Lynceus, who has just won the favours of Propertius' mistress, Cynthia:

Who, who will be the next man to entrust his girl to a friend?
Love interferes with fidelities;
The gods have brought shame on their relatives;
Each man wants the pomegranate for himself;
Amiable and harmonious people are pushed incontinent into duels,
A Trojan and adulterous person came to Menelaus under the rites
      of hospitium,
And there was a case in Colchis, Jason and that woman in Colchis;
And besides, Lynceus,
          you were drunk.

Could you endure such promiscuity?
          She was not renowned for fidelity;
But to jab a knife in my vitals, to have passed on a swig of poison,
Preferable, my dear boy, my dear Lynceus,
Comrade, comrade of my life, of my purse, of my person;
But in one bed, in one bed alone, my dear Lynceus
      I deprecate your attendance;
I would ask a like boon of Jove.

And you write of Achelöus, who contended with Hercules,
You write of Adrastus' horses and the funeral rites of Achenor,
And you will not leave off imitating Aeschylus.
      Though you make a hash of Antimachus,
You think you are going to do Homer.
      And still a girl scorns the gods,
Of all these young women
      not one has enquired the cause of the world,
Nor the modus of lunar eclipses
      Nor whether there be any patch left of us
After we cross the infernal ripples,
      nor if the thunder fall from predestination;
Nor anything else of importance.

The passage displays with zest an intense variety of tones of voice, gay, bitter and sardonic, and a keenly ironic sense of self and of situation. It is a dramatic monologue, projecting a set of attitudes and a speaker of distinct social manner and *empressement*. Pound's Propertius—leaving aside the ascertainable nature of Propertius himself—is an indulgently self-aware and confident person, whose accents imply the mocking understanding he has with the metropolitan society to which he, his mistress and his few readers belong. The voice is languid, conversational, given to arabesques of reverie and sallies of wit, yet Pound does not indulge these traits of personality at the expense of communicating meaning. The amused cuckold ironizes restlessly on his own trustfulness, on the infidelities of the gods and heroes, the shamelessness of Lynceus, the weakness of Cynthia, the treachery of Lynceus and the bombast of his verse; lastly, on the gormlessness of the 'pomegranate' girls who inspire these inelegant antics and excessive emotions, notably in himself. The comic self-mockery of 'Meditatio' is here put to biting use.

The implied subject of the *Homage* is the nature of the poet's vocation. Pound picked out of Propertius' love elegies the verse *ingenium nobis ipsa puella fecit*: 'my genius is no more than a girl'. The highly reproachable Cynthia is the inspiration and theme of the elegies, and Pound presents a self-scathing Propertius who knows how degraded and foolish his passion makes him but persists in his devotion to an irresponsible muse, because it is only of her (and not of 'imperial order' or Olympus) that he can write. The truths of moral conduct, of natural philosophy, of man's destiny, are important (more so than politics), but they must be weighed in a balance with the passion inspired by a witless girl; and it is of the girl that he must write. If this sounds like Hollywood's view of Byron or Pushkin, the effect of the lines is dry rather than wet; a suave irony puts an edge on these attitudes. Pound makes us believe that Propertius, for all his joking, is not enjoying his situation. It is with painful fidelity that the poet records the follies and splendours of his undignified passion.

As a fragment, this passage resists full commentary. But we can notice its easy command of a conversational mode of discourse, a manner of speaking easily able to rise and dispatch an irritant or to deepen to register the exact quality of a loss or a regret. The Latinate irony is from the epigrams, the long lines are from *Cathay*, as are the repetitions; but the assurance is new, the paragraphs are longer, and the range of tones is larger.

This relaxation is important. Pound, previously tense and intense, here seems to be able to do what he likes with his words; his rhythms incorporate his iridescence of mood. He is talking in verse—the talk is measured, turned, urbane, but it is impromptu and often high-spirited. Finding a stance from which to pursue his quarrel with the world, he finds a form and a voice. Far from being a character-study of Propertius, the *Homage* allows Pound to present his own vocation in a satisfying and coherent relation to 'current exacerbations'. The vehicle for this complex bundle of attitudes and values is the tone of his voice. Sometimes they emerge broadly enough:

> And besides, Lynceus,
> > you were drunk.

From this series of personae, each more developed in a different way than
its predecessor, we come to a more fully dramatized piece. Canto 13 is a
presentation of Confucius; it stands well on its own and is reproduced
entire:

Kung walked
     by the dynastic temple
and into the cedar grove,
     and then out by the lower river,
And with him Khieu, Tchi   5
     and Tian the low speaking
And "we are unknown," said Kung,
"You will take up charioteering?
     Then you will become known,
"Or perhaps I should take up charioteering, or archery?   10
"Or the practice of public speaking?"
And Tseu-lou said, "I would put the defences in order,"
And Khieu said, "If I were lord of a province
I would put it in better order than this is."
And Tchi said, "I would prefer a small mountain temple,   15
"With order in the observances,
     with a suitable performance of the ritual,"
And Tian said, with his hand on the strings of his lute
The low sounds continuing
     after his hand left the strings,   20
And the sound went up like smoke, under the leaves,
And he looked after the sound:
     "The old swimming hole,
"And the boys flopping off the planks,
"Or sitting in the underbrush playing mandolins."   25
     And Kung smiled upon all of them equally.
And Thseng-sie desired to know:
     "Which had answered correctly?"
And Kung said, "They have all answered correctly,
"That is to say, each in his nature."   30
And Kung raised his cane against Yuan Jang,
     Yuan Jang being his elder,
For Yuan Jang sat by the roadside pretending to
     be receiving wisdom.
And Kung said   35
     "You old fool, come out of it,
Get up and do something useful."

2

And Kung said
"Respect a child's faculties
"From the moment it inhales the clear air,   40
"But a man of fifty who knows nothing
          Is worthy of no respect."
And "When the prince has gathered about him
"All the savants and artists, his riches will be fully employed."
And Kung said, and wrote on the bo leaves: 45
          If a man have not order within him
He can not spread order about him;
And if a man have not order within him
His family will not act with due order;
          And if the prince have not order within him   50
He can not put order in his dominions.
And Kung gave the the words "order"
and "brotherly deference"
And said nothing of the "life after death."
And he said   55
          "Anyone can run to excesses,
It is easy to shoot past the mark,
It is hard to stand firm in the middle."

And they said: If a man commit murder
          Should his father protect him, and hide him?   60
And Kung said:
          He should hide him.

And Kung gave his daughter to Kong-Tch'ang
          Although Kong-Tch'ang was in prison.
And he gave his niece to Nan-Young   65
          although Nan-Young was out of office.
And Kung said "Wang ruled with moderation,
          In his day the State was well kept,
And even I can remember
A day when the historians left blanks in their writings, 70
I mean for things they didn't know,
But that time seems to be passing."
And Kung said, "Without character you will
          be unable to play on that instrument
Or to execute the music fit for the Odes.   75
The blossoms of the apricot
          blow from the east to the west,
And I have tried to keep them from falling."

This Canto is a selection of 'gists and piths' (one of Pound's definitions of poetry) from the *Analects* of Kung Fu-tsu, arranged into a semi-dramatic scene.[14] The arrangement looks casual but proves to be calculated. The Canto is a heavily cut version of an informal Platonic dialogue on Order; the logic is not a progressive one, but from the precepts and examples Pound's Confucius emerges clearly.[15]

As the presentation of an ethic is the purpose of the Canto, our first concern would normally be with the meaning, and the validity of that meaning both in itself and in the *Cantos*. Yet our present concern is with qualities rather than quiddities; and despite its didactic purpose, this Canto exhibits the same formal and qualitative characteristics as the verse addressed to more aesthetic subjects. The principle of its organization is, first, the collation of concrete samples into a sequence, and, second, so arranging the parts of the sequence that the eliciting of their congruities and incongruities, the appearance of coherence and significance, is for the reader a natural process. The coherence is implicit, intrinsic: we are not told what to think, and the props and labour-saving devices of expository writing are eliminated. There are no 'buts', 'howevers' or 'nathlesses'; few subordinate clauses, one simile, none of the superstructure of argument. Things are allowed to speak for themselves, linked by simple narrative 'and's. Things, thus abandoned, have the habit of speaking little and looking inscrutable. But one of Pound's seven labours was 'to unscrew the inscrutable' (Canto 101); not for him the despondency of Eliot in 'East Coker':

> And so each venture
> Is a new beginning, a raid on the inarticulate
> With shabby equipment always deteriorating
> In the general mess of imprecision of feeling,
> Undisciplined squads of emotion.
>
> (v, 7–11)

On the other hand Pound does not show that optimism about the self-evident significance of unmediated phenomena that we find in Gertrude Stein's rose or William Carlos Williams's red wheelbarrow. Pound, like Kung, offers 'something useful'. His method is do-it-yourself, but purposive rather than aleatoric. His data, clear in themselves, gradually make their combined meaning clear; the bits are clear, the whole becomes clear. We have to do some thinking, or some looking.

Contemplation of Canto 13 is a pleasure. The connections between the blocks are simple: in the grounds of the temple (not the academy, the church or the mental hospital) the disciples are asked how they intend to 'become known'. The first three scorn the suggested courtly accomplishments: they are going to 'put order into' their chosen domains; the fourth declines the active pursuit of fame. All, to Thseng-sie's surprise, have 'answered correctly', because each speaks out of his own nature, the right starting point.

This opening movement is answered later, but first Pound disposes of a false inference that might be drawn from ll. 28-9 by a Westerner accustomed to think of philosophy as academic, and of Chinese as quietists invariably respectful of their seniors. The child's nature is good, but it must be cultivated (rather than caned); education and the arts, rather than the army, the administration and the church, are the personal basis of such cultivation and order. The ordering of one's self is the basis of civic order (rather than the putting of one's neighbour's self in order, which, Pound maintained, was the priority of Christians). The discipline of archery has a point after all.

Put to the test, Kung gives a firm and a moderate answer; again it is not what the Westerner, or the questioner, expects. One notes the discrimination between 'protect' and 'hide', and the unspoken corollary. Kung spreads order about him by respecting his own child's faculties and letting his niece marry an unknown. Modern savants 'run past the mark', unlike Wang; again, one notes the discrepancy between 'well kept' and the wording of Khieu's boast.

The coda, addressed to the lute-player Tian, substitutes 'character' for 'order'. Kung himself had been the musical editor of the ancient Chinese poetry classic, the *Book of Odes*, a task requiring attention to 'character'.[16] Orthography, like music or administration, requires 'order'. Just as the time of the old simplicities has passed, so the Odes and their music—like the blossoms of the apricot—will fall, unless men renew the principles of natural order.

This skeleton 'argument' is designed to suggest, without spelling out, the connections between the data; the externals of exposition are missing, but the structure is there. Despite its apparent incompleteness, this is a coherent presentation of a thesis and a way of life. An expository incompleteness is here part of the poetic coherence—a dangerous paradox one would not readily extend to most modern poems, nor to all of Pound.

The incompleteness consists not so much of such Poundian elisions as not telling us who Kung is or that he edited the Odes (a sufficient curiosity is supposed) as the omission of Tseu-lou's name from the first list of disciples, or of Tian's name from the preface to the closing speech. Deduction has to fill these gaps. Deduction, too, makes all the links suggested above: the distinction between 'putting order into' and 'spreading order'; between 'protect' and 'hide'; between 'suitable' and 'fit for'. We discriminate easily enough between the personalities of the disciples. The important relationship is between Tian's answer and Kung's reply to it ending the first and third movements of the Canto, and chiming in length and emotional timbre.

The informality of the presentation extends to such possible accidents as the inconsistent use of quotation marks and the blurred paragraphing at ll. 31 and 73; but much of this sibylline carelessness is deliberate casualization. The use of rural American not only by Tian but by Kung is only the most striking example. The remarks on Wang and the historians are full of character, and all Kung's replies have a dead-pan humour; so Pound dispels any misconceptions that all Chinese are like Tchi and Thseng-sie. Yet this 'de-mandarinizing' is compatible with the beauty of the opening and the close, and with the dignity of the central teaching on natural order. Pound varies the weight and the inflection of the speeches by quiet dramatic contrasts; the 'incompleteness' tactfully invites our consideration: we join up the points with our pencil, and the picture emerges.

The claim that incompleteness—the casual and impromptu appearance —helps poetic coherence is best supported by the surprising exchange between Tian and Kung. Before Tian appears there are no redundancies, yet his gesture is given a lingering close-up and onomatopoeia, an indulgence confirmed by the affectionate Tom Sawyerishness of Tian's reply. This fullness is otherwise accorded only to Kung's maxims on 'order' and to his closing speech in reply to Tian's diversion. The first sentence of Kung's last speech has condensation and precision—the declarative virtues which Kung and this Canto explicitly recommend; the second—the dénouement of the scene—is a poignant definition for the young man of the master's own life's work. 'Order' has its limits as well as its virtue.

Thus the emotional and aesthetic effect of the Tian–Kung exchange is to right the balance of the Canto. Dramatically, musically and logically, it resolves the anti-utilitarian theme raised by Tian. We come to feel the truth of what Kung says earlier about order being natural in the child and latent in society and about the role of 'savants and artists' in bringing out that potentiality. Kung teaches the centrality of the arts and the use of beauty; his closing words, acknowledging, Prospero-like, the limits of his own success and of human power generally, alter the effect of his earlier maxims. For though Canto 13 is entirely didactic in intention, the variety and tact of its presentation make its lessons humane and its farewell a moment of deep though controlled emotion. This is art of maturity, wisdom and of immense though self-deprecating skill. In such writing Pound's achievement, and the success of his technique of implication even when applied to a most complex subject, are beyond doubt.

For a last sample, I take from Canto 81 a relatively self-contained passage, the latter part of which is familiar from anthologies. It is a critical passage in Pound's later work.

81 is one of the *Pisan Cantos*, so called because they were written in the U.S. Army's Detention Training Center outside Pisa.[17] The sixty-year-old poet, whose dreams of Italy and America had crashed about his ears, had been given a tent in which to recover from the breakdown brought on by his confinement in an open-air cage. This is the end of the Canto:

Ed ascoltando al leggier mormorio
  there came new subtlety of eyes into my tent,
whether of spirit or hypostasis,
  but what the blindfold hides
or at carneval   5
                          nor any pair showed anger
  Saw but the eyes and stance between the eyes,
colour, diastasis,
  careless or unaware it had not the
    whole tent's room   10
nor was place for the full Εἰδὼς
interpass, penetrate
  casting but shade beyond the other lights
    sky's clear
    night's sea   15
    green of the mountain pool
    shone from the unmasked eyes in half-mask's space.
What thou lovest well remains,
                          the rest is dross
What thou lov'st well shall not be reft from thee   20
What thou lov'st well is thy true heritage
Whose world, or mine or theirs
                          or is it of none?
First came the seen, then thus the palpable
    Elysium, though it were in the halls of hell,   25
What thou lovest well is thy true heritage
What thou lov'st well shall not be reft from thee

The ant's a centaur in his dragon world.
Pull down thy vanity, it is not man
Made courage, or made order, or made grace,   30
  Pull down thy vanity, I say pull down.

Learn of the green world what can be thy place
In scaled invention or true artistry,
Pull down thy vanity,
                    Paquin pull down!   35
The green casque has outdone your elegance.

"Master thyself, then others shall thee beare"
        Pull down thy vanity
Thou art a beaten dog beneath the hail,
A swollen magpie in a fitful sun,   40
Half black half white
Nor knowst'ou wing from tail
Pull down thy vanity
                How mean thy hates
Fostered in falsity,   45
                Pull down thy vanity,
Rathe to destroy, niggard in charity,
Pull down thy vanity,
                I say pull down.

But to have done instead of not doing   50
                this is not vanity
To have, with decency, knocked
That a Blunt should open
                To have gathered from the air a live tradition
or from a fine old eye the unconquered flame   55
This is not vanity.
                Here error is all in the not done,
        all in the diffidence that faltered. . .

We are here two-thirds of the way through the *Cantos*. If transitions
seem oblique, this is partly because Pound is relying on the network of
themes and procedures he has built up, and partly because the crisis
of the author's life has brought the need to resolve these themes under
a painful pressure.

One might well compare, from 'Little Gidding', Eliot's meeting with
the 'familiar compound ghost'. Immediately, Pound's is a less coherent
and unified statement; his view of reality is more physical and external
than metaphysical: he achieves inclusiveness by counterpointing diverse
aspects of 'hard' reality rather than by a symbolist fusion of the Many
in the One. Pound directs attention outwards.

Nevertheless, he speaks here *in propria persona*, and what he sees is
personal. He is visited by a goddess, who gives him words of reassurance.

He asserts the reality of his vision of a lasting natural paradise (as against the Christian 'life after death' and the artificial paradise of Baudelaire). Nature rebukes the vanity of human art; Pound castigates, among other human excesses, his own artistic vanity, and, above other human arrogances, his own. Yet (and this is less like Lear on the heath) all action is not in vain: to know, to attend the unconquered flame, to cultivate and have faith in human virtue and hand it on, is not in vain.

Apart from identifying the initial 'subtlety of eyes' experience, the above commentary is redundant, unless it draws attention to unnoticed relations between the divine visitor and the reassurance she brings; and, again, between the castigation of vanity and the exception from that castigation. This movement between these four larger blocks is the formal life of the passage.

In Canto 13 the parts were clear and the whole became clear. As a description of the strategy of Canto 81, as of the *Cantos* as a whole, that is accurate enough. Yet here the finesse or bearing of the surface detail will at times elude a reader, through ellipsis, idiosyncrasy, too private a reference on Pound's part, or the reader's ignorance. It is relatively unimportant if, say, *ascoltando*, Εἰδὼς, Paquin, even Blunt remain opaque: Blunt's function is clear enough, though if we know, or discover, who he is, he gains in point.[18] The bringing of apprehension to comprehension is a continuous process in the *Cantos*, but the immediate recognition of particular references is curiously dispensable. If Paquin is not known to be a *grand couturier*, the context tells us he is something of the sort. The *Cantos* are among other things an encyclopaedia of what we ought to know; the introduction of new information is part of their designs on us.

Yet if Pound was insouciant about the availability of such references, it can be no sensible part of his intention that we should experience equal difficulty in discerning larger patterns. It is of prime import that this extract, for example, should resolve itself readily enough into the blocks designated above as vision, reassurance, castigation and exception. Only if the articulation becomes clear can there be the sense of sequence and counterpoint that bring the Canto gratefully to its point of rest.

These changes in direction are not signalled by paragraphing, though the unpunctuated, lower-case 'vision' is thus distinguished from the more typographically systematic statement of the rest. When he wished, the master of free verse made all that can be made of the expressive possibilities of typographical layout, the insetting, breaking and dropping of lines, etc., to direct the reader. But his avoidance of formal and regular explicitness of presentation often makes a severe demand on the reader's powers of divination.

Yet even a reader who finds himself at a disadvantage with this passage will, I think, be seized by Pound's fervour, anguish, gravity. The visitation and the illumination it brings save the poet's balance, and this natural epiphany enables him to apply criteria not so far from those of the 'familiar compound ghost'—of 'love' and 'hate'—to the lofty artistic ambitions he and others had flaunted. After this chastening the final affirmation comes with a tempered firmness that earlier has been missing.

This autobiographical Canto seems improvisatory, compared with the calmness of Canto 13; yet the structure is similar—blocks are juxtaposed, movements are counterpointed and finally resolved. When the language of the two Cantos is compared, a greater eclecticism is noticeable: not merely in the use of Italian and Greek, which follows from Pound's international ambitions for his 'tale of the tribe', but in the cross of archaic Biblical diction and idiom with a great variety of free rhythms. The decorum of 13, whether formal, informal, expository or lyrical, was clear and consistent. 81 can be shown to suit its style to its subjects, but its decorum is vastly wider, looser, more flexible and idiosyncratic. Pound soliloquizes, and the voice, as in a reverie, changes its tones almost constantly; the reader notes the larger stages in the development, but he will need a fine ear to catch the extraordinary modulations. Pound demands here a deep inwardness with his world and with himself. This demand arises from something central to Pound's sensibility and native procedure, but is intensified by the set of transformations of poetry that go under the various names of modernism, experimentalism, Imagism, Vorticism. The discarding of rhetorical inessentials can leave the reader clueless; immediacy can be baffling.

For example, it takes considerable attentiveness to register promptly that it is the 'it' of l. 9 who addresses 'thou' (Pound and the reader) from l. 18 onwards, or that ll. 22–5 are an aside from Pound. Does the address end at 'down'? What is the force of 'your' (l. 36)? We may answer 'yes' to the first question, but the second remains a puzzle, albeit a very minor one. (I take Pound himself to be making a contemptuous aside, but the dramatic personae are not clearly distinguished.) Pound, like Browning, is sometimes to be found in an in-group of one.

This extract shows a further development in self-dramatizing power so remarkable as not to need immediate comment. Yet it would be wrong to leave it without recognizing that—whatever preconceptions we may have of Pound as poet or political malefactor—he is here experiencing a form of purgatory. Whether or not he is 'restored by that refining fire' we cannot miss the agony of this revaluation of himself and of his art. He reveals himself as a stoic, though with a Pauline temperament. It is extraordinary to feel how completely he communicates his passion when

2*

one considers the fugacious oddity of the materials he uses. His command
of voice permits him to compel the subjects of his conversation into
coherence.

The poems or extracts thus reprinted and reviewed should at least dispel
the idea that Pound is unintelligible. More importantly, a similar pattern
emerges in each of them, despite their differences. Simply put, all the
poems seem to arise from the comparison of two instances. In 'Meditatio'
or 'Fan-Piece', whatever their eventual rarefactions, the two bases are
simple: man and dog; girl and fan. In 'The Tree' we have two ways of
looking at natural forms—vision and myth; in 'Poem by the Bridge' two
relationships between nature and human activities; in Cantos 13 and 81
the two bases are again natural order and human order, though each
base is really a set or series of values. In *Propertius* we are comparing
two sources of poetic inspiration—the personal as against the official.
    What is the significance of this pattern of comparison? When we
carefully consider the curious data offered us, we are invited to discriminate, and conclude that x is the superior animal. The critique is aesthetic,
but the conclusion is moral; the process, an instinctive discernment.
    The relationship between the instances is not, however, one of mere
superiority. The correlation is made through a presence whose perceptions sharpen our attention, a speaker whose voice dramatizes the comparison. The mode is not completely dramatic, however, as there is
usually only one speaker, and so the presentation is also objective and
epic. In so far as the reader identifies the speaker with Pound, the 'drama'
will seem, at the same time, romantic self-projection. Thus, where
Pound is the hero as well as the speaker of the *Cantos* we have a curiously
naked presentation of the self.
    This analysis into a speaker and two instances makes a Pound poem
sound excessively triangular, like a billiards player making a cannon;
in the experience of reading, this closed triangularity is less clear because
Pound's poetry is a continuing process rather than a product. For all
their polish, Pound's poems are unfinished; the parts are highly finished,
but they require the reader to compose and complete them. The particular instances are so stated that, when taken in conjunction with each
other, they project unspoken corollaries, and it is the relation between
these unspoken corollaries—in the reader's mind—that brings out the
counterpoint. The contemplation of the parts is an aesthetic process;
the unfolding of their implications a detective one; the result is catalytic,
emotional. Thus a Pound poem is static and may be blank until it is
understood, when it becomes dynamic and delivers its charge. There is

a tension between the parts, initially palpable, ultimately meaningful. In 'The Tree' the tension is almost a sexual one; in 'Meditatio' it is ironic; in 'Fan-Piece', plangent; whereafter it is too complex to be fixed in a formulated phrase. In the *Cantos* the sets of objects to be held in play by the reader grow into a number of series, and the tension or counterpoint becomes quasi-musical. For example, in Canto 13 the reader attuned to Pound will, with the certainty of the reader of detective stories, be waiting for Kung to return to the theme introduced by 'Tian the low speaking', and will find in the Master's last words not a trailing enigma but a satisfying symbolic resolution of the Canto. The dialectic of Canto 81 is evidently much more dynamic and anguished, but is to be followed by the same combination of instincts.

Pound's condensation undoubtedly makes him cryptic at times, and his ruthless cutting-out of rhetoric leaves the new reader of the *Cantos* without a handrail; but the enigmatic face of his work, seized on early by anthologists of such poems as 'In a Station of the Metro' and 'The Return', is not merely the result of modern technique (or modernized Nineties-ism). Pound's obliquity, though it has to do with his dislike for obvious conceptualization, is the semi-dramatic strategy natural to a sensibility inwardly in awe of life, and the product of a temperament possessed of deep instincts, though normally reticent in their expression. The mysteriousness and refinement in Pound is not an affectation, in spite of his striking of attitudes; it is rather that his inner life was not for direct export. In this he resembles the other 'men of 1914'—Joyce and Eliot, and Wyndham Lewis—if not D. H. Lawrence. As the reader comes to know Pound's poetry, he will increasingly recognize and go beyond the multifarious objects of knowledge that at first dominate the landscape of each poem, and he will become more interested in the poetic character of the presence, seer, protagonist who presents the data. The data are variously instructive, diverting, beautiful or awe-inspiring, and the patterns of emotion and moral value that they create are fascinating or rewarding. Eventually, however, it is the richness and quality of the mind, rather than the *virtù* of the objects it contains and which it salutes, that continue to fascinate and to instruct. It is only at first that Pound's purism of surface and form seem clinically to exclude the presence of a known human speaker. Not that Pound is often predictable; but he becomes easier to locate. The reader of Pound is forced to develop his senses and his antennae. The art of reading him is, in a phrase he applied to Henry James in Canto 7, 'drinking the tone of things'.

3. *Personae*

Pound is still best known in Britain through the 1928 *Selected Poems*, selected and introduced by T. S. Eliot, and indeed this still offers the best approach to Pound; it includes all the poems dealt with here, apart from *Propertius*. Eliot's Introduction gives an authoritative account of Pound's development up to *Mauberley*—'a great poem' and 'a document of an epoch'.[1]

If Eliot's estimate sustained Pound's reputation, Leavis's revision of it influenced academic notions. Writing in 1932, he thought that *Mauberley* had 'almost wholly escaped recognition'.[2] Adopting Eliot's opinion of the poem as the basis of his critique, he nevertheless disparaged Pound's earlier work and Eliot's account of his development. Consequently candidates in the appreciation of modern poetry were led straight to *Mauberley*; but touchstones make tough teething rings, and many retired hurt. In 1928 Eliot omitted *Propertius*, pronouncing himself 'quite certain' only of *Mauberley*. I should like to restore the proportion of his Introduction,[3] and add that the best of the Provençal, Chinese and classical adaptations are not only more attractive, but, within their limits, more successful and more characteristic of Pound than *Mauberley*, which in some ways is more suitable to the faithful than to the catechumen. The early verse is not merely of preliminary interest, and will be read by those whom the precarious sophistication of *Mauberley*, for all its brilliance and anger, leaves cold.

Before opening the early poems, a minimal consideration is required of Pound's origins and education, for his cultural formation shaped his early ideas of what it was to be a poet—a career he proposed to himself on being admitted to the University of Pennsylvania at the age of fifteen.[4] Ezra Pound was an American, and of a particular epoch. The circumstance of his nationality could have escaped no one who had the pleasure of meeting him; nor would he have wished it to do so.

Though Pound was brought up in the East, he was born in 1885 in the West, in Hailey, a small mining town in Idaho, where his father, Homer, ran the U.S. Land Office, a key post in a mining town. Homer Pound had himself been the first white male child born in northern Wisconsin, and had an Indian nurse. Homer's father, Thaddeus, had set up a lumber business there; he ran the business himself, enjoyed wrestling with his lumberjacks, built three railways, and served as Lieutenant-

Governor of Wisconsin, and also for three terms as Congressman. Pound had it that it was his grandfather's taking to himself 'a second feminine adjunct, without sanction of clergy' that lost him a place in the cabinet of President Garfield. Homer soon left Hailey to become Assistant Surveyor to the Mint in Philadelphia, and Ezra, the only child, was brought up in the modest suburbs of the old capital. His family was American on both sides back to the seventeenth century, and his mother claimed relation to the Captain Joseph Wadsworth who in 1687 had saved the Connecticut Charter from the Governor-General by hiding it in the Charter Oak. Even this compressed sketch will show that Pound's background was as American as Joyce's was Irish. Pound's autobiographical *Indiscretions* indicate how American Europe made him feel, even in 1921, and his family story can be seen to touch on historic American issues at several points: pioneer enterprise, public office, government service, monetary control, even morals. The relevance of his grandfather's career and his father's occupation should not be overlooked by any reader of the *Cantos*.

Like Eliot, Pound was long a student. From 1901 he attended the University of Pennsylvania and then Hamilton College, Clinton, New York, where he took a Ph.B. in Romance Languages, followed by an M.A. at 'Penn' in 1906, and a postgraduate year. After four months teaching Romance Languages at Wabash College, Crawfordsville, Indiana, he lost this modest entrée to an academic career in January 1908 after a cele-brated but obscure incident involving hospitality to a stranded chorus girl; he was thought to be too much 'the Latin Quarter type'. The curricular facts of these seven university years are known, but the nature of his training in Comparative Literature may not be so readily appreciated. *The Spirit of Romance* (1910), a survey of the literature of the romance languages from the fall of Rome to the Renaissance Latinists, was the fruit of these studies.

In 1908, then, Pound had left the only regular job he was ever to have and failed to publish his poems. He sailed for Europe (his third visit) equipped only with his M.A., a determination to succeed, probably as a poet, and a feeling that he would not do so in the U.S.A. By the end of September 1908 he had reached London (with £3 in his pocket), after visiting Spain, France, and Venice, where he had published his first volume, *A Lume Spento*; within a year or two he had decided to stay.

The impression he made on some few of the subjects of Edward VII is best gleaned from Ford Madox Ford's rich reminiscences of this period. The quixotic Ford, a generous backer of other writers, under-stood Pound: they shared Pre-Raphaelite and Flaubertian tastes.

Ezra . . . would approach with the step of a dancer, making passes with a cane at an imaginary opponent. He would wear trousers made of green billiard cloth, a pink coat, a blue shirt, a tie hand-painted by a Japanese friend, an immense sombrero, a flaming beard cut to a point, and a single, large blue ear-ring. . . . He once challenged a *Times* reviewer to a duel because the reviewer had too high an opinion of Milton.[5]

Comparative Literature had evidently had its effect on Pound. His rainbow clothing recalls the charge of eclecticism, brought against him by Leavis and Winters among others. Leavis objects to Pound's dilettante eclecticism as indicating the rootlessness of the cosmopolitan aesthete. One can understand how, viewed from Cambridge twenty years later, the dancing fencer of Ford's sketch might have lost in colour and gaiety. However, it is natural for an educated American to take a catholic view of European culture, and from a less local stance. American poets are the grandchildren of Europe, not merely of Wordsworth and Whitman, and may regard Europe's past as theirs also. Pound's enthusiasms are not the scattered offspring of a course in world literature but the findings of a trained student of romance languages and literature. Holding the culture of his day up against 'the best that is known and thought in the world',[6] he found it wanting, and his 'classics in paraphrase' from Provence, China and Rome are efforts to nourish Anglo-Saxon roots.

From his study of early romance literatures Pound chose to imitate the troubadour origins of modern lyric poetry. He supplied the first truly poetic translations of classical Chinese poetry. His selective revival of Catullus and Propertius showed how the less public poets of our first metropolitan, imperial and corrupt Western civilization had resisted 'current exacerbations'. These translations and adaptations were the fruit of a deliberate survey of civilized poetry, an exploration growing out of the methods and materials of Comparative Literature. Pound was not subject to that provincialism in time which Eliot diagnosed as a modern illness; on the contrary, he preferred Homer and the Chinese *Book of Odes*.[7] His interest in history, though its motive is partly educational, is not academic nor Parnassian; indeed he took history only too personally. 'Provincia Deserta' ends: 'I have thought of them living'. The eclecticism was not lotus-eating but rather missionary in purpose; part of his moral education, it became part of the education of his readers. Naturally, its particular forms have more personal motives also, but they are not arbitrary.

Criticism of Pound's early poems has related him to his Victorian roots, to his brandished slogans or to his later achievements.[8] The reader new to the *Collected Shorter Poems*, if he wishes to take them on their own terms, may be more immediately concerned with their kaleidoscopic variety of subject and attitude. The last chapter indicated some characteristic elements in the form of a Pound poem; an account of the contents of his volumes published between 1908 and *Propertius* in 1919 might be useful here. Arranged by provenance, the largest groups of poems are, in order of appearance, the Provençal, Chinese and classical imitations. Pound developed his early style and extended his range and his sense of self by copying the old masters. Overlapping with these translations and imitations from twelfth-century Provence, eighth-century China and first-century Rome, and developing out of the latter, is a large set of poems on modern life: epigrams and imagisms, parodies and sketches. There are also manifestos, such as 'A Pact' and 'Salutation'; a group of phantasmagoric poems; and 'The Seafarer' and 'Near Perigord'. The remainder is an assortment of small translations and pastiches, especially in earlier volumes. Yet the 1977 *Collected Early Poems* (containing a great many poems which Pound chose not to keep in print) shows that the man whom Yeats and Eliot allowed to blue-pencil their work was a severe critic of his own.

The *Collected Shorter Poems* can be thus categorized by provenance or by form. As they are read through, volume by volume, in order of writing, a hardening of Pound's sense of society and of the artist's role in society is noticeable, especially in the modernization of his language in *Lustra*. When, finally, the early Pound is approached by means of such questions as, What does he have to say? What are his typical attitudes?—questions which do not seem often to have been asked—one notices a set of variations upon the theme of the poet, singer, seer or sage—the friend of nature, of beauty, of wisdom, of refinement—engaged in the study of beauty or society, or, more frequently, of both. The emotions are those of exile—aesthetic, ironic, elegiac or indignant. One speaks of emotions and attitudes rather than of thought, ideas or 'message' in discussing Pound's verse before *Mauberley*, where he first denounces

> usury age-old and age-thick
> and liars in public places.
>
> (iv)

Emotion, indeed, is the origin and end of Pound's poetry, despite his concern for 'direct treatment of the "thing"', objectivity, technique, and despite his surgery of rhetoric and gush.[9] What Pound 'has to say' is 'the world is thus and thus'; but what he communicates is always emotion and attitudes charged with emotion.

This may need saying because the critical rhetoric of the Moderns was all neo-classical hardness, science and irony. Indeed, Pound's poetry has been criticized as unfeeling, perhaps on account of this early rhetoric; such critics have not read *Cathay*. All the Moderns who survived into middle age, even Wyndham Lewis and Pound, outgrew their debunking, yet the rumour of their youthful anti-subjective, anti-Victorian and anti-Romantic propaganda lingers on; the sixth-former who disapproves of Wordsworth's daffodils is being modern. Touches of a defensive smart-ness can be observed even in Eliot on Wordsworth and Shelley as late as 1933.[10] The reaction against Romanticism, even for the Moderns themselves, was only a partial reform; indeed many of the next generation of poets went back to their throbbing personal pronoun as if nothing had happened.

So Pound's poetry arises from emotion and evokes emotion; indeed, the sensibility he started with was Victorian, and, 'seeing he had been born / In a half savage country', was 'out of date'.[11] But, like Yeats, Tennyson and Browning in their dramatic monologues, Pound attributes the emotion to another speaker, a persona; his first London volume was called *Personae*.[12] He does not openly or directly avow passion: he either wears a mask, as in 'Impressions of [. . .] Voltaire':

> You'll wonder that an old man of eighty
> Can go on writing you verses. . . .

Or he distances it in some other way, as in 'The Picture':

> The eyes of this dead lady speak to me,
> For here was love, was not to be drowned out.
> And here desire, not to be kissed away.
> The eyes of this dead lady speak to me.

The lady is dead, and painted; Pound's note tells us that she is '*Venus Reclining*, by Jacopo del Sellaio (1442–1493)'. This citation of the precise source of a moment of personal experience should be understood as salute and acknowledgement, not as showing-off.

The emotional basis of Pound's poetic impulse is clearly evident in *Personae* (1908, 1909, 1910), now the opening volume of the *Collected Shorter Poems*. Equally clear is the age of his clothing: the curious diction of 'The Tree' is found throughout, even to such a Miltonism as 'what time the swallow fills her note'. The themes and motifs, too, though varied, are literary and dated: Tristan and Isolde (at 'Tintagoel'); Villon, Browning, troubadour imitations. One first line tells us: 'It's the white stag, Fame, we're a-hunting'. The hunt is tireless, but the equipment, though well maintained, is out of date. And too often the sentiments of *Personae* are immature:

> Aye, I am wistful for my kin of the spirit
> And have none about me save in the shadows
> When come *they*, surging of power, 'DAEMON',
> 'Quasi KALOUN.' S.T. says Beauty is most that, a
> 'calling to the soul'.

This is from 'In Durance' (1907), which begins 'I am homesick after mine own kind . . .'

> that know, and feel
> And have some breath for beauty and the arts. . . .

The effusion ends: ' "Beyond, beyond, beyond, there lies . . . " '. Pound's yearning is for the company of master-spirits, not only of fellow artists but also of beautiful daemons and of Samuel Taylor Coleridge. Thus did Tennyson's Ulysses wonder if 'we shall . . . see the great Achilles, whom we knew'.

The transcendentalism from which Pound began is evident in the aspiration of such personae as 'Threnos', 'Praise of Ysolt', 'Night Litany', 'The House of Splendour' and, a poem which may serve as representative, 'The Flame':

> 'Tis not a game that plays at mates and mating,
> Provençe knew;
> 'Tis not a game of barter, lands and houses,
> Provençe knew.
> We who are wise beyond your dream of wisdom,
> Drink our immortal moments; we 'pass through'.
> We have gone forth beyond your bonds and borders,
> Provençe knew. . . .

The excess of sensibility over its object, the unsatisfied longing, the appetite for the unattainable, these traits are familiar: for a century the exponent of spontaneous overflow, 'all breathing human passion high above', had glutted his sorrow on a morning rose and flung his soul upon the growing gloom. Like Eliot, Pound seems to have been touched by Shelley fever in adolescence. He 'passes through' out of 'durance' into the 'beyond'.

'The Flame' has other motives of interest. It asserts that Provençal poetry was about something better than barter and bonds; then the exclusive 'we' and the disdainful 'your' proclaim that such gnostic wisdom is reserved to poets and other adepts of the absolute, and that the *trobar clus* is not to be understood of bourgeois scholars. 'The Flame' continues:

And all the tales of Oisin say but this:
That man doth pass the net of days and hours.
Where time is shrivelled down to time's seed corn
We of the Ever-living, in that light
Meet through our veils and whisper, and of love.

O smoke and shadow of a darkling world,
These, and the rest, and all the rest we knew.

This couplet proclaims a gnosticism ('we know' that the temporal world
is but smoke from the flame of 'our' eternal reality) that sorts oddly with
the subject of the veiled whisperings of the Ever-living—'love'—also,
evidently, the true subject of the *trobar clus*. Gnosticism about love is a
paradox deriving from nineteenth-century French scholarly speculations
linking the Provençal troubadours and the Courts of Love with the
Albigensians who flourished and perished mysteriously in that same
Provence. The apparently adulterous nature of Courtly Love held an
immense fascination for Romantic mediaevalists, as did the nature of the
true beliefs of the Albigensian 'Catharist' heretics whom the Church
suppressed at the same time.[13] French and German interest in the
possible spiritual justification for illicit passion offered by these two
mysterious and non-matrimonial movements was reflected in England by
the Pre-Raphaelites, Pater and the Decadents. The romance of this kind
of love is the motive for four of the Provençal studies at the core of
Personae. 'The Flame', only partly Provençal and less coherent, tells us
much about the nature of Pound's interest:

We are not shut from all the thousand heavens:
Lo, there are many gods whom we have seen,
Folk of unearthly fashion, places splendid,
Bulwarks of beryl and of chrysoprase.

Sapphire Benacus, in thy mists and thee
Nature herself's turned metaphysical,
Who can look on that blue and not believe?

These lines define what Pound in the *Cantos* calls the 'arcana', the
heavens from which he is 'not shut', although his final rhetorical question
is provocatively mysterious. The only thing quite clear from this description of the heaven of love is that the home of Catullus on Benacus (Lake
Garda) is the next thing to it. The poem ends:

Search not my lips, O Love, let go my hands,
This thing that moves as man is no more mortal.

If thou hast seen my shade sans character,
If thou hast seen that mirror of all moments,
That glass to all things that o'ershadow it,
Call not that mirror me, for I have slipped
Your grasp, I have eluded.

He has indeed. This seems to mean that if 'Love' seeks the poet's soul in his body or among the local habitations in which he has drunk his immortal moments, she will fail, for his soul, if anywhere on earth, will be found merged in Benacus. Thus the melodious twang with which 'we of the Ever-living' disappear is more important than Pound's literal meaning, since the poem is a fantasy.

Yet we saw in 'The Tree' that Pound is serious about his dreams. The young poet's ecstatic daydream, like Milton's 'At a Vacation Exercise' or Keats's 'Endymion', is a possible programme. It summarizes the earliest phase of Pound's poetic aspirations: it shows us his concern with 'love', his naked sensibility, his awareness of the opportunities and dangers of shape-shifting, his love of playing the part of a transcendental pimpernel. 'I have eluded' recalls the disappearing trick of Old Possum's 'Macavity's not there'.[14] Pound's 'personae' and Eliot's 'impersonality' were in part the reactions of serious American graduate students from Idaho and Missouri adjusting to Edwardian London. It is worth looking hard at Pound before responsibility began and before he modernized himself. 'The Flame' may be callow, but the author has some definite ideas about what he is playing at.

Further evidence is supplied by words Pound wrote in 1914.

In the 'search for oneself', in the search for 'sincere self-expression', one gropes, one finds some seeming verity. One says 'I am' this, that, or the other, and with the words scarcely uttered one ceases to be that thing.

I began this search for the real in a book called *Personae*, casting off, as it were, complete masks of the self in each poem. I continued in a long series of translations, which were but more elaborate masks.[15]

All self-expression involves self-dramatizing. It would be misleading, then, to restrict what is 'real' in Pound to the directly autobiographical, and mistaken to read anything he wrote before the *Pisan Cantos* as simply autobiographical. In adding what he calls 'the real' to 'the sincere' Pound challenges conventional ideas of what is poetic, much as his criticism challenges accepted valuations and classifications in the curriculum.

The core of *Personae* is the Provençal series of 'masks of the self'; in them the aspirant whom we have seen scattering his leaves before the mellowing year shows a control of vehicle, form and dramatic idea as well as of technique and local poetic effect. The title salutes Browning's *Dramatis Personae* (1864) and Pound includes 'Mesmerism', a homage to Browning. Browning is praised for the qualities he himself praised in Chaucer: a generous insight into human motive, a love of truth and a grasp of essentials: 'Clear sight's elector!' Yet as this concluding phrase indicates, it is really Browning's style that mesmerizes Pound; he admires the 'seventy swadelin's' in which the 'old mesmerizer' is 'tyin' [his] meanin'.'

The mesmerizer's apprentice offers us six dramatic monologues from 'Provence', giving us Cino da Pistoia, Arnaut de Mareuil, Piere Vidal and, thrice, Bertrans de Born. Considerations of space forbid recourse to ample quotation. But Cino is a vagabond Don Juan who now prefers to sing of the sun rather than of women; Marvoil a poor clerk who hides his passion from all save his lady, the Countess of Beziers. Both poems expand in the time-honoured fashion of Sir Walter Scott upon hints in the lines or the lives of the poets. Pound takes the love in Marvoil's poems seriously, imagines an intrigue and idealizes a passion. Cino is a gay deceiver of the open road, unlike the bitter Arnaut; and he too is a dreamer, though he prays to Apollo not Venus. Pound's interest is in the seventy complications that conceal and then reveal the intrigue and the personality of the speaker—in the management of effect. The ingredients are stock motifs: wandering minstrel, Don Juan, 'pagan' sun-worship; also husbands, suitors and cuckolds. This admission has to be made for the theatrical tradition of historical romance that Pound is working in here. But how well is it done? Pound's 'stale creampuffs' have their moments, especially at their endings when sentiment and situation pull together: 'Marvoil' has a touching triple variation on a theme, 'Cino' a successful piece of 'celestial' imagery:

> 'I will sing of the white birds
> In the blue waters of heaven,
> The clouds that are spray to its sea.'

This is 'Prufrock' without the irony.

'Piere Vidal Old' is a grotesque melodrama:

> Swift came the Loba, as a branch that's caught,
> Torn, green and silent in the swollen Rhone.

Yet the old man is not a stock character and the projection of his mad love

has a vigour which though rhetorical is not assumed. His final defiance
is remarkable:

> O age gone lax! O stunted followers,
> That mask at passions and desire desires,
> Behold me shrivelled, and your mock of mocks;
> And yet I mock you by the mighty fires
> That burnt me to this ash.

There is something in the legend of this hunted martyr of Eros which
engages Pound deeply and rescues this vehicle, for all its rhetoric, from
being ludicrous.

The dexterous 'Planh' is a close translation of Bertrans's original,
whereas 'Sestina: Altaforte' is a fantasia on the themes of the troubadour's
sirventes inciting his neighbouring barons to war. Pound wrote in 1913: 'I
wanted the curious involution and recurrence of the Sestina. . . . Technically it is one of my best, though a poem on such a theme could never
be very important.'[16]

With 'Na Audiart' we come at last to the lady—Bertrans's lady, and
the source of the long 'Near Perigord'. It is a case of *ingenium nobis ipsa
puella fecit*, the girl herself inspires the song. The girl is still a lady here;
Pound was not really a 'Latin Quarter type'. But, whether with Audiart
or Venus Reclining, he was, after his fashion, faithful to feminine beauty
and attraction as the source of his inspiration; even as, in 'Impressions
of [. . .] Voltaire' (1916), 'an old man of eighty'. Beauty renews perception:

> Grass showing under the snow,
> Birds singing late in the year!

This shorthand has a purity of style and a lightness of idiom unattainable
by the Pound of 1908. 'Na Audiart' is encumbered by the English of
Rossetti's version of the *Vita Nuova*; it is not 'a perfect limning'. Yet the
first model for that purity of style and perception which is the instrument
of all Pound's achievements in poetry was Provençal verse, not modern
French verse or prose, nor even modern American speech.

Provence was the discovery of the nineteenth century, and it is not
possible to separate it entirely from the fascinations it held for its dis-
coverers: the mystique of an idealized yet adulterous Courtly Love, of
honourable devotion in an illicit cause, of a treacherous seduction
sanctioned and transfigured by the Ideal. This profane religion is close to
the heart of the 'mediaeval' poetry of Tennyson, Morris and the Pre-
Raphaelites, not forgetting such other Poundian enthusiasms as the
swoons of Swinburne, and the French novel from Dumas to Flaubert.
Pound escaped *Lo Gai Saber* of Nietzsche and the opera of Wagner, but

that he was far from immune to the tradition is confirmed by his essay 'Psychology and Troubadours', added to *The Spirit of Romance*.[17] One of the reasons Ford, 'the last Pre-Raphaelite', was so dear to Pound was that he was a direct link to that circle through his grandfather Madox Brown. Ford's father wrote a book on the troubadours; Ford's *Provence* (1938), a masterpiece of his late style, enshrines all that piety, and his poem 'On Heaven' is about driving down to Provence (in a large red car) with a beautiful woman. Pound once thought it 'the first successful long poem in English *vers libre*, after Whitman'.[18]

It was debated in the last century whether the implicitly adulterous nature of troubadour song should be taken literally, and also how Dante could have so completely idealized Beatrice. Pound's Provençal personae encompass both these extremes, though his contemplation is aesthetic, mystical and transcendental rather than Christian and allegorical. In the lyric style of the troubadours, known as the *dolce stil nuovo* when it came into Italy, Pound found a model of the greatest importance, pre-Petrarchan and free from rhetoric. At first he re-expressed Provence in the cluttered, opaque and Gothic mediaeval style of Rossetti; the English mediaevalizers of Victoria's reign, whether in 'Goblin Market', or in 'Work', or in Puginesque, tended to the late Gothic richness of detail and colour. Pound, who in 1907 had walked the roads between Spain and Venice, was drawn to the Romanesque style of the earlier Middle Ages, the style which in Italy survived into the Renaissance because of its simplicity and proportion, a discipline which kept Gothic ardour and fantasy within intelligible bounds.

In the vulgar tongues, this began with the troubadours. Only in the best of the Church's hymns was a classic sense of form preserved. Not since Venantius Fortunatus had European poetry seen anything as fine as Bernart de Ventadorn's:

> Quant ieu vey la' lauzeta mover
> De joi sas alas contral ray. . . .
>
> (When I see the lark a-moving
> For joy his wings against the sunlight. . . .)[19]

The vernacular lyric is best known to readers of English through such Harley lyrics as 'Alysoun':

> Betwene Marsh and Averil,
> When spray biginneth to springe

or religious lyrics such as 'I sing of a maiden that is makeless'.[20] More germane to Pound is the opening of Cavalcanti's 'Ballatetta':

Perch'io non spero di tornar giammai,
Ballatetta, in Toscana . . .[21]

now familiar from the beginning of Eliot's 'Ash-Wednesday'. Again,
Pound often quotes:

Your eyen two wol sle me sodeynly
I may the beaute of hem nat sustene

from Chaucer's 'Merciless Beaute'. The qualities of such lines—limpid
diction, clear image, melody—are precisely what Pound was about to
campaign for in his Imagist purges. He had been studying them for
nearly ten years, through Victorian varnish and vertigo, but as yet he
could not imitate them properly, as 'Na Audiart' shows.

Na is Provençal for 'Lady'; between the epigraph and the first line
which translates it we find a headnote of eleven lines of small type; at the
end there are two footnotes, both Gothic. The feeling of the poem is
overlaid by an antique patina in the diction which obscures its freshness.
Pound makes the terse 'Que be-m vols mal' the pivot of his adaptation;
but his 'Though thou well dost wish me ill' loses the sharpness. The archaic
element in the diction doesn't go with the 'bodice', 'laces' and 'stays', nor
does the promise of reincarnation with the *carpe diem* implication. Yet the
extraordinary combination of old clothes is made to dance by firm control
of movement both in the line and in the pacing of the poem overall; the
return to the beginning in the coda has some of the inevitability we
noticed in Canto 13. There is good use made of pause and the inflection
of a teasing, taunting voice, rising to a pride worthy of Browning in:

Bertrans of Aultaforte thy praise
Sets forth. . . .

Whereafter the poem turns neatly on its keynote and slips rapidly into
mystagoguery; the speed of hand almost deceives the eye. But formally
'Na Audiart' is markedly original and, in its musical organization of
themes, anticipates that of many Cantos. Some of the thematic motives
also reappear in the *Cantos*, notably the dendrophilia, which makes a
startling entry:

Where thy bodice laces start
As ivy fingers clutching through
Its crevices. . . .

Pound can't look long at a girl without thinking of trees, and vice versa;
of trees, flowers, grass, birds in flight or in song. Women merge into
nature; but also into supernature—they 'pass through'; not, in this case,

very happily. The scale of plant–human–goddess is one Pound runs up and down very easily; for him it is a way of expressing mythically or metaphorically certain perceptions of intimate importance to him, a nature mysticism that must antedate his acquaintance with Ovid's *Metamorphoses* or any conscious neo-paganism. This mysticism is to find another expression in his use of landscape, in which he eventually projects an uncanny evocativeness that at this pitch of development is remarkable, though not as original as his cult of Daphne.

The use of the image of a woman to express physical and spiritual reverberations and affinities is again something he got directly from Provence, as well as via Renaissance love poets and Rossetti. Provence cleansed his perception and allowed him to read classical love poetry in a slightly different way, just as Chinese poems were to alter his poetic use of landscape and nature.

'Na Audiart' contains, though it does not embody, those transcendental and 'spiritual' aspirations that were to crystallize later in Pound's versions of Cavalcanti; here they receive a cloudy and half-hearted formulation in the 'reincarnation' passage. The headnote makes play with the armchair notion of 'una donna ideale', a Pygmalion composite of the best physical features of the local beauties. Despite the old clothes, however, a feminine presence and masculine reaction do make themselves felt. For all the circumlocutory quaintness of 'Where thy torse and limbs are met', one can expect a limit to this poet's spiritualizations of the physical; Donne's 'Ecstasy' offers a parallel to Pound's range of attitude. If Audiart is ideal, it is not in Dante's sense. And if 'Na Audiart' is not better, in point of accomplishment, than Belloc's 'Tarantella', it has more interesting ambitions; if it is imperfect and quaint, it remains a gay, stimulating poem, and, in its first half, truly Provençal.

Further in *Personae*, 'Ballatetta' is a conceit on the ennobling power of love, like those in Dante's *Vita Nuova*, recast by Pound into his 'Quattrocento' spring–dawn–light imagery; it runs out beautifully:

> no gossamer is spun
> So delicate as she is, when the sun
> Drives the clear emeralds from the bended grasses
> Lest they should parch too swiftly, where she passes.

The 'Latin' epigrams are also mnemonic of sunlit hours of love, pre-Imagist complexes caught in an instant. In 'Satiemus' Dante's Amor becomes a more familiar form of *amour*, 'As crushed lips take their respite fitfully'. In 'Horae Beatae Inscriptio' Pound looks forward to looking back, savouring his *nessun maggior dolore* in advance. 'Au Salon' signals the emergence of the modern butterfly from the Rossetti chrysalis—he sits in the metropolitan light waving his wings: a Whistlerian dandy in a tea house, scorning the mob, preferring the elect and 'the absolute unimportant'. The poem is a manifesto of sophistication; *Propertius* is in sight.

The versions of Heine, especially iv, v and vi, are also amusing variations on the persona of the lover, and Pound displays an unexpected talent for slackwristed humour:

> In evening company he sets his face
> In most spiritu*el* positions,
> And declaims before the ladies
> My *god-like* compositions.

The conversations between Ezra Pound and Max Beerbohm beside the tennis courts of Rapallo are, alas, not recorded.

The worst of *Personae* is the 'Goodly Fere' and the bracing transcendentalism of the Villon pieces. *Punch* saw in it 'a blend of the imagery of the unfettered West, the vocabulary of Wardour Street, and the sinister abandon of Borgiac Italy'.[22] *A Lume Spento* would have provided more evidence of the chaos that existed before the poet Ezra Pound was born:

> But I was lonely as a lonely child.
> I cried amid the void and heard no cry,
> And then for utter loneliness, made I
> New thoughts as crescent images of *me*. . . .

('Plotinus')

> Ye blood-red spears-men of the dawn's array
> That drive my dusk-clad knights of dream away,
> Hold! For I will not yield.

('To the Dawn: Defiance')

> Christus, or John, or eke the Florentine. . . .

('Histrion')

But juvenilia that Pound repudiated should not detain us.[23]

The best of *Personae* are those masks that are not mere transparencies for Pound's desire to be a poet, namely the troubadour adaptations; they too have their Wardour wardrobe and their abandon, and the voice behind the mask is at times too transcending. Yet in 'Marvoil', 'Na Audiart', 'Vidal', the vehicle is used, and with skill. Another uncollected adaptation, combining a line from Vidal with an anonymous *alba*, indicates what it is that drew Pound to Provence:

"Of that sweet wind that comes from Far-Away
Have I drunk deep of my Belovèd's breath,
Yea! of my Love's that is so dear and gay.
Ah God! Ah God! That dawn should come so soon!"

This is Vidal's

Ab l'alen tir vas me l'aire
Qu'eu sen venir de Provensa

(Breathing I draw the air to me
Which I feel coming from Provença)

plus

Oi deus, oi deus, de l'alba tan tost ve![24]

plus Romance in its most spirited form. Pound has all Keats's love for unattainable beauty 'Forever young and still to be enjoyed', but without the chagrin of love disappointed because its object is *sans merci* or because enjoyment brings 'a heart high-sorrowful and cloyed / A burning forehead and a parching tongue'. In Pound's version of the lover's dawn song, his love may be 'Provence' and her breath may come from Far-Away, but the warm South also comes from one of Provence's handmaidens, and from nearer at hand. Love also has its aesthetic and mystical aspects for Pound, but the chief use of Provence to him at this stage was that it offered him a stage and a scenario. He found indirect conventions necessary, and Provence offered him a poet, a lady, Eros, Amor, and a sophisticated set of conventional relationships involving passion and secrecy. The poets also gave him a pure model of lyric style: lucid in diction, melody and image. With these ingredients, thematic and formal, he could explore a set of variations which engaged some of his own deeper concerns and allowed him to dramatize his feelings as poet, lover, idealist or mystic. The results show mastery of cadence and also of overall rhythmical organization. And despite the old-fashioned melodrama, there is a stirring of a sense of audience and of tone, a performer's sense of self within a situation, which does indeed dramatize; and there are signs of a command of speech, improvisatory speech, that is the test of the dramatic monologue form. These elements do not often hold together over long stretches, but when they do there is a three-dimensional sense of recession and inflection, of life in the rhythms of a voice speaking intently, that is promising.

Other aspects of *Personae* that we shall meet again are its imagery of metamorphosis, of natural analogies, of light, of love in a natural setting;

its heroes, poets, lovers, men of action, gnostics, sacred outcasts, old contemptibles; its moments of direct self-questioning or self-justification. And in poems like 'Blandula' and 'Francesca' there are the seeds of those fragments of uniqueness, those intensely focused moments of solitary perception, that define the essence of Pound's talent. Finally, there is 'Night Litany'.

Pound had visited Venice with an aunt in 1898 and again in 1908, when he had nearly ditched his first book, *A Lume Spento*, in a canal.[25] 'Night Litany' is a hymn to the city, an aesthete's Magnificat, converting themes, rhythms, idioms and actual phrases of Biblical prayer to the praise of the beauty of Venice. The impudence of the transposition is compatible with humility, for the polytheism is genuine. A gratitude for beauty is found again and again in Pound, as in the *Pisan Cantos*; so also is the use of French to cool the *vox humana*. Pound's awe and wonder at the miraculous existence of Venice 'floating upon the waters', his simple sense of not having deserved all this, testifies to a radical innocence, humility and receptiveness before nature and human art that is fundamental in him. Indeed, his response to the city was indelible: Venice was a home to Pound, not only in the Sixties, but also in the Thirties; a home, as well as an image of the beauty man has been capable of when he works in harmony with nature; and a numinous image of the divine. Pound asks God to 'make clean our hearts within us'.

A passage apposite to this and to *Personae* as a whole occurs in *The Spirit of Romance*, where Pound is discussing how the spirit got into romance:

... we are a fair distance from Catullus when we come to Peire Vidal's: "Good Lady, I think I see God when I gaze on your delicate body."
You may take this if you like *cum grano*. Vidal was confessedly erratic. Still it is an obvious change from the manner of the Roman classics, and it cannot be regarded as a particularly pious or Christian expression. If this state of mind was fostered by the writings of the early Christian Fathers, we must regard their influence as purely indirect and unintentional.
Richard St Victor has left us one very beautiful passage on the splendors of paradise.
They are ineffable and innumerable and no man having beheld them can fittingly narrate them or even remember them exactly. Nevertheless by naming over all the most beautiful things we know we may draw back upon the mind some vestige of the heavenly splendor.

I suggest that the troubadour, either more indolent or more logical, progresses from correlating all these details for purpose of comparison, and lumps the matter. The Lady contains the catalogue, is more complete. She serves as a sort of *mantram*.[26]

Pound must have been aware of the Hebrew and Christian sources of the language and cadences of praise he used in 'Night Litany', but the poem, for all the boldness of the transposition it makes from the Virgin Mary to the Queen of the Adriatic, is not intended to be taken with a grain of salt. The light irony of the prose just quoted is absent. 'Night Litany' offends literary and more than literary propriety—it is *à rebours* and almost preposterous; yet one can be convinced by it, as by 'The Tree' and other *Personae*, while knowing that Pound has not yet found the proper language.

4. *Ripostes*

'There is a definite advance in *Ripostes* of 1912 beyond *Personae* of 1910,' wrote Eliot in 1928;[1] in *Ripostes* Pound gets off his high horse. The raillery which surfaced in 'Au Salon' is confirmed in the title and the opening gestures of *Ripostes*. Yet other ripostes are from the same cloaked and sworded gallant that caroused with Villon and sailed with the Goodly Fere, notably 'The Alchemist' and 'The Needle' (. . . 'Mock not the flood of stars, the thing's to be'). Ford's dancing fencer did in fact try to teach Yeats how to fence, and was often to be glimpsed playing tennis or chess. Fencing supplies analogies to the caperings of these years: feint, cut, thrust, pass and counterpass. He occasionally miscalculates, and beats his reader too easily.

In considering how far Pound is 'in ernest or in game' in this or that poem, we should not underestimate the part of make-believe in literary composition. After Shelley's directness of lyrical and emotional expression, Victorian poets had tried wearing their hearts off their sleeves, Browning most contortedly. If the young Pound seems both excessively romantic and excessively nervous of straightforward feeling, one has only to think of the young Yeats; of Eliot's nervous views of Wordsworth, Coleridge and Shelley;[2] of Joyce's poems and his use in *Portrait of the Artist* of *The Count of Monte Cristo*. Even Wyndham Lewis, the bouncer of the Modernist club, wore a cloak and sombrero.

We should not be surprised then to find Pound opening *Ripostes* with a poem entitled 'Silet' ('He is silent'), taking his panache from his musketeer's hat, inverting it to more clerkly uses—and then putting it back in his hat again:

> When I behold how black, immortal ink
> Drips from my deathless pen—ah, well-away!

The next poem begins:

> 'Time's bitter flood'! Oh, that's all very well. . . .

—a riposte to Yeats's 'The Lover Pleads with His Friend for Old Friends':

> . . . But think about old friends the most:
> Time's bitter flood will rise. . . .

This dialogue between Sancho Panza and Don Quixote in Pound goes back at least to the critical moment when he all but quenched *A Lume Spento* in the canal. A self-doubt appears in *Personae*'s 'Famam Librosque Cano'; in *Mauberley*'s 'no adjunct'; and throughout the *Cantos* to the end, when the poet would freely remark that he had made a mess of them.[3] The doubt, the modesty, the self-mockery are always at the elbow of such arrogances as 'In vain have I striven, / to teach my heart to bow'.[4] Pound knew as well as Prufrock about 'the diffidence that faltered'. Consequently it is mistaken to see his irony merely as the effect of reading French prose or of living in London. True, he felt pre-war poetry was too far away from the realities of life as customarily dealt with in French prose and from 'established and natural fact / Long since fully discussed by Ovid'.[5] But the Sancho Panza–Don Quixote dialogue was endemic in him and forced further upon him by being an American in Europe. The Moderns often spoke of starting a new Renaissance; they too were 'new men'— rational and realistic humanists exposing the 'mediaeval' aspirations of their chivalrous seniors. Coincidentally, Pound's formal studies had ended with those humanists of the Renaissance—Rabelais, Cervantes and Lope de Vega—in whom the irreverent spirit of the comic servant is prominent. In challenging an official adulator of Milton to a duel, Pound seems to combine both roles.

The true advance in *Ripostes* is in style and language, to be seen in the ironic first group of poems, and also in the greater concentration of meaning and economy of rhythm in poems like 'Δώρια', 'The Plunge' and 'The Return'. Having looked at Pound's palette in *Personae*, we can pass over some of the epigrams, adaptations and fragments of imagery in *Ripostes* as continuations. The longer poems in *Ripostes*, with the exception of 'The Seafarer', can also be neglected. 'Portrait d'une Femme' is an essay in something new, but the comparison with Eliot's 'Portrait of a Lady' is to Pound's disadvantage. Like Masefield's 'Quinquireme', the woman is interesting chiefly for her cargo; she is a Sargasso Sea of quaint wrecks, of cultural trophies and memories.[6] Like other ladies in early Pound, Eliot or Lewis, she is and has long been a hostess in the *salon* world, the object of ambiguous feeling on the part of the iconoclasts who drink her tea. The lady is a collection of curiosities, not a person; her identity is defined by her trophies. Very good; but Pound is too interested in the cultural rarities, too much the museum visitor. And the pot-hunter is not saved by his irony. His 'brilliant' dismissal of the dear old relic at the end 'falls heavily among the bric-à-brac'; but, unlike Mr. Eliot's young visitor, he doesn't notice.[7]

Ironic detachment is more appropriately maintained in the epigrams 'An Object' and 'Quies'. Indeed the Pound who glimpsed land from the top of a wave in 'Au Salon' is beginning to wade ashore, more high-spirited and looking more dangerous than when in 'Altaforte' he had cursed his jongleur Papiols or when, in 'La Fraisne', he had hidden his face. Something has crystallized behind the gaiety: both incisiveness and sparkle are necessary to wit, and Pound has begun to strike the balance. Thus the end of 'In Exitum' is too brutal; the end of 'Quies' has a saving impudence; but the sting of 'An Object' is followed by a nice mock-benevolence.

'Phasellus Ille' is an interesting poem, and makes a convenient example of the power and limitations of allusiveness.

> This *papier-mâché*, which you see, my friends,
> Saith 'twas the worthiest of editors. . . .

It does not require much wit to see that this 'thing' is a magazine editor; nor to notice the same technique in 'An Object' ('This thing . . .') and 'Quies' ('This is another . . .'). The satirist turns his human butt into an object; Pound returns to 'this thing' in the last line of 'Phasellus Ille'. Readers with small Latin would link the repeated use of the demonstrative 'this' with the *ille* of the title. Classicists will know *phasellus* means 'bean' or 'boat shaped like a bean'; but only if they recall Catullus' poem iv will they take Pound's poem as he intended it. Catullus points out his boat, 'Phasellus ille quem videtis, hospites . . .':

> My bean-pod boat you see here
>> friends & guests
> will tell you
>> if you ask her
> that she's been
>> the fastest piece of timber
> under oar or sail
>> afloat.
> Call as witness
>> the rough Dalmatian coast
> the little islands of the Cyclades
> Colossan Rhodes
>> the savage Bosphorus
> the unpredictable surface of the Pontic Sea
> where
>> near Cytorus
> before you were a yacht
> you stood
>> part of some wooded slope

where the leaves speak continuously in sibilants together.
Pontic Amastris
    Cytorus
—stifled with box-wood—
    these things
my boat affirms
    are common knowledge to you both.
More:
    you witnessed the beginning
    when she stood
straight on a hill-ridge behind the port,
in your waters
    you saw the new oar-blades first flash,
thence through the impetuous seas
carrying her owner
    the call
first to lee
    then to larboard
sometimes the wind-god falling full on the blown sheet.
Finally,
    no claim on the protection of any sea god
on the long voyage up to this clear lake.

These things have all gone by.
Drawn up here
    gathering quiet age
she dedicates herself gratefully to you
the heavenly twins
    Castor & Pollux
the Dioscuri.[8]

Catullus is a hero of Pound's, not only as a passionate lyric, erotic, satiric and mythological poet, a casualty of Victorian prudery and the exemplar of the edged emotive poetry he himself wanted to write, but as upholding Mediterranean values. Pound saw Catullus as the Roman Sappho, and poem iv is full of the Aegean, and of 'epic' mythical and genetic thought. In view of Pound's recurrent use of Mediterranean voyages, not only that of Odysseus, the import of the citation seems beyond doubt, especially as *phasellus* is a Greek-derived word, and an Alexandrian usage on the part of Catullus.[9] The conservation of a tradition by citing a single word is characteristic of Pound's own Alexandrian procedures. The accurate echo is as neo-classical as the recapitulation in

'Lycidas' of the genealogy of pastoral poetry back to its source in Orpheus, or the synthetic use of Homeric formulae in Tennyson's 'Ulysses.' By giving his squib against a stuffy editor this particular title, and by his return to the theme in his last three lines, Pound is summoning up, in opposition, a whole cultural tradition and a countervailing standard of colour, gaiety and fine life.

Yet this standard—Catullus at his villa at Sirmio pointing out to his guests the boat on Lake Garda below—is so glancingly set up that it will not be noticed by our 'generation witless and uncouth'. It is not easy to get this in perspective. In California I met a university student of English who believed that Christ was killed in a cavalry charge. Nearer home, some recent British undergraduates in English Literature, uncontaminated by contact with foreign languages, classical literature or the Bible, are not obliged to have more than a slight knowledge of Shakespeare or of English literature before Wordsworth. Indeed, in his *Guide to Ezra Pound's 'Personae' (1926)* K. K. Ruthven concludes that Pound 'tried to be a learned poet at a time when the conditions that foster learned poetry had ceased to exist'.[10] While one is grateful to (and sympathetic towards) Pound's editors and commentators, this seems a little pessimistic. In *A Midsummer Night's Dream* Duke Theseus declined to hear

> 'The thrice three Muses mourning for the death
> Of Learning, late deceased in beggary.'
>
> (v,i, 52–3)

Pound resisted the advance of Universal Darkness in a lively manner that has rallied support, though he met with opposition from other quarters. As he put it in poem ii of *Mauberley*:

> The age demanded an image
> Of its accelerated grimace,
>
> .   .   .   .   .
>
> Better mendacities
> Than the classics in paraphrase!

'Phasellus Ille' is a reminder that literature, for all its universal pretensions, belongs only to the literate. 'Phasellus Ille' relies upon Catullus; Pound's 'The Lake Isle' upon Yeats's 'The Lake Isle of Innisfree'. Today even the latter allusion may not be caught by some; for others Pound's titles may, if with the help of the commentator, open for the first time a view on 'the Lesbian shore' as well as on Co. Sligo. Without its title, 'Phasellus Ille' remains amusing, but the allusion greatly increases its interest, range and effect. If it is considered recherché to refer to a Catullus

3

poem other than 'Vivamus, mea Lesbia, atque amemus' or 'Odi et amo', this is only because these poems have been so much imitated by later poets. Pound brings things to life.

The poem on the next page of *Ripostes* is far from the Mediterranean and from mockery. 'The Seafarer' is subtitled 'From the Anglo-Saxon'—a long way from it, some experts have thought. The poem, however, is not intended for those who can recite the original in the bath, but for those who have no Anglo-Saxon. It is the only translation of Pound's that I am qualified to judge, though I should declare an interest. As an under-graduate student of Old English, I was aroused to emulate Pound's trans-lation and inscribed my version of the Old English poem 'The Ruin', 'to E.P.'. I later sent the version to E. V. Rieu, the editor of Penguin Classics, who replied: 'Who is E.P.? Not Ezra Pound, I hope—my *bête noire*.' Not-withstanding, Dr. Rieu kindly asked me to do a selection of Old English poems, which, when completed, I wished to dedicate to Pound. Offered the dedication, the poet replied, revolving many things in his mind, among them perhaps the likely effect of such a dedication upon philo-logists: 'If you think it can be done without *ir*rony.'

Scholarly reaction to 'The Seafarer' is a rehearsal for the reception of *Propertius*—if reception is the right word. There are circles in which Pound's 'translations' have made him more unpopular than his 'treasons'. Yet the nettle must be grasped. It requires a discussion of some length to produce conclusions which may have application to Pound's translating activities in general.

Translation has become a minor art, and that kind of modernizing adaptation known as 'imitation' a neglected one, but from Chaucer to Johnson it was a major part of the output of most poets. The Romantics preferred spontaneity; and only with Rossetti and Swinburne was translation much practised again. Alongside the ideal of the poet as a free spirit arose the literal ideal of scientific accuracy, and word-for-word construing, the basic drill of classical schooling, became the paramount form of translation; instead of Pope's *Iliad*, which Johnson thought 'a performance which no age or nation can pretend to equal',[11] we had the 'timeless prose' of Butcher, Leaf and Lang; in the age of the novel a prose Homer seemed natural. Bentley had thought Pope's poem was not Homer, and his descendants hold that 'accurate' prose translation is less misleading than a poetic version in that it gives 'the sense' without pretending to 'be' Homer. This maintains the serious study of language, and, ideally, respects the priority of the original text; it is axiomatic with the old school of classicists that translation should be modest, to avoid any possible confusion with the original. It is a view shared by many poets; Frost once defined poetry as 'that which gets lost from verse and prose in translation'.[12]

Translation was not for Pound either an instrument of pedagogical discipline or the sort of aid to popular education that inspired the Everyman or Penguin Classics series—'readable modern English prose'. For Pound translation was a personal medium of cultural transmission; with his romantic sense of the immortality and transcendence of souls, and his classical belief in 'permanent' traits of human nature, he was aware, from his education in Comparative Literature, of the prevalence through literature of certain constant ideas, motifs, beliefs, images, myths. Thus Canto I transposes into 'epic' English a Renaissance Latin version of Odysseus' descent into Hades—an English which realizes both the starkness and the primordial nature of the experience.

Pound's version of du Bellay's sonnet, 'Rome', is a re-translation of a different kind; du Bellay was translating a Renaissance Latin poem.[13] There is a similar source problem with some of Chaucer's translations; we are dealing with a pre-Petrarchanmentality, a mentality not disciplined by the demands of textual criticism, a mentality for which there is 'a story', not a sacred and unique text. Pound's radicalism was always for the cleansing of the spring, the preservation of the seed corn, the getting back to first principles, elements and roots: 'make it new' presupposes an 'it'.

Pope's 'what oft was thought, but ne'er so well expressed' is often taken as a rhetorical theory where art is the sugar on the pill of truth.[14] It is nearer to Johnson's belief that men require more often to be reminded than informed; both stem from the classical idea that Nature or reality is the only subject of art. Thus Pope says that Virgil found that Homer and Nature were the same; Johnson also praises Shakespeare as the poet of Nature.[15] Pound's approach is anthropological rather than philosophical, but it is not dissimilar to the neo-classical view on the one side or a Jungian view on the other. His belief in the 'it', the prime material to be made new and translated, recalls Lévi-Strauss's idea that myth is what can be translated without loss of meaning: all forms of a myth are true and legitimate.[16] If Frost's definition of poetry is correct, what Pound is translating is myth and not poetry. Pound has the common-sensical view that there is a reality 'out there', however impalpable at times: *res, non verba*. He has not the solipsism of the symbolist, the belief in 'the word' as the only mode of access to reality. Consequently he is happy to translate the spirit rather than the letter.

Certainly his translations are not literal. Indeed he takes Pope's view of pedants in the *Epistle to Dr. Arbuthnot*:

Pains, reading, study, are their just pretence,
And all they want is spirit, taste and sense.

(ll. 159–60)

Pains, study and patience are necessary to exact scholarship, and Pound
was not a patient man. Some of his prosaic versions in *The Spirit of
Romance* are conventional cribs, but most of his translations vary between
fidelity and free adaptation. Some—'Impressions of [. . .] Voltaire',
Propertius, Women of Trachis—are selections freely run together. Others,
from Cavalcanti for example, are in places so literal as not to be translations. Such inconsistency would not have worried Pound, who commented approvingly on Joyce's technique in *Dubliners*: 'His . . . most
engaging merit, is that he carefully avoids telling you a lot that you don't
want to know.'[17]

The poem called 'The Seafarer' by a Victorian editor was written a
thousand years earlier, and is, even more than other Old English elegies,
a peculiarly problematical poem. It has regularly been edited and re-
interpreted, yet I could not offer a universally acceptable account of it
without qualification at many points, though the bulk of the scholarship
has been done. However, it can be shown that Pound was consciously
giving a particular and personal interpretation to the poem.

The nature of his interest in the poem is itself open to interpretation.
From his translation it appears to be largely in the language and rhythm,
but he also speaks of the poem as containing the 'English national
chemical' and of his version as 'a major *persona*', so the theme too held an
attraction for him.[18] He detected what he calls a 'lyric' behind the more
dramatic and meditative poem that has survived; and he divides this
'fragment of the original poem' into ' "The Trials of the Sea", its Lure,
and the Lament for Age', discarding a fourth moralizing section of the
text as a later addition.[19]

Pound's paragraphing of his version emphasizes this tripartite division;
his Trials are a boast of things endured as well as a complaint, his Lure
proclaims a faith in the seafarer's heroic destiny, his Lament is an
excoriation of the unheroic age—and of Age itself. The moral of his
version would seem to be that the call to a life of solitary heroic endeavour,
however desperate and ultimately unavailing, is better than a decadent
and comfortable land-life in an unheroic age.

The interest in the significance of the poem, or even in its detailed
meaning, would seem to be a secondary one for Pound, for he has
lavished on the reproduction of the formal qualities of the poem all his
art, even at the expense of the sense. This is his longest poem, and
perhaps makes the most impact of any so far. Considered as a speech, a

soliloquy, it is fiercely emphatic, and has an exceptional energy of utterance; despite the density of the phrases, locked in their alliteration, the sentences go driving onward. At the same time it has a heavily 'measured' rhythm, far more abrupt than that of 'Night Litany' or 'By the Bridge' but with a similar chanting intonation. Line 71,

> Beats out the breath from doom-gripped body

is reminiscent of the final battering stresses of 'Altaforte':

> And through all the riven skies God's swords clash.

Pound wrote in Canto 81, 'to break the pentameter, that was the first heave'; yet the iamb had never been his norm.

The line I cite from his 'Seafarer' is technically irregular—'doom-gripped' should begin with a 'b', and 'body' should not, in these metrical positions—yet it gives an excellent idea of what reading the original of this characteristic line is actually like. The omission of the article before the adjective is defensible on the same grounds, that this is what reading the original is like. This feeling of rightness comes off the surface of his Trial and Lament sections, and even the Lure, the difficult section of the original, has patches like this:

> Bosque taketh blossom, cometh beauty of berries,
> Fields to fairness, land fares brisker,
> All this admonisheth man eager of mood,
> The heart turns to travel so that he then thinks
> On flood-ways to be far departing.

This gives the sensation of the check and run of Old English syntax and versification: Pound has seized on and reproduced the interplay between the two which makes the life of Old English verse. He achieves, therefore, full marks in a department of translation where prose translators get no marks at all.

Again, the sentence above breaks the 'rules' for stress and alliteration. It also tramples exultantly in the ruins of the 'no archaism' and 'no inversion' rules that Pound is sometimes thought to have contributed to the Modern game. Thin partitions divide the bounds between traditional and archaic diction, and to outlaw traditional diction from poetry is parricide; this was Coleridge's reproach to Wordsworth in *Biographia Literaria*. The Wordsworthian notion, revived by Pound, that one should not write anything that a man under stress of emotion might not actually say, is, like many attractive ideas, itself conceived under the stress of emotion; the diction of good poetry is Poetic Diction.[20] A more helpful approach in this case is indicated by Eliot: 'Throughout the work of

Pound there is what we might call a steady effort towards the synthetic construction of a style of speech.'[21] But we had better not take his 'Seafarer' as the text for a discussion of Pound's language.

Pound's aim in this translation was to recreate the experience of reading 'The Seafarer' by reproducing its language and versification. Though he does not keep to the rules of stress and alliteration, he succeeds in giving the impression of a metre based on stress pattern rather than syllable count. Metrically, then, the translation is faithful rather than accurate.

Linguistically, the translation is equally mimetic of the original: it avoids Latinate words and construction, selects harsh consonants and dark vowels, drops particles of syntax and is fantastically archaic. It uses correct traditional archaisms such as 'not a whit' and the '-eth' form, alongside incorrect ones—'daring ado' is a late corruption of Spenser's 'derring-do', itself a false formation via Lydgate from Chaucer's 'durrying don'. Perhaps 'daring ado' is an incorrect *new* archaism; there are also correct new archaisms in 'narrow nightwatch' and in all the compound words calqued on the originals. No department of Poetic Diction is more poetical than the Homeric formation of compound epithets. When, at about this time, Pound prescribed the renunciation of poesy and pleonasm, he was himself practising slimming rather than total abstention.

Pound's 'Seafarer' is a late sport of the Saxonizing school of Morris, Barnes, Hopkins and Hardy, reviving obsolete words on the principle that Tolkien dubbed 'the etymological fallacy'.[22]

> "forloyn" said Mr Bridges (Robert)
> "we'll get 'em all back"
> meaning archaic words and there had been a fine old fellow
> named Furnivall and Dr. Weir Mitchell collected
>
> (Canto 80)

This is ironic, as is, in the light of the inversions in this translation,

> "He stood" wrote Mr Newbolt, later Sir Henry,
> "the door behind" and now they complain of cummings.
>
> (Canto 80)

Distortion of word order in imitation of the original is an organic principle of Pound's translation; the idiom is as archaic as the words themselves. Sometimes this succeeds strikingly, as in:

> May I for my own self song's truth reckon

where the involution is the outward dramatic form of an inward strength of identity and purpose. Elsewhere there is no compensating intellectual firmness behind the oddity adopted to 'throw it out of prose':

Nor may he then the flesh-cover, whose life ceaseth

(l. 94)

Indeed there are passages where the syntax is very hard to follow, for example at the ending. This distortion of idiom is thoroughly calculated, usually correctly. Yet, for example, 'Nor winsomeness to wife' is meant to mean either 'Nor winsomeness in women' or 'towards women'; but doesn't. The syntax, and even the intended sense, of the following are likewise obscure:

> For this there's no mood-lofty man over earth's midst,
> Not though he be given his good, but will have in his
>   youth greed;
> Nor his deed to the daring, nor his king to the faithful
> But shall have his sorrow for sea-fare
> Whatever his lord will.

(ll. 39–43)

I suppose the third line of this to mean: 'not even if his deed is to be found among daring deeds, nor even if his king is among faithful kings'. The chief blemish of Pound's translation, taken as a poem in its own right, is its obscure syntax.

This fault, however, is the result of the same radical effort to reproduce the impression created by the form of the original that gives the poem its astonishing effect, etymologically fallacious or no. There is also an archaeological fallacy in the notion that the reading of a lexicographically accurate version in readable modern English prose, rather than Pound's phonetic simulacrum, would be nearer to the experience the original audience had of the original poem; the loss of formal quality and imaginative life in the one is as serious as the loss of exactitude in the other. So rooted in our schooling has been the primacy given to accuracy, that this proposition is not likely to command very ready assent. Yet any humane teacher of language and any teacher of literature knows that a crib is a study-aid, not a substitute for the original. The majority of readers, who are not gifted students of language, are rather pleased to find such a scholar as W. P. Ker remarking (of Anglo-Saxon translators of the Bible): 'The fault of Bible versions generally was that they kept too close to the original. Instead of translating like free men they construed word for word, like the illiterate in all ages.'[23] The pursuit of exactitude via classical studies produced good textual critics and civil servants. It also produced in some an idea that nothing happened in literature or philosophy between the fall of Rome and the Renaissance; or that Catullus' obscenity disqualifies him from our attention.

There is only one 'Seafarer', just as, at the other extreme of literalness, Milton did only one translation of Horace; one would not wish either to be imitated directly, yet no one else could have done it. Pound's 'Seafarer' is a powerful dramatic monologue:

> Coldly afflicted,
> My feet were by frost benumbed.
> Chill its chains are; chafing sighs
> Hew my heart round. . . .

(ll. 8–11)

The resource of speech evident here is extraordinary; it has the 'concrete' and 'enacting' virtues praised in Hopkins's English, without the factitiousness. 'Hew' has the onomatopoeia of Hopkins with more tact; 'afflicted' has his etymological precision. (Hopkins's poetry, released by Bridges eleven years after 'The Seafarer', also uses a synthetic poetic language much given to the etymological fallacy.)

So far we have considered Pound's 'Seafarer' as a poem, and as a translation of Old English language, rhythms and effects. Considered as a translation in the examination sense of the word—that is, as a registration, in an English free from solecism, of the dictionary meanings of the words of the original run together into 'prose'—Pound's version is a nonstarter. It is easy to imagine the examiner's report: 'Grasp of language uncertain; identification of individual words in glossary unreliable; understanding of accidence rudimentary. Grammar poor, syntax worse.' Such might be the reaction not only of Furnivall, but also of the more modern mind of Thomas Jefferson, the author of an essay on Anglo-Saxon.[24]

Scoffing at Pound's howlers is easy enough, and was encouraged by his cavalier defence of their correctness; *Propertius* was the main battleground and I am not equipped to rehearse Roman campaigns. It is quite clear, however, that as regards 'The Seafarer' Pound knew what he was doing with the translation, whatever misinterpretations of his position he allowed subsequently. He stated at the time of publication that he was 'translating' the 'original'—the 'lyric' which had been corrupted or improved by a monastic hand. As this 'original' does not exist, Pound's readings—whether general or particular—cannot confidently be questioned on grounds of mere accuracy. He adopted what Homeric or Biblical criticism used to call an Analytic approach to his text, discerning an 'original' lyric overlaid by clerkly additions. The Analytic approach, commonplace in Pound's authorities, is less in favour today, partly because there are no criteria for determining what is original and what corrupt, especially when there is only one manuscript as in this case, and partly because modern critics find a holistic approach both safer and more convenient. Certainly Analysis ran to excess in Homeric studies; but even today the orthodox editorial position on 'The Seafarer' is that the moralizing fourth section is an addition.[25] Analysis cannot be excluded altogether. However, Pound's 'Philological note' tells us that he translates a word which he *knew* meant 'angels' as 'Angles', so we are confronted with the fact that he was prepared to adapt rather than translate, to amend the text where he mistrusted its reading.

This complicates the judgement of translations of particular words and phrases; it is clear enough, however, that he misread or misunderstood a number of words and lines. Thus, notoriously,

> wuniath tha wacran and thas woruld healdath,
> brucath thurh bisgo. Blæd is gehnæged. . . .

(ll. 87–8)

is rendered:

> Waneth the watch, but the world holdeth.
> Tomb hideth trouble. The blade is layed low.

whereas it means that 'the weaker men remain and possess this world; they enjoy it by means of their labour; honour is brought low. . . .' Pound mistook the common *thurh* ('through') for the uncommon *thruh* ('tomb') and misunderstood *wacran* ('feebler') for a form of *wacu* ('watch'); this led him to put every other word in l. 87, with the exception of 'and', into the wrong case and number. A beginner might misread *thurh* and misunderstand *wacran*, but the discordant endings of all the other words in these clauses should have put him wise. Yet Pound preferred intuition to taking pains. It may be conceded that his confections do not sound wrong when one is reading his version. The translation of *blæd* as 'blade' might seem another mistake; but he translates the same word literally in l. 79 as 'blast', a rather etymological but very acceptable poetic rendering. Pound understood the word, and his 'blade' is a synecdoche for heroic glory. Indeed, since the original is concerned here with the superiority of swords to ploughshares and of heroism to anxious survival, this is a happy translation. It might have cost Pound another mark in an examination, however, as it breaks the rule of caution which dictates the choice of a duller word if the more metaphorical word might allow the examiner to think that you have misidentified the original. 'Blade' is better than 'glory' for Pound, because it is more concrete, less obvious, closer to the sound of the original, and rhymes with 'layed' (Pound's spelling). Such reasons seem good to a poet.

3*

Closeness to the original sound is Pound's aim, of course, and he pursues it in unexpected places, for example in the first line, where he renders *wrecan* as 'reckon', a homophone in his pronunciation; like 'blade' it is a more than acceptable translation. *Maeg ic be me sylfum sothgied wrecan* means something like 'I can tell a true story about myself' or 'I am able to compose and declaim a true song about myself'. Translation cannot bring out the full force of this *sothgied*—a word associated with traditional and historical feats of war—applied to the singer's self. Such autobiography was reserved for boasts within heroic poems or for riddles. The novel combination of *sothgied* and *sylf* is enforced by the word order, stress and alliteration of the original; the poet's opening words give his subject—as a literary poet would use a title—and the combination gets the maximum prominence available in Old English verse. The situation, *mutatis mutandis*, is not unlike that to which Wordsworth admitted when writing to Sir George Beaumont about *The Prelude*: 'it was a thing unprecedented in literary history that a man should talk so much about himself'.[26]

Pound begins: 'May I for my own self song's truth reckon'. The closeness to the sound and word order of the original forces the reader's tongue to twist through the articulation of the original, right down to the gristly sounds themselves. He is not rendering the sense of the Anglo-Saxon into standard literary English but rather making the minimum modernization of the Old English to accommodate it to modern understanding; that is why his syntax is so tortuous elsewhere. He breaks the mould, gets beneath the reader's guard, by this dislocation of conventional responses; one is forced to consider the Old English not as notation but as actual speech, so refractory are its patterns. The pastness, the uncompromising difference of the past, appears; and yet what it says is intelligible, dynamic, even compelling.

The technique of calquing the original word is employed again in *monath* (l. 36), rendered as 'moaneth' instead of 'admonisheth', which in l. 50 renders *gemoniath*, a perfective form of the same verb. Pound understood *monath* but preferred to render its sound as well as its sense; the extended sense works well in context, as in the case of 'blade'. The translation of *gemoniath* also echoes its sound.

This establishes that Pound was doing something new with translation. Examples could be multiplied of words not so much translated as transferred from Old to Modern English, much as Picasso stuck pieces of newspaper into his collages. Pound has written *wrecan*, *blæd* and *monath* into modern sentences, punning on their meanings with a cunning that subverts the steady one-to-one relationship with the original text that is expected of translations. The motive is perhaps a magical one, that the original virtue of the word should survive. This challenges the common idea that a translator should write what the original author would have written had he been alive today.

A sceptic could likewise collect examples of Pound's calques, puns and homophones that do not work. Thus *byrig* (l. 48) means 'towns' not 'berries', and *stearn* (l. 23) means 'tern' not 'stern'. These *faux amis* look and sound like modern English words, but they have betrayed Pound; in simple terms, 'berries' and 'stern' are howlers. Alas, simplicity has been left far behind.

In detail, then, we have found 'The Seafarer' to contain both simple mistakes and good, if unorthodox, translations that look like mistakes. This untidiness is repulsive to the mind of Dr. Syntax, who is moved to declare Pound a charlatan. The poet's admirers, on the other hand, can at times be detected in a sophisticated defence of his every impudence and impatience. But Pound, though a pirate, is not a charlatan, and, though the sense of 'The Seafarer' bears no consistent relation to the sense of the original, the sound of 'The Seafarer' is an authentic if new kind of translation. As a translation of the sense, it is usually not incorrect, sometimes brilliant, often wildly wrong. I do not think Pound's 'Seafarer' can be defended as a translation of *the* 'Seafarer'—if the word 'translation' is to bear its normal sense—but only as a translation of the experience of reading *a* 'Seafarer'. Poundians cannot condone the mistakes on the ground that they are all deliberate jokes, for some of them are clearly accidental. If they could all be proved conscious, this would equally be proof that Pound was not writing a translation. But if Dr. Syntax thinks that I concede his case, he is mistaken. *The* 'Seafarer' begins *Maeg ic be me sylfum sothgied wrecan* and, in absolute terms, it cannot be translated. All translations, even the most literal and scholarly, are versions of *a* 'Seafarer', and time will render all of them more obsolete and archaic than the original.

It might be less misleading to call Pound's poem an adaptation or imitation. His own later reference to it as 'a major *persona*' implies a degree of identification with the speaker that is far from the detachment needed for the production of a literal translation. The version first appeared in the *New Age* under the heading ' "The New Method" in Literary Scholarship' and was soon being described by its proud father, in words that come easily to a translator, as being 'as nearly literal, I think, as any translation can be'.[27] Yet the 'Philological note' that accompanied publication indicated not only that Pound was deliberately translating a word meaning 'angels' as 'Angles' and omitting the 'dignified but platitudinous address to the Deity' at the end, but also that he was cutting l. 76b. This turns out to be a reference to the Devil, which, with the reference to the angels, is the most unmistakable Christian reference in the part of the poem translated.

The cuts and changes Pound made in 'The Seafarer' amount to a complete purge of Christian words; one does not have to be the devil's advocate to say that Pound edited the poem into heathenism.[28] Indeed, his 'Philological note' implies as much. It is this indifference to the integrity of the text, more than the errors, that seems a *trahison* to the *clercs*: it makes his 'Seafarer' an adaptation rather than a translation Today scholars are aware of the interpenetration of heroic paganism and Christianity in Anglo-Saxon poetry, and Pound's editing looks mischievous; but he was carrying to a logical conclusion the interest of much mainstream philology in seeking, by an analytic approach to the text, to eliminate monkish 'improvement' and isolate the original, primitive folk-essence—here, the 'English national chemical'. Some scholars think that such cavalier surgery as Pound performed is as indefensibly arbitrary as Bentley's rewriting of Milton; others cannot reconcile themselves to the final banishment of the monkish improver. Pound's editing, then, if bold, was declared and not unreasonable in view of scholarly attitudes standard in his day. But it confirms that his version is an adaptation, not a translation. Such literalness as it possesses is confined to the occasional reproduction of the sounds represented by the letters of the original.

It was in 1920 that Pound called 'The Seafarer' a 'major *persona*'—along with 'Exile's Letter' and *Propertius*; perhaps keeping his piece nine years had enabled him to see better quite what he had put into it. His involvement had indeed been personal. If the reader forgets the Old English, certain features of this supposedly literal translation stand out. As well as being markedly non-Christian, the speaker, like Pound, is fiercely anti-bourgeois:

> Not any protector
> May make merry man faring needy.
> This he little believes, who aye in winsome life
> Abides 'mid burghers some heavy business,
> Wealthy and wine-flushed, how I weary oft
> Must bide above brine.
>
> (ll. 25–30)

Again:

> ... Burgher knows not—
> He the prosperous man—what some perform
> Where wandering them widest draweth.
>
> (ll. 55–7)

If we read 'modern artist' for 'Seafarer', 'patron' for 'protector', the wealthy and wine-flushed burghers begin to resemble the after-dinner audience at the Lord Mayor's Banquet whose duty, could they but see it, is to provide 'protection' for the garret-dwelling seekers after perfection.

That Pound should see the poem this way is less surprising in view of a poem of 1905 entitled 'At the Heart o' Me', dated A.D. 751, included in *Umbra* (1920), the volume in which 'The Seafarer' is first described as a 'major *persona*'.[29] 'At the Heart o' Me' is spoken by a seafarer, trader, pirate and singer, whose one fear is that his Penelope should be stolen away by the fairies:

> An thou should'st grow weary
>   ere my returning,
> An "*they*" should call to thee
>   from out the borderland,
> What should avail me
>   booty of whale-ways? . . .

This early effort gives vent to the wanderlust of the self-reliant voyager that eventually crystallized in the figure of Odysseus in Canto 1.

Pound had himself been a 'man faring needy' all the way from Wabash to Venice to Kensington; the open road and the open sea always invited this scholar gipsy to 'plunge himself in strangeness'. The translation of 'The Seafarer' was not, I suspect, something Pound suddenly took up in 1911 for technical reasons, because he was interested in Old English metre and diction, or because here was a manly 'chemical' that needed to be reinjected into Georgian rotundities. There are Saxon and seafaring hints throughout his early work, notably in his Kingsleyish 'Goodly Fere', and we know that he had studied Old English at Hamilton in 1903–5.[30] This persona poem gave him a suitable vehicle for the emotions of youthful exile—restlessness, isolation, contempt for the comfortable, pride in self-reliance, belief in one's star, dreams of an ideal company. Hence the commitment of several passages in the Trials, the Lure and the Lament. Already by 1920 the Lament must have seemed prophetic to the departing Ezra Pound; his original impact on London had worn off, the blade was layed low, and among the 'lordly men' who were 'to earth o'ergiven' were such different 'gone companions' as Henry James and Gaudier-Brzeska; they are remembered thus in Canto 74. Others, like Ford, had been discarded by the 'gold-giving lords' and 'unpaid, uncelebrated' had taken refuge from 'the world's welter' in a leaking cottage, as *Mauberley* had just chronicled.

Although the alienation of the poor artist from society is a very different theme, it would appear, from the theme of the Old English *wræcca*, and the inhabitant of the *burh* equally remote from the wine-flushed rentier philistine dear to bohemian legend, there is yet enough similarity for the 'translation' not to be a travesty. The Old English elegy is about the trials of the lordless adventurer, his ambiguous attitude to settled society, his heroic preference for solitary life, his castigation of an age 'gone lax' compared with a previous heroic age, and his lament for the passing of valour and of life itself with time. All these fit Pound's situation in 1911. The de-bowdlerizing of the poem's Christian references accommodated it to Pound's own views. 'The Seafarer' is itself an unspecific and enigmatic poem, so paradoxical to us seems its blend of pagan and Christian sentiment. So the ambiguity of the Lament—partly an elegy for heroism, partly a reminder of the vanity of earthly glory—corresponds to the belated knight-errantry of our transcendental reviver of ' "the sublime" / In the old sense' when confronted with an over-ripe literary society in London: a salon world that spoke to him of the existence of a previous civilization in a way that America—as yet—did not.[31] Scholars do not know quite what to make of the Seafarer's aspirations, which seem to be both heroic-reactionary (secular) and heroic-progressive (spiritual); this too finds an echo in Pound. One view of the Old English poem is that it expresses the ardours of the Christian missionaries, hermits and *peregrini* In the heroic feudal vocabulary of the secular society that they were leaving and seeking to replace; certainly it is a poem arising from some such tension and transition. The ideals of the aspiring Pound likewise defied the reigning materialism whose official religion appeared to him to be Protestantism. Whether or not the reader is convinced by the parallels I have suggested, I do not say that they were consciously perceived by Pound, but that they supply the ardour which speaks out again and again in the poem, fiercely and eloquently for the most part, less coherently at other points. One may be amused by the errors and irritated by the distortions and incoherence, but this passion makes 'The Seafarer' the most powerful realization of Old English poetry we are ever likely to have.

Pound's 'Seafarer', then, is both a translation, a poem in its own right, and a persona. It is an adaptation and an imitation, though he does not make it clear that he is extensively modernizing his original, perhaps because he did not realize how far he was doing so; in *Propertius* the process is much more conscious. In so far as it is not a complete modernization, it is not strictly an imitation. It is, however, a remarkable imitation of the formal speaking qualities of the original. As a translation it is brilliant, stimulating, inaccurate, misleadingly heathen and at times rather loud. As an interpretation it is radical and heterodox, though not indefensible. As a model to translators it needs to be handled with care, except by translators of comparable gifts. But as an adaptation and as a poetic performance it is a work of genius.

There remain, of *Ripostes*, such poems as 'Δώρια', 'The Plunge' and 'The Return'. Here is the 'advance' remarked by Eliot, who mentions 'the lovely small poems in *Ripostes*', and cites 'A Girl' as a moving poem where 'the "feeling" or "mood" is more interesting than the writing'.[32] The Eliot who in 'Preludes' wrote:

> I am moved by fancies that are curled
> Around these images, and cling:
> The notion of some infinitely gentle
> Infinitely suffering thing . . .

also wrote: 'I am not prepared to say that I appreciate epigrams: my taste is possibly too romantic.'[33] Certainly he himself does not wield the same gay sabre, and his whole discussion of Pound has a romantic response to the poems of 'feeling' surprising to those who take literally the essay 'Tradition and the Individual Talent'.

While Eliot does readers of Pound a service in stressing the new personal feeling in these poems, it is demonstrable that the clear language and light rhythms of these 'lovely small poems' are equally to be found in the poems he calls Epigrams; both groups have a new concentration of meaning and feeling, a strength and spring lacking in earlier heroics. In fact the characteristic poem of this new phase is the romantic epigram or cameo-lyric in the line of early Greek lyric poetry, such as 'The Spring', an adaptation of Ibycus which introduces *Lustra*.

The mood of 'The Plunge' is a straightforward expression of Pound's own impatient desire for independence, disentanglement and the new. It is not mediated through a persona, and though it has the anonymous quality of some Greek, mediaeval and Tudor lyrics, it is undoubtedly sincere. 'Δώρια' also expresses personal feeling, but the impalpabilities it reaches towards are given classicized values, and these values tend to objectify the otherwise private feelings. 'A Girl' is further along the scale from 'personal' to 'real' in Pound's vocabulary: Daphne's change is first felt from the inside then perceived from the outside. Pound's intuitions on seeing this girl are personal: the metamorphosis lends it 'reality'—not enough reality, as the last line concedes. However, these states of feeling forbid robust expression and the presentation of the encounter itself delicately defines their scope. The 'folly' of the last line shows the shyness of the original feeling. Typical of a more completely realized mood is the anthology piece 'The Return'. Pound said that this poem was 'an objective reality' with 'a complicated sort of significance'.[34] It seems that the pagan gods are returning to us after an absence at the hunt; their attendants are 'pallid'. The transition from gods to hounds to 'leash-men' is beautifully delayed. 'A Girl' gives us fantasy described as actuality followed by fantasy admitted as fantasy. 'The Return' confidently presents vision as real, with only a gesture towards the origin of the mystery.

Pound was soon to articulate his doctrine of the natural object as the proper and perfect symbol, a formulation which contains William Carlos Williams's two opposing principles: 'No ideas but in things' and 'Only the imagination is real'.[35] Pound's classical realizations of romantic fantasy recall the 'Greek' imagism of H. D. and Richard Aldington.The classical/modern dress should not conceal the romantic impulse of these visions. On the other hand, fantasy and actuality are no more mutually exclusive than are the realms of the ideal and the real, and such foundation documents of Romantic thought as Wordsworth's 'Tintern' and Coleridge's 'Frost at Midnight' guaranteed for their successors the use of the creative imagination as a divinely ordained mode of imitating reality. This inheritance of the Romantic poets has never been repudiated by these successors, however sceptical or materialist, and its continuing validity makes nonsense of any simple dismissal of Victorian or subsequent poetry on the grounds that it is escapist.

5. *Lustra*

Lustra is Pound's first successful volume. We behold him fully arrived in Kensington—not only physically, in his triangular flat in Church Walk —but in full cosmopolitan fig, vastly ironic, immoral and well-travelled. Not a page without an erotic impropriety, a learned foreign title to a squib, or a poem that is Too Short. Diners in hall in some Oxford colleges can still be 'sconced' for talking about work, for using a foreign word or mentioning a lady's name. The equivalent rules of Kensington social life were not observed by the author of *Lustra*; nor is it to be wondered at that he made more impression upon the ladies than in St. James's.

The role of Kensington gadfly seems to have suited Pound, as *Lustra* is also the first and perhaps the only book which shows its author as happy, if not contented. The Bohemian viper found the high bourgeois bosom accommodating, at least from 1912 to 1914. He was 'coming into his force' and throve on opposition. He came, saw and conquered, and seemed at least a Hannibal.

The dedication page of *Lustra* sounds the first blast of the trumpet, with its snarling 'Definition', its veiled *senhal*, its dedication (from Catullus)[1] and its epigraph (from the author himself):

> And the days are not full enough
> And the nights are not full enough
> And life slips by like a field mouse
> Not shaking the grass.

Lustra has gaiety, effrontery and incandescence, and my own delight at discovering it has not worn off. Many of its libations are irresponsible café poems, putting to comic use an insolent persona, as Catullus did, and our Cavalier poets after him.

These magazine poems are preceded, as in Herrick's *Hesperides*, by a series of poetic preliminaries which show how critically aware Pound was of his own rapid evolution, and offer certain *prises de position* to warn the reader and the critic that he knows what he is doing; these skirmishes over, we come immediately to 'The Spring', a version of the first lyric in the text of Ibycus, a poet of the sixth century B.C.[2] It is the perfect example of what appeals to Pound in Greek lyric poetry, and is the type of the romantic epigram. 'April', 'Gentildonna', the first set of Chinese poems in *Lustra*, the Greek 'Papyrus', 'Ione. . .', 'ἱμέρρω', even 'Shop Girl', and 'Heather'—all these are variations on the erotic–natural–aesthetic moment of vision. This in its turn leads to the visions of gods, which form another group of *Lustra*; and to the Imagist 'In a Station of the Metro' and 'Alba'. Nearly all the ironic or satiric poems in *Lustra* are also concerned with sexual–aesthetic values turned to the wrong ends by social fashions or institutions. The placing of 'The Spring' is, then, deliberate. Pound, having warmed up the audience, gives us his new piece; it is the keynote for all that follows. 'In *Lustra* are many voices', wrote Eliot; but they are in tune.[3]

While *Lustra* has a unity lacking earlier, not all its parts are equally successful; some are very light and close to journalism (now Pound's means of earning a living). A few relate to the central theme only distantly. But Pound has found a way of expressing or implying the core of his interest in life, and even where he strikes a false note, we can see how it is meant to sound; we can allow him a little grace, as he is beginning to include the great range of tone, including some very conversational notes, that can make him, in the *Cantos*, so diverting a companion.

'The Spring' is very loose translation, and the last three lines are all Pound's invention. The point of the original is that spring comes but once a year whereas love afflicts the poet's heart all the year round. Pound's Spring kindles desire, uniquely and irreplaceably, and, though spring returns to the trees and vines, the poet's heart is blasted and the object of his desire 'Moves only now a clinging tenuous ghost'. Pound has both reversed the point of the original, and made it more complicated, spiritual and elegiac. Not that he mutes the joy of Spring—on the contrary, the first half of the poem is as springlike as anything between Boccaccio and Botticelli—but he adds to Ibycus' fierce celebration of the pangs of present love a temporal dimension—a before and, especially, an after. The family of poems that descends from 'The Spring' in *Lustra* contains both the 'new brilliancies' and the 'clinging tenuous ghost'. She 'clings' again in 'Gentildonna', 'Liu Ch'e', 'Ts'ai Chi'h' and, residually, in the 'Petals on a wet, black bough' of the 'Metro' image. And *Lustra* proper ends with an 'Epilogue' that bids farewell to all the songs it contains as if they were 'An homely, transient antiquity'—yet adds: 'Only emotion remains'. This last sentence is the first firm pronouncement of Pound's maturity, and states a theme that runs throughout his whole work. It also implies the mnemonic function of his art.

It is easy to take the introductory poems in *Lustra* and Pound's envois and epilogues generally as part of the gay trappings of artifice, but this would overlook not only the strategy of this volume but the poet's awareness (most memorably expressed at the end of Canto 13) of how even the finest lyric fails to capture the essence of what it tries to express and does not itself become truly permanent. From all the 'new brilliancies' *Lustra* contains—and there are among them epigrams as exquisite as any in English—'only emotion remains'.

Having advanced a claim for the thematic unity of *Lustra*, and having surveyed the earlier Pound in a detail which will serve to establish his interests and attitudes in the period before his output was subject to a conscious critical programme, it might seem time to turn to its best pieces. Yet I think it is possible to recognize that the arrangement of the poems in *Lustra* also has a conscious programme, to which the variety of personae of earlier books is now subordinated. Pound is creating an audience—his relationship with it is conspiratorial and mock-antagonistic, at times uneasy, yet more confident of understanding. The days of 'all this is folly to the world' are over.[4] The advance is personal, social and artistic—it enables him to relax and to perform. This goes beyond the rapport of performer and public towards the kind of critical and cultural awareness required by Matthew Arnold of an art which shall be fully equal to the life of its time. In this connection, Arnold wished that Wordsworth had read more widely; in *Lustra* Pound shows the critical advantage of his 'literature'. In a specialized sense, the author of *Lustra* had understood the recent cultural and artistic life of the West better than his London contemporaries, partly because he was an out-of-date outsider for whom the aesthetic faith of the Nineties was still alive, and partly because he had read a great deal of literature before and beyond the dominant Shakespeare-to-Tennyson tradition and could see the parlous state of English poetry. With the exclusion and suicide of the aesthetes in the Nineties, heartiness was in the ascendant: Kipling, Galsworthy, Shaw, Wells, Bennett. And in the English reaction, when it came, to this philistinism, whether in Bloomsbury or in Auden's generation, there was too much of a snigger at Victorian earnestness and Edwardian vulgarity. Pound's understanding of the transition from Rossetti to Kipling was very different, as *Mauberley* witnesses. Like Yeats, he had absorbed via Symons, Pater and Swinburne enough to make the arts in France seem at once both finer and more inclusive of modern life than what England had achieved in the nineteenth century. Pound was thus exceptionally well informed. In an island or an epoch where the appreciation of beauty or art was so habitually taken as evidence of preciousness that such appreciation had actually become precious in self-defence, Pound also found, besides the philistinism, a complacent lack of artistic dedication, intelligence and seriousness. That this critical realization has not dawned in Britain is evidenced by

the current offering of the English poets of the Great War not as witnesses
to a great national tragedy, but as modern poets of real stature.

The use Pound made of his literature is very clear in *Lustra*—not in
the un-British scattering of foreign words but in the instinctive and
critical formation of his whole approach. 'Mr Ezekiel Ton', as *Punch*
called him, showed extremely poor form in this regard.[5] The opening
of *Lustra* prepares us for the polyglottal excesses of the *Cantos*; the first
page adds to the promiscuity of the dedication page a poem with a
Provençal title and another with an epigraph from Lope de Vega. The
British reader concludes that Mr. Pound is ill-bred and—*ignoramus odi*—
not possessed of the learning to which he pretends. This harrumph is
not entirely without justification; but the notion of Graves, Bowra (and
Winters) that Pound is a barbarian decked with erudite gewgaws is
absurd.

The display of *Lustra* is display all right, but the nerve of appropriating
Catullus' 'to whom shall I present my neat little new book?' is not empty
panache. Pound opens his books with care: there was a propriety in
his placing of 'The Tree' in *Personae*; and, in the *Ripostes* sequence of
'Phasellus Ille', 'An Object' and 'Quies', a nicely inconspicuous use of
ille to link the poems. *Lustra* is a more sustained example of decorum:
a Catullan disdain and amusement are required for the Augean hygiene
Pound proposed to administer. The irony is the obverse of the amatory
motive announced in these same poems.

A 'Tenzone' is a challenge to a flyting, or, in the case of Bertrans de
Born, to actual fighting. Pound's is less serious:

> Will people accept them?
> (i.e. these songs).
> As a timorous wench from a centaur
> (or a centurion),
> Already they flee, howling in terror.

Propertius will make the mock-heroic aside and the overheard query
familiar; likewise the de-mythologizing transposition of 'centaur' into
'centurion' and the hyperbole of 'timorous', 'already' and 'howling'.
The conscious Latin translatorese of 'procure' and 'recesses' in the lines
which follow is also part of a conspiratorial joking relationship with the
Latin epigrammatists. 'Tenzone' continues in similar vein with a play
on *virgo intacta*:

> Will they be touched with the verisimilitudes?
> Their virgin stupidity is untemptable.

In English poetry this play with invisible inverted commas and the

provenance of phrases is done best by Pope; as in the incident in the
Epistle to Arbuthnot (ll. 39–44) when the poet, besieged by poetasters
who importune him for a recommendation for their plays, is forced to
reply—

> And drop at last, but in unwilling ears,
> This saving counsel, "Keep your Piece nine years."
> Nine years! cries he, who high in *Drury-lane*
> Lull'd by soft Zephyrs thro' the broken Pane,
> Oblig'd by hunger, and Request of friends,
> Rymes e're he wakes, and prints before *Term* ends.

Pope's play on 'saving' and 'piece' both re-states and improves on Horace's
advice to poets, without making fun of it.[6] Pound's assimilation of the
spirit of Catullus exemplifies the vitality of his amateur knowledge of
the classics and the freedom of his use of them. At the same time, curiously,
his comic use of translatorese acknowledges their antiquity and remote-
ness, their need to be brought up to date. Yet his mock-heroic style is not,
of course, intended to mock the classics, but to mock an unheroic present
by a modern use of the classics.

Another use of the classics is also operative in *Lustra*. On the one
hand, the broadly comic:

> We were not exasperated with women,
>   for the female is ductile.

> ('The Condolence')

On the other:

> Nor has life in it aught better
> Than this hour of clear coolness,
>   the hour of waking together

> ('The Garret')

The erotic theme is elaborated in 'Salutation the Second', a progress
report which concludes the preliminaries of *Lustra*. The balance of its
first sections is not fulfilled in the new theme announced later:

> Dance the dance of the phallus
>   and tell anecdotes of Cybele!
> Speak of the indecorous conduct of the Gods!

This neo-paganism descends to naughtiness:

> Greet the grave and the stodgy,
> Salute them with your thumbs at your noses.

The American graduate student who in 1907 wrote back to Dr.
Felix Schelling, that 'since the study of Martial there is nothing I
approach with such nausea and disgust as Roman life (Das Privatleben)'[7]
was a proper and ungross person, as indeed his scatological vision of
Hell in Cantos 14 and 15 perversely confirms. He dislikes pornography
(see 'To a Friend Writing on Cabaret Dancers'), and his 'anecdotes of
Cybele' are, like 'the hour of waking together', rather daring. As is
well known, the reign of 'Edward the Caressor' (Pound's phrase) was
easygoing. The classicizing of the erotic is itself an antique practice,
but in the age of the Cambridge anthropologists it was enjoying a new
vogue, as, for example, in Forster's short stories. But Pound would have
found the mysteries at Eleusis rather alarming in reality; the more
mysterious the better. For all his Swinburne and his de Gourmont,
Pound found the later Joyce, for example, rather dirty.[8] His own 'orgy'
in Canto 39 is a clean, tasteful and ideal sensuality—attractive indeed,
but as splendid in its modern style as Frederick, Lord Leighton's painting
of the *Daphnephoria*.

While the eroticism and its accompanying paganism have their merely
aesthetic and fashionable components, they can crystallize, as in 'The
Spring', into something important and new, something well beyond
the mere anti-Victorianism so delightful to readers of Lytton Strachey.
Pound's neo-paganism developed a considerable range of themes, acting
as a metaphor for primitive intuition and visionary experience. It became
a vocabulary rather than a programme.

It was, nevertheless, at about this point that the new pagan apostasized
from Christianity. The *Cantos* are, among other things, a personal
history of Western man, and some readers—Noel Stock, for example—
are astounded at the total absence of Christianity from the poem; doubtless this was part of Eliot's disagreement with Pound's 'philosophy'.[9]
(The *Cantos* also have other conspicuous lacunae when compared with
the conventional landscape of British, European or even American
thought. Notable absentees from Pound's literary history are not only
Milton but, less noisily, Shakespeare, the Romantics and the English
novelists; Pound's history and economics have equally surprising
omissions.)

Christianity survives in Pound chiefly as a fierce moral and not un-
puritanical emotion about certain intellectual, social and cultural issues,
erupting occasionally in Biblical language and cadences. Paradoxically,
he is extremely anti-Hebraic, anti-monotheistic and anti-moralistic,
finding most of the artistic interest of Christianity in Hellenistic, Roman
and heterodox contributions to it, especially in the 'neo-Platonic' imagery
of light in so memediaeval theologians. Dante indeed provided an inter-

mittent model for the structure of the *Cantos*. But the essential religious basis of Christianity seems to have meant as little to Pound as it did to Lawrence, and partly from the same revulsion from the Churches' repressive sexual morality. Like Swinburne, he felt the pale Galilean had turned the world grey with his breath.[10] Pound, following the enlightened founders of his Republic, was also opposed to dogma; yet he liked the Catholic Church as a protective cultural institution tolerant of an assimilated Mediterranean polytheism and mythopoeia, and insisted that for a thousand years all the best thinking had gone on *inside* the Church.[11]

Paganism provided an otherwise positivistic Pound with some mythology for his humanism and naturalism. A very personal interpretation of Greek myth, out of Homer and Ovid, becomes his essential notation for a transcendental (not metaphysical) possibility in a world that is otherwise the unfurnished world of modern experience, the rational world of Voltaire, the civic world of Jefferson, the moral world of Flaubert, the physical world of the natural scientists and Joyce. Paganism is, at this stage, germinal in Pound, little more as yet than an aesthetic way of dealing with possibilities.

> We went forth gathering delicate thoughts,
> Our *'fantastikon'* delighted to serve us.
> We were not exasperated with women,
> for the female is ductile.

('The Condolence')

The ductility of the female was not so evident to a recent acquaintance, whose portrait of Grishkin was to seem to Pound incomplete.[12]

Exasperation was a state of mind that grew on Pound until his old age. He begins 'Salvationists', prophetically enough,

> Come, my songs, let us speak of perfection—
> We shall get ourselves rather disliked.

Pound and Eliot were both salvationists, though of different stripes, and it would be wrong to leave this out of even an initial sketch of Pound's 'religious' position.

Nature itself—especially the Mediterranean landscape—is the instinctive basis of many of Pound's religious values. Ethically, he was attracted to such purely humanistic social philosophies as those of the Enlightenment or of Confucius. Politically, he starts off as a liberal, and philosophically as an experimental pragmatist. His attitudes changed, hardened and changed again, but Pound always avoided defining his philosophy; he listed himself in the British *Who's Who* (1957) as 'a follower of Confucius and Ovid', which we may perhaps translate as Civilization and Myth. Like William Carlos Williams he was an unsystematic and provisional thinker.

The religion of *Lustra* is the religion of love, and 'The Spring' is its theophany. Other devotions are 'Surgit Fama', 'Dance Figure', 'April', 'το καλόν', 'Ancora', 'Dompna. . .', 'The Coming of War: Actaeon', the 'imagisms', 'The Faun' and 'Coitus'.[13] The last poem in *Lustra*, 'Provincia Deserta', announces the theme of landscape, a principal subject of *Cathay*. These religious experiences, visions and affirmations are accompanied by an equal variety of comminations upon the infidel, namely the Bourgeois and his wife (e.g. 'The Garden', 'Salutation', 'Salutation the Second', 'Albatre', 'Commission' and 'The Social Order'). Epigrams proper form a third group running from 'The New Cake of Soap' to 'Coda', plus 'Society'; there are also contemporary sketches overlapping with the anti-bourgeois pieces. Setting aside the poems after 'Epilogue', the largest remaining group is autobiographical: some boasts —'Causa', 'A Pact', 'The Rest', 'Dum Capitolium Scandet'—and poems about 'this damned profession of writing' ('The Study in Aesthetics', 'The Encounter', 'Tempora', 'Tame Cat'). The first and third groups of his catalogue—the love-visions and the epigrams—contain the successes.

I believe that the sequence of poems is arranged in a pattern, which one might recapitulate thus: preliminaries and announcements; 'The Spring'; further announcements; love-visions; egotistical variations; epigrams; 'imagisms'; social sketches; love-visions; sketches and epilogue. *Lustra* is organized around the blocks of love-visions and epigrams, with a calculated variation of intensity, subject, type, tone and length, though all in the key of Eros. If we consider the volume as one connected sequence instead of as a series of independent items, the loose organization of the sequence into blocks and troughs is an anticipation of the pacing, format and policy of the *Cantos*. This strategy—if it is no accident— lends piquancy to the collocation of such items as 'Society' and 'Image from D'Orleans', and makes their representative significance as instances of moribundity and vitality all the more striking. . . .

How far to take the process of seeing significance in collage and juxtaposition is a matter of judgement; for the reader of Pound this is a constant process, of discrimination and sometimes divination. The 'lack of form, grammar, principle and direction' characteristic of 'the contemporary plight' for F. R. Leavis was found by him to be reflected in the *Cantos*.[14] Certainly we found ourselves groping at times in Canto 81. But in the blankness and nakedness there is a challenge to go beyond the four entities so robustly demanded—by confronting the words on the page and finding their coherence by apprehension of their 'field', their sequence and immediate context. Such an understanding, though it involves intelligent moral discrimination, is mediated by means less purposive than the Miltonic quartet summoned up by Leavis, and the communication is less positive, full and commandingly eloquent.

Forswearing the more obvious directional aids, Pound relies greatly on context. If, for example, 'The Spring', 'Society' and 'The Three Poets' are taken out of *Lustra* they lose the force that comes from their timing in the sequence of the volume. Likewise the absurdly short 'Papyrus', held up to isolated ridicule by Robert Graves, makes sense in context. It is a squib and a *reductio ad absurdum* of a method by self-parody; but it is also the fragment of a papyrus containing words of a poem by Sappho, and stands at a critical point in the line of Greek lyric poems that runs from 'The Spring' to 'ἱμέρρω', and forms the spine of *Lustra*.

Pound, like William Carlos Williams and Marianne Moore, came from a culture where the traditional expressive forms of poetry were at that time much weaker than in England. All three write in the understated, inexplicit, unapologetically empirical way that, to Europeans, often seems lacking in traditional resonance and significance. Pound lacked the rootedness that gave Hardy's direct concentration on the object a meaning and a bearing. Hardy's significance comes from an integrity between himself, his speech and his given world. The bleakness of a world of objects and passions is felt and expressed in his speech. Pound, who had a deep respect and understanding for Hardy's aims and methods, had no Wessex.[15] In order to endow his objects and his passions with significance he had to rely on what he embarrassedly refers to as Kulchur and on the creation of a personal voice.

Lustra is the first extended exercise of Pound's voice; there is more recitative than aria, but gone are the histrionics of 'The Goodly Fere', 'Altaforte' and 'The Seafarer'. It is a conversational, a talking voice, and, in order to give salience to the poignancy and bite of its more intense moments, it must also be allowed a fair amount of chat to create the role. Exiles have to operate through the stereotyped misunderstandings of their hosts; Pound needed to establish his personality. If we allow the voice room and scope, the 'form, grammar, principle and direction' of *Lustra* will emerge—informally, indirectly and in an unprincipled fashion. Grammar, as the examiner of 'The Seafarer' noted in his report, is not Mr. Pound's strong point, but the juxtaposition of poems, casual though it appears, has a kind of thematic and tonal logic. *Lustra* contains several poetic jokes, test cases for sensitivity to Pound's tone ; for example, 'Meditatio', 'The Seeing Eye', 'Epitaphs' and 'Ancient Wisdom, Rather Cosmic'. 'The Three Poets' is a more elaborate joke

and an excellent epigram. And 'Papyrus' indicates that Pound knows
that such poems as 'April' are dangerously near to being jokes, so extreme
is their stylization. It is an axiom that you must first draw the circle
in which you are to perform: Pound the dandy, Bohemian, lover and
censor is better than 'Christus and John and eke the Florentine'.[16]

The 'advance' of *Lustra* consists, then, in the way earlier voices are
now caught up into a modern, Catullan personality. The book works
in a discursive and semi-dramatic way, with lesser poems grouped around
the blocks of love-visions and epigrams.

To take 'το καλόν' as a representative combination of the two styles:

> Even in my dreams you have denied yourself to me
> And sent me only your handmaids.

This has both lyric emotion and epigrammatic economy, and is a definition and an example of Pound's aesthetics. The Greek ideal of 'the
beautiful and the good' is real and to be loved, but it seems that its
perfections cannot be grasped. Though an ideal, it remains apprehensible
to sense; the erotic metaphor should not be taken too literally. The
precise rhythmical articulation of the sentence silhouettes its vocal
outline, and also its simple cannon-like 'triangularity' as noted in Chapter
2: you—me—handmaids. The incompleteness of the first line calls
for the response of the second, spoken resignedly, like 'Fan-Piece'.
Yet, though it is so clearly to be spoken, it reads as an anonymous verse
or inscription from some pre-individualistic age, Greek, mediaeval or
Chinese. This is a product of its measured simplicity; of its brevity and
isolation; of its antique title and closing word; of its 'overheard' lack of
context. A poem of this sort obviously meets the ideals of economy,
directness and 'absolute' rather than metronomic rhythm.[17] These
'imagist' qualities are techniques, but it is important to enquire what
ends they serve.

Imagism attempted a new purchase on reality ('direct treatment of
the "thing"') by a process of limitation ('*the* "thing"') and exclusion
of inessentials by a formal purism.[18] The pursuit of the essential, the
illuminating moment caught in the significant detail, was Pound's
habitual aim, an empirical mysticism involved in the origin of descriptive
poetry. Though he outgrew the static simplicity of Imagism, this
kind of Acmeist poem is Pound's signature, and it has instantaneous
immediacy and a simple identity of form and sense that pierces the
outer layers of customary perception and appreciation. If the response
Pound evokes in a reader is indeed of this sort, the reader will not lose
interest in what Pound has to say. Someone blind to the crystalline
quality of this little poem might see it, I suppose, as pretentious, abstract,

vague, archaic, romantically vulgar. Such a critic might at least have
sensed that 'το καλόν' is a declaration of aesthetic faith, of a neo-
Platonic sort. 'What Pound has to say' is unparaphrasable of its nature
because so inexplicit and condensed. It is, however, germane to suggest
that the poem is concerned with the possibilities of ecstatic experience
and that even though its tenor is disappointment, the possibility of
ecstasy is implicit in the expression of disappointment. The speaker
is at once rapt, floating, sublime, free of specific reference, and in the
same breath ironic towards himself and grudgingly respectful of his
ideal. Such a combination of ecstasy and wit recalls the metaphysical
love poems of Donne, such as 'Air and Angels':

> Twice or thrice had I loved thee,
> Before I knew thy face or name;
> So in a voice, so in a shapeless flame,
> Angels affect us oft, and worshipped be.

('I dare say it is meaningless unless one has drifted into a certain vein
of thought': Pound on 'In a Station of the Metro'.)[19]

> But we by a love, so much refined,
> That our selves know not what it is . . .
> ('A Valediction: Forbidding Mourning')

> And whilst our souls negotiate there,
> We like sepulchral statues lay;
> All day, the same our postures were,
> And we said nothing, all the day.
>
> ('The Ecstasy')[20]

> 'It rests me to converse with beautiful women
> Even though we talk nothing but nonsense,
>
> The purring of the invisible antennae
> Is both stimulating and delightful.'
>
> ('Tame Cat')

Compared with Donne, Pound has not here that fine complexity nor
that dominance of the predatory mind over the senses; but the ecstatic–
ironic emotional temperament is similar. The accent in Pound is at once
more vatic and comic; but the quasi-religious intensity is, as in these
particular love poems of Donne, accompanied by self-awareness, a
self-awareness less keen and sparkling than his, but clearly audible.
As well as a protestation, 'το καλόν' is also a superb compliment.
Pound defined an image as 'that which presents an intellectual and

emotional complex in an instant of time'.[21] Though he has not Donne's intellectual force and extravagance of wit, and though, like Jonson's, his poems distill classic simplicities and commonplaces, they themselves are not simple.

If 'το καλόν' is too short an example of the love-vision for the reader who has not 'drifted into a certain vein of thought', let him again consider 'The Spring', and its fine emotional quality. This is not the beauty of an artefact, but the bodying-forth of a delicate yet strong complex of feelings. It is balanced, flighted, articulated; but it also has urgency and outspokenness, together with a poise previously lacking when there was any fierceness of emotion. Here indeed is the 'brilliant improvisator translating at sight from an unknown Greek masterpiece' of Yeats's image; for once he has 'got all the wine into the bowl'.[22]

The best of the epigrams are 'The Bath Tub', 'Amities', 'Ladies', 'Phyllidula', 'Society' and 'The Three Poets'. As with the first crop of epigrams in English at the time of Donne and Jonson, the Attic salt was attracted by the bland expansiveness of prevailing fashion; the contemporary impact of a poem like 'The Temperaments' can well be imagined. The impudence of the poems addressed to women again recalls Donne, the Donne of the Elegies and of 'The Indifferent':

> I can love both fair and brown,
> Her whom abundance melts, and her whom want betrays. . . .[23]

Compare 'Phyllidula':

> Phyllidula is scrawny but amorous,
> Thus have the gods awarded her,
> That in pleasure she receives more than she can give;
> If she does not count this blessed
> Let her change her religion.

Pound is perhaps less full-blooded, more mannered.

> The family position was waning,
> And on this account the little Aurelia,
> Who had laughed on eighteen summers,
> Now bears the palsied contact of Phidippus.

('Society')

'Palsied' and 'Phidippus' are like Beardsley or Bakst—exquisite, aesthetic, near to self-parody in their attenuation; one of Pound's Kensington friends was the illustrator Edmund Dulac. But the vigorous, Poundian, contribution to the line is 'contact'. As this suggests, there is broadness and high-spiritedness in the epigrams, a verbal comedy, that preserves

them from becoming either the curmudgeonly insults of Ben Jonson
or the self-regarding witticisms of Wilde. They all deal with the distortions that social and commercial pressures wreak upon Eros. The
chief targets are sexual dishonesty, cowardice, vanity and corruption—
and also folly and deception in those bourgeois institutions, marriage
and family life. (The obverse of these negatives is to be found in such
poems as 'Coitus', 'ἱμέρρω' or 'Dompna. . . '.) Although such single
epigrams as 'Epitaph' and 'The Bath Tub' are the most striking, the
sequences 'Amities' and 'Ladies' may last better, in that here the exact
tone is more firmly established and subtleties are thus more easily
managed. The epigrams proper are 'objective' but the projection of
personality seen in these two little sequences shows again in 'The Three
Poets':

> Candidia has taken a new lover
> And three poets are gone into mourning.
> The first has written a long elegy to 'Chloris',
> To 'Chloris chaste and cold,' his 'only Chloris'.
> The second has written a sonnet
> > upon the mutability of woman,
> And the third writes an epigram to Candidia.

This illustrates Pound's critical theory of that day, and is a true epigram.
The neatness of the logic and plot is brightened by the bromidic 'Chloris'
and barely suppressed exultation of the last line. Exultation is much in
evidence in the autobiographical *causerie* poems of *Lustra*, of which
'Ancora' is perhaps the most attractive.

The love-vision is crossed with the epigram in the most celebrated
poem in *Lustra*, 'In a Station of the Metro', celebrated because Pound
explained how, like his third poet, he boiled it down from twenty lines
to two, making it the diploma piece of Imagism. It has often been discussed, and we have already discussed 'Fan-Piece'. Imagist condensation
and juxtaposition apart, one should not underrate the role of the word
'apparition' in the poem.

'Liu Ch'e' may be less familiar. The opening onomatopoeia for silk
takes rank with Herrick's 'liquefaction' and Donne's 'whistling'.[24]
'Discontinued' uses understatement and detachment to intensify emotion,
where in an epigram these would serve an ironic purpose. The heavy
double stress alliterating at the beginning of the second line helps to
create a rhythm of timeless slowness; the dust drifts endlessly. One
might compare, from *Cathay*, 'Blue, blue is the grass about the river.'[25]

While the poem powerfully evokes a regret for a love and a civilization,
its second half is less successful. The leaves scurry while dust is only

drifting; and the wetness of the leaf is more emotional than physical. While the sequence silk–dust–leaves–wet leaf is calculated to express the peeling off of the layers of memory and perception to reach the heart of the scene, the natural objects are perhaps too clearly arranged in a symbolic and rhetorical hierarchy. There is in Pound always a drama buried in the landscape, but the emotional colour of the leaf is too clearly an attributed quality. The leaf that clings to the threshold is the 'half-regained Euridice' still perceptible to the backward look of Liu Ch'e. Pound, like the hounds of 'The Return' 'sniffing the trace of air', points to the physical presence that is still vivid there for the lover's memory and imagination: 'only emotion remains'. In conclusion, it could be restated that the emotional tonality of this last line is, despite all the gaiety, the most enduring note of *Lustra*.

Its pendant, 'Provincia Deserta', one of the best sustained of Pound's early poems, has many interests: the rhythm, the successful use of a litany of names, the direct autobiography without embarrassment, the historical imagination, the landscape, the ebb and flow of emotion rising to a fine climax:

> I have walked over these roads;
> I have thought of them living.

Here we have a crystallization of the Provençal experience in a truly personal form, integrated much more firmly round a speaker whom we now know. We could notice that Pound's picturesque scene is a platform, ultimately, for a romantic adventure such as that which ended 'Poem by the Bridge'—an adventure of a wandering minstrel; and that this story of love and war is called 'a second Troy'. Adulterous elopements tend to be heroic in Pound.

The mixture of love and war, historic romance and modern experience succeeds so notably here, I suggest, because it is 'fixed' in landscape. The landscape is imbued with 'the spirit of romance': 'Sharp peaks, high spurs, distant castles.' This line of romantic landscape was perhaps first struck out in the *Chanson de Roland*—'Halt sunt li pui e li val tenebrus'—and developed in mediaeval romances.[26] Pound's landscape here includes personal observation:

> I have crept over old rafters,
> > peering down
> Over the Dronne,
> > over a stream full of lilies.

And personal memory:

> I have looked south from Hautefort,
>> thinking of Montaignac, southward.

As Bertrans de Born had looked from Altaforte, thinking of Maent of Montaignac.

'Provincia Deserta' is a new kind of Pound poem, narrative and direct; the relation between Pound and the Provençal world is emotional without being confused. The power of the poem is also due directly to a rhythmic and syntactical staple used so skilfully that it is surprising to discover how simple it is. The poem is a litany, like the famous 'Usura' Canto, based on a simple antiphon–and–response. The full line is answered by the inset half-line or dropped line, and these pairs are grouped into little verse paragraphs; the paragraphs are rendered syntactically parallel by the repetition of 'I have'. The sequence runs: 'I have walked—I have crept; I have walked—seen—looked back—gone —climbed; I have said—looked south—lain—seen—seen—said—seen— seen—seen—said—thought; I have walked—I have thought'. So insistent is this recital of what the poet has directly experienced that the few parts of the poem which are not personal assertions attract special attention. These are the opening, the end of the first paragraph and the culminating story of Pieire de Maensac. The emotion in the long third paragraph has already risen to a climax with the 'distant castles', and intensity is built up again through the repeated 'I have' up to 'I have thought', so that the length itself of Pieire's story both demonstrates its importance and asks for a return to the personal formula that is then satisfyingly restored in the close. It is not easy to think of a simpler method of ordering a poem than repeating items of personal experience prefaced by 'I have walked', 'seen', 'said' or 'thought'; it ought to sound like Whitman, but he makes it sound like Chopin.

The places mentioned here have a meaning for anyone who has visited this region or knows anything of the troubadours. They have romance names, but are real places with personal and literary memories. Some of the associations are reported, some understood, some cryptic. Yet the progress from the outer 'I have walked' to the inner 'I have thought of the second Troy' is readily apprehended. The claim of the poem's last line is obviously true; Pound has indeed thought of the troubadours as living, and his slang ('En Bertrans' old layout') and solemnities ('Glad to lend one dry clothing') are more vivifying than the tactful commonplaces of literary history. The presences that Ford brings to life in his *Provence* are sensed, felt and communicated more intensely if less obviously by Pound. His own involvement (he has 'lain' where Coeur-de-Lion was 'slain') is at once poignant and controlled. Much of the *Cantos* consists of walks and conversations with the dead, and it is clear from 'Provincia Deserta' why Odysseus and Dante should appeal to this wandering poet. It is his first completely successful poem of any length, and like many of his latter successes it is the tale of a traveller in time as well as space, peopling a real landscape with real but invisible presences—or felt absences.

6. Cathay

Cathay (1915) deserves a corner of its own, as the most attractive single volume of Pound's poetry. Its winning qualities were perceived on its début, but later it fell among experts.

If we wish to approach the poetry we must make at least a passing acquaintance with Fenollosa and ideogram: that is, first, the relation of Pound's versions to Fenollosa's notes and to the Chinese originals, and secondly, Pound's Fenollosan essay *The Chinese Written Character as a Medium for Poetry* (1920). Pound's translations were not based on any previous knowledge of Chinese but on notes made on Chinese poems by the American Orientalist and art historian Ernest Fenollosa. Fenollosa had studied Chinese poetry with the Japanese scholar Mori at the turn of the century, and his copious unpublished notes were given by his widow to the author of 'Fan-Piece'. Pound's work on the notes to 150 poems resulted in the 14—later, 18—poems of *Cathay*.

Pound, then, did not know Chinese and was working from the post-humous notes of an American learning from a Japanese.[1] The reader might well be wary if I, who am ignorant of Chinese, should seek to lead him through this forest of roots and branches: I shall skirt it. We should not, however, lose hold of two considerations: (1) Pound did not know Chinese; (2) many competent judges of Chinese and of English poetry think these the best translations of Chinese poems into English poems that have been made.[2]

Dissent from such a valuation of *Cathay* has normally been *a priori* where it has not been *ad hominem*: since Pound did not know Chinese, it is impossible that his translations should be good. Scholars irritated by the inaccuracies in *Cathay* had their doubts confirmed by the later Fenollosan essay on the Chinese written character, which propounds an etymological view. As the ideograms are pictures of things—the essay argues—the Chinese script is by its very nature more concrete and poetic than alphabetic writing: reading the character for sunset, the Chinese actually sees the descending sun tangled in a tree's branches. Sinologists point out that the English may just as easily 'see' the sun actually setting when they read the English word 'sunset'; that usage, in Chinese as in other languages, dulls original metaphor and turns words into counters; that most characters are not simple pictograms but of compound, confused or forgotten etymology. Nevertheless there is the ghost of a truth

4

in Fenollosa's view of the ideogram, and some modern scholars are now more aware of the role of latent visual etymology in the Chinese script when used by poets.[3] This concrete theory of Chinese language that Fenollosa developed, together with his dynamic stress on verbs at the expense of nouns, naturally appealed to the activist who wrote 'go in fear of abstractions' and demanded 'direct treatment of the "thing"'': Fenollosa helped crystallize certain ideas in Pound's propaganda for modern poetry.[4]

Fenollosa's ideas, however, do not account for the success of *Cathay*. Fenollosa's notes on the poems, and the work that Pound put into his study of them, produced *Cathay*; Fenollosa's ideas about Chinese script may have helped to give Pound's versions a certain vividness and particularity. The credit of *Cathay* does not depend on Fenollosa's theories and only partly on his glosses; Pound had to interpret the glosses. The credit goes to Li Po and to Pound.

Like 'The Seafarer', *Cathay* contains many mistakes. And as Pound had studied Old English at university, whereas he was at the outset quite ignorant of Chinese, *Cathay* exhibits wilder mistakes. Even A. E. Housman might have had some difficulty in interpreting the private notes of a dead art historian on sessions held with Japanese scholars about Chinese poems as old as 'The Seafarer'. He would certainly have had more discretion than to print the results.

However, it was not Pound's principle to avoid making mistakes at all costs. It is remarkable that he fished anything worthwhile out of this scholarly soup, yet a sceptic might concede that he achieved and communicated an extraordinary understanding of how some Chinese poems work without, in all probability, having enough everyday Chinese to figure out his laundry bill. Such feats of poetic realization of the scholarship of others are not without precedent among English poets translating from the classics. Dr. Johnson's account of Pope's translation of the *Iliad*— the centrepiece of his *Life of Pope* and so of the *Lives of the Poets*—can be consulted. Johnson awards this translation the supreme place among the poetry of his age. Yet he has no anxiety in allowing Bentley's 'pretty, but not Homer'; nor was he under any illusions about Pope's learning: 'At an age like his (for he was not more than twenty-five), with an irregular education and a course of life of which much seems to have passed in conversation, it is not very likely that he overflowed with Greek.'[5]

That Pound managed *Cathay* 'blind' from so foreign a tradition as the Chinese seems an astonishing anomaly. But Europe had been interested in the language and arts of China for centuries; chinoiserie had recently risen to its greatest heights since the eighteenth century; the specialist had not yet triumphed over the amateur among educated readers; and to the London 'vortex' of Pound, Wyndham Lewis and Gaudier, anything in the arts of the whole world seemed both accessible and possible. Besides, Fenollosa's notes, due allowance made for his shortcomings and those of his tutors, were full and rich; and Pound was a gifted linguist of courage and energy, who lived for poetry.

Cathay has been much studied *qua* translation, and I can do little more than report on the discussion.[6] It is clear that its mistakes are at times gross; at times unlucky accidents growing out of the glosses; and at times wholly deliberate. Thus 'The River Song' all unwittingly runs two poems into one, incorporating the title of the second as if it were simply another line. Egregious among the howlers, proper names are sometimes rendered as if they were mere lower-case nouns; and, though some poems are done as closely as possible, others are made over into something sweepingly at variance with Fenollosa's glosses. The degree of conscious adaptation here goes far beyond anything in 'The Seafarer'. In such cases Pound edits out the necessity for notes; what he cannot bring across, he cuts; and what he leaves, he is prepared to change.

Though sinologues naturally have the greatest difficulty in accepting such inspirational procedures, other readers who prefer half a loaf to no bread would be perverse to disown evidently successful poems merely on hearsay academic principle. Some poems in *Cathay* may be travesties, but they are read. Unlike other translations, they are vivid and beautiful, they read like poems, they move the reader. This is, of course, unfair; the method is wrong and not to be imitated; a successful translation by an untrained outsider, an amateur, an earring-wearer, and one who, on top of this, dares to cut and reinterpret, like the most abandoned modern producer of Shakespeare.... It is not surprising that some of the reactions of those in receipt of academic emolument were frigid. Indeed there is something miraculous about the appearance of *Cathay*, over and above the providential collusion that gave rise to it; to quote Johnson on Pope again: 'Those performances which strike with wonder, are combinations of skilful genius with happy casualty'.[7]

Those who wish to consider *Cathay* principally as translation can be referred to Wai-lim Yip's study *Ezra Pound's 'Cathay'*. 'One can easily excommunicate Pound from the Forbidden City of Chinese studies', he concludes, 'but it seems clear that in his dealings with *Cathay*, even when he is given only the barest details, he is able to get into the central concerns of the original author by what we may perhaps call a kind of clairvoyance.' Of other translations, 'none . . . has assumed so interesting and unique a position as *Cathay* in the history of English translations of Chinese poetry.'[8] The example of Pound's *vers libre* has been extremely influential: Yip shows that Pound, 'the inventor of Chinese poetry for our time', according to T. S. Eliot, may indeed be said to have invented Chinese translation by phrase.[9]

Before coming to *Cathay* itself, it should lastly be said that Pound does not pretend to originality. The acknowledgement prefixed to the volume is an open disclaimer: 'For the most part from the Chinese of Rihaku, from the notes of the late Ernest Fenollosa, and the decipherings of the Professors Mori and Ariga.' Rihaku is the Japanese name for Li Po, and Pound gives Japanese forms throughout in acknowledgement of the tradition by which *Cathay* came to him. (That Pound, who had previously published an Epitaph on Li Po, did not know that Rihaku should 'really' be called Li Po, is a *canard*.)

The analysis of 'Poem by the Bridge' and the discussion of 'The Seafarer' show how long it takes to educe unstable critical essences out of a technical inquest on a translation. The poems of *Cathay* are approached here primarily as poems and invitations. Critics have discussed *Cathay* in terms of the extension of rhythmic control over longer lines and verse paragraphs. By whatever techniques it has been gained, it is the beauty of the poems that strikes the reader.

Beauty, the supreme term of literary commendation in the century before Oscar Wilde, has fallen on hard times and ought to be rescued. Some Sunday reviewers still seem to believe that Verdun or Auschwitz—or Peterloo—somehow make it for ever indecent to remark on or seek to emulate beauty. In the homeland of relevance, Pasternak and Mandelstam were ostracized for writing about trees. ('To the question: "What is Acmeism?" Mandelstam once replied: "Nostalgia for world culture."')[10]

What is the beauty of *Cathay*? 'People of today who like Chinese poetry', Eliot sagely remarks in his Introduction to his selection of Pound, 'are really no more liking Chinese poetry than the people who like Willow pottery and Chinesische-Turms in Munich and Kew like Chinese Art.'[11] A full assent to this proposition involves a scepticism about the possibilities of human knowledge that Pound would scarcely accept. However, Eliot's prophecy that *Cathay* will be called 'a "magnificent specimen of XXth Century poetry" rather than "a translation"' still sounds good.[12] Certainly, much of the original and some of the surviving charm of *Cathay* is to do with chinoiserie, the exotic colours, quaint customs and refined sensation of a world that is different-yet-the-same. This is in part a conscious exploitation: Pound's own sensuous enchantment with China dominates some poems, notably 'The River Song' and 'Old Idea of Choan by Rosoriu'. So the beauty of *Cathay* cannot easily be separated from the appeal of the exotic. Indeed, the 'abandon' of Li Po—deprecated by disconcerted mandarins down to Arthur Waley—must have drawn Pound's 'pagan' sympathies; sensuous indulgence in beauty (or wine) is not taboo in the poems Pound has chosen to translate; the ecstasy in 'Sennin Poem by Kakuhaku' is consciously aesthetic, as is the parenthesis in 'Exile's Letter': 'Eyebrows painted green are a fine sight in young moonlight'.

Yet the beauty of *Cathay* is more than a delight in wine, women and song or in the strangeness of old China. Certainly the aesthetic appeal of *Cathay* is keenly and often frankly sensuous, but its beauty is more than skin deep. It is a fitting economy of means to ends: the simple, intimate and direct apprehension of the world of nature becomes the discreet yet powerful formulary of human and spiritual feeling. The emotions of exile and homesickness; of friendship and convivial joys and pleasures; of war; of contemplation—these are projected strongly or subtly in *Cathay*. Before trying to divide the credit between China and America, we can see that the beauty of *Cathay* is not merely exotic, alien or sensuous—it comes from a recognition of humane emotion. As often with openly sensuous poetry, transience and nostalgia may predominate in the impression left by the poems; but this nostalgia is not feebly aesthetic, it always has a human depth.... *Cathay* has also been open to another charge, that of naïvety, simplicity, sentiment, lack of complication. To a sensitive reader the precision and freshness with which such complex 'simplicities' are recreated is answer enough.

As Pound chooses only a few of Fenollosa's poems to make up *Cathay*, the selection itself tells us something about his responses. The particular emotional quality of *Cathay* is regretful and plangent, and its themes meet on this note. These themes embrace departure, exile, estrangement, separation, love, war, travel, escape, pleasure, heroism, rapture, ecstasy. War is a theme that (in 1915) gets special prominence; and there is a subsidiary interest in the place of court and folk values in an ideal society. But the keynote is struck at the conclusion of the first poem, 'Song of the Bowmen of Shu':

> Our mind is full of sorrow, who will know of our grief?

the central poem, 'Exile's Letter':

> I call in the boy,
> Have him sit on his knees here
> > To seal this,
> And send it a thousand miles, thinking.

and the last poem:

> 'But however we long to speak
> He can not know of our sorrow.'

This sense of a painful fullness of emotion being accepted, together with the sense of the relations of Time and Beauty, is the taste *Cathay* leaves in the mind. The value of emotion, the preciousness of the emotional life however painful and however incompletely expressible, is also constantly asserted, most memorably in the lines immediately preceding the conclusion of 'Exile's Letter':

> And if you ask how I regret that parting:
> It is like the flowers falling at Spring's end
>   Confused, whirled in a tangle.
> What is the use of talking, and there is no end of talking,
> There is no end of things in the heart.

Wistfulness pervades the lyric poetry of Victoria's century, from Keats to Tennyson to the Nineties; here the associated whimsy and attenuation are absent. An exquisite delicacy remains, but the directness, the lack of inhibition, is new, and, even at this distance in time from 1915, liberating.

In seeking to illustrate the various qualities of *Cathay* in detail, one is hampered by ignorance of the originals and of Pound's exact route to them. One can however speculate that the timbre I have pointed out is specially characteristic of one side of Li Po, rather than of Chinese poetry in general.[13] More generally Chinese is the non-allegorical, or seemingly non-allegorical, use of nature and landscape to express emotion: 'it is like the flowers falling at Spring's end'. This use of nature as a language is a permanent contribution of China to Pound; of course all descriptive poetry, all nature poetry, uses nature as a language, but China opened Pound's eyes to a nature unsanctified by Palgrave or Dante, and employed the language in new ways, both subtler and simpler; certainly fresh. By 'Palgrave' I mean to indicate the English tradition from Chaucer to Tennyson, and particularly the richer, rhetorical side of the lyric tradition, from which Pound was now trying to advance; and by Dante I refer only to the intellectual framework of inherited patterns of significance that informs the cosmos of Dante and his Christian-allegorical successors—not to his austere imagery, to which Pound responded positively.

One cannot disinherit one's father: Pound never renounced the early Yeats;[14] and *Cathay* is in many ways a deeply Tennysonian volume in its matter, its colour, its emotion. But its versification, melody, use of image and directness of language are indeed very different. This difference presents itself primarily as a difference in the 'nature', in the actual landscape:

The clouds have gathered, and gathered,
   and the rain falls and falls,
The eight ply of the heavens
   are all folded into one darkness,
And the wide, flat road stretches out,
I stop in my room toward the East, quiet, quiet,
I pat my new cask of wine.
My friends are estranged, or far distant,
I bow my head and stand still.
               ('To-Em-Mei's "The Unmoving Cloud" ')

The same freshness, the same feeling of material that is actually new, I find in 'The Beautiful Toilet' and in 'Taking Leave of a Friend'—to choose simpler examples. The latter, one of the 'Four Poems of Departure', illustrates well Pound's imaginative use of natural landscape to create enormous resonances:

Blue mountains to the north of the walls,
White river winding about them;
Here we must make separation
And go out through a thousand miles of dead grass.

Mind like a floating wide cloud,
Sunset like the parting of old acquaintances
Who bow over their clasped hands at a distance.
Our horses neigh to each other
       as we are departing.

Perhaps one should give the credit to Li Po. So far as it is Pound's, critics have analysed the rhythm to account for it. Certainly, the confident use of a new kind of long line, the resource of emphasis and the delicate use of echoes, create much of the effect.[15] And the use of direct language and strong clear imagery contributes as much as the rhythmic invention. It seems to me, however, that in a natural concern to attribute to Pound only the stylistic successes of *Cathay*, critics may have directed readers away from the content. It is more important, in my view of poetry and of translation, when reading 'Taking Leave of a Friend', to picture the leave-taking and feel its consequence, than to decide what the poem owes to its father and what to its mother, still less whether it is legitimate. Pound absorbed a great deal from Li Po, and he also transmuted it. It is usual to prefer *Cathay* to *The Classic Anthology* and to say that Pound translated better when he knew less Chinese, that he was right by instinct rather than by learning; without disagreeing with the spirit of this—for there is something very like a meeting of old acquaintances in *Cathay*—I do not think that the genius of Li Po or the help given by Fenollosa's notes should be neglected.

Constant re-reading cannot detect a weak poem in *Cathay*, though the astonishing profusion of glamour is occasionally reflected a little too clearly by Pound himself, e.g. in a couple of lines in 'The River Song': '... And heard the five-score nightingales aimlessly singing' and 'The wind bundles itself into a bluish cloud and wanders off'. This casualness is merely the extreme of the naturalization of these poems into English; Pound enters personally into the poems, he 'thinks of them living'. The finest of the poems in *Cathay* are by consent 'Exile's Letter' and 'Lament of the Frontier Guard'; the strength of 'Song of the Bowmen of Shu' and the delicacy of 'The River-Merchant's Wife' have always been admired; I would add 'The Unmoving Cloud' to these. The balance of sentiment and irony at its conclusion seems to me very characteristic of Pound, and inimitable. I am not surprised to learn from Hugh Kenner that it is mostly Pound's imagination.[16]

'Exile's Letter', rather than the war poems, seems to me the core of *Cathay*; Arthur Waley's comment, 'at most a brilliant paraphrase', must remain the verdict of the specialist.[17] Pound does, however, suggest a personal freedom of manner very proper to an intimate letter; a man's whole life is set out here, with neither the joys nor the sorrows distorted or constrained. The voice is mellow or lamenting, full or keen, never stinted or stilted as in other translations. As in 'Poem by the Bridge', the balance of emotion is again fully realized. The musical variety and sweep of 'Exile's Letter' are much richer. If the feeling were not intimate and personal, one might compare it, as a rhetorical and musical performance, with Dryden's large odes; as it is, it is more reminiscent of Coleridge's 'Dejection' Ode or Arnold's 'Dover Beach', the current of emotion swelling and fading according to the rhythms of the speaker's voice. The title suggests a theme close to Pound, doubtless rightly, but I do not find the intimate similarities of 'The Seafarer'. The failure to find a post, the deprivation of friends, the sense of a break-up of the Round Table—these correspond to a view of Pound's actual situation as an alien in 1915 (see the extraordinary final note attached to the first edition of *Cathay*).[18] But the situation in 'The Seafarer' seems closer; 'Exile's Letter' offered a sensibility with deeper affinities, hence the sweetness and rightness of tone throughout. Ecstasy, regret, wonder, ceremoniousness, outspokenness, stoicism—this more civilized gamut of feelings offered something richer and more promising. Consequently there is much more sense of strain in 'The Seafarer', a gap between speaker and persona detected in the anti-bourgeois rant, that is nowhere in 'Exile's Letter', though I take this to be a less autobiographical poem; in real life Pound was not a famous drinker. It is the flashing fineness, subtlety and volatility of Li Po's lyric temperament that he responds to.

7. *Propertius* and *Mauberley*

Cathay appeared in 1915, that is, at the time of the magazine *Blast* and before the completion of *Lustra*. The translations of the Noh plays came out in 1916, some early *Cantos* in 1917, *Homage to Sextus Propertius* in 1919 and *Hugh Selwyn Mauberley* in 1920. The War, then, saw a diversification of Pound's activities, not without signs of an understandable distraction. The polemics from *Blast* are described by Pound's most understanding scholar as 'almost wholly unfortunate'; they closed several publications to him and made his living even more precarious.[1] And the later *Lustra*, with the exception of 'Near Perigord', are colder continuations of the Provençal and contemporary-satirical strains. The War dispersed the Vorticists of *Blast* and brought to an end, among other things, the first phase of English Modernism. But Pound was more seriously occupied in these years with how to start the *Cantos*, and much engaged with Yeats, Joyce and Eliot. He and Eliot planned a reform of *vers libre*, the results of which were *Mauberley* and Eliot's *Poems, 1920*, unlyrical ballads which could have appeared in one volume. The War divided Pound's youth from his maturity.

The poems between *Cathay* and *Propertius* offer straws in the wind, but only 'Near Perigord' calls for attention, as the consummation of the early style. It is a solid, full-length treatment of many of the old Provençal themes, and suffers a little from our ignorance of Bertrans de Born; even Richard Coeur de Lion, who discusses Bertrans with Arnaut Daniel in the poem, can scarcely be counted today among those whom every schoolboy knows. But a look at the passage to which Pound refers us in the *Inferno* is all that is needed to follow the poem, and the gist of it is actually translated for us here.

'Near Perigord' is a poem with plenty of old-fashioned attractions and, perhaps because of this, has been neglected.[2] We have met Bertrans in 'Altaforte', 'Planh for the Young English King' and 'Na Audiart'; 'Near Perigord' attempts to rescue him from Hell, where Dante put him for having encouraged the sons of Henry II to fight one another. The three sections of the poem are respectively 'historical', imaginary and dramatic. The first sets the problem: 'Were Bertrans's poetry and strategy motivated by Mars or by Venus?' The second speculates, but leaves the reasons of the head and of the heart still separated; the third, in the first person, is a lyric projection of the psychology of the Lady Maent, Bertrans's true inspiration. As the poem is designed as a riddle, if a fairly open one, it is not too readily to be explicated; but it calls for a few comments.

First, in no other poem is the conception so reminiscent of Browning nor the picturesque mediaeval colour so clearly Victorian. Then, the 'imaginary conversations' approach is prophetic of Pound's later poetry; he gets Cino, Papiols, Arnaut Daniel, Coeur de Lion and Dante into the poem. Again, the theme itself is recurrent in the *Cantos*; a man of action/artist/lover at odds with fate, embedded in a rich historical and mythical setting which makes the nature of his motive all the more enigmatic. Romantic love is often enigmatic in Pound; the third part, though it opens splendidly, ends:

> And all the rest of her a shifting change,
> A broken bundle of mirrors. . . !

These lines might have been found in another poem, 'Portrait d'une Femme' or 'Villanelle: the Psychological Hour', contemporary efforts in the manner of James or Eliot; but as the climax of this poem they represent a permanent feature of Pound's own bundle of attitudes. Love is bewildering, overmastering, complex and impenetrable, and it is to be honoured and obeyed. In context, the conclusion focuses the riddle: Maent hates Bertrans's mind, not *him*, and has married another; yet he is possessed by the knowledge that she who is now 'unreachable' can only live through him. The last line is an image of her which suggests why the distracted Bertrans created (in 'Na Audiart') a composite image, a borrowed lady to approximate to her; it is also a self-definition of the poem. The image is arresting—certainly 'an intellectual and emotional complex in an instant of time'—suggesting the fragmented brilliance of her personality as of his poetry. Visually, the image is reminiscent of Vorticist paintings, and is an early example of Pound's characteristic swirl of constellated particulars moving in different planes to imply larger complexes.

Pound believed that 'the heart of another is a dark forest',[3] and had much sympathy with that nineteenth-century tradition of presenting motive, especially in romantic tragedy, in a darkly brilliant light. The continental tradition of intrigue and complication appears in Browning, James, Conrad and Ford himself, and also in the historical fiction of Stevenson and Maurice Hewlett. This mysterious mode can become heavily saturnine, occluded and reliant on dénouement, though Pound is rarely heavy. 'Near Perigord', however, remains a bit of a galleon.

This does not apply to the beautiful and eloquent Part III, where the identification with Bertrans intensifies the poem beyond the intended urgency of 'a lean man? Bilious?' of Part II. The identification between poet and persona is dramatically most effective, for the theme of unfulfilled passion for unreachable beauty vibrates deeply in Pound. The vehicle here is infinitely more satisfactory than in, say, 'Piere Vidal Old'. Yet there is a limit to what can be done with putting new psychology in old clothes—the voice remains the voice of Ezra. This was to be the last of his mediaeval personae.

Certain Noble Plays of Japan: from the Manuscripts of Ernest Fenollosa, Chosen and Finished by Ezra Pound, With an Introduction by William Butler Yeats (1916) is a little-known cousin of *Cathay*.[4] Yeats's eighteen-page introduction is longer than any of the four Noh plays, which belong as much to Yeats's career as to Pound's. Though Pound is credited with finishing Fenollosa's texts, and his hand is clear in the poetic imagery, the prose speeches are often very Irish, as the opening of *Nishikigi* shows:

WAKI: There never was anybody heard of Mount Shinobu but had a kindly feeling for it; so I, like any other priest that might want to know a little bit about each one of the provinces, may as well be walking up here along the much-travelled road.

So the plays are very much a work of collaboration: Japanese, American, Anglo-Irish, with a dash of translator's Greek.

The plays, with their unfamiliar conventions, are not to be judged unseen, but their plots and incidents are simple, and the language clear and fine. The themes 'chosen' by Pound are not surprising: parted ghosts of lovers; dialogue with a goddess; the return of a great hero to praise the lad who had killed him; a daughter searching for a father now fallen on evil times. It is a world of primal affections, heroic romance, sacred landscape and of communication with gods and heroes. The example of Noh as upheld in Yeats's Introduction certainly took Pound further away from declamation and rhetoric into economy and an intensified allusiveness.

The title of *Homage to Sextus Propertius*, Pound wrote to Hardy, is borrowed 'from a French musician, Debussy—who uses "Homage à Rameau" for a title to a piece of music recalling Rameau's manner. My "Homage" is not an English word at all.' Hardy had suggested Pound might have called the poem 'Propertius Soliloquizes', which, although suggesting a character study too much in the manner of Browning, might have prevented anyone supposing that Pound intended literal translation.[5]

The study of the classical languages and literatures is so peripheral to modern education that it is easy to forget how effortlessly it occupied the centre of English education from the foundation of the Grammar Schools until recently. Ben Jonson thought Shakespeare had 'small Latin and less Greek'; and Dr. Johnson remarks of him: 'It is most likely that he had learned Latin sufficiently to make him acquainted with construction, but that he never advanced to an easy perusal of the *Roman* authours.'[6] Johnson, who composed Latin verse with ease, may seem to set his standard high with 'easy perusal', yet that is what for centuries schools aimed at and their best pupils achieved. Today there will be few Professors of English with as much Latin or Greek as Shakespeare, or Pound, and fewer poets. Those who experienced the fag-end of the old tradition will remember how the first authors at school were Caesar and Virgil, the most imperial and Augustan of Roman authors; less character-building poets, such as Catullus and Propertius, came later. Cicero might replace Caesar, but nothing could replace Virgil. Among the best-known lines of Propertius to one schooled in this tradition would be:

> cedite Romani scriptores, cedite Grai:
> nescioquid maius nascitur Iliade.[7]

Gantillon, in the Bohn Classical Library, translates: 'Yield, ye Roman writers, ye Grecian poets, yield; something greater than the Iliad is arising.'[8] To public schoolmasters turning out public servants, Aeneas was a more suitable model than any of Homer's heroes, and, to those with less Greek, Virgil a more convenient author. He held a special place in their hearts. Pound's Propertius is a burlesque-show barker:

> Make way, ye Roman authors,
>   clear the street, O ye Greeks,
> For a much larger Iliad is in the course of construction
> (and to Imperial order)
> Clear the streets, O ye Greeks!

(xii)

The sentiments of classicists on reading 'much larger' for 'greater' can be imagined; what they chose to print was much milder.[9]

Pound's *Homage* is a free rendering of selections from Propertius' love elegies to Cynthia, rearranged in Pound's order. The sexual relation with Cynthia, and the inspiration that this, rather than 'Martian generalities', provides Propertius as a poet, are the leading themes of the *Homage*, and the mythology is either dropped or burlesqued. Omission or burlesque is the treatment given to Propertius' eulogy of pious, patriotic or imperial themes, as in the raspberry reference to Virgil's *Aeneid*.

The *Homage* is thus a one-sided presentation of Propertius, and
and deliberately so. It is a critique of the accepted Propertius, a reinter-
pretation that finds irony as much as melancholy to be his prevalent mood.
As a view of Propertius it has until recently met with little success among
British classicists, few of whom may have recognized the mode of Pound's
poem. Pound persuaded Eliot, and has impressed A. E. Mason and
J. P. Sullivan and the *Arion* school. The relation of the public and the
private, the august and the ironic, presents a genuine problem in Propertius; the elegies beginning his fourth book, for example, have been taken
as piously if stiltedly patriotic, while the eighth elegy of the book is, as
Gantillon notes, 'a very lively account of the manner in which the jilted
poet retaliated on Cynthia, and how she caught him in the fact and took
summary vengeance upon him and her rivals'.[10] Gilbert Highet begins
his version thus:

> After so many insults offered to my bed,
>   I moved to the offensive, led the charge.
> There is a girl called Phyllis on the Aventine—
>   when sober, unattractive; charming, drunk.
> Then there is Teia—lives near the Tarpeian Park—
>   a lovely thing, but hard to satisfy. . . .

and ends:

> So, after she had changed each separate sheet and blanket,
>   I kissed her. We made peace, all over the bed.[11]

This scabrous passage, which Pound calls the 'Ride to Lanuvium' but
doesn't include in the *Homage*,[12] is clearly comic, chiefly at the poet's
own expense. Propertius' capacity for mockery cannot be doubted by a
reader of this elegy. It is less simple to read the tone and draw the lines
in elegies such as that which becomes section ii of the *Homage*, where
Propertius dreams of epic themes but is warned by Apollo and Calliope
to stick to the love elegy; or the next elegy, a vision of the divine Augustus
Caesar's Parthian campaign. At the Triumph, Propertius concludes, 'it
will be enough for me to be able to applaud on the Sacred Way.'[13]
Propertius is not easy about becoming fully and publicly 'Augustan';
there is a clear possibility that the straight-faced modesty with which he
accepts his position as impotent onlooker may conceal an irony not unlike that with which Mauberley is to contemplate his own irrelevance.
Such irony is a problem with other Roman poets, Lucan and Ovid for
example, and it is at times equally hard to know exactly how to take
Chaucer or Donne; or, in places, Eliot or Pound.

Dogmatism is inappropriate in such cases. Yet many classicists have been categorical enough about Pound's *Homage*; Highet was not unrepresentative when he called it 'an insult both to poetry and to scholarship, and to common sense'.[14] Yet, writing elsewhere about his first encounter with Propertius, Highet alludes to a problem similar to this problem of tone and irony: '... the most difficult thing to understand, even to sympathize with, was his habit of breaking suddenly away from violent personal emotion and introducing a remote Greek myth, not even as an interesting tale to be told, but as a decoration, which every reader was apparently expected to understand and appreciate.'[15] Pound cuts out this mythology. What with his irony and his mythology it would seem that Propertius is a very problematical poet.

Quite apart from the irritation caused to classicists out of range of the tradition of imitation that flourished in England before the triumph of Germanic literal translation, it would seem to the visitor to classical studies that the modern poet, in cutting out or mistrusting the mythology, and in sensing and highlighting the irony, has at least shown critical acumen.

Setting aside as irrelevant here the issue of literal translation, we may ask: 'Is it legitimate for a poet to raid Propertius for what he needs, leave what he doesn't, to alter what he takes, and still to call the result a Homage?' If his poem is successful, the answer must be Yes. The *Homage* seems to me an almost wholly successful performance, and so will it I think to an unprejudiced reader with an interest in the classical world. The interest is needed because Pound presumes some acquaintance with that world, and the success is not outright only because many with that acquaintance will be irked by some superficial blemishes. Pound does not fully transpose and update Propertius into the modern world, as English Augustan imitators did to their Roman originals; consequently there are references to identify.

To take the opening line for an example:

Shades of Callimachus, Coan ghosts of Philetas

Understanding this melodious invocation involves a resolution of the epithet 'Coan', and knowing or guessing that the owners of the plural shades and ghosts must be poets—better still, Alexandrian poets. A little Latin helps with the 'later nephews of this city' (l. 38); to appreciate '(associated with Neptune and Cerberus)' (l. 59) one has only to have been 'weary with historical data' (l. 71) of the notes to a school edition. Yet even so modest a preparedness to deal with proper names might prompt surprise at the forms in 'Polydmantus, by Scamander, or Helenus and Deiphoibos?' (l. 32) or 'Threician' (l. 47). These forms are idiosyncratic

and deliberate; and every edition published by the poet has a rash of
accidental errors in proper names: the *Collected Shorter Poems* has
'Oetian' and 'Phaecia'. To take the possible significance of these variations
from the normal forms, one goes back to the Latin text, and the result
can disconcert. 'Polydmantus', looked up because of the lack of concord
between Latin -*us* and Greek -*os* endings, is a misunderstanding of a
Greek accusative inflection; doubt is sown about Pound's detailed
understanding of the language.[16] This carelessness may involve the
attentive reader in the kind of pedantic worries that Pound was concerned
to rid us of. A reader accustomed to Pound knows that he frequently
insists on the particular form of a name in which he—*ego scriptor*—chooses
to remember it; an allowable idiosyncrasy, reflecting Pound's sense of
linguistic flux. But it is distracting, in a Homage which is not a literal
translation, to be sent back to the minutiae of the text.

Suspicions raised by Polydmantus might extend more generally to
Phoebus' 'vote' (surely Propertius' *vow*?), to Polyphemus' 'dripping
horses' and the 'Marcian vintage'. And the enquiry pursued will lead to
further doubt; in fact, those with examiner's eyebrow may be led into a
savage Housmanic joy in uncovering Pound's cavalier path. Pound is
unsound; and there is undoubtedly something about the *Homage* which
affects British blood pressures, not only in such classicists as Highet, but
also in some ordinary poets.

Yet—to be ordinary—Pound has produced an intelligible Propertius, a
lively Propertius and a modern Propertius. The relationship between the
public and private responsibilities of the writer engages us, the summons
to Art abashes as much now as in 1917, if not in the same way. More
important, the personality disclosed intrigues us—not only in its brilliant
display but in its underlying seriousness. Seriousness is not perhaps the
obvious quality of this spectacular literary spoof, whose principal defects
are its entertaining but overindulged parody of Latinate English and its
broad guying of the corny and unacceptable in poetry; as G. S. Fraser
says, 'for a very discreet irony in the original, Pound substitutes a violent
satirical contempt'—and, I would add, a wild humour.[17] If this paradox
seems somewhat strained, it reflects the strain of Propertius' paradoxical
position perceived and exaggerated further by Pound.

I suspect that Pound began the 'poems for the Propertius series'[18]
light-heartedly enough, having seen the need for a modern Propertius
and having discovered a kindred spirit. The experiments engaged him
deeply, he worked them into a sufficient dynamic and psychological
coherence, and allowed them to stand. He was in no position to keep his
piece nine years; John Quinn could not rival Maecenas. The result is not
Augustan, perhaps not even Propertian: it still seems a little unfinished,

unresolved, it is too many things at once, partly dependent on the Latin, partly about Pound and his London. Yet it subsists, a little desperate and undetermined in tone at times, but held together by a deep conviction that his poetry celebrating Cynthia will survive death. This commitment is eloquently and dramatically realized at the end of several of the sections, notably i, iii, vi, vii and xii, and is the unifying feature of the poem. Unity might at first seem to be what the poem lacks, and the unity I am claiming for it is dramatic and psychological, a dynamic unity coming from the possessed personality of the speaker, Pound's imagined 'Propertius'. This view may seem to grant too little to the formal unity of an accomplished poem: some of the sections, such as i, ii, vi and xii, have perfect logic and self-subsistency, and there is a strategy to the whole work. But several of the episodes are autobiographical, vii and x for example, and the reader is clearly invited to make connections between the literary and the personal—between i and ii is the first such leap—which involves his conceiving Propertius as a character. This is not difficult, as Propertius' tone of voice, constantly varied, pulls the reader along and into the poem. Pound himself may be a little nervous that the dynamic of the poem is not a formal or logical but a dramatic one: he often reinforces the first lines of later sections by repetition, as in 'When, when, and whenever death closes our eyelids' or 'Light, light of my eyes'. Anaphora is a mannerism that was never to leave him. There is a similar, though quieter and more successful, intensification at the end of each section. As the process of the poem is intrinsically dramatic, there is really no need for the sections to begin theatrically.

If Pound found Propertius not only a convenient but an inspiring persona, this was due not to external correspondences of position but to a deeper analogy of interest. If the splash made by the *Homage* is due to the brilliance with which Pound plays on an irony that had been neglected, the enduring value of the poem lies in his successful realization of the tragic source of that irony in Propertius' knowledge of his own value and his simultaneous knowledge that this value is not appreciated by his age, still less by Cynthia, but only by the Muses and by his posthumous readers. This awareness fills the declarations of the poem's splendid opening and closing paragraphs and is strongly felt whenever death is considered, as at the end of i, of iii and of vi. The sense of a difficult fate recognized and accepted, of dedication alongside a rueful perception of personal irrelevance, is implicit in all the best lines of the poem:

We, in our narrow bed, turning aside from battles:
Each man where he can, wearing out the day in his manner.

(v, 2)

I shall triumph among young ladies of indeterminate charact er,
My talent acclaimed in their banquets,
  I shall be honoured with yesterday's wreaths.
And the god strikes to the marrow.

(xii)

or:

  No, now while it may be, let not the fruit of life cease.

   Dry wreaths drop their petals,
    their stalks are woven in baskets,
   To-day we take the great breath of lovers,
    to-morrow fate shuts us in.

 Though you give all your kisses
     you give but few.

 Nor can I shift my pains to other,
   Hers will I be dead,
 If she confer such nights upon me,
     long is my life, long in years,
 If she give me many,
   God am I for the time.

(vii)

Has the *carpe diem* theme of classical love poetry had better modern expression?

The *Homage* is an uneven poem—iv is not a success, for example—and it is irritatingly messy in detail: some will find it too stridently anti-Augustan. Its allusiveness has restricted its audience; its accomplishments, its insolent ease, have offended those jealous of their Latin or their earnestness; and those who admire the technique and enjoy the sallies have often not allowed the poem its full weight. For all its sophistication, its strain and its attendant problems, I find it a more positive, genial and genuine achievement than *Mauberley*. The voice is much nearer to Pound's own voice than that of any of his previous personae; the inflections of Catullus in *Lustra* have proved prophetic. Pound's imagined Propertius may not be all of Propertius, but he liberates much of Pound.

If *Propertius* has never quite arrived, *Mauberley*, having made its impact, shows signs of retiring. It spoke immediately to the disgust and the reaction that followed the War. Commended in literary circles by Eliot and, later, to universities by Leavis, its success with critics perhaps led to too much being expected of it; some have now succeeded in finding it a confession of failure, as has happened with that other 'impersonal' poem, *The Waste Land*. This is a mistaken overreaction against the success of its presumed 'message', its anatomy of society. I have seen *Mauberley* represented in an anthology simply by poem v ('There died a myriad'), which can be assimilated to a familiar view of the Great War. The irony of the poem is then safely directed against the Establishment (poem iv) and the élite (poem xii); the rest can be welcomed as unintelligible but nevertheless cultured sophistication. The polemic of the poem —that the finer life of our society, and especially its art, is poisoned by universal commercialization of values—can thus be neglected, as if 'getting on' no longer affected the artistic life of Britain.

Complex 'readings' of the poem have quite sufficiently attended its allusiveness. A prior problem, however, is the nature of the poem's structure.[19] *Hugh Selwyn Mauberley* is a sequence of eighteen poems in two parts, of which the first thirteen—which we may call Part I—are concerned with Pound, the last five—Part II— with his invented hedonist poetaster, Mauberley. Poem i is a funerary 'Ode' on E.P., the age's epitaph on the disappearing Pound; poems ii to xii are his reply to the age; 'Envoi', the thirteenth poem, is Pound's poetic riposte and farewell. Part II is subtitled 'Mauberley (1920)', and takes this representative aesthete through the same literary world as Pound has just encountered; all Mauberley can manage is the final poem 'Medallion', an anaesthetized version of the same experience that produced Pound's glowing 'Envoi'.

Critics have got into some terrible tangles in interpreting *Mauberley*, partly because Pound does not trouble to provide signposts for those who do not happen to know what he knows. The outline given above can be deduced from an attentive reading of the text alone. Applying Occam's azor to the interpretations that have grown up, this basic structure, assumed by Kenner and expounded neatly by Espey, is simple and answers well. The structural problem arises because the title misled readers into thinking the whole sequence was about Mauberley, even though poem i, 'E.P. Ode pour l'élection de son sepulchre', is clearly about Pound. Other readers have thought that the whole sequence is from the pen of Mauberley.* These confusions arise naturally enough, and Pound is much to blame, but the overwhelming argument for the

---

* If all Part I were by Mauberley—a possibility which cannot be disproved—Mauberley's recounted experiences would then have exactly to coincide with Pound's; which leads directly to the confessional interpretation assumed by Leavis among others. 'Life and Contacts' is the subtitle, in parody of 'Life and Letters'—Mauberley's 'letters' amount to the solitary 'Medallion'. This may again suggest that poems ii to xii are Mauberley's life and contacts, whereas it is crucial to recognize that they are Pound's; they may incidentally be Mauberley's also.

structure outlined above is that the author clearly divides the sequence into two parts, and entitles the second part 'Mauberley'. After the first poem in Part I—the funeral Ode on E.P.—the ensuing eleven poems are vigorous and critical, whereas the whole of Part II parodies passivity and anaesthesia. From this it is clear enough that there is a contrast intended between the active Pound of Part I and the aesthete Mauberley in Part II, a contrast enforced by their two versions of the same event offered in 'Envoi' and 'Medallion': Pound responds to a woman singing by offering his own song, a song that echoes both the enchantment of English lyric poetry and its collapse, whereas poor Mauberley sees something that reminds him of art objects in books and museums and drifts finally into an aesthetic analysis of the singer's 'face-oval'.

That this apologia and explanation have to be offered is no doubt an admission of the difficult nature of *Mauberley*'s structure; there are perhaps elements of confusion or supersubtlety in Pound's conception as well as in his presentation of the poem. But the bulk of the poem remains clear and strong, and the criticism I wish to offer is not new and only incidentally a commentary, as several detailed readings are available.

It may be that the desire for a consistent and clear model of fictional structure for the reader to hold in his mind, as in 'point-of-view' criticism of the Novel, is inappropriate here. The poems in series make a great impact, whether the hero is Pound or Mauberley. Nevertheless, the question seems a primary one.

The force of poems like ii, v and ix, as sheer statement, is astonishing, even shocking:

> Better mendacities
> Than the classics in paraphrase!
>
> (ii)

> Accept opinion. The 'Nineties' tried your game
> And died, there's nothing in it.
>
> (ix)

These nostrums are held under an ironic lens and so turned for us to inspect that our invited contempt operates unimpeded. Intensity of feeling comes near to clouding the statement in the 'lies' of iv, the 'botched civilization' of v, or the 'foetid' of vi; yet the invective is controlled and disciplined. In poems vii and x, based on Victor Plarr and Ford Madox Ford, admired figures discarded by the age, the implied feeling is superbly balanced and restrained, as the close of each shows:

> Neglected by the young,
> Because of these reveries.
>
> (vii)

He offers succulent cooking;
The door has a creaking latch.

(x)

Pound borrowed the quatrains and the isolating cameo-technique from Gautier's *Emaux et Camées*. Elegance and efficiency of exposition cannot go much further.

The intelligence, pattern and authority of these vignettes stamp *Mauberley* as a mature achievement, and these qualities are found again in the more complex poems i and ii, and in the 'Envoi'. Pound speaks to the world at large in a way he has not done before, and his passionate indictment of the blindness of that world is moving, especially in the feeling for the casualties of the war and of the peace. His critical sense of himself in the 'Ode', however ironically expressed, lends the whole sequence a dimension suggested more diffusely in *Propertius*. Here he admits some inappropriateness in his earlier heroic manner; his hubris ('Capaneus') and his obstinate Odyssean susceptibility to and cultivation of beauties that lie off the straight and narrow path of return to his 'true Penelope', Flaubert. This last is a doubly ironic line, as Kenner pointed out, for the speaker means 'Flaubert' to indicate a sterile aestheticism, whereas Pound sees Flaubert not as the martyr to art but as the painter of the essential reality of his time—the 'histoire morale contemporaine'.[20] The last quatrain is an equally ironic testament, as Pound has been so deeply affected by what is feebly referred to as ' "the march of events" , that he is leaving, slamming the door. The reason he passes from (English) men's memory at the age of thirty (viz. as the author of *Cathay*) is that he is leaving this obstinate island for his destiny as a Flaubertian realist.

The withering reply of poem ii still seems, in its analysis of contemporary demand, a classic statement: I take 'the obscure reveries / Of the inward gaze' as referring not only to Plarr but to Eliot's Prufrock; the paraphrased classics as his own *Propertius*; and the ' "sculpture" of rhyme' as the Pound–Eliot reaction against *vers libre*, of which this is the manifesto. Literary history records, however, that *The Waste Land* rather than *Hugh Selwyn Mauberley* was to prove the *Hernani* of English Modernism.

The more general critique of contemporary society in poem iii seems to me sketchier and lacking in the personal authority and drama of the opening; not that the critique of democracy is untimely. The music of the lyre is clearly preferable to that of a pianola, though it is less clear that Christ, macerations and Caliban form a syllogism. The symptoms of cultural decline are extreme and rather esoteric, except to readers of Gautier, but the idea is more commonplace, however brightly expressed.[21]

The versification is brilliant, the wit crackles in the 'tawdry cheapness', and rises to something much finer in the famous last quatrain. Pound as a Pindar with no one to praise is amusing, and his wreath sounds tinny indeed—which does not detract from the truth or seriousness of what he is saying here. But the glorious pagan past, however phallic, is too theoretical an ideal to sustain such sweeping pottedness as:

> Even the Christian beauty
> Defects—after Samothrace;

This is crabbed and cryptic. Much more typical of Pound at his best is the growl of 'in the *market place*'. On the whole, poem iii is, by the standards of its exceptionally solid predecessor, a rather patchy treatment of too vast a theme. However, the transitions between the 'mould in plaster' and the 'tea-gown', and between 'What hero shall I crown?' and the war poems are disciplined and powerful.

Poems iv and v are admired; they are certainly very striking. Poem iv has a panoramic disillusion that includes the civilian and after-war phases, a feeling familiar from the other war poets. There is a characteristic Poundian admiration for courage—and for nobility of lineage. But despite the heightening effect of the litany, this generous, sincere and right-thinking lament remains—apart from the beginning, the *non dulce*, and the end—not so very extraordinary; much of the thought is, in no discreditable sense, naïve, overwhelmed by events, like the reaction of Sassoon and many others. Poem v tries to strike a very summary balance. Can a civilization be 'botched'? Is God an art historian? It is true that art without life is lumber, and that the British Museum without Pound's beloved Gaudier is pointless; the War finished Pound and his friends, and the bitterness is passionate. Yet the War finished both more and less than is realized here—as the *Pisan Cantos* in part record. The judgement here is, for an English reader, too archaeologically remote; from what tenable point of view can it be maintained that the 'high blood' was spilt to defend nothing more than the British Museum?

'Yeux Glauques'—beginning the historical explanation for the mess—has been criticized as inaccurate cultural history, whereas it is merely syncretic and unorthodox; Swinburne and Rossetti are referred to by a Cambridge critic of this passage as 'two poets remarkable (to us) for their meretriciousness', a remark which in itself seems to demonstrate Pound's continuing relevance.[22] The poem, as an epigram on the Pre-Raphaelites, is a brilliant foreshortening of the effect of a hypocritical official morality repressing and distorting the lives of artists, stifling the *Rubáiyát* till Rossetti discovered it, and robbing Elizabeth Siddal's eyes of their natural 'quickness'. We may not accept the implicit theory, nor even

admire the poetry nor the Latin Quarter morality of these three lyric
poets and translators; but 'poor Jenny's case' has undoubtedly been put.

In poem vii, 'Siena mi fe . . . ', the case of the Nineties, even more
sadly pickled and stillborn, is put with a wild and tender sense of farce
that for all the indignation below the surface preserves a curious tact.
The arrangement of details to suggest essences is worthy of Joyce (or
Flaubert): the utter deadness of Verog's inward-turned 'reveries', their
preciosity, can coexist in Pound's even-toned recapitulation with a
pathetic sense of loss and waste. Poem vii is a very funny poem, but 'the
flippancy', as Leavis said, 'subserves a tragic effect'.[23]

Of viii, ix and x—perfect, complete statements—there is nothing to
add, except that the unpleasant reference to Max Beerbohm (who was
not a Jew, incidentally) conceals, however unwillingly, a compliment.
Beerbohm may or may not have erased his true nature in order to appear
impeccably conformist: but his stuffed shirt would not be included in
this 'series of curious heads in medallion' were it not that he too conserved
something of the aesthetic and irreverent tradition of the Nineties behind
his 'limpid eyes' and 'infant's face', even if at too great a cost. The
reference to the 'forty years' of exile, though hostile, is not devoid of
fellow-feeling.

Poem xi is the slightest of the cameos and depends upon too *recherché*
a reference to be widely intelligible, though the obscurity is partly
decent: the Ionian 'habits' referred to by Remy de Gourmont were
erotic bites;[24] they contrast with the 'mouths biting empty air' of poem ii
in Part II.

Poem xii, though it completes the sequence and brings the review
up to date, and though it opens with a brilliant image, exposes the edge
of Pound's range; compare it with Eliot—or with Max Beerbohm—and
the satirical tone seems a little forced. The mock-tentative words—
'precisely', 'somewhat', 'uncertain', 'possible'—become predictably
Prufrockian and the satire, however accurate, rather obvious; Pound
seems to have expected a lot of the aristocracy. The possibilities of a
modern heroism, and the absence of a role for the artist, are both themes
of *Mauberley*. As Espey suggests, the poet finally has to crown himself
under the asterisks.[25] The conclusion of the twelve poems is not that
Fleet Street is nowadays inhabited by haberdashers rather than by Dr.
Johnson, but that those who accept the patronage of Fleet Street—Shaw,
Wells, Bennett—are condemned to turn out, not even the tea-roses of
Kensington, but half-hose.

'Go, lovely Rose' is the 'song of Lawes' referred to in the 'Envoi', and
the rose evokes the Tudor lyric tradition summarized in Waller's words,
which themselves echo a further tradition stretching back to Sappho's

roses. The 'Envoi' is meant as a farewell rose for the English lyric Muse
to add, not to her Museum diadem, but to her living bouquet. The first
stanza reproaches Pound for not having been able to live up to the material
he had known; the second is a superb amorous compliment in the
Campion tradition; the third is addressed both to the singer, and also to
the English language. 'Envoi' is a wreath for the English lyric tradition,
and thus reverses the verdict of the 'Ode'. (The question lingers: What
adjunct to the Muses' diadem has England presented since 1919?)

Part II, 'Mauberley (1920)' bears a complicated parody relationship
with the first part—complicated in detail and minor implication, though
simple enough in essence; Mauberley is what Pound or any artist might
have become had he indeed been merely the aesthete in the out-of-date
tradition represented by the cipher of Brennbaum. (Mauberley bears a
certain relationship, too, to Prufrock and to Stephen Dedalus, earlier
selves outgrown by their creators.) His 'fundamental passion' is an effete

> . . . urge to convey the relation
> Of eye-lid and cheek-bone
> By verbal manifestation. . . .
>
> (II, ii)

It is only a year after the end of his 'romance' that he realizes he has
missed his chance, his 'mandate of Eros'. He drifts, daydreams like
Prufrock of the South Seas, drops out of 'the world of letters' and
produces a 'Medallion' of the singer whose song Pound had answered
in 'Envoi'; all Mauberley can manage in response to his Venus Anady-
omene is a glazed look.

Though accomplished, witty and subtle, Part II reads as a pendant to
Part I, and its wonderful cleverness is perhaps more apparent than its
efficacity as a foil. It has some of the thinness of its subject, and little of
the impact of Part I. Of course, this is part of Pound's plan, and the
quality of the art, the perception and the excellent humour are not in
doubt. Mauberley is the sort of charming person Pound was always
meeting in London, and Pound is notably nice to him, much nicer than
Wyndham Lewis would have been. It is pleasant to see that the balance
of sympathy and clear-eyed perception is so firmly kept. Consider, as a
solitary example, the bathos and pathos of:

> As Anadyomene in the opening
> Pages of Reinach.
>
> ('Medallion')

Superficially, however, there is some overcomplication, the entropy of an
in-joke.

Some would apply this last judgement to the whole sequence, and there is no doubt that *Mauberley* is a learned, allusive and difficult poem, difficult in its compression ('Capaneus; trout for factitious bait') and in its cultural exhibitionism. A knowledge of *Mauberley* is something that has to be acquired by study. Pound wrote to Hardy: 'If—as in the case of Mauberley's own amorous adventure, I compress Henry James's novel into two pages—even unsuccessfully—I have the right to some of the attention that would have gone to the 298 pages omitted.'[26] *Mauberley* is indeed extraordinarily concentrated and complex—a more disciplined poem, more unified in its imagery, than *The Waste Land*; and with the sharpest and wittiest use of rhyme. It can be seen from *Mauberley*, too, how profoundly Pound wished to reclaim for poetry areas which the lyric tradition lost to the novel in the nineteenth century—areas of social, public and cultural life, including both 'l'histoire morale contemporaine' of Flaubert and the epic ambitions represented by 'the sublime' and 'Achaia'; though these were to be the material of the *Cantos* and the future.

8. The Cantos

In 1920 Pound moved to Paris and in 1924 settled in Rapallo. Henceforth he was to devote himself principally to the *Cantos*, the epic 'long poem' he had intended from his college days. The comparison with Milton is not unilluminating, despite the disparity in aims and achievement; Pound and Milton have in common early essays in many poetic forms, and a 'synthetic construction of a style of speech'. There are similarities, too, in their characters and careers: a Hellenic–Hebraic division in the sensibility; virulent pamphleteering; courage, innocent self-belief, stubborn idealism; political disillusion, leading to a reluctant postponement of paradise.

When he left England in 1920 Pound had an entire career behind him, the poetic achievements of which are set out in Eliot's Introduction to the 1928 *Selected Poems*; we have merely reviewed them at greater length. He had also been the recognized actor-manager of the Modernist company. But the company had broken up with the War, and the sequences he produced during it record a disappointment. He had not, after all, 'arrived' in England, nor had his causes; his poems were increasingly reviewed in terms of his *Blast* persona; the magazines could not support him; and he did not like what he saw of British public life after the War. He left, and perhaps was not much missed. He returned in 1965 for Eliot's memorial service.

The Provençal, classical and Chinese inventions and imitations had always been preparations for the long poem. He published the first three Cantos in *Poetry* (Chicago) in 1917, before both *Propertius* and *Mauberley*. The slightly improvised air of these sequences suggests distraction. Pound was occupied with how to begin the *Cantos*, and made one or two false starts. Tentativeness is marked in the title, *A Draft of XVI. Cantos of Ezra Pound for the Beginning of a Poem of some Length now first made into a Book*, which appeared in Paris in 1925 in an edition of 90 copies. Cantos and parts of Cantos had appeared and continued to appear in different magazines in three countries.[1] *A Draft of the Cantos 17–27* appeared in 1928 in London in an edition of 101 copies; *A Draft of XXX Cantos* was published in Paris in 1930 in 200 copies. Only in 1933 did London and New York see the first thirty Cantos. From this point onwards new instalments of the *Cantos* appeared in commercial editions of 1000 or 2000 copies; Eliot was now at Fabers. Before the Second

World War Pound sold slightly better in London, after it in America; the criticism sold better than the poetry. Throughout this period Pound wrote fast for a large number of fugitive or eccentric magazines, as well as for the *New Age*, the *Criterion* and the *Dial*.

In retrospect it seems that, leaving England, Pound did indeed 'pass from men's memory', aged thirty-five. If we except limited editions, no new poems appeared in book form between 1920 and 1933—a virtual abdication from the public stage. The motives for absenting himself from Anglo-Saxondom were those of Achilles as well as those of Odysseus; Pound pointed out how many English poets from Byron onwards had chosen to live in Italy. The departure from England lost Pound his fragile publishing base and separated him from whatever tiny readership he had. Gallup's bibliography lists him as publishing one contribution to a periodical in 1926; in 1918 there had been well over 100. But the retreat was also strategic; away from the centre, he was working on his long poem, the epic for which he felt he had at last found the right form.

The form of the *Cantos* is, as those who have read Pound's critics will be aware, an insistent question. Unfamiliar subject-matter and idiosyncratic reference would scarcely matter if the reader could feel confident that he knew where he was going. It must be admitted that he rarely has felt this, and sometimes has wondered whether the author did.

Upon what principles could a long poem which intended to contain both the modern world and how it got into its present state—a modern epic—be organized? The three original Cantos show Pound knew what he wanted to do and had many subjects in mind, but that he felt uneasy about that predominantly discursive, talkative, Browning-like monologue form—the 'Near Perigord' form—to which he could see little alternative in a poem which was to contain both history and poetry. What is now Canto 2 begins with a relic of the original beginning of the poem:

> Hang it all, Robert Browning,
>   there can be but the one "Sordello."
> But Sordello, and my Sordello?

This poses Pound's problem of how to establish his own version of essential cultural history when (a) some of it has been done inimitably already, and (b) historical facts are recalcitrant to imagination and to personal need. In the event, the *Cantos* now start with Odysseus telling how 'we' went down to the ship. The example of Joyce and 'myth' came to replace the example of Browning and 'history'—of ancient and universal myth that was at the same time modern; *Ulysses* was to give Eliot the same idea.[2]

The first Canto offers Odysseus as an heroic explorer and experiencer;

self-reliant, he cultivates only the gods and the great dead, in search of knowledge; lieutenant of Athena, yet follower of Aphrodite; lover of Circe, faithful to beauty and to his own form of duty. Like Dante's (and Tennyson's) Ulysses, he is in search of *knowledge*—as well as, like Homer's Odysseus, on the way back to Penelope and home. Odysseus/Ulysses was a natural persona for Pound. Canto 2 presents a mythical transformation, like that worked by Circe; 3 begins autobiographically in Venice, like Odysseus telling his life story at the court of Alcinous. If the *Cantos* are not cast consistently in the form of a voyage of discovery, they are conducted in the spirit of such a venture, and continents or islands of knowledge, like Enlightenment America or Siena, or corners of Renaissance Italy, or China as seen via Confucianism, are explored and reported on. The amorous encounters of Odysseus with Calypso and Circe, and his interviews with other nymphs and goddesses, also serve as models for other realms of Pound's experience. The visit to Hell, initiated in Canto 1, is resumed *in propria persona* in 14 and 15. Incidents from the *Odyssey* are specifically used as ways of dealing with actual experience—shipwreck, landfall, passing the Lotus-Eaters, the encounter with Proteus, the loss of companions.

Yet the *Odyssey* is only one model, and an intermittent one; the visit to a modern hell in 14–15 is conducted more in the manner of another traveller, Dante, though without guide or 'familiar compound ghost'. The *Cantos* are also arranged with some deference and reference to Dante's *Divine Comedy*—the graduated ascent to knowledge and illumination via Hell, Purgatory and Paradise. Again, the model is intermittently invoked; this is a humanist *Commedia*.

Both the *Odyssey* and the *Commedia* are narratives, unlike the *Cantos*. Pound refers to the framework of their stories occasionally—stories so well known that they have become the myths of the literate. The *Odyssey* and the *Commedia* also have it in common that they are travelogues, accounts of a voyage and a journey, containing sacred incidents and encounters with figures from myth and history. This broad figural quality they naturally share with much of the world's literature—with other epics and other mediaeval and Renaissance dream-visions for example, and also with the historical novel, the *Bildungsroman* and the autobiography of the nineteenth century.

Allusions to Homer and Dante are made by Pound throughout the poem. These analogies are made much of by some commentators, as are such other hints of models as Pound threw out in letters or conversation.[3] None of these models, however, is reliably of use, for they are not used consistently: Odysseus is not like Dante's Ulysses, for he does not drown. Pound is not like Dante, for he is without an 'Aquinas map' and, outside

Pisa, found himself in a real Purgatory worse than the cultural Hell of Cantos 14 and 15. Nor are the *Cantos* really like a fugue, as is claimed, for large new subjects are introduced towards the very end. Nor are they truly epic, for the epic should be objective narrative, and Pound speaks too often in his own voice. Those familiar with the *Cantos* sometimes sidestep the problem of form. Donald Davie wrote: 'And meanwhile we can forget about such much debated non-questions as whether this poem has a structure, and if so, what it is.'[4] There is much in a 'meanwhile': the structure question may not be the first to ask, nor to answer, but it is a question which rises up and assails the reader opening a page of Greek and Chinese, of mingled mythology, history and autobiography. . . . Readers have perhaps no rights, except the right to skip or stop. ('*Paradise Lost* is one of the books which the reader admires and lays down, and forgets to take up again.'—Johnson)[5] But all books, even *Tristram Shandy* and the aleatoric deal-your-own novel, have a form and a structure, even if they have invented it. Forswearing all traditional forms, the *Cantos* inevitably dissolve into autobiography—an autobiography cast in the form of a mythical narrative, so that Pound does not at first appear to be the protagonist, though incidentally and at last he is discovered to be so; 'the *Cantos*, which are wholly himself . . . ,' wrote Eliot in 1928.[6]

Yet are not the *Cantos* supposed to be an epic ('An epic is a poem including history'7)? They certainly included history, especially in the Thirties, and at times have an epic dimension. At times, they are also drama, satire, documentary, catalogue, sermon, reportage, lyric, diary, meditation, descriptive set-piece, blasts and blessings, hymn, elegy, eclogue, asides, doodle, history notes, epigram, abstract, essay, paradigm, peroration, fanfare. Despite the slabs of 'fairly tough and unblastable' documented fact, the poem becomes autobiographical, intentionally or otherwise, most of it intellectual autobiography. That which is not intellectual but emotional is often, indeed characteristically, mediated through mythical and literary prototypes, as from the epics of Homer and Dante. These background forms provide a shadowy design inside which a chaotically various foreground occupies the eye—a foreground whose conventions can be as curious as those of the mediaeval or Renaissance romance—those inclusive and often unfinished forms, such as those of Chaucer, Spenser and Rabelais, where 'point of view' is often lost in the local contrast of foreground and of sequence.

The 'much debated non-question' of the structure of the *Cantos* arises and has to be faced, though it cannot be solved, at the outset, and an answer, which may be a debatable non-answer, has to be offered; for the difficulty of the *Cantos* lies more in its structure than in its allusiveness, a point admitted involuntarily by the way long-time students of Pound will still rather print exegesis of some newly cracked *locus desperatus* than commit themselves firmly and publicly to a view of the structure. Certainly the *Cantos*, Canto by Canto, have intelligible structures; the meaning of each Canto can be apprehended; and this more or less continuous understanding can pleasurably get the reader through the 800-odd pages. But the overall design, the sense of direction between Cantos, is not so intensely and continuously present that the unity of the poem can be said to rise far above such almost-circular categories as a 'unity of sequence' or the unity of the author's mind. It can be granted that the sequence is not merely linear but polyphonic and involves recurrence; and that the author has a remarkable mind with some forcefully organizing axes of interest—all this can be granted without granting until after further debate the structural success of the enterprise.

It is persuasively argued that Pound did not intend the kind of evident intellectual coherence intended by Milton nor the kind of formal harmony and fullness predicated as essential, even to the short poem, by Yeats. Yeats says that Pound had style without form, and Yvor Winters that he is 'a sensibility without a mind';[8] observations which have formed the praise of admirers who dislike the notion of art *imposing* order on life, or the assumption that the intellectual order of a poem consists in a skeleton of conceptual propositions. While it is now clear that Pound quite deliberately eschewed formal completeness and proportion, and likewise did not want to subject artistic means to thematic ends, it remains to be calculated whether he was wise in this. There is sense in Aristotle's warning in the *Poetics* not to make a work of art like a creature one thousand miles long, and in his observation that a poem is not a unity simply because it is about one man.

In Canto 74 Pound quotes Aristotle to the effect that young men's generalities 'cannot be born from a sufficient phalanx of particulars'. He describes as 'ideogrammic' the establishment and arrangement of a 'sufficient phalanx of particulars', which is one of the chief motives of the poem. Much of the documentation in the *Cantos* is 'evidence' in a 'case' —the case against the historical corruption of Western civilization by usury. The case consists of the evidence and—in the 'Usura' Canto— the indictment, without the connecting arguments or a summing up. But this 'case', which dominates the polemic middle reaches of the *Cantos*, is only the local form of the general mode of operation—a 'hermeneutic', discovering mode, which is used by Calliope as well as Clio in the poem.

Augustine remarked that what is grasped with difficulty is perceived with pleasure and retained.[9] This principle of communication arises in his vindication of the allegorical interpretation of particulars; whereas the positivist Pound is offering us sets of instances arranged so as axiomatically to project their inherent significance. The heroes of the *Cantos* include medical scientists, anthropologists, naturalists and journalists—connoisseurs of observed facts. At the same time, however, there is an implicit allegorical or typical significance in the figure of Odysseus going down to the world of the dead in Canto 1, a *nekuia* Pound repeats in Canto 3. The *nostos* of Odysseus is itself myth as well as event.

One therefore cannot say that the *Cantos* have no form. Their form, it is often claimed on the other side, is imitative of the flux, variety and multifariousness of life—an 'open' form. The first words of Canto 1 are 'And then . . .', the last 'So that:'. The first volume of the *Cantos* was *A Draft of* . . . , the last *Drafts and Fragments*. The working title, *Cantos of a Poem of some Length*—formulated in the experimentalist days of Joyce's *Work in Progress*—became *The Cantos of Ezra Pound*, the poem modestly giving way to its author. (Another ambivalence is revealed by a question of etiquette: is or are the *Cantos* singular or plural?) In 1965 Pound made a *Selected Cantos*, prefaced by his 'call the thing an art-form', the suppressed beginning of the original Canto 1. So there is plenty of evidence that Pound changed his mind about the nature and direction of the *Cantos* over the six decades during which he was composing them. It would be rather worrying if he had not; besides, there is a closer connection than has been remarked between his personal circumstances and the concerns of the poem even before 1945.

And yet an open form is still a form, however flexible. The extreme theory adopted by some followers of William Carlos Williams, that form should be no more than a posthumous and accidental aspect of content or of 'utterance', is a rationalization and a fallacy. Language can never become entirely reflexive or self-referring, it remains a communicative medium, referring to realities outside itself. A piece of writing is not in itself a slice of life; as Williams himself admits, there are no apples in poems.[10] Art is incurably mimetic and only by illusion can it assume the same ontological status as the reality which it imitates. It necessarily represents by selection, and selection involves a point of view and, however informally, an order. A man believing as strongly as Pound in the controlling and discerning power of the mind, the judgement and the will could never have lent his name to the random aleatoric excesses of the more beatific of its invokers. Indeed, *abouleia*, lack of will, is for Pound a greater sin even than usury.

It is obvious that Pound had certain convictions, opinions, passionate preferences and dislikes and that these help to pattern the *Cantos*. They do not, however, amount to categories of thought. The only filing system left to us, he once observed with regret, is the alphabet.[11] (It is also the method of the *Annotated Index to the Cantos of Ezra Pound*.) Pound felt strongly the desirability of a graduated hierarchy of values—a graduated scale like that of Dante, graduated rather than simply polarized. He does, however, revert under emotion to ecstasy or outrage. The measured graduations he observed in Dante, or in Confucius, in Coke, in Jefferson or in Henry James, he envied. He also envied Eliot's 'more symmetrical' education and envied as well as resented the metaphysical categories of his morbid friend. For a humanist *Commedia* is an enlightened mirage, a Temple at once of Reason, Astraea and Aphrodite; and all autobiographies are inconclusive.

It is important to be completely candid about the initial difficulties presented by the *Cantos*, and to make it clear that some of the models provided for the structure of the *Cantos* by their admirers are actually present only intermittently. I cannot accept the theory that the *Cantos* have no structure or form; nor that this alleged aformality does not matter because life itself only reveals its own coherence ultimately, progressively and even then incompletely. Nor could I accept it if it were demonstrably Pound's own view.

We can venture, then, that Pound had plans for the form of the *Cantos* which were consciously modelled on 'mythical' elements in Homer and in Dante; and that the composition was to be musical, polyphonic rather than symphonic, and developing cyclically or spirally rather than in a straight line of narrative. These plans, even from the outset, included room for the topical, the new, the accidental; no end was clearly foreseen. The epic ambition meant the inclusion of history, to be presented in a would-be objective, though also a dramatized form. The historical aim also meant the exclusion of mere subjective self-expression, though the transfiguring moments of historical *aristeia* would be of the poet's choice, and would also aspire to the universal status of myth. The poet's attitude to history was always personal and ethical, and combined the documentary with the romantic, the statistical with the hero-worshipping. The celebration of the heroic man and moment is often paralleled by a mythopoeic handling of visual and sensual experience in terms of a Mediterranean polytheism. The heroic man lives in and produces a just and/or heroic epoch when the human 'nerve-set' can remain open to and in tune with a natural universe full of vital forces, intuited directly as factual experiences but expressed as myths.

The compositional process can be described as polyphonic in that the elements do not mingle or blend but remain vigorously distinct, though the planes may be superimposed. Locally this may seem merely accumulative of circumstantial evidence—the ideogrammic, 'Aristotelian' or documentary method—but the arrangement within each Canto is meant

to lead to perception; as the block within each Canto, so the Cantos
within the whole poem. But the process of composition is so flexible as to
allow Pound to incorporate unforeseen discoveries, such as the Malatesta
papers, and biographical accidents, such as the Pisa confinement. On
the other hand, the Chinese and American Cantos, whether or not they
were originally planned, have a clear purpose, coming where they do in
the middle of the poem, as Enlightenment examples of just societies; and
the intended *Commedia*-like progression of the poem is increasingly
evident as we proceed.

Why or how Pound adopted this mixture of methods of composition
is a difficult question. He wanted not just a *Prelude* or an *Excursion*, but
to 'get it all in'. Whatever else, this was no mean ambition. Despite the
serendipity or opportunism of this process of composition, it is clear
that the poet who issues his work in wholly separate volumes intends a
lesser unity than Pound did. His would not be a philosophical unity
such as we can see shaping the work of Eliot, Yeats or Stevens, but a much
simpler inclusiveness and openness of sensibility, a trustingness. It
would be useless to spend longer on divining Pound's intentions: whatever the *Cantos* are in 1978, they are surely not what he may have intended
in 1917.

After these preliminaries, it may do no harm to offer a table of contents
of the *Cantos*. Such a step may seem unduly modest, but it provides a
basis.

The *Cantos* were published in nine volumes:

1   1–17. The subject-matter of the first seven Cantos is mythical,
legendary and visionary, introducing a rich mixture of themes:
Odysseus' journey to Hell; Helen's beauty as cause of the Trojan war;
the metamorphoses of Dionysus; troubadour and Italian parallels to
Ovid's metamorphoses. Modern lifelessness presents, in contrast, only
'rooms, against chronicles'. The Graeco-mediaeval legendary setting

5

gives way in 7–11 to the activities of Sigismundo Malatesta, master of Rimini in the fifteenth century, condottiere and patron, striving against larger economic forces. 12 introduces sordid modern monopolists. 13 is a vision of Confucian order. 14–15 return us to the monopolists, in an obscene Inferno of war profiteers and usurers, from which Pound, with the help of Plotinus, escapes into Elysian fields (16) where he dreams of heroes and nymphs, gods and goddesses, principally Dionysus (17) and sails back to Venice.

2 18–30. Modern exploiters (18, 19, 22) are contrasted with passionate Renaissance life and natural and pagan pleasures (20, 21, 23–26). The constructive energies of the Quattrocento also contrast with modern drift, diffidence and destructiveness (27–29). 30 celebrates a passionate ruthlessness in Renaissance civilization.

3 31–41 (Jefferson: Nuevo Mundo). The initiative of the Founding Fathers, their intelligence, their rational and practical resource, is the theme, contrasted in 31–34 with European darkness, to which Bonaparte is an exception. (35 contrasts Viennese decadence with North Italian care for quality; 36 is a translation of Cavalcanti's 'Donna mi prega', an expression of a submerged neo-Platonic tradition.) 37: President Van Buren continues Jefferson's struggle against the Bank. 38: Modern war profiteers. 39: A 'Pervigilium Veneris'. 40: Institutionalized swindling and vulgarity versus Hanno's voyage and the crystal. 41: Mussolini's *virtù* against monopolists is compared with Jefferson's.

4 42–51 (*Fifth Decad*: Siena: The Leopoldine Reforms). The Monte dei Paschi a distributist bank based on the abundance of nature; Siena in the eighteenth century a benevolent dictatorship where money was spread, not hoarded. 45: Usury anathematized. 46: England corrupt ever since the foundation of the Bank in 1694; the resulting slums; Roosevelt a parallel. 47: 'sailing after knowledge' to the bower of Proserpine. 48: Monopolists against adventurers; the crushing of the Albigensians. 49: The peace of life in the Chinese countryside. 50: Waterloo a victory of usury over enlightenment. 51: Usury against light and nature.

5a 52–61 (The Chinese Cantos). A Confucian presentation of Chinese imperial history, beginning with the Book of Rites, the first emperors and Confucius, up through the dynasties to the Manchu. Taoists and Buddhists enfeeble the empire, which flourishes only when Confucian ethics rule. French Jesuits a partial exception to the rule that religion is a distraction from human affairs. Yong Tching (d. 1735) an ideal emperor.

5b 62–71 (The Adams Cantos). A detailed presentation of John Adams

(b. 1735) as the father of his country: integrity, energy, study of law, negotiations, foresight; his domestic life; impressions of France, England. Founds Constitution upon a study of the English constitution from Magna Charta through the Civil War to the Stamp Act, in terms of the people's right to their own money. Adams in favour of peace, nature, balance, against exploitation, slavery. The art of government.

6   74–84 (*The Pisan Cantos*). The contrasts used on a larger scale in early Cantos are here applied to small details, and various themes interweave in each Canto, making summary difficult. The situation of the poet in the D.T.C. among the criminals of the Army, and of the D.T.C. in the Pisan landscape, form a background to a meditation on the fall of Mussolini and the end of Pound's dream of society, except as an ideal; the meditation is also an elegy for the life he had known in the old Europe, especially in London. There is a daily struggle between love and despair, in which personal memories and observed natural events act as a 'raft' until nightfall. 'I surrender neither the empire, the temples nor the constitution.' Visions of the gods, and Confucian maxims, sustain him, as does birdsong, and the kindness of the petty thieves around him. 'What thou lovest well remains.' Tension between ecstatic celebration of nature's paradisal possibilities and a dark night of the soul. Unconvinced by the Democracies.

7   85–95 (*Rock-Drill*). The standard of government upheld by the Confucian history classic (85) used to judge usury (87) and government in nineteenth-century Europe (86) and America (88–89). The first half of *Rock-Drill* refers back to the American and Chinese Cantos; the second looks, not without self-reproach, to the poet's *paradiso*: 'the dream remains' (90); 'waiving no jot of the arcanum' (91). Pound celebrates civic virtue and courage (Randolph of Roanoke; Elizabeth I; Italian ministers); pagan mysteries (Castalia, Dionysus); a neo-Platonic strain in mediaeval thought from Apollonius of Tyana to Dante, via the Albigensians; and an animistic vision of the natural universe. The section ends with the shipwreck of Odysseus and his rescue by the nymph Ino.

8   96–109 (*Thrones*). The title comes from Dante's *Paradiso*; the two themes of *Rock-Drill*, the examination of history and the celebration of virtue and intelligence, are pursued with a more positive accent. To the further study of nineteenth-century European and American government is added a new exploration of the early Christian Empire, especially the regulation of civic and guild life in Constantinople; this is connected both with down-to-earth Chinese imperial practice and with philosophers of Light in the Dark Ages. Early English history yields parallel examples of enlightened government, from the Saxons

through Magna Charta to Elizabeth and the parliamentary crisis of the seventeenth century, with its American sequel. The history is punctuated by 'flashes' of Eleusinian mysteries, pagan theophanies and the celebration of nature and light.

9   110–117 (*Drafts and Fragments*). A return to Venice and to the poet's own situation; reflections on the failure of the enterprise but the beauty of life. Fragmentation. Humane affirmations.

The sheer size of the poem suggests that to cast this summary into an even more tabloid form may have a (temporary) usefulness:

1–7	Mythic beginnings: Odysseus, Troy, Dionysus, metamorphoses, troubadours
8–11	Malatesta's struggle
12–15	Confucius versus modern Inferno
16–17	Limbo, Elysium
18–30	Quattrocento life versus modern avarice
31–34	Jefferson 35–36 Vienna versus Cavalcanti 37 Van Buren
38–39	War profiteers against *Pervigilium Veneris*
40	Swindlers against Hanno's voyage 41 Jefferson and Mussolini
42–44	Siena well ruled 45–46 Usury and the Bank of England
47	Sailing to Koré 48 Monopolists versus sailors 49 Chinese country life
50	Napoleon against usurers 51 Usury against life and nature
52–61	A Confucian account of Chinese dynastic history
62–71	John Adams as the father of his country
74–84	Pisa: wreck, survival, memories, nature, visions
85–90	Usury in the nineteenth-century West
91–95	The arcanum, the dream
96–109	Usury in the nineteenth century. Early Western and Eastern empires; guilds, charters, constitutional laws. Seekers of light
110–117	Venice, quiet, fragmentation, affirmation

So drastic a reduction is clearly open to dispute; all poetic quality and all questions of significance or intention are excluded, and the headings are crude, though not, I hope, inaccurate. Any answer to the question, What do the *Cantos* contain? must be based on a list of the subjects Pound treats in the order in which he treats them. As his blocks of material become smaller and more fragmentary, the subjects of the later Cantos are less easily indicated.

The fragmentation of the later Cantos does not, however, preclude significant combination or conversational weave. This arranged fragmentation has its origins in *Lustra*, and is present from the outset of the *Cantos*. The close of Canto 1 and the opening of Canto 2 are already extremely tessellated and compressed; only in the Chinese history Cantos and the Adams Cantos is there a relatively continuous progression over a score of pages devoted to a single subject.

If the contents tabled above were to be sorted into subjects, easily the largest heading would be History, the material of perhaps three-quarters of the poem. The history is of several kinds—economic, constitutional, dynastic, cultural—and concerns states as small as Rimini and as large as China; but all is conducted in terms of personalities and moral ideas. Even the dynastic history of China is presented as a Plutarchan chronicle of individual men and their deeds, powerfully interpreted and slanted, although apparently objective in that it is presented in the form of documentary evidence. The documentation is more for authenticity than to convince the reader of impartiality, for Pound's didactic design is always palpable.

Even more striking than the didactic intent is the selectivity which has been applied to the documents; despite the mosaic of citations, the cutting is done on an entirely personal basis. Sources are generally not given, quotations are not reliably accurate and rarely complete. Yet the poet clearly intends to be just, if not fair, and is passionately committed to the moral truth of his presentation of men, events and cultural periods.

After history, the two other chief categories of subject-matter in the *Cantos* are myth and anecdote, or 'permanent' and 'quotidien'.[12] By 'myth', I mean to designate a complex of visionary experience, often cast in a Homeric or Dantescan or 'Quattrocento' form, which Pound eventually summarized as 'the arcanum'—the mysteries, whether of Eleusis, of Dionysus, of Pythagorean, Gnostic or neo-Platonic origin, which express Pound's mythopoeic perception of the elements of the natural, human or divine universe. The anecdotal contribution consists of personal memories and impressions of contemporaries, some at second hand; at times this passes into myth and legend, at other times remains obstinately journalistic. There are, of course, many other elements in the *Cantos*—a thematic analysis would show the prominence of Eros—but most of them fall into these three loose categories of history, myth and anecdote. Indeed, much of the history is anecdotal or mythical, and much of the personal anecdotage is intended to have representative historical value, for example, the often-reported 'bizniz' of modern war profiteers or monopolists.

The purpose of the table of contents and of these simple generalizations about kinds of subject-matter has been to allay some of the disquiet spread by the notorious obscurity of the poem; it is, reassuringly, *about* something, even if the something is as vast as the evolution of our civilization. Pound used to be quoted on book jackets as saying that, contrary to a prevalent impression, there is no mystery about the *Cantos*;[13] but his own striking confidence in the poem's coherence flickered and often went out towards the end, as he confesses in *Drafts and Fragments*. . . . The present purpose is only to remove *undue* mystery; some of the mysteriousness is intrinsic and intentional, and the poem does not live by reason alone. The furibund author of *Jefferson and/or Mussolini* and the rapt student of Apollonius of Tyana was not as common-sensical a man as his plain John Adams.

One formal principle springs so clearly from the mere listing of the contents of the *Cantos* that its operation may be admitted as part of these initial data. That is, that Pound's habitual method of arrangement and of presentation is based on *contrast*, as in the setting of Confucius amid the modern Inferno of Cantos 12–15; of Vienna against Cavalcanti in Cantos 35–36; of the Sienese Monte dei Paschi bank (Cantos 42–44) against the Bank of England (Canto 46). The contrast of these good and bad banks is so stark that the intervening presence of the famous Canto 45 against Usura is not logically necessary, however much it adds rhetorically. Contrast—elaborated into more complex forms of comparison and counterpoint—is the basis of Pound's appreciation and presentation of experience; the contrasts may at first seem oblique, but Canto 45 is not the only editorial comment in the *Cantos*, and to the understanding reader these contrasts become more and more direct.

In view of all this history, it may give surprise that I see the poem as so autobiographical:

> This is not a work of fiction
> nor yet of one man.
>
> (99)

Eliot observed that Pound's hell was 'for the *other people*', which is true of Cantos 14–15.[14] But the poem changed. Canto 113 ends: 'but the mind as Ixion, unstill, ever turning'. In which Pound is himself the tortured Titan. From the *Pisan Cantos* onwards, his own presence at the centre of the poem is acknowledged.

In approaching the poem itself, it is hard to avoid what Pound wrote in preface to a *Selected Cantos* in 1966:

> the best introduction to the *Cantos* . . . might be the following lines from the earlier draft of a Canto (1912):

> Hang it all, there can be but one 'Sordello'!
> But say I want to, say I take your whole bag of tricks,
> Let in your quirks and tweeks, and say the thing's an art-form,
> Your Sordello, and that the modern world
> Needs such a rag-bag to stuff all its thought in;
> Say that I dump my catch, shiny and silvery
> As fresh sardines slapping and slipping on the marginal cobbles?[15]

The anxiety about form, pushed aside by a blithe determination to go ahead anyway, surfaces occasionally in the *Cantos*, and from Pisa onwards it becomes overt, emerging and taking over Canto 116 entirely. In 1969 the poet was saying that he had devoted insufficient attention to questions of structure[16] and, more important, published his last words on these doubts in the last complete Canto:

> I cannot make it cohere

adding later

> i.e. it coheres all right
>   even if my notes do not cohere.
>
>   (116)

Doubt and affirmation—Sancho Panza and Don Quixote—carry on this dialogue through the poem, and the bringing of this oscillation into the open is evidence for Pound's eventual acceptance of his own role in his poem. The draft of 1912 quoted above continues:

> (I stand before the booth, the speech; but the truth
> Is inside this discourse—this booth is full of the marrow of wisdom.)[17]

Despite the clumsy mixture of metaphors, this (suppressed) passage shows that from the outset Pound saw himself as an impresario separate from, and subordinate to, his 'discourse'. He is merely 'the instrument for his work', as he said in 1966, quoting Jung. Yet he eventually came to recognize the relationship between his hero Odysseus and himself, and to allow the loss of companions, the shipwreck of his hopes and his rescue by a nymph, into the poem. Thus the epic became autobiography.

However, it can be seen that autobiography was there from the outset. The 'earlier draft' quoted above was originally Canto 1, but it now begins Canto 2, thus:

> Hang it all, Robert Browning,
>   there can be but the one "Sordello."
> But Sordello, and my Sordello?
> Lo Sordels si fo di Mantovana.
> So-shu churned in the sea.

There follows a series of metamorphoses: a seal appears in the sea, a wave speaks of Helen, the voices of the Trojan elders are heard, the seal becomes Tyro, raped by Poseidon; Dionysus turns some slavers who attempt to kidnap him into fish; coral is seen as formed from sea nymphs, like Daphne turned into laurel. This Ovidian material may seem impersonally mythological.

Then, once more,

> . . . So-shu churned in the sea, So-shu also,
>   using the long moon for a churn-stick. . .

So-shu is the Japanese form of Chuang Chou, a Chinese Taoist philosopher who 'dreamt he was a butterfly; but when he awoke said he did not *know* whether he had dreamt he was a butterfly, or whether he was not now a butterfly dreaming he was Chuang Chou'. Pound's 'Ancient Wisdom, Rather Cosmic' in *Lustra* is a variation upon an 'Old Poem' by Li Po based on Chuang Chou's paradox. Arthur Cooper's translation begins:

> Did Chuang Chou dream
> he was the butterfly,
>   Or the butterfly
> that it was Chuang Chou?
>
> In one body's
> metamorphoses,
>   All is present,
> infinite virtue![18]

The similarity felt by Pound between his own poetic processes and those of Chuang Chou and Li Po is suggested by the lighter type in which the first of the two lines from Canto 2 is printed in the original edition, a device marking a shift of consciousness. For it is the magical churning of the sea that produces these phantasmagorical changes.

Pound's invocation of So-shu churning the sea with a moonbeam is an image of divination or sortilege, and suggests the flux of perception, imagination and memory which makes up experience. Nothing could be less solid than the sea, less reliable than moonlight, less ordered than churning; it makes the consultation of the blood-bibbing Tiresias in Canto 1 seem relatively straightforward. Yet the line preceding So-shu's introduction is a quotation from an early life of the Italian troubadour to the effect that Sordello was from the country of Mantua—a documentary 'fact' which rebukes the accretions of pseudo-historical fantasy in Browning's poem, 'Sordello'. It seems, then, that Pound is intending to keep history and myth, Truth and Calliope, distinct in *his* 'Sordello'. The Canto ends with 'the fauns chiding Proteus', in which the junior satyrs appear rather shocked by the naughtiness of the old shape-shifter. So Pound balances the unreliable power of fantasy against its poetic value; for Pound, Proteus' knowledge of the arcane and numinous Mediterranean sea world is indispensable wisdom.

Coming where it does, Canto 2 seems to proclaim both the flux of phenomena and the necessity of imagination as the source of primal knowledge. The epistemology is magical, Orphic, and 'by no means orderly' or 'Dantescan' (Canto 74). Pound was to write in Canto 113:

> The hells move in cycles,
>> No man can see his own end.
> The Gods have not returned. "They have never left us."
>> They have not returned.

This cyclical, 'flowing, ever unstill' nature of reality, and of the mind, is what has made an orderly and Dantescan rising from Hell, via Purgatory to Paradise, an impossible task, though the intention and the framework remain. That Pound knew he had to deal with a Protean reality from the outset seems clear, though his efforts to pin Proteus down grew more and more determined, until the Pisan experience smashed his favoured practical version of his dream of a new terrestrial order.

The fluidity of the mass of materials he had to deal with is announced more obviously in the 'And' which begins Canto 1 and the 'So that' which ends it. Canto 2 opens: 'Hang it all'. This joky expostulation with the 'old mesmerizer' contrasts so violently with the mantic intentness of 'Bearing the golden bough of Argicida' that the gentle reader's nose is rubbed in discontinuity. Why so? What has Canto 2 to do with Canto 1? Proteus, at the end of the Canto, corresponds to Tiresias. Each tells a wandering hero what he must do to get home after the fall of Troy and the loss of companions. Menelaus (in *Odyssey*, v) has to disguise himself as a seal in order to surprise Proteus. Thus phenomenal disorder hides real correspondence and significance. Wisdom is to be sought in many forms and under many disguises in the *Cantos*. The deliberate discontinuity continues with 'And . . .' at the end of 2, and 'I sat on the Dogana's steps', opening 3—transferring us to an apparently straightforward piece of autobiographical experience: 'For the gondolas cost too much, that year.'

The penultimate fragment of the *Cantos* contains:

> that I lost my centre
> fighting the world

5*

This seems to lend support to the view that Pound has an uncertain identity, though the very concession also suggests a simple honesty: ' "Missing the bull's eye seeks the cause in himself" ' (77). The fight with the world—like the struggle to impose order on experience —was never wholly abandoned: the imperial thrust of the moral will went on asserting itself, from habit, to the very end. The disintegration and incoherence which at times overwhelmed the poet result from the frustration of that fight. But the 'lack of centre' is endemic to the whole method of the *Cantos*, the fluid evolutionary process of empathy—'I have thought of them living'—which prodigally animates so many periods and persons, states of mind and landscapes. Canto 2 shows that fixity in such a flux can only be local and temporary. The moral weight, authority and self-consistency of some of the anthologized Cantos—1, 13, 45 and 49—and such passages as the end of 81, which we have looked at earlier, may suggest otherwise, but that is not the impression of the *Cantos* as a whole. Though it has landmarks and axes of reference the whole enterprise remains essentially exploratory, even where it appears authoritative, for its authoritative stands are always taken in conscious opposition to the age—they are radical, heterodox, reactionary, visionary and idealistic. However traditional the authorities behind Pound's condemnation of usury or behind his distributism or his Enlightenment principles, the propaganda cannot be reduced to conformity with any extant modern consensus, whether capitalist, socialist, sensitive liberal or dogmatic Christian, or even Italian Fascist or American populist, though in favour of both. Yeats was right: 'Ezra Pound has made flux his theme; plot, characterisation, logical discourse, seem to him abstractions unsuitable to a man of his generation.'[19] As for 'fighting the world', he was not the only man to be blown off course in the 1930s.

The discontinuousness which marks the exposition on almost every page of the *Cantos* was, then, not merely a function of Pound's impatience, volatility or incompetence, but involved in the very nature of his idea of the poetic process. His poem 'including history' also included a polymorphous mythopoeia, where honesty to perception involved a shifting focus and the use of superimposed images and dissolving forms. There is also a deliberate reason of technique, an anti-explicitness noted by Yeats in his ironical allusion to Pound's Imagist war cry, 'Go in fear of abstractions.' This particularism is what Pound meant by his 'ideogrammic method', and Chapter 2 was spent in establishing its nature. Whether Pound was wise to use it—even in the modified form signalled by the change from Imagism to Vorticism—as the staple compositional method for such a very long poem will always be doubted by most readers.

Most readers, too, will be dubious of the inclusiveness and allusiveness, and this must be the last of the preliminary topics which will detain us before we too 'go down to the ship'. Pound is undoubtedly optimistic about the learning of his readers.

> "but that kind of ignorance" said the old priest to Yeats
> (in a railway train) "is spreading every day from the schools"—
> to say nothing of other varieties.

> (113)

But it is among his more learned readers that Pound finds some of his most intolerant critics: they do not wish to know about China, still less about the Na Khi culture introduced in Canto 98. As Pound requires of us a vital intellectual and moral curiosity rather than vast erudition, he will not much mind the absence of a few scholars. He cheerfully admits he wishes to 'extend the field of understanding', to 'make people think' and even to make them learn some Greek.[20] It is among the young and the enthusiastic that Pound makes converts. Yet the learned have a point: Pound so often gets things wrong. He misuses his sources or does not check them against other sources, so that his Chinese history is as one-sided as his Chinese philology is amateur. His denunciations of Christians are as irritating as his phobia about Jews is horrifying. Buddhists and Taoists are not invariably 'slobs', and 'Adolf' (Hitler) is not usually considered to have become 'furious from perception' (Canto 104).[21] Naturally Pound is, often enough, challengingly right, or we should not be interested in him, but there is no point in glossing over his blunders and his sins of prejudice; especially as in his last years he made efforts to put many of them right.

Returning to his allusiveness, one can have little quarrel in general with Pound's grand ideas of our curiosity about civilizations other than our own; I find such rash expectation exhilarating in an age where ignorance of the past is indeed spreading every day, and not only from the schools. His use of mythology is a glorious strength. His learned errors are in the cause of imaginative truth and fullness of knowledge. But whereas I make no apology for his eclecticism and little for his inaccuracy, one cannot avoid a little pedantic irritation with his arbitrary and incomplete methods of reference. I have enjoyed lessening my ignorance of, for example, the American founding fathers, but it is confusing to have them referred to by their initials, nicknames, first names and surnames indiscriminately, or, quite often, by a completely ambiguous personal pronoun. Even Sherlock Holmes could not solve an affair with unidentifiable suspects. I rarely find Pound's slang annoying (his abusiveness is a different matter) and his whimsical personal references to his grandfather by his initials, or to Senator George Tinkham, a non-relation, as 'Unkle George' (Canto 76) are easily detected and forgiven. (The American detailed to transcribe Pound's Rome Radio broadcasts had a difficult time: Abelard appears in Davy Crockett disguise as Abe Lard.) I can put up with Mussolini as 'the Boss'; I do not read Chinese. But there is a knowingness in the inflamed Cantos about modern arms manufacturers, war profiteers, monopolists, financiers and news managers —a knowingness which runs too often to name-dropping, hunches and guesswork. Pound wanted us to judge; but no jury can convict on a series of dark hints.

Sigismundo Malatesta is an interesting final example of allusiveness —'Siggy, me darlint' as Pound calls him on one occasion. He earns several Cantos; it is quite clear what he is there for, and one is glad to meet him. It is refreshing to find that Pound's views of Sigismundo and of his enemy Pope Pius II are precisely the opposite to those of Jacob Burckhardt, one of the few authorities one can easily consult on Sigismundo. Everything we are told about him is interesting. Yet all we are allowed to get is a fragmented kaleidoscopic impression—it is difficult to discover his relatives, employers, enemies and friends, or even his dates, so cavalier is Pound's presentation. What did Sigismundo achieve beyond his victories, and the Tempio? What of his alleged murders of various of his relatives? Pound is silent. Our curiosity is certainly aroused, and we can go off and satisfy it. Or can we? Sigismundo is so obscure a figure that the non-Italian non-researcher rapidly runs out of information. Why is it that a man so important is so little known? Why is a man so little known so important?

It is very often the case that Pound writes about figures so unfamiliar that we cannot pursue them far beyond his pages. Lorenzo di Medici, Confucius, Jefferson and Adams, Cavalcanti, Homer, Ovid—these are certainly important exceptions, as are Pound's own contemporaries in the arts. But the majority of Pound's subjects are not well known, and many of them are already as unknown as Pope's grubs in *The Dunciad*. Readers may be inclined to suspect that Pound is deliberately choosing obscure subjects, so that, blinded by his science, we cannot answer back; in my experience, such suspicions are not well founded. Pound's discoveries in the past are as rewarding as those among his living contemporaries in the arts; they are merely unconventional and unexpected. This eccentricity, the non-mainstream nature of his interests, has to be faced up to, as a very practical difficulty. Eliot succeeded in creating the taste by which he is appreciated: his work can be seen to 'conform' to his Tradition, a Harvard–European–Anglican tradition. Not so Pound; and though Pound is not as antiquarian as some of David Jones, nor as 'far out' as Charles Olson, his enthusiasms, though culturally comprehensive, are by no means symmetrical.

Yeats provides an interesting comparison: his mystical interests, for example, are odder than anything in Pound, yet his poetry is notably more accessible and public and not only for reasons of form. He naturally makes his private occasions themes for public meditation. Whereas Pound at times wants precisely to teach us some history that he knows we do not know. He wishes to give us new foundations. The pattern of his interests will emerge quite comprehensibly as we read the *Cantos*—it is an American pattern, and an old-fashioned one—but the practical difficulty remains; we quite frequently do not know what he is referring to, and he sometimes makes it worse by the compressed throw-away manner in which he makes the reference. Even this idiosyncrasy can become attractive to admirers.

9. Cantos 1-17

> And then went down to the ship,
>   Set keel to breakers, forth on the godly sea.....

There is no more splendid testimony to Pound's resource as a translator than the account of his visit to Hades with which Odysseus opens the *Cantos*. A salute to Homer is traditional in epic openings, yet to begin with a translation of a translation of Homer is exceptional, as Pound acknowledges with his placatory

> Lie quiet Divus. I mean, that is Andreas Divus,
> In officina Wecheli, 1538, out of Homer.

This epic, which Pound described as 'the tale of the tribe', is also a tribal encyclopaedia, and in places resembles an archive.

This is the first acknowledgement of a source in a poem much given to quotation and adaptation. Bibliographically speaking, it is a much fuller style of reference than we usually get—author, edition, date, subject—and it comes in the right place. We are to know that Pound has been translating, or cannibalizing, a Latin translation of Homer. Those who consult Pound on Andreas Divus in the *Literary Essays* will find the Latin sources of Canto 1, though little about the translator or his printer, Wechel.[1] Yet, to understand what the poet is doing here, we must turn to his prose. At such points, however available the ancillary material, the primary communication of the poem must be weakened. The bond of continuous understanding between poet and reader is broken, although appreciation of this interplay between poem and source may eventually strengthen a reader's involvement. Direct access to Pound's masters—Homer, Ovid, Dante, Confucius, Jefferson—is more worthwhile than such a cross-reference to the poet's own prose, and is equally a part of reading Pound. Both source and cross-reference, however, must remain subordinate to the uses they assume in the poem.

'And then went down to the ship' is a genuine plunge *in medias res*, into an action immediately invigorating and significant. The *res* here— Odysseus' *nekuia*, or journey to the underworld, seeking direction from the dead—being older than the matter of Homer himself, has conscious symbolic intention for Pound. Like Eliot's recourse to Sanskrit in *The Waste Land*, it goes back to the original ground of knowledge for its author, a respectful if enquiring relation with nature and with the human past, gained through arduous submission. We ascend to the source of Western literature and wisdom in order to get our bearings. This consultation of the oracle declares the huge cultural role of the *Cantos*, the epic of knowledge. But Calliope as well as Clio is the Muse of this poem, and the role of Odysseus the solitary explorer also has a more personal as well as a cultural significance. The Canto is strikingly prophetic of the course of Pound's life; it records a dedication.

Pound translates from a Renaissance humanist crib, making a point about translation and tradition. Divus had helped him to see a Homer without a Victorian halo. The last line taken from Divus—the suppressed reference to Odysseus' mother—is printed in lighter ink in some editions; but there is no typographical device before 'Lie quiet' to indicate a change of speaker. In effect, Odysseus, the first-person speaker of the Canto, is deliberately not distinguished from Pound, and the identification is significant. Pound half-dramatizes his relationship with what he is rendering by glossing his aside to Divus for our benefit; but we are meant to see that Pound is protagonist as well as author.

The remaining lines begin the movement of the next Canto: 'And he sailed, by Sirens . . . and unto Circe. . . . Aphrodite . . . thou with dark eyelids.' The direction towards a different kind of knowledge is adumbrated in the progression of these names and fulfilled in the sensory, then carnal, then visionary awareness of nymphs and of Dionysus in the next Canto. We can distinguish three levels of interest for the reader of the envoi to Canto 1: the subject-matter (sexual and mystical knowledge); the poet's relation to his subject-matter (intent, rapt, awed); and the sources. Just as in the body of Canto 1 we perceived clearly Odysseus' journey, and, more briefly, Pound's identification with Odysseus, and then, more briefly and less clearly, Andreas Divus 'out of Homer', so in the end of the Canto we have the same diminishing scale of *intelligibilia*, though the scale is compressed.

To recapitulate: we gather (1) Odysseus sails on his appointed voyage past the Sirens to Circe's enchantment, leading to a worshipful encounter with Aphrodite; (2) Pound, not easily distinguished from his hero, repeats her praises in a fervent cadence until he conjures up her presence; (3) Pound the craftsman is dealing with a Latin text in praise of Aphrodite, from which he cites and renders phrases.

The third level of interest, the involvement with sources, is the least important. In order to make the examination of this sample more complete, we may add, from the *Literary Essays*, that the 1538 Latin *Odyssey* which Pound picked up on a Paris bookstall also contained a Latin version of the Homeric Hymns to Aphrodite by Georgius Dartona

Cretensis, 'the Cretan'. The Latin tells us that she is to be venerated; that the cities of Cyprus are devoted to her cult; and that the girdles etc. are 'golden' because they are of yellow metal ('orichalchi', Graeco-Latin). 'Argicida' is a name for Hermes, who with his golden wand slew Argus so that Zeus could get at Io—thus manifesting Aphrodite's power.[2]

If the involvement with the source is the least important aspect, it is also the most alchemical, and it is deliberately 'closed', a mystique. Pound could not expect anyone to have a copy of this universally neglected humanist; so the citation of 'the Cretan', though it hints that this Greek islander is like Divus translating into Latin and, to the literary detective, that he is translating the Hymn to Aphrodite, is ultimately for the researcher and the initiate. . . . Initiation is the ultimate subject of Canto 1, but it can be read with understanding and pleasure, without taking it all in at first. Indeed the concluding invocation is so written that it is not possible to take it in at first.

The occultation of 'sources' may strike the lucidly minded as charlatanry; they will regard this 'least important' level as merely the least satisfactory. This mysteriousness is certainly more appropriate to mysteries such as these than to the later histories. It is pointless to deny that Pound is a magician, the question is whether his magic works. Here we have a translation into archaic English of a Latin version of the oldest piece of Homer; plus a partial translation of another Latin version of Hymns by a follower of Homer; in each case it is the *res* not the *verba* which is being translated, recovered, re-used. We have, co-present here, Homer, pre-Homer, post-Homer; two obscure Aldine humanists; Odysseus, Dante's Ulysses, and Pound's virile explorer; 'the glory that was Greece'; Aphrodite 'with dark eyelids', and Sir James Frazer. These are superimposed on a base of heroic English. It is eclectic, unorthodox and improbable—but how powerfully it works! The sense of dark recession and access to the beginnings of civilization is common in Pound: his 'permanent' arcana are both archaic and still alive. Recalling the equally complex bloodlines of *Cathay*'s descent into English, it becomes clear that Pound has a faculty for what might be called palimpsestuousness, the literary romance of the past carried to new depths of verbal resonance. He also, by an act of neo-humanism, brings the past alive into the present.

The contention here advanced, that the minutiae of Pound's dealings with his sources are of secondary interest, and that the main drift or drive of his work is often quite clear where these complex questions of provenance are not at all clear, is an important one, for if this is so it means one can read the *Cantos* without worrying that one is not understanding parts of them. This describes quite well my own experience in

reading them. One has to accept that Pound makes mention of secrets
between him and his Muse, some of which we will never penetrate.
Private reference, of a more confessional and trivial kind, is the staple of
much bad modern poetry, but I am more prepared to accept it in Pound's
case, in view of civilizing and not merely personal compensations. To
say 'Some of this I do not understand, more I cannot explain, yet I
continue to trust' goes against the claims of reason, and the scholiastic
and explanatory tendency of professional literary studies today, but it is
true to the exploratory experience of much valuable reading outside
Pound and beyond the modern period.

Canto 1 ends with 'So that:' and the attentive reader of Canto 2 will
discover in Proteus the link back to Tiresias' directions to the wandering
Greek. Canto 2 ends with 'And . . .'. Canto 3 opens with Ezra Pound *in
propria persona* recalling his youthful experience of Venice, when,
though he could not afford a gondola, he could see

> the clouds bowe over the lake,
> And there are gods upon them,
> And in the water, the almond-white swimmers. . . .

The second half of the Canto contains the reaction of Myo Cid, the epic
hero of mediaeval Spain, to proscription; followed by a condensed
evocation of the tragic fall of two Renaissance families.[3] These four
subjects (Pound in Venice; his vision of the gods; the Cid's setting out;
Renaissance dynastic tragedies) are jammed into two blocks of print in
such a way as to suggest there must be a relationship between A and B
and between C and D, and may be a further relationship between A:B
and C:D. The observable pattern is not so symmetrical. Between the
situations of Pound and his Cid, as presented, there are certainly similarities: both are excluded, exiles; one reacts with a vision, the other with an
action involving vision. The reason for the exclusion is ideological and
financial; and the defiance is resourceful, heroic, quixotic. Thus A, B
and C; what of D?

> Ignez da Castro murdered, and a wall
> Here stripped, here made to stand.
> Drear waste, the pigment flakes from the stone,
> Or plaster flakes, Mantegna painted the wall.
> Silk tatters, "Nec Spe Nec Metu."

Ignez had been killed by nobles who did not wish the young King Pedro
of Portugal to marry her; he set her dead body on the throne and made
them honour her. 'Neither with hope nor with fear' is the motto of the
Este family of Ferrara, also ruined by a tragedy of jealousy and passion;

both stories recur in Cantos 1–30. Pound had seen these waste walls: the ruins of time are a common theme in these Renaissance Cantos, especially of the Albigensian Montségur, of Malatesta's unachieved Tempio in Rimini, and of Troy. Pound as Odysseus saw London as Troy. Canto 4 begins:

> Palace in smoky light,
> Troy but a heap of smouldering boundary stones.

There appears at first sight no connection between the visions of the impecunious poet and the *virtù* of Myo Cid; and even second sight does not immediately disclose the germaneness of these Websterian catastrophes. The 'smoky light' of Priam's burnt palace thickens the atmosphere through which we see Mantegna's flaking fresco in the palace in Mantua; and there is perhaps a whiff of it in the remembered Morosini palace in Venice (l. 5). There is a clear contrast with the bright Venetian gods who 'float in the azure air' before the poet's eye. We could suppose, then, an intended contrast between on the one hand Quattrocento clarity and action, and on the other a later Renaissance pomp, passion and skull-duggery; between ideal sensuous life, free and active, and a corrupt, jealous pride which repressed it—as in Browning's 'My Last Duchess'. There is also a financial aspect, for example in the pawn-brokers who no doubt keep up the cost of the gondolas. Yet we are not dealing with a contrast superficially complicated but morally crude. For Venice is presented with all her ambivalence: she is both pure and corrupt, both the Venice of 'Night Litany' and the Venice of Shylock, Volpone and Burbank, where 'the smoky candle end of time / Declines'.[4] The peacocks in Koré's house, with their Argus-eyed tails, suggest the theophany which follows them. The walls which are 'made to stand' at the end, the flaking pigment, the tattered silk, regret the beautiful corpse of the bride and the stoic pride of the buried Este. There is a tension between beauty and time and not merely an opposition between good and bad; Pound makes us feel fascination as well as repulsion. He is not always averse to flat contrast: *usura* is piercingly declared to be *contra naturam*. But flexibility is the norm: the *donne* of the *Cantos*, a goodly company, are astonishingly *mobile*, from the Sirens through Circe and across to Aphrodite. Venice herself—like the Venus on whose name Pound, like Pope,[5] could pun—is peculiarly self-contradictory: the city, like Venus born from the sea on a shell, is at first a model of what man's hand and mind can do in co-operation with nature, and later a warning of monopoly capitalism gone rotten. She features more as a nymph than as a painted woman in the *Cantos*, but there is always power as well as beauty, a power inspiring, beneficent, bewildering and hypnotic by turns:

The silvery water glazes the upturned nipple,
As Poggio has remarked.

(3)

The dynamic relationship between the contradictory elements in Canto
3 is emphasized by the detail of the transitions, which are by association
as much as by contrast. The 'tower like a one-eyed great goose / cranes up
out of the olive-grove' in Canto 2 and the vision fades 'in the smell of
hay under the olive-trees'; Canto 3 opens on the Dogana's steps, across
the Grand Canal from the Campanile in the Piazza San Marco. The
parallel between the natural architecture of trees in a grove and the
marble architecture of a temple's columns is often made by Pound;
and the phallic Campanile, though not mentioned here, is certainly to be
seen 'craning up' in the view from the Customs House steps which it
dominates. The peacocks' tails in Koré's house suggest the bright gods
in the air, and the Venetian scene supplies the base for the fantasies of
the vision that follows. The 'green veins in the turquoise' are in the
Venetian marble as well as in the water; and the line 'Or, the gray steps
lead up under the cedars' is another metamorphosis of the marble steps
and columns of the Venetian Customs House, forming the threshold of
another, alternative paradisal vision. 'My Cid' rides *up*, as the steps 'lead
up'; and he ends by 'breaking his way to Valencia', with a constructive
violence contrasting with the destructive 'murdered' and 'stripped' of the
next lines on the corpse 'made to stand' to be worshipped. The fluid and
associative nature of the transitions suggests that those commentaries on
the *Cantos* which, to help the rationalizing mind, block out Pound's
values in geometric black and white, are suppressing the play and iridescence of his myth-making imagination, its constantly altering relation
with what it presents to us, and overlooking the connecting filaments
between the pieces.

The unfolding of the *Cantos* is full of curious surprises and the texture
is rich with invitation to the imagination of the reader—the new reader—
though this can be neglected by the dry-eyed stalker of sources and of
rational and moral designs. In actuality, Pound's plan is often elusive, and
his values normally emerge by accretion, not announcement. In the
suggested schema tried earlier, we found that D related more to A than
A did to B: there is a loose counterpoint, but no symmetry. And as for the
relationship of Canto 3 to its predecessors, this is something that has to
be sought for and then remains potential, a parallel: the awareness shown
by Odysseus or by Acoetes, and the objects of that awareness in 1 and 2,
are akin to the adventurous self-reliance of Myo Cid and the mythopoeic
imagination that transforms Venice into its ideal counterpart. This
should not be put more strongly: the eliciting of meaning, of design, in

the *Cantos* is a process of noting family resemblances and allowing the pattern of the instances to assert itself without too ready a conceptualization. A sceptic will say that the emperor has no clothes: there are no connections; it is the reader who has to supply all the vital relations; the *Cantos* are a disorderly record of Pound's enthusiasms. Noel Stock, for example, as a former disciple, knows Pound's sources well—but the bewildering variety of the separate items that make up the work is no longer redeemed for him by an intellectual current between them. As he explains in *Reading the Cantos*, and implies in the *Life*, Stock has come to disagree radically with Pound's ideas, and denounces the conventions by which they are implied. But for those who are approaching the *Cantos* for the first time, I would enter a caveat against too early a recourse to even the best of the available critical kits, useful though they are for information. The ideas of the *Cantos* are embodied and latent rather than explicit, and had best be discovered by the reader; information can be picked up by the curious in Pound's own prose, in direct access to Pound's sources and in encyclopaedias. *Solvitur ambulando*—because the poem, even to its end, contains unresolved attitudes, and its organizing principles come to consciousness in the process of composition; like much modern work, the *Cantos* were made up as they went along, which is not to say that they do not have an argument: they have an argument with themselves, a dialectic.

The first seven Cantos are particularly demanding and particularly imetamorphic'.[6] They establish a norm of fluid relations between the realms of the mythical, the historical and the anecdotal, and there is an unusually high proportion of myth. The myth is part Greek, part Romance ('Romance' in the special sense of Pound's *Spirit of Romance*: the *matière de Provence*, the loves of the troubadours). The two are first linked in the eleventh line of Canto 2:

> "Eleanor, ἐλέναυς and ἐλέπτολις!"
> And poor old Homer blind, blind, as a bat,
> Ear, ear for the sea-surge, murmur of old men's voices:
> "Let her go back to the ships,
> Back among Grecian faces. . . ."

Here Pound alludes to the incident in the *Iliad*, III, when the Trojan elders discuss Helen; though she 'moves like a goddess', to them she has brought only evil. The blind Homer imagines their words as he walks *para thina poluphloiosboio thalasses*, and hears their voices in the murmur of the pebbles.[7] The many voices of the sea have whispered earlier a line derived from the *Agamemnon* of Aeschylus: Helen is a destroyer, of ships and of cities. But Pound's Helen is Eleanor of Aquitaine, daughter of the first troubadour, William IX of Aquitaine; wife of Louis IX of France and then of Henry II of England; mother of Coeur de Lion and his brothers. As Helen's beauty 'caused' the Trojan War and, indirectly, the poems of Homer, so Eleanor's gave rise to Anglo-French strife, and to the poems of Bernart de Ventadorn, the most famous of the troubadours. The historical accuracy of these notions is immaterial; they retain a legendary force from the gossip of those days, and more especially from nineteenth-century interpretation of that gossip, an interpretation coloured by romantic views of Woman and Beauty—illustrated, for example, in Keats's 'La Belle Dame Sans Merci', Rossetti's paintings, Dowson's 'Cynara' and Yeats's earlier love poetry. Helen and Eleanor are types of the power of beauty over men, terrible, destructive and irresistible, examples of the consequences of trying to bind Eros by social conventions. Pound is extreme in his opposition to any sexual possessiveness.

This thesis is illustrated by the Provençal example of Guillaume de Cabestan, Piere Vidal, Poicebot, Pieire de Maensac, Arnaut Daniel and Eleanor herself; and the Italian examples of Sordello and Cunizza, and Cavalcanti. The stories differ in their outcome according to the degree to which Amor is thwarted or respected; the former end tragically in madness or death, the latter well. *Romeo and Juliet* is the best-known expression of this idea of love-tragedy in English, and Tristan and Yseult were the chief of love's martyrs for the nineteenth century; Chaucer's *Troilus and Criseyde* contains more of the mediaeval philosophy of love.

Classical, or rather pagan, parallels are offered to this pattern or set of patterns in the legends of Actaeon, Leda, Danaë, Gyges, Theseus, Dido and Sicheus; and the erotic poems of Sappho and Catullus. The examples are interwoven in a complicated way, though there are direct comparisons, or fusions: 'Actæon: Vidal' and 'Cabestan, Tereus' in Canto 4. The implied necessity of honouring Eros—if life and song are to flourish—is not in doubt. There is difficulty in establishing exactly what happens in some of the stories—they are recounted incompletely or spliced into each other—but their tenor is clear: the loves of the troubadours recreate the loves of the pagan gods and heroes. The gods punish not only possessiveness but also those whom they themselves possess: Cabestan and his mistress; Actaeon; and Vidal. But the *furor* which drives these martyrs is divine, and a blessed state compared with the indifference to beauty of Poicebot, de Tierci, Louis, Richard St. Boniface—all of whom like Menelaus lost their wives to the heroes and saints of love.

Mixed into these phantasmagoric and syncretic Cantos are the visions of the gods which bewitch their devotees, and Oriental and Christian analogies to these ecstasies. Catholic processions are interpreted, as commonly by enlightened ex-Protestants, as crypto-pagan rites; thus the

Salve regina at the end of Canto 4 is 'really' addressed to Venus. Pound swirls the kaleidoscope so that the cinematic shots dissolve into each other. The Garonne 'becomes' the Adige; Mary's procession 'becomes' the Madonna painted in Verona, 'as Cavalcanti had seen her'. The equation makes sense for Pound not only because of his neo-pagan interpretation of these two expressions of worship but also because he himself has seen and remembered these two things. The element of personal experience which informed 'Provincia Deserta' is allowed in here too casually: '(as at Gourdon that time)'. The phantasmagoric and fragmentary nature of Cantos 4-7 is explicitly related to Pound's own state of mind as he sits by the arena at Verona. The use of dots to show one train of thought giving way to another, and the use of explanatory stage directions like 'Dawn, to our waking, drifts in the green cool light' or 'Titter of sound about me, always' or 'The lake of ice there below me' reminds us again of Pound before the booth, lifting the curtain on his show. At times the impression that he is letting us in on the phenomena of his own fancy, and is a little unsure that we will follow, is unmistakable. Thus an occasional touch of Madame Sosostris:

> Topaz I manage, and three sorts of blue;
> but on the barb of time.
> The fire? always, and the vision always,
> Ear dull, perhaps, with the vision, flitting
> And fading at will.

(5)

The Adige, we are informed, is 'a thin film of images' (the Garonne is 'thick like paint'); the stream of consciousness beckons the self-conscious artist.

A number of detailed expositions of the meaning of these early Cantos are available, such as Pearlman's *The Barb of Time*; the intention here is more general, to suggest how they may be read and to show their place in the poem. After the bold introduction of Canto 1 there are six phantasmagoric Cantos introducing various motifs of love, vision, action and passion, held together by the consciousness of the impresario, and by the patterns and polarities we have noted.

Canto 7 summarizes this phase, introduces new matter and alludes to a motif I have barely mentioned—the murders of John Borgia and Alessandro dei Medici. These dynastic murders exemplify for Pound the violence and disorder of the Renaissance as opposed to the clarity and life of the making of the Middle Ages, and also the disordinate effects of an indulged passion for power; he compares the murder of Agamemnon. (If Medici and Borgia Popes behaved thus, it is permissible for Sigismundo Malatesta of Rimini to use force in order to create his vision of paradisal order, imaged in the Tempio.) At the same time, the energy and resolve of the murderers has an appeal for Pound ('John Borgia is bathed at last'), as, less fortunately for the reader, does the intrigue, business and resource which they employ. Borgia is not much mourned, and Alessandro is guilty of the prime Poundian sin of *abouleia*, lack of will, rudderlessness, whereas their murderers are men of intelligence and will, and their elimination is cleansing and constructive. The Canto thus offers a spectrum of heroism ancient and modern.

The passion and *virtù* of these men is contrasted in Canto 7 with the emptiness of the rulers of the world of Pound's youth. Early twentieth-century French and British civilization is presented as desiccated, dead at the top, like Homer's sexless elders; over their tawdry table the 'locust-casques' who make decisions 'make sound like the sound of voices'— 'Lorenzaccio' (the murderer of Alessandro) 'Being more live than they, more full of flames and voices.' This is Dante's imagery, but Machiavelli's world; Dante ranked Brutus with Judas.

> "Beer bottle on the statue's pediment!
> "That, Fritz, is the era, to-day against the past,
> "Contemporary." And the passion endures.
> Against their action, aromas. Rooms, against chronicles.

Pound finds the rooms of Paris or London full of ghosts, among whom the spirit of Henry James acts as a Virgilian guide, 'drinking the tone of things'. Canto 7 is the most ambitiously complex of the early Cantos, and, as a critique of its time, resembles *Mauberley*.

Cantos 8-11 are concerned with Sigismundo Malatesta (1417-68) and form a historical block, as do the Chinese and Adams Cantos later. They open, however, with a bridge passage that looks like a digression, a characteristic manoeuvre to suggest that the order of the *Cantos* is based on internal correspondences, not on external symmetry. Pound begins, as often, by walking backwards on to the stage, arguing with someone in the wings:

> These fragments you have shelved (shored).
> "Slut!" "Bitch!" Truth and Calliope
> Slanging each other sous les lauriers:
> *That* Alessandro was negroid. And Malatesta
> Sigismund: . . .

The first line offers a rejoinder to the conclusion of *The Waste Land*, a poem Pound had helped into the world between the appearances of his Cantos 7 and 8. (The resemblances between Eliot's poem and Canto 7, both in their antique fragmentariness and their disillusioned attitude to 'the era', indicate that Eliot learned from Pound's example as well as his editorship; Canto 7 antedates *The Waste Land*.) The comment is both impatient with Eliot's weariness and an admission of kinship.

The couplet that follows epitomizes the flyting in the *Cantos* between what 'Near Perigord' called 'fact' and 'fiction'. Truth is bitching about Pound's own epically promiscuous imaginings, and demands some 'facts'; perhaps Eliot is reproved here too. The conversation takes place in an Elysian field, an argument blessed by Daphne's shade.

This plunge *in medias res* (and, in this cyclical epic, every new *res* will demand a new ducking of the reader's head into its middle) is especially vertiginous: we are immersed in a flurry of letters from Sigismundo to Giovanni dei Medici; of documents and records relating to Sigismundo's employ as a condottiere by various city-states; of campaign chronicles; of letters from his agent about the building of the Tempio; of the text of the papal proscription of him. Vorticism and the documentary approach to history make a demanding combination. The effect is exciting but also confusing—like, say, sitting in a café in the Campo at Siena during the rehearsals for the Palio, and trying to read *The Duchess of Malfi* in a copy from which some pages, including the list of dramatis personae, are missing; meanwhile neighbouring tables debate with suitable animation the recent elections, in which their relations have been involved. . . . The pleasure is increased if you know the plot, the political situation, and the language, though it remains vivid even if you do not. We are *in medias res* with a vengeance. Since the Twenties it has been rediscovered that immediacy, urgency and authenticity are not all that are required to make a good story; at times Pound's cross-cutting method can seem like someone twiddling the tuning dial on a powerful radio receiver.

However, print can be reread, just as a Cubist picture can be stood back from, and out of the whirl of jagged detail the various aspects of Sigismundo—fighting, negotiating, protecting his family and his city—assert themselves and imply a personality, the centre of which is the construction of the Tempio Malatestiano at Rimini. 'A splendid church,' admitted his enemy Pope Pius II, 'dedicated to St Francis, though he filled it so full of pagan works of art that it seemed less a Christian sanctuary than a temple of heathen devil-worshippers. In it he erected for his mistress a tomb of magnificent marble and exquisite workmanship with an inscription in the pagan style as follows: "Sacred to the deified Isotta".'[8]

The Tempio, though never finished, is a great achievement; Alberti was the architect, the bas-reliefs are by Agostino di Duccio, Piero della Francesca and others, the marble was brought from San Apollinare in Classe. It is unique, perhaps the most original church of its time, a monument of beauty and power. Like many a Renaissance church it is really a monument to the greater glory of its patron and to his ideals; in this case, to his love for his third wife, Isotta. The Tempio is a monument very similar to the *Cantos*. It stands off the beaten track in the old town, which is now a dusty annexe to the popular beach resort. From the outside it is powerful and austere, the masterpiece of the first architect of the Renaissance; inside, it is a cabinet of beauties, disregarded.

Not many miles away is the Ducal Palace of Urbino, the very much better-known monument to a more orthodox Renaissance prince and all-round man, Federico—or Nicknose, as Pound calls him—the hero of Castiglione, and of William Butler Yeats, and also of Jacob Burckhardt.[9] ... Another hero of the Swiss historian of the Renaissance is the elegant Aeneas Silvius Piccolomini, Pope Pius II, Burckhardt's favourite humanist, apart from his lapse in calling the last Crusade. Pius's acts and works are prettily glorified by Pinturicchio in the Library of Siena Cathedral. The Pope and the Duke were Malatesta's two worst enemies. Pound admires anti-establishment heroes who go down with all guns firing, not with a whimper. Mussolini, like Malatesta, came from the Romagna.

The family life of the Malatesta, though dynastic, might not have appealed to Confucius as an example of 'order'. Certainly Sigismundo's ancestor Giancotto had not shown 'brotherly deference' to Paolo when he found him with his wife, Francesca da Rimini.[10] In his portrait of Sigismundo, Pound is at pains to show the love of son and father, the trust of lover and mistress, the humanity of the leader; he also admires his courage and force. In a disorderly age you have to fight to realize your ideal of order and 'keep it against armed force'. Principled action will take revolutionary or conservative form according to the corrupt or harmonious nature of society. 'In the gloom, the gold gathers the light against it' (Canto 11).

Malatesta's tireless campaigning energy, his enquiring mind, his patronage of the arts, his neo-paganism, his devotion to mistress and child, his independence and courage, give the Odysseus theme its fullest statement. The detail is magnificent illustration for the theme, and the choice of concrete evidence shows Pound's eye for 'gists and piths' at its best. The life, colour and vigour of the condottieri (in an Ezratic eavesdrop in Canto 10, Federico and Sigismundo are heard threatening to cut each other's guts out) contrasts not only with the hollowness of the men at the Council of Versailles but also with the paralysing image of the Renaissance Humanist as University Professor unveiled in the last century. The indecorous language of these civilized bandits is a jolt and a pleasure. It remains a criticism of the Malatesta Cantos, however, that they presume too far on our acquaintance with the history of these families and consequently fail in exposition and hence as 'instigation'. The historical novels of more recent times have abandoned even the Medici, let alone the Malatesta. This criticism applies to other historical Cantos. Selectivity, rearrangement, slant, imaginative reconstruction—these one gladly accepts; but a habitual incompleteness and allusiveness are self-defeating: too much escapes us, we cannot follow, we cannot judge. This miscalculation imposes important limits, for all but the instructed, on the comprehensibility of these Cantos. But the last word must be of admiration for the exultant and spirited handling of material new to poetry. The result is a shot across the bows of received ideas of the Renaissance. And it furthers the poem.

A subordinate theme of these Cantos is Ruin. Canto 12 begins:

> And we sit here
> under the wall,
> Arena romana, Diocletian's, les gradins
> quarante-trois rangées en calcaire.

This picks up, from Canto 11:

> And we sit here. I have sat here
> For forty four thousand years . . .

and, from Canto 9:

> And the old sarcophagi,
> such as lie, smothered in grass, by San Vitale.

The Renaissance thirst for glory in stone mingles with the later note of loss. Pound describes the Tempio as being 'in the style "Past ruin'd Latium"' (9). That is, he sees it with all the regret of Landor's 'Past ruined Ilion Helen lives', an extraordinary condensed allusion-cum-revision.[11] Landor intends that 'one name, Ianthe, shall not die', and Sigismundo's Tempio is likewise a monument to the beauty of Isotta. In Canto 11 Sigismundo sits in the Tempio noting 'what was done wrong' and knowing that it would not be finished. So Ravenna, last Western memorial of Ilion and its descendant Latium, lives—and dies—again in the Tempio; and again in Pound. In this he is more of a Virgilian humanist than a Homeric hero. The struggle to re-edify, to make it new, is seen, as in many humanist poems of the Renaissance, to be endless.

In the lines quoted above there is an implied stage direction: Pound 'is discovered' seated on the steps of an old building. The epigraph to 'Near Perigord' is 'A Perigord, pres del muralh', near the wall. This is the scene-setting gesture in many neo-classical paintings and poems of meditation, from du Bellay on Rome to Gray's 'Elegy', and it is an instinctive one with Pound, a professional *genius loci*. (It is perhaps noteworthy that Pound's main complaint about Florence was that there is nowhere to sit down in it.[12]) I make this point because, just as one does not forget the figure in the bottom left-hand corner of the Claude landscape, one never quite forgets that it is Pound's voice that is reading the document (throwing in *argot* when he feels like it) and Pound's eye that is seeing the landscape: 'with the road leading under the cliff', or 'where the water comes down over the cobbles' (8). The allusion to the 44,000 years and such lines as:

> And the wind is still for a little
> And the dusk rolled
> to one side a little
> And he was twelve at the time . . .
>
> (8)

indicate, too, Pound's latent notion of himself as a dreamer or seer, a Tiresias to whom Time is a mere illusion. The action of the poem is at such moments interior to his own sensibility.

The Malatesta Cantos mark a departure by including in the text whole documents of prose with no pretence at being verse. The prevalence of 'and' as the chief connective device of the poem is confirmed. This 'adding style' gives the impression of a chronicle, intensified by the condensation Pound imposes upon events. Whole pages are tacked together by this simplest of principles, though the monotony of Hemingway's later manner is avoided. Pound has relaxed the constraints of verse to a dangerous extent here. Such recourse to unedited quotation remains rare in the poem, however, and the documents in these Malatesta Cantos bring out 'a touch of rhetoric in the whole' (9): the magniloquent forms of address in the letters, for example, contrast with their firm grasp of practicalities; the pageantry of the processions acts as a foil to Sigismundo standing 'in the water up to his neck / to keep the hounds off him' (9). The documents give us 'the tone of things'; Pound's taste for the style of Italian social life keeps the detail lively, and the 'ands' keep things rattling along. Few can vary the pace better than Pound—compare the lightness of the incident of Sigismundo filling the fonts with ink (10) with the lines on the sarcophagi by San Vitale. In a musical contrast with the grandiose myth and complexities of the foregoing Cantos, the Malatesta group is quick, external, a record of action: chronicles, against rooms.

I intend to treat Cantos 10–17 as a group; although 17 stands first in the second published volume of Cantos, it completes a pattern of contrasts. Thus, 12: Modern monopolists: Baldy Bacon; Dos Santos; Quinn's tale of the honest sailor. 13: Kung's order. 14: Hell of usurers. 15: More Hell; Pound's escape and (16) arrival in the Elysian fields; heroes of the Great War. 17: Zagreus and Nerea (Venice); Koré and the condottieri. Thus 12, 14 and 15 contrast with 13, 16 and 17.

The first contrast is between, on the one hand, monopolists, obstructors of distribution, English capitalists behind the Great War, and, on the other, Kung's serene 'order', the active heroism of Malatesta, and the vision of a perfected natural order in Elysium, of which Venice is a part. Cantos 12 and 13 are clarified by the violence of their contrast, and 14–17 are united by the first-person narrative of Pound. For once, the pattern is straightforward.

Canto 12 is an example of material where explanation of the main elements is fortunately superfluous. Baldy and Dos Santos buy cheap and sell dear, whereas the Honest Sailor becomes rich respectably. The moral correlatives of these tales of enterprise are interesting: Baldy and Dos Santos are rogues and swindlers who use Odyssean ingenuity to exploit the poor and credulous; whereas the Honest Sailor's improving story of self-betterment, told by John Quinn (the patron of Pound and Eliot) to edify the Presbyterian bankers, ends in the sailor's deathbed confession to his heir, who has great expectations, that he owes everything to having been buggered by a rich merchant in Stambouli. Baldy, however base, is livelier than the bankers; and the sailor, for all his gullibility, is at least honest. This Rabelaisian Canto has its moral axis in the old Catholic principle that usury and sodomy are equally sins against nature, since money should be a non-reproductive means of exchange rather than a commodity, true wealth growing from the abundance of nature through procreation, and from the labour of man. The bankers are Presbyterians, and, like Baldy, they invest only in money (bank buildings): they are as barren as the reformed sailor.

This Mark Twain side of Pound has been reproved not only at the Court of King Arthur but also by those Yankees who want their great writers more dignified. Pound sees the desire for imperial dignity as absurd, whether in person or in literary style: 'De Gama wore striped pants in Africa' (7): ' "to the main shack brought 'em," / As Henry would have said' (12).

But crudity of language does not always entail crudity of thought: the sting in John Quinn's tale is superb. And the benign irony of the following lines is urbane enough:

> Porkers, throughout all Portugal,
> > fed on the cargo,
> First lot mortgaged to buy the second lot, undsoweiter,
> Porkers of Portugal,
> > fattening with the fulness of time,
> And Dos Santos fattened, a great landlord of Portugal
> Now gathered to his fathers.
> > Did it on water-soaked corn.
>
> > > (12)

Canto 12 is a more successful exposé of usury than 14-15.

Pound's Hell has not prospered: it invokes its own nemesis by comparing itself with Dante and Blake. Even the comparably scatological visions of Jonson, Swift and Pope show that the satirist must keep his temper. Yet, though it is not a success (weak theology, repetitive imagery, shrill in tone), Pound's Hell has a curiosity value, for example in its pique against the *English* establishment. There is genuine power and genuine obscenity; there is ingenuity and some humour ('the circle of lady golfers'); the sins, or rather crimes, are consistent with the values of the rest of the work. It is tempting to relate the phobias to an American puritanism or to Pound's preference for Botticelli beauties whose arms are never 'downed with light brown hair'. Yet, when all is said, it does not even fit in; perhaps it is there because of a desire to keep up with Joyce, Wyndham Lewis and Dante Alighieri.

The exit from Hell is contrived with the aid of the neo-Platonist Plotinus and an adapted shield of Perseus, perhaps to suggest the saving power of ideals preserved. Plural models of salvation are offered in Canto 16: Blake, like Pound, shouts at the evil; Dante looks at it in his mirror; Sordello in his shield; Augustine gazes towards the invisible. Pound goes via a magic passage into the Elysian fields to see the heroes, including the Malatesta, and to overhear Victor Plarr's account of Gallifet's triple charge at Sedan. Both the narrative and the allegory remain confused.

This transition to modern wars is not unnatural, but three pages into the Canto we find a marginal note: *Plarr's narration*. Is this a helping hand, or a cry for help? It is difficult to crack *Plarr's narration* unless one recognizes Victor Plarr ('the author of "The Dorian Mood" ' from *Mauberley*, vii). Is Pound aware how impenetrable he is, and trying to help, extending a hand in the form of a marginal gloss? Whatever it is, it is a sign of nerves. Only those who have undergone total immersion in Pound could have been expected to recognize Sir Henry Newbolt in 'as Henry would have said'; the unbaptized might consider *Plarr's narration* rather as Dr. Johnson received Lord Chesterfield's belated offer of help.

The roll of heroes proceeds via Lord Byron to a list of Pound's friends who went to the First World War, and wanders with a dream's true inconsequence into some demotic French impressions of the horrors of the trenches and hearsay rumours of the (unplanned) Russian Revolution. All of which loops back to the theme of the decay of Europe in Canto 7, but doesn't make the writing hereabouts any more interesting.

Now that the *Cantos* are published in one volume, Canto 17 reads as a paradisal finale to the first cycle, beginning with the words that end Canto 1: 'So that.' Spoken by a man lying exhausted in Elysian fields, it is a vision of Zagreus (Dionysus) feeding his panthers, 'Nerea' in her cave, and 'the great alley of Memnons'. This vision is not only arcane and syncretic, but, like a dream, subject to metamorphoses. The speaker seems at the beginning to be clearly distinct from the Zagreus whom he then observes. Pound's invented Nerea, daughter of Nereus, the Old Man of the Sea, is thus born of the sea, like Venus in the painting of Botticelli; and like the Istrian limestone of Venice herself. The 'one man' who comes holding the sail of his boat and babbling of Murano and gondolas is suspiciously like Ezra Pound (whom we left watching the sailor's arrival); and the speaker (who certainly has been Pound throughout the preceding Hell Cantos) is then embraced by Koré and addressed as 'brother of Circe' in an improved version of Odysseus' arrival on the shore of Phaeacia. He enjoys three days of 'Splendour, as the splendour of Hermes'; Hermes has previously been glimpsed with Athene:

                    As shaft of compass
          Between them, trembled—

so it seems that the embrace conferred knowledge; the initiations and visions of Cantos 1–3 have borne fruit. Pound–Odysseus is then shipped to Ithaca–Venice to face some barbed arrows.

My aim in giving this dry account of a Canto full of Quattrocento pictorial enchantments is not to suggest that it is a farrago of nonsense, but that it only makes sense if it is read as a fantasy, a dream or a vision; 'God am I for the time.' (Like so much else of the *Cantos* it is curiously prophetic of Pound's own life.) The powerful enchantment of Nerea in her cave is indeed hallucinatory. But to see it as a poetic gem without looking at its setting is to lapse into a Palgravian particularism. Considering this discontinuousness, we may recall Dante's curious dreams and rude awakenings, and the unexpected things that, if we are to believe him, happened to Odysseus. But such comparisons merely bring out the differences between Pound and his exemplars. He has a fissile personality; and the confusion admitted in his work is in himself as well. Part of the difficulty is that he is trying to express things that he can see but we can't. The incoherence of the man who tries to give an account of Venice is a conscious device on Pound's part, and the modulation of the figure of Nerea is artful, but the constantly dissolving and merging personality of the speaker of the Canto may not be so conscious; certainly there is little in Pound's published literary theory which would allow for so Coleridgean a psychological fusion between subject and object. A conclusion is forced on us: for all his hard shell, his finish and his learning, Pound is one of those romantic dreamers who play so little part in his public pantheon. Despite his frequently hearty tone, his interest in the natural object and the external world, his connoisseurship of the visual image, and his reformist attitudes to such practical issues as 'the nature of coin, credit and circulation', Pound's subject-matter is very often internal and symbolic. The arcane lies near the centre of his work.

The arcane can be regarded as either escapist or idealist; as inaccessibly private, useless fantasy, or as reaching magically towards genuine sources of religious value, whether metaphysical, ethically ideal or naturalistic, in a language consciously symbolic and unavoidably hermetic. The positivist, pragmatic and analytic strain that has contributed so powerfully to English literary criticism in the earlier part of this century, particularly at Cambridge, may here see Pound as an escapist, an American dreamer. And the Christian and neo-classical strains in English thought, the tradition to which Eliot appealed, may find the expression fragmentary and the ideals suspect. Eliot was eventually to write to Leavis saying that he found the *Cantos* 'arid and depressing'.[13]

The question about the value of the 'arcanum' cannot be answered at this stage, though the heterodox underground neo-Platonist tradition which Pound increasingly invokes in the *Cantos* indicates a conscious alliance, as does the neo-paganism of his mythology. An examination of the first cycle of Cantos, however, does allow one to answer positively the question of the *Cantos'* coherence. Faint and arbitrary though the pattern may appear at times, the main design of this first *Draft* is certainly intelligible; it is equally certain that it is neither clear nor explicit throughout, particularly at the beginning. The opening Cantos show a bewildering variety of purposes, and Pound introduces a number of themes of

exploration, perception, passion and metamorphosis from a wide range of
sources, with some spectacular elisions and connections. One of his chief
means of linking materials in more discrete Cantos is his habit of reminding us of his presence in the corner of the picture, as a dreamer, observer
or seer, sometimes only by a tone of voice; though this linking does not
always raise the coherence to a level much above that of a diary. But the
use of interior monologue and dialogue, of stream of consciousness
techniques and asides to the reader, animates and dramatizes the diary.
Further, the whole metamorphic and mythopoeic mode of perception
and presentation creates a drama between the poet and his materials in
which—a crucial step—his own consciousness becomes the principal
actor. It is not clear, however, that Pound is in firm control of this
development nor at all times sure of its effect on the poem's professed
analogies to Homer or Dante, still less to such formal analogies as the
fugue, the vortex or the spiral that critics have hospitably entertained.
Putting it more crudely, it is the presence of Pound which unites the
Cantos or gives them what coherence they have; our awareness of the
poet himself, shy though he is, rather than the professed rational
and narrative designs he has on us. This is not altogether a limitation,
but the extent to which this autobiography is unacknowledged is
problematical.

The inherited cosmologies and myths of Homer and Dante can only
operate as metaphors and models in the twentieth century. Homer
supplies Pound with a providential voyage, a resourceful explorer, an
underworld, a polytheistic overworld, miraculous encounters with wise
men and beautiful women, shipwrecks and landfalls. Dante supplies a
disdainful persona, an omnivorous system of moral philosophy, a hell, a
purgatory, an earthly paradise, a Ulysses, and a firm episodic structure.
Beyond these there is the chaos of the author's personal experience, of
modern life and of recorded history. The metamorphoses of Ovid offer a
model of coping with the mythical substrate Pound perceived in the
natural order and in personal imaginative experience.

For all their energy, perception and splendour, these early Cantos
exhibit a pattern of frustration: the 'baffled' Pedro and the heroically
overwhelmed Malatesta, robbed of their ideal brides, construct them
monuments 'braving time'; Actaeon and Vidal, Cabestan and his mistress,
suffer the nemesis of those who have seen too much beauty; the heroes of
the Great War are destroyed by the war profiteers. There are also
successes—Myo Cid, and, in part, Malatesta; and Odysseus–Pound
escapes the usurers' Hell with the enlisted help of Plotinus and Koré.
There is wanton destructiveness in the murderous rivalries of the
Renaissance, and a worse negativity in a modern world controlled by

money men. And there are the ideal and idealized worlds of Confucius—Pound's Aquinas—and of the natural beauties of the Elysian fields. Like Milton, Pound is beginning to turn to a 'paradise within'; like Blake, he constructs a heaven in hell's despite.

The first seventeen Cantos are in many ways the most difficult; the remainder of *A Draft of XXX Cantos* can be approached more simply. Cantos 18–30 mark no change of direction—they complete the volume which ends *Il Papa mori* in Canto 30, the end of the Italian Renaissance. The categories of history, myth and anecdote remain in much the same proportions, though the anecdote is less personal, designed more to indicate the trend of contemporary history. Canto 18, for example, illustrates further the role of the modern arms manufacturer via the figure of Zenos Metevsky. Themes of dynastic passion in the Renaissance are pursued further through the history of the Este family, notably in Canto 24. Mythical scenes from Pound's Elysian fields recur throughout the group. So there is much material that repeats or reinforces earlier themes. Other Cantos extend these themes: the history of the Este is linked to that of the Malatesta, the Borgia and the Venetian republic; in Canto 20 the Lotus-Eaters episode of the *Odyssey* is adapted to Pound's purposes; in Canto 28 American obtuseness in Europe is contrasted with native American vigour. There are also new subjects in the appearance of Jefferson in Canto 21, the Compleynt of Artemis in 30, and the juxta-position of Eliot with Joyce in 29. But the mixture is as before, and the cross-links are of the same kind. Pound is discovered dreaming on the Dogana's steps or in the arena at Verona; he again connects troubadour song with a pagan theophany in 20; he has unconstructive Russian revolutionaries chorusing from Dantescan stone quarries. There is, in comparative terms, much less to surprise us in the latter half of Cantos 1–30. There are new thickets here and there in the wood of error, but they are not unlike the old thickets; their obscurity is almost inviting among the paths and clearings. The reader's progress is easier, the views are similar, there are a few new achievements; Canto 20, for example, is a new and successful fusion of personal, historical and legendary themes.

It will appear from this summary that the chief gain in 18–30 is in intelligibility. Zenos Metevsky is no advance on Baldy Bacon; the Este tragedy is less immediately decipherable than Malatesta's effort; and, Cantos 20 and 30 apart, there is little new visionary material.

A gain in intelligibility is not however to be despised, since the reader's process of apprehension is part of the work, and certainly there are new

delights, like the Compleynt of Artemis, but most of these delights—
the detailed Venetian Cantos 25 and 26—are of a kind we know. In
short, the work does not seem, apart from the exceptions indicated, to
grow quite as much in stature and depth as it does in meaning. The
complicated kind of decadence that Pound finds in the middle Italian
Renaissance is made clearer; so is the kind of structural link Pound is
employing between subjects and between Cantos. We have a growing
sense of the poet's values and of his role in the poem. We have, then,
after the explosive opening Cantos, a consolidation requiring less
comment.

The significance of the history of the Este carries the main thematic
burden of the sequence, but before we come to that, two doubts must be
faced up to. One is the anxiety about form betrayed by Pound himself;
the other concerns the anecdotal treatment of contemporary history,
which becomes repetitious. The gossipy parts of Cantos 18, 19, 22, 27
and 28 are, despite surface animation, not particularly satisfying. To
take Canto 18 as representative: Zenos Metevsky (Sir Basil Zaharoff)
profits by the Great War, and his activities are made to typify the
technological and financial exploitation of men and nature which leads to
destructive wars. The rapacity of modern civilization becomes a leading
theme of the *Cantos* generally—a theme larger than the word 'usury'
might suggest. Indeed the weakness of our sample Canto 18 lies not in
any simplicity of its moral ideas, but rather in a certain ambiguity in
their application.

Initially a counter-theme is introduced, by the standard of which
Metevsky is to be judged: Marco Polo's report on Kublai's paper money,
an example of Western readiness to learn. The lesson is not learned,
however, and the Cathaian traveller languishes in an Italian prison.
Metevsky, in contrast, takes Western capitalists for a ride, and does well
out of the war; further, the effect of his machinery on more primitive
peoples is seen to be purely destructive. We have, then, a tableau,
'Ingenuity, applied and misapplied'. Polo's intelligence about superior
Chinese techniques of exchange is unwelcome back home; whereas
Metevsky's cunning is allowed to operate under the guise of philanthropy.
Western stupidity stifles the discoverer and honours the swindler and the
vandal.

Metevsky's Quaker agent in Ethiopia sees one of his employees put
a buzz-saw

                    . . . through an ebony log: whhsssh, t ttt,
          Two days' work in three minutes.

Pound comments:

War, one war after another,
Men start 'em who couldn't put up a good hen-roost.

The moral contrast between putting things up and cutting them up is clear enough, but the force of it is queered by Pound's excessive interest in Metevsky's success; the poet's resentful fascination at the triumph of the entrepreneurial outsider—he is compared with Napoleon—modifies our horror at destruction. The local colour and stage business also distract. Perhaps the vivid detail of Kublai's superior postal and fiscal arrangements is in intended contrast with the mundane detail about primitive worship of Western machinery; but what also comes across is an undifferentiated Yankee interest in quaintness on the one hand, and in technical acumen and expertise on the other. Alongside the moral and intellectual programme of this Canto, but imperfectly co-ordinated with it, goes an awe for men and methods that get things done—that 'work'. The ebony log—a natural miracle of vegetable life, with divine, animal and human correlatives—is, for Metevsky's operatives, a mechanical and commercial problem solved by the buzz-saw. Pan is sacrificed to Midas, and by a good hard-working Protestant; for time is money. We draw appropriate conclusions from these instances, we recoil from the violation; but we also feel the *virtù* of Metevsky and the power of the saw. Pound, so often his own Boswell, plays Metevsky's Bourrienne too well. Critics may explain that Metevsky's cunning is a perversion of Malatesta's *maestria* or of Odysseus' resourcefulness; probably this is what Pound intended, but his inexplicit method courts misunderstanding.

The last words of 18 are 'Also sabotage . . .', and 19 opens 'Sabotage? Yes, he took it up to Manhattan'—and the dialogue between Pound and the reader, or between Napoleon and Bourrienne, continues. The anecdotal episodes are often half dramatized by this 'conversational' method: 'Ever seen Prishnip. . . .'; 'Vlettmann?'; 'So I said to the X. and B. Central' (all from 19). As a device it lacks the confidence and conviction of the Cantos introducing Odysseus or Kung, and nowhere is Pound so near to seeming a barker as in these hooks to catch the passer-by's attention.

Canto 19 repeats the Polo–Metevsky pattern of the unrecognized inventor frustrated by the industrial exploiter, and enlarges on the monopoly economics which abort intelligence and abuse nature. We are then taken, though scarcely introduced, to the London office of the *New Age*, with Pound, Major Douglas and its editor, Orage—all unnamed. Journalism is further glorified in the person of Lincoln Steffens and his impressions of the Russian Revolution, hovering between contempt for

Russian stupidity and anarchy (Tovarich is invariably benighted *chez* Pound) and an admiration for Lenin. Half-hose has superseded the cultivation of roses.

The uneasy wise-guy tone of these low-downs and exposés is shown up by the genial opening of Canto 20. If, as Eliot says, Pound's Bertrans de Born 'is much more living than his Mr Hecatomb Styrax',[1] his Arnaut Daniel is more rewarding than the Inside Story of the Russian Revolution. Pound's need to account for the War, the break-up of the old Europe and the incident dispersal of the pre-war avant-garde, leads him into recrimination. He takes his ammunition from the fall-out of journalistic gossip. Technically, much of it is effective propaganda, but philosophically it is unsatisfactory: the villains of the piece, the Blankendorfs who subvert or allow subversion of the *ancien régime*, are no more credible than Eisenstein's animated caricatures of the Russian Revolution; perhaps less so, as it is not so clear that they are caricatures. Pound accounts for the war by showing that foreigners of Levantine origin exploited the defective intelligence and purpose of the West—a simple, technical, Darwinian interpretation: we wuz robbed. And there is some admiration for the burglars. Empirically unsatisfactory, there is little room either, in such an ideal explanation, for metaphysics, and even its morality is confusing.

The unsatisfactory nature of the anecdotal Cantos of contemporary history is, in a curious way, deliberate. Pound's exasperation with contemporary realities mounts palpably as he compiles the records of infamy, and he means, by a mimetic miscalculation, that we too should wish to escape from them, to 'bust thru from quotidien into "divine or permanent world" '.[2] But we want to get away not so much from this sordid modern world as from Pound *on* the modern world. Unlike Joyce (or Dante's Virgil) he tells us many things we don't want to know, and some that we do not believe.

The other doubt concerned Pound's anxiety about form, and it recurs at the end of the remarkable Canto 20. The opening is a moment of extraordinary synthesis and lyrical vision—we are back in the Elysian fields, in front of a Dantescan shrine of the love poets: Catullus, Homer and Bernart de Ventadorn contribute to the composite glimpse of the singer; we are told, in Italian, that Propertius and Ovid are also present. *Ligur' aoide* refers to the Sirens' 'sharp song' from the *Odyssey* (XII, 183); but the presiding genius is the Amor of the troubadours.[3] Bernart's 'neo-Platonic' line, 'Se no'us vei . . .', is translated in Canto 92: 'And if I see her not,/no sight is worth the beauty of my thought'. Pound then adopts Emil Lévy's solution of a crux in Arnaut Daniel—*noigandres*—into an imaginative reconstruction of a Mediterranean garden of love in which 'the smell of that place' creates not only an intelligible reading but leads on to another erotic incarnation from Daniel:

> And the light falls, *remir*,
> from her breast to thighs.

The singer opens the vision, the beloved closes it. Spliced happily into the middle is Pound's account of a visit to consult the Provençal scholar 'old Lévy' in Freiburg. The whole passage is a test case—in my view entirely successful—of Pound's intensely allusive method. It will, however, be quite lost on the reader who has only English and who is also unwilling to go beyond the text to see where Pound's talismanic words— his 'radiant gists'—come from. The *bel pensar* of the glimpsed singer at the beginning is fulfilled by the physical reality of his glimpsed mistress at the end; the visionary tension between them, expressed in the *remir* of the light, has an erotic power and refinement rare in English poetry since the seventeenth century. Both the scene and the vision are traditional in romance art and poetry, but the method of implication is, despite its reliance on fragments of tradition, entirely Pound's own. The spiritual ancestry of such a passage in his work goes back at least to 'The Tree'.

Pound's natural paradise receives no better adumbration in the *Cantos*, though the erotic generally brings out the crispest imagery and tone in his writing. There is nothing left of the spiritualized sensuality of the Pre-Raphaelites, much though Pound owed to them. It is a vision, not a swoon, neither sickly nor ethereal nor lacking in urbanity:

> You would be happy for the smell of that place
> And never tired of being there, either alone
> Or accompanied.

There is also a sane and amiable quality in the account of the visit to Lévy and in the neat contrast of unhelpful German cleanness and helpful Italian smells.

The note is struck again later in Canto 20 in the lament for Odysseus' crewmen:

> "That saw never the olives under Spartha
> "With the leaves green and then not green,
> "The click of light in their branches. . . ."

The image is clear and solid, the language ceremonious but natural, the subtlety of the mythopoeic glance from 'the click of light' back to *remir* is unforced, magical. The nymphs of Forster and Lawrence are much more oncoming; Pound really possesses the inwardness with immanent natural myth to which he lays claim. And it is, curiously, in his dealings with

'Courtly Love', a defunct—if not invented—love mysticism, that he is
at his sanest.

The anxiety about form, referred to above, comes out in the passage
in 20 beginning:

> Jungle:
> Glaze green and red feathers, jungle,
> Basis of renewal, renewals;
> Rising over the soul, green virid, of the jungle,
> Lozenge of the pavement, clear shapes,
> Broken, disrupted, body eternal.
> Wilderness of renewals, confusion
> Basis of renewals, subsistence,
> Glazed green of the jungle;
> Zoe, Marozia, Zothar,
> > loud over the banners,
> Glazed grape, and the crimson,
> HO BIOS

This raises form as an issue: out of the jungle of formlessness, the chaos
of life, emerge glimpses of civilization, of the temple of the gods, of the
'body eternal' of some plenum or arcanum of reality. The jungle is that
primitive nature where Lawrence and other contemporaries of Pound
found the source of 'Life'; it sounds better in Greek. The Greek guise
recalls the evolutionary theory proposed in Jane Harrison's *Ancient Art
and Ritual*:[4] civilization arises from the primitive through communal
rites and mysteries from which art is derived. Pound's Eleusinian
mysteries lead to his Parthenon via processions, as well as orgies and
sacrifices, and it is in one of these processions, presumably, that this
strange device is borne, 'loud' indeed but curiously abstract and rhetorical.
This anthropological view of civilization implies also a neo–Platonic idea
of inspiration, the psychology of which is much like that of Shelley's
Defence of Poetry. The passage has its oddities: the obscure triad of
ladies;[5] the relation of the 'soul' to the 'body'; the 'red feathers'. But it
may be taken generally as dramatizing the poetic process of the *Cantos*,
where clarity is continually interfered with by a return to the multifariousness of the actual 'quotidien', and then by a return to the ideal 'permanent';
a process where both stages are necessary, though the relationships
between bits of jungle and bits of eternal are not at all necessary but
contingent and admittedly disruptive: 'confusion basis of renewals'.
(Are *all* disruptions renewals?) The intellectual and stylistic coherence
of the passage is deliberately incomplete, and might be acceptable as a
tentative model for the form of the *Cantos*, were it not for the conclusion,

which only the decent obscurity of the Greek can make interesting. A spell should not conclude in a slogan; 'the world's welter' should not end in a catchword, however much of a bang it makes. The need Pound feels to produce a banner (more than the actual words on the banner) suggests an anxiety about form; also, perhaps, an anxiety about the jungle.

This 'Jungle' passage occurs after a strange synthesis of three stories cross-cut into each other:[6] (1) Niccolo d'Este's madness after he has put to death his young wife Parisina and his son (her stepson) Ugo after discovering their incest; (2) Roland's destruction of the horn with which he has, too late, summoned Charlemagne to Roncesvalles; (3) an episode from a play by Lope de Vega where the King is sexually aroused by the sight of a woman on the walls of the city—a woman who turns out to be his sister. There are other references to Niccolo's son Borso, to the legendary Trojan foundation of the house of the Este, and to the elders on the walls of Troy murmuring about Helen. The 'confusion' of the three stories takes place in the mind of Niccolo, as is made clear in parenthesis. Roland's insane pride, which led to the slaughter of the Franks' rear guard in the name of his honour, is d'Este's projection of his own pride which has made him take violent revenge upon Eros; likewise the King's attraction to his sister is evidence of the naturalness and rightness of the instincts which can lead to incest. The reference to the fall of Troy reminds us that Menelaus' sexual possessiveness and jealousy are in legend the cause of war and destruction, even if that destruction can be the basis of renewals ('condit Atesten'). D'Este's execution of his nearest and dearest drove him mad (he later orders the execution of all adulterers); his other son Borso can no longer 'keep the peace' between Sigismundo Malatesta and Federico d'Urbino, and the dynasty thereafter declines; the whole is an illustration of Kung's words on Order in Canto 13. The last line of the passage refers to the scene of the celebrated murder of Paolo Malatesta and Francesca da Rimini, victims in Dante of their own sexual passion, though for Pound they are victims of a husband's sexual jealousy.[7] Shakespeare's *Measure for Measure* offers an instructive range of comparisons.

The theme of sexual possessiveness leading to wider destruction is enlarged on in Cantos 23, 24 and, indirectly, 25 and 26, and 29 and 30. In the Venetian Cantos 25 and 26, the theme is connected with the supremacy of financial values and showiness on the one hand, and with an abstract and restrictive Christianity on the other:

> The dead concepts, never the solid, the blood rite,
> The vanity of Ferrara. . . .

(25)

The thickening and ostentation of later Renaissance art, contrasted with the purity, intelligence, fluidity and grace of the Quattrocento, is the most convincing part of Pound's case; for him art is a direct index of the changes taking place in private and public mores and in religion between the twelfth and the sixteenth centuries. A preference for Italian primitives as against the Baroque was general in the nineteenth century—here Pound's values are Ruskinian. Ruskinian, too, are Pound's views about usury and changes in social values. But the interpretation of the proto-Renaissance as a period of pagan vitality and healthy polytheism ruined later by a totalitarian and corrupt Church is a peculiarly Poundian version of merrie Catholic Europe.[8] The suppression of the Albigensians, or, say, the private life of Alexander VI, are historical indications in favour of his views, as perhaps are the histories of Florence and Venice. But his chief 'source' is the stimulus given to his imagination by the poems and the superb paintings of the period, interpreted as in the 'Renaissance' poems of Browning, according to the tradition of a romantic scholarship and backed up by evidence selected from the lives of those Renaissance rulers, like Lorenzo de' Medici and Sigismundo, who were patrons of the arts. The moral and conceptual rigour Pound associated with a repressive Christianity is present in Dante, where he ignores it, as he does Eliot's version of 'the blood rite'. Despite Artemis' Compleynt against Pity, it is not easy to imagine Pound enjoying a 'solid' blood rite like, say, the Taurobolion. (Indeed, Yeats seems to have found Pound's habit of going out at night to feed Rapallo's stray cats puzzlingly reminiscent of the R.S.P.C.A.)[9]

The Este theme is summarized in Canto 30, where Alfonso d'Este is married by proxy to Lucrezia Borgia, whose 'Papa' is the Pope Alexander Borgia who dies at the end of the Canto. Alfonso, the degenerate scion of the Este line, is bought up by the predatory Lucrezia Borgia, referred to allegorically by Pound as Madame *Hyle*—the Greek word for 'matter'. Alfonso feebly fails to turn up at his own wedding, thus providing an example of the triumph of materialism over mind and nature. This 'wedding' is preceded by another perverted wedding, where Ignez da Castro's corpse is rendered 'homage', like Lucrezia's money:

"Honour? Balls for yr honour!
Take two million and swallow it."

The Borgia corruption of the Papacy completes the picture: 'homage'; Lucrezia's 'balls'; and the Pope who is no longer a father to his church, all are inversions of natural sexual roles. Earlier in the Canto, Venus, alas,

> . . . goeth not with young Mars to playe
> But she hath pity on a doddering fool.

Artemis complains that 'Nothing is now clean slayne / But rotteth away.' If post-fascist perspectives make this maypole neo-paganism sound rather theoretical, that is Pound's misfortune. The positive side—'Beauty on an ass-cart' in Canto 29—is much more effective.

Canto 30 lastly includes a letter to Cesare Borgia, the Pope's son, describing the introduction of printing: Aldus Manutius' types were taken, it says, from two texts:

> from that of Messire Laurentius
> and from a codex once of the Lords Malatesta. . . .

The letter is written from 'Caesar's Fane' i.e. from 'Caesaro-Papal' Fano, once part of the lands of that glorious Malatesta who built the Tempio and renewed the art of letters.

Whatever the moral truth of this lively cultural history, its edged use of brilliant instances in an organized strategy makes it a virtuoso finale to Pound's presentation of the Renaissance. The ideas have an instrumental value in bringing out the tendency and the coherence of these Cantos. The spoken drama, the surface animation, yield up their moral and human significances at last in a curiously satisfying and solid way. . . . Always supposing readers are alert enough to follow the poet's drift. They will see exciting correspondences everywhere: the Borgia reap the reward of the Malatesta, just as Metevsky reaps the rewards of Marco Polo. Such history has many cunning passages.

Cantos 31–41 deal with 'Jefferson: Nuevo Mundo'; the *Fifth Decad of Cantos* (42–51) with 'Siena: the Leopoldine Reforms'. Cantos 52–71 are preceded by a Table,[10] in which 62–71 are entitled 'John Adams'; 52–61 digest Chinese history from its origins to 1735, the year of John Adams's birth. Thus Cantos 31–71 form one section, in that, as these subtitles suggest, their material is primarily historical; there is a change of direction in Canto 47, and 52–71 are wholly historical. This historical section of the *Cantos* was written in the political context of the Thirties, and is separated from the *Pisan Cantos*, 74–84, by the unpublished Cantos 72 and 73.

The theme of the forty history Cantos is the Enlightenment, the effort of intelligence to bring new order into the chaos and corruption of old Europe; Jefferson and Adams cast themselves naturally in this role; so, on our making their acquaintance, do the enlightened despots of Siena, whose economics, for Pound, preserved a mediaeval sense of social justice; so, from a certain point of view, does Napoleon the liberator; so, in Pound's eye, did Mussolini, the modern avatar of a new order for 'ruined Latium'. Even to readers accustomed to the inverse relationship Pound's views bear to modern expectations, the inclusion of China in this scheme may seem a little surprising. What 'renewal' will this 'confusion' bring? If we adjust the angle of our vision, Confucianism is of course the answer—the Confucianism in which the Age of Reason found a humane non-Christian equivalent for the values enshrined in the Declaration of Independence and the Napoleonic Code.

If the good subject of Queen Elizabeth II is now convinced he has wandered through the looking-glass, his confusion is understandable. Pound's effort in his middle years was to construct an alternative view of the world to that once enjoyed from London, the centre of usurocracy, or, less contentiously, of modern finance, from 1694, the date of the foundation of the Bank of England, to 1939. The view of English history offered by Adams in Canto 68 stops with the Civil War, whereafter Pound's interest transfers to America, and England becomes principally the fief of George III and the home of the rotten borough. American reverence for Magna Charta—and subsequent British constitutional developments until the stand of Coke and Hampden against Stuart usurpations of the liberties of the (property-owning) people—reflects the views of those who wanted no taxation without representation. The enlightened republic drafted in the U.S. Constitution reposed on a Whig interpretation of British history, fortified by an admixture of the ideals of the French Encyclopaedists. From the point of view of an old American constitutional liberal, the defeat of Napoleon by England was the victory of the financier over the reformer, and not, as in British memory, a police action against a bully.

The disillusion with London recorded in *Mauberley*, and Pound's withdrawal to Rapallo, represented a general disillusion with metropolitan life, the plutocratic perversions of which were now as evident to Pound as its deprovincializing advantages had been on his arrival (see *Ripostes*). The commercial, industrial and financial world, the modern world whose capital was London, now became the enemy, as it had been for Tom Paine and the intellectual leaders of the American and French Revolutions, for whom British capital meant tyranny, obstruction, and depriving the people of the fruits of their labour. For Pound in the Thirties, this Enlightenment critique of modern capitalism inherited from the radical mediaeval synthesis the ideal prestige which, as we have seen, nourished his critique of early capitalism in Italy. Pound's return to his American radical roots is obscured for the modern liberal by his simultaneous discovery of Mussolini, whose populist and anti-capitalist side seemed to Pound more significant than his contempt for democratic process. Such a view of Fascism allowed Pound to see Mussolini as the complement rather than the antitype of the author of the Declaration of Independence. Civic order, for Pound, was primarily a question of just economic distribution, with a fair deal for the producer (and artist) and a just price for the consumer; representative institutions, despite 1776, came a poor second, universal suffrage nowhere.

Such are, as I take it, some of the considerations which led Pound to displace from his account of European history what for the British reader of Burke and Mill might be the centre, namely the modern history of England and France; in the *Cantos* the French Revolution merely derives from the American. For Pound, England and France were not 'the democracies' but the usurocracies, an unfamiliar perspective to the British reader. The absence of Christianity from Pound's history of Europe, and of Shakespeare and the Romantics from his history of English literature, are, however, circumventions much less notable for an American, and indeed orientations perfectly natural to a man brought up on the 'Roman' traditions of the American Republic.

The first two 'decads' of the forty history Cantos are interspersed, in a familiar way, by comparisons with modern swindlers and slitherers, and by paradisal intervals; whereas the Chinese and Adams Cantos are history unrelieved. Jefferson is a Renaissance man who is successful in creating in his Nuevo Mundo, unlike Sigismundo Malatesta. The death of a Borgia Pope closes Canto 30, the magisterial correspondence of Jefferson opens 31. The intervening 284 years (of usury) are for Pound something to keep quiet about: *tempus tacendi*. With Washington, Adams, Jefferson, the New World had a chance to carry on where the Renaissance had left off or gone wrong. Jefferson's letters, in 31-34, show the mind and character of the man and of his correspondents, particularly Adams; also the active concern of the Founding Fathers for the good government of the United States, and their scorn for Europe, courts and reformers alike. There are inserted for contrast the reflections in old age of Adams and Jefferson on the popular politicians of that day—Clay, Calhoun and Webster—and on further instances of Western decline of principle, especially in Britain; and 34 ends with a maxim and a warning. The maxim, that of Adams and Jefferson, is that:

> Science as a principle of political action. . .
> Proportioned to free inhabitants.

The warning is the appearance of the Jews in America. For Pound, as for too many Gentiles, Jews—or 'jews'—were the archetypal usurers: men who cash in on the work of others and strive to get the nation into debt, the funding of which debt by a national bank means that the people are renting their own money, and are hence no longer 'free inhabitants'. 'Usurer' was for Pound a dirtier word than 'Jew'. The usurers, in this simple model of the world, are the parasites who bring down Napoleon and have corrupted (in Canto 35) 'Mitteleuropa'. Vienna is contrasted in 36 with the credit policy of Leopoldine Siena. 36 translates Guido Cavalcanti's Canzone on Love, an example of mediaeval Mediterranean clarity of intellect about immaterial qualities; hence a reminder of what Mitteleuropa has lost in its materialism and sentiment, and also a parallel to the proper use of the mind, as in the case of Adams, to clarify and articulate experience. 37 is devoted to Martin van Buren, a neglected continuator of the Jeffersonian dynasty, especially as a champion against the Bank of the United States.

These seven Cantos contain the Jeffersonian statement, by the method of selecting letters, with effects at once lively and locally confusing, as in the Malatesta Cantos; perhaps less lively because less romantic and more documentary, but also less confusing because the overall message is clearer. Van Buren's epitaph is 'Hic Jacet Fisci Liberator'. The modern decline from this standard is recorded in 35, 38 and 40: Mitteleuropa; arms manufacturers; J. P. Morgan; and the destructive effects thereof in the exploitation of nature.

39, part of 40, and 41 represent a positive push: Odysseus; Hanno; Mussolini. The fourth 'decad' of the Cantos is, generally, positive, in the face of a historic decline, the beginning of which is registered in the first three. Pound hoped that the usurious system, which America joined with her Civil War, might be coming to an end with Mussolini, or that he represented a promising new departure, 'ad interim 1933'—the last words of Canto 41.

The pattern of 31–41 is clearly an antithetical one, dualistic; in its values, its heroes and villains, and its conception and presentation. Although it is clear which side Pound is on in the interrelated struggles he presents, he is not yet irrevocably *within* that side, as in the 'Confucian' or Adams Cantos. Nor yet is his own mind and memory the theatre where the dialectical process takes place, as in the Pisan Cantos; he is not yet presented as the protagonist. The exemplars—Jefferson, Cavalcanti, Van Buren, Odysseus, Hanno or the Duce—are entities distinct from the poet, though not always distinguishable from the poet's perception of them.

The dogmatic trend of these Cantos is clearer than in 1–30; flux is not itself a theme. Increasingly it is possible to see quickly just what this or that item in the *Cantos* is to stand for. Although, in the ordinary universe, Cavalcanti's philosophical definition of love might seem to have little to do with the physical union of Odysseus with Circe in Canto 39, and neither might seem to have any ordinary connection with the founders of the American system or of the Italian corporate state, Pound's use of contexts and contrasts makes apparent the coherence or, better, the compatibility of these elements, especially when they are set *against* relationships of exploitation in politics, economics and 'civilized' sexual mores.

Pound does not present us with a system, but with an alliance of attitudes which one might term natural, or respectful of nature; this cousinhood of attitudes is defined by contrast with the greed that inspires their opposites. The antagonism is of sets or series rather than systems openly advocated, because Pound is interested in praxis rather than programme. The more clearly his views on, say, money, are spelt out by interpreters or even by himself, the more the web of the poem may be pulled out of shape, as the isolation of one strand—even the fiscal— suggests for it a centrality which will often be denied by the next Canto, about a mythical sexuality, a geographical exploration, a ritual or a joke. Though the sense of an intelligible polemic develops very strongly, it is never completely reducible, despite its insistences, its King Charles's heads, and its blessings and blastings, to simple terms, and it is rarely predictable. The unpersuaded will see the heroes as extensions of Pound's idea of himself, and relate the 'programme' quite closely to the politics of the Thirties (thus, Hanno = Mussolini). But the act of reading shows the poem to be irreducibly many-sided. Even the title of Pound's tract *Jefferson and/or Mussolini* challenges the reader to find the concord of this discordant conceit. Though their names are used as tokens for democracy and dictatorship, these rhetorical pragmatists shared an interest in the land, as Pound thought, and acted upon it; though Abyssinia is an odd parallel with Louisiana.

The attacks on arms cartels and usurers (Gentile or Jew), like the later fulminations against non-Confucians, are not rewarding. The documentary Cantos of American history I value more highly than other readers of Pound appear to: I find them stimulating, not only as specimens of prose, but even as history, regardless of Pound's 'case'. Perhaps this is an antiquarian taste for authentic novelty. Here, for example, is Adams on tyranny:

> Is that despotism
> or absolute power . . . unlimited sovereignty,

is the same in a majority of a popular assembly,
an aristocratical council, an oligarchical junto,
and a single emperor, equally arbitrary, bloody,
and in every respect diabolical. Wherever it has resided
has never failed to destroy all records, memorials,
all histories which it did not like, and to corrupt
those it was cunning enough to preserve. . . .

(33)

Cantos 36 and 39 deserve attention as defining much further the principle of love implicit in earlier pagan and Provençal mythopoeia, of which Cavalcanti provides the metaphysics, Odysseus the physics. Pound edited the works of Dante's friend, Guido Cavalcanti, the key to which he finds in the canzone 'Donna mi pregha', translated in Canto 36. The most pregnant lines for Pound's natural mystique of love are:

> Be there not natural demonstration
> I have no will to try proof-bringing

and

> Cometh from a seen form which being understood
> Taketh locus and remaining in the intellect possible. . . .

Daniel, Sordello and Cavalcanti are Pound's favourites among the troubadours and their followers in the 'sweet new style'. All three are amorous and (to Dante) heterodox, and in Canto 36 Pound links them by a secret tradition to Scotus Erigena, who 'was not understood in his time/"which explains, perhaps, the delay in condemning him".' Pound identifies himself with this fragmentary, unofficial tradition, against the tradition of Aquinas, Dante (and T. S. Eliot). Aquinas is 'head down in a vacuum', according to 36.

> Aristotle which way in a vacuum?
> not quite in a vacuum.

This last half-line[11] is in lighter type, representing a (necessary) after-thought in Pound's interior dialogue; the echo of 'vacuum' continues in the first words of the next line: 'Sacrum, sacrum, inluminatio coitu.' And 'coitu' again rhymes immediately with 'Goito', Sordello's castle. The weaving together of this 'tradition' consciously admits to its own Joycean play and fantasy.

The rite of illumination by coitus is celebrated in Canto 39, a spectacularly syncretic piece of mythography, a fantasia based on the Circe episode of the *Odyssey* but involving Catullus, the *Pervigilium Veneris*, Pound's own 'Dionysian' cats and even Mussolini ('by Circeo', where he drained the marshes). The passage cited from the *Odyssey* gives Circe's directions to Odysseus for getting to Hades (and Tiresias); we are referred forward to Canto 47 for a translation. Canto 39 is a key Canto for the 'plot' and thematic development of the poem, and is intensely vivid and memorable in detail. Briefly, the Canto moves from (1) the actuality of Pound's own 'desolate' sense-world, lacking a miraculous though very real cat, via the sound of a loom on a hill path and 'a song/ under olives'; to (2) Circe's ingle, as experienced by Elpenor metamorphosed to a swine; to (3) Odysseus (with Frazerian variations) meeting Circe and conquering her (*not* vice versa); to (4) a ritual coition which renews the spring (the hero becomes a god); to (5) the final mating with Penelope, presented as a fertility myth.

Towards the end,

> Can see but their eyes in the dark
> not the bough that he walked on

returns us momentarily to the originating impulse of the whole 'vision' —the glimpse of the eyes of a cat, attendant of Dionysus. We are far from the cats of Cheshire, but the vestigial image has its similarities.

The Greek, the mythology, the allusiveness and the sex have produced much commentary[12] on Canto 39, and rightly so, for the complexity of organization and reference is as great as in the later work of Joyce. The reader of Pound will rarely be primed with all the information, yet the Canto operates satisfactorily with less than half of that information; it is perhaps more important that the associative, metamorphic nature of the Canto be recognized than that each detail be understood: it begins in and returns to Pound's personal observation, and its transformations take place in Pound's own imagined reality rather than in its sources or in the syntheses of Sir James Frazer. That is, the Canto is true to Pound's usual process from actual experience to visionary transformation: the parent image remains a natural object, a natural object now retaining a talismanic power. Cats, henceforward, are harbingers of Dionysian mysteries, and of sexual union as a source of the indispensable knowledge to be gained by joining in the primitive natural order, and hence a source of renewal. Without this, Love, 'wild often', as Pound has Cavalcanti say, remains incomplete; though Cavalcanti's intellectual discrimination is equally indispensable. (The conscious, voluntary and intelligent role of Odysseus needs to be underlined. Pound's Orphism is not Lawrence's, and his orgies, though ecstatic and genuinely erotic, are orderly: *fac deum* is the ritual word, 'fuck' is the language of the 'sensual sty'. (Indeed, Pound's view of Circe is not diametrically opposed to that of the author of *Comus*.)

'Out of which things seeking an exit': Hanno's *periplum* or sailing around of North-West Africa is an Odyssean and Ulyssean image of the discovery of a Nuevo Mundo. Hanno arrives, apparently, in the stratosphere, the 'temple' both of the Carthaginians and of pure mind, where the map of his personal exploration is hung. The mess of modern exploitation is confronted in Canto 41 by Mussolini, Jefferson and C. H. Douglas, 'ad interim 1933'.

The second decad of history Cantos begins, despite its subtitle, not with Siena but with some very sundry asides which clearly 'belong' elsewhere; another renewing confusion for the helplessly tidy-minded. . . . The Sienese Cantos record the good government of Siena between the foundation of the Monte dei Paschi Bank in 1622 and the coming of Napoleon. The enlightened Medicean Grand Dukes of Tuscany ruled Siena without the city incurring public debt to bankers, and without lining their own pockets. This illustrious example of probity is offered by Pound in implied contrast to the corruption of British values during the two centuries following the foundation of the Bank of England. The Grand Dukes entered into partnership with their people by means of a permanent arrangement with the public Monte dei Paschi Bank: this Mount, or bank, of the Pastures, was set up with capital from the Grand Duke's public income to finance public and private works and to pay fixed dividends. It was not a profit-making institution and debtors were treated leniently. The bank's income came from the produce of the public grazing lands.

Cantos 42–44 document in some detail and with much local colour the setting up of the bank. The sketch of the bank's mechanism is incomplete, though the purpose of the model remains clear: it exhibits a harmonious organic relationship between Duke, people and nature. The bank is bottomed upon nature, not upon the discounting of paper, and is run for the public good. Pound has the rural American mistrust of big money. The scheme was—appropriately—dreamed up by Della Rena, the 'illegitimate father of the bastards of Pietro de Medici' (43). A generous, non-proprietorial attitude to propagation and 'the abundance of nature' is therefore observed in private as well as in public affairs by the good Dukes.

Whether this picture of Siena under the good Duke Leopold is credible or not—and the appearance of the city today does not contradict it—its function is like that of the fresco of Good Government by Lorenzetti in the Palazzo Pubblico, ideal and exemplary. The 'Monte' appeals to Pound as much for its poetic as for its pecuniary meanings: the Mount of Purgatory, the mount of Venus, the *Collis, o heliconii* of Catullus, the hill upon which the U.S. Senate is built, the steep streets of Siena itself.

> The kallipygous Sienese females
> get that way from the *salite*
> that is from continually plugging up hill.
>
> (43)

Finally, the emblem of Siena and of the Monte dei Paschi Bank is , which appears in Canto 42. The 'local colour' of modern and ancient Sienese life suggests the liveliness and harmony of such an enlightened natural and organic economy. Here Catholicism *works*:

> Respectons les prêtres, remarked Talleyrand
> 1800 a good grain and wine year
>   if you wd/ get on well with the peasantry
> of the peninsula.
>
> (44)

This Canto ends with a list of the Leopoldine Reforms, followed by two entries which make a positive contrast with the ending of Canto 30: 'Madame Letizia' (the mother of Napoleon) for 'Madame *Hyle*' (Lucrezia Borgia); and 'Piccolomini, Provveditore' for the greedy Piccolomini who excommunicated Sigismundo.

Canto 45 must be an 'adjunct to the Muses' diadem'—perhaps the clearest and most cogent statement of principle in the poem. Its Old Testament litany of the effects of usury on natural life is full of torrential moral indignation, a passion which remains, in spite of reservations, deeply impressive. I once heard Christopher Logue reading the Canto to a respectful Albert Hall poetry 'happening' in 1965, substituting 'Ursula' for 'Usura' throughout; even this portent has not dented the poem. It is curious nevertheless to see an accepted masterwork of modernism so utterly archaic in its diction and cadence and so entirely dogmatic and moral in intention. Its values are no less reactionary: it is a proclamation of mediaeval values which could be signed without reservation by William Morris and Pope Leo XIII, and, with a few, by Enrico Berlinguer.

The destructive effect on the quality of human activity of scarcity economics, and the equation of time with money, has not been put more trenchantly. With Usura,

    no picture is made to endure nor to live with
    but it is made to sell and sell quickly

and the same goes for buildings, and bread, and even for procreation:

        Usura slayeth the child in the womb
        It stayeth the young man's courting.

The closing lines of the Canto resume the themes of Cantos 30 and 39.
In a commercial society which marries late the sexual mysteries are
available only through the brothel; fruitfulness doesn't pay.

The radical integrity Pound finds between economics, the life of the
arts, craft, nature, procreation and religion is nowhere more startlingly
announced. It is both a critique of and a jeremiad against the modern
industrial world, and its positives are mediaeval and Quattrocento. The
proper names which contain the positive instances are not conventional
—each is the prize and record of experience—but they are a logical
development of the Ruskinian tradition. Pound was a virtuoso in the
arts of this period, and in some respects a pioneer.

The critique of modern civilization proclaimed in Canto 45 is spelt
out in 46, a deliberate anticlimax or desperate scherzo treatment of the
same theme, bringing it home to London and the Empire, and up to
date in F. Roosevelt's America. Against usury are Orage's *New Age* and
Mussolini's *Il Popolo*.

        19 years on this case/first case. I have set down part of
        The Evidence. . . .

The deliberately mimed exhaustion, distraction and discursiveness of
the writing tell us that after the thunder of 45, Pound is relaxing:

                . . . This case, and with it
        the first part, draws to a conclusion.

Appropriately, Canto 47 initiates a departure in Pound's Odyssey:
'Yet must thou sail after knowledge', developing a new side of a theme
introduced in Canto 39. There, the ritual love-making has a regenerative
effect; here, the personal *inluminatio* is dwelt on less than the changes in
the natural world itself. The Odysseus/Adams passage at the beginning
is a reprise of 39, a Poundian version of Ovidian and Frazerian material.
Several themes are orchestrated: the death of Adonis; the sexual penetra-
tion of Circe by Odysseus; the entrance of Odysseus into the gate or

cave of the earth, seeking knowledge; springtime ploughing or sowing.
The original biological natures of woman and man are inescapable:

> Two span, two span to a woman,
> Beyond that she believes not. Nothing is of any importance.
> To that is she bent, her intention
> To that art thou called ever turning intention,
>
>   . . . . .
>
> The stars are not in her counting,
>   To her they are but wandering holes.

It is for men to do the reckoning:

>   Begin thy plowing
>   When the Pleiades go down to their rest. . . .

The Canto is full of the lore of this natural religion, a reconstituted pagan
Deuteronomy. The young Pound's nature-mysticism has taken on an
objective and communal side; Hesiod has been added to Eleusis. There
are still personal elements, though cast in an impersonal form, and these
provide some remarkable lines:

> Here the mules are gabled with slate on the hill road.
> Thus was it in time.
> And the small stars now fall from the olive branch,
> Forked shadow falls dark on the terrace
> More black than the floating martin
>   that has no care for your presence,
> His wing-print is black on the roof tiles
> And the print is gone with his cry.
> So light is thy weight on Tellus
> Thy notch no deeper indented
> Thy weight less than the shadow. . . .

Here the rarefied and oblique implications lend a mysterious resonance
to personal observation. In this vein Pound has a power of suggestion
quite transcending that of any of the Imagists in whose company he
started out, and he has refined his polytheism.

The new start signalled by 'Yet must thou sail after knowledge' is
confirmed by Cantos 49 and 51. 49—'For the seven lakes, and by no
man these verses'—celebrates the peace of the country life of ancient
China, and 51 re-states 45 more calmly, with less stress on the artist, more

on the peasant, who, under usury, 'does not eat his own grain' and 'has
no gain from his sheep herd'. It continues with an impassioned 'Look
here upon this picture and on this': directions to fishermen for tying
flies to suit the seasons; against an evocation of Geryon, Dante's monster
of Fraud. It can be seen in retrospect that the decad 42–51 marks a
change of focus away from the individual artist or doer in 1–30, to
society, the corporate life, either sane or twisted by usury. 'Peasant has
no gain from his sheep herd' is the last reference to the Monte dei Paschi
theme. The Leopoldine Reforms summarized in Canto 50 are set alongside the principles of the American Revolution, Napoleon (and Dante!)
against 'the slough of Vienna'.

The *Fifth Decad* contains, in 45, 47 and 49, three of the most remarkable
of the Cantos, together making the climax of the poem before the Pisan
sequence and indicating a change of direction. No account of the *Cantos*
would be complete without a pause at Canto 49; but before this major
plus is reached, two considerable minuses have to be registered. Cantos
48 and 50 are alarming portents, 50 (' "Revolution" said Mr Adams . . .')
more obviously, in its abuse of Vienna's 'embastardized cross-breeds', and
'Pus was in Spain, Wellington was a jew's pimp' and

> 'From the brigantine Incostante'
> for a hundred days against hell belch
> Hope spat from March until June
> Ney out of his saddle.

The Russian mud which stops the enlightened Napoleon may be an
acceptable emblem of obscurantism; but pus is not acceptable as the
emblem of the Spanish (i.e. English—i.e. Jewish!) resistance to Napoleon.
If Pound's epic scheme has Geryon (Fraud) as an emanation of 'hell
belch', then Hope may with propriety 'spit' for a hundred days: but this
is not Rabelaisian or Swiftian, it is not even like Milton's God the Father
locking the Devil in the privy. It is an entirely black-and-white, or rather
shit-and-sunlight, view of the world, with a dash of *Führerprinzip* and
diabolism, where everything is shiningly good or stinkingly bad. When
Hitler has become as remote as Bismarck this will not seem good history,
sound morality or sane poetry. It is moral allegory masquerading as
fact, with a romantic identification operating unacknowledged. The
'brigantine' and 'Ney' are, in their attractive way, as silly as the absurd
'jew's pimp'.

Less alarming but more puzzling is Canto 47, a miscellany of excellent
fragments with no sense of order or coherence. Viewed through Pound's
spectacles, all the instances take up their proper places in the spectrum
from light to mud, but the relevancy or necessity is highly obscure. 47 is

perhaps a reservoir of imagery for phase two of the *Cantos*, as 1–7 were for phase one. The splicing of anecdote, scraps of reading, mythopoeic invention, a letter from his daughter etc. is not casual—on the contrary it bears the weight of a strong set of personal meanings, when interpreted by a set of attitudes earlier implanted in the mind of the reader; but unless there is naturally a self-evident quality in the examples, the process becomes too arbitrarily allegorical. The natural object becomes not an 'adequate symbol' but a counter evacuated of its natural meaning. Thus, the last line of Canto 48 is: 'and if the wind was, the old man placed a stone.' It seems that the man placed a stone on the long beach costumes. The point of the anecdote is the futility and wrongness of so trivial and servile an employment: an old man ought not to have to anchor against the wind the long beach costumes of rich elderly ladies. When its context has been restored, this becomes an image both comical and poignant, but without the gloss it remains irrecoverably cryptic. A bad sign.

The Seven Lakes Canto, 49, is the still point in the kaleidoscope, like Canto 13, the Kung Canto, to whose principles it is related, since the stability and endurance of the Chinese empire results directly from its adherence to Confucian practice:

> This canal goes still to Ten Shi
> though the old king built it for pleasure.

The Canto adapts a number of Chinese and Japanese poems to make a composite picture of a country life in rhythm with the seasons, and adds glosses, of which the most important is: 'Imperial power is? and to us what is it?' The well-run empire does not interfere, and the peasant eats of his grain. But this corporate aspect co-exists with a mystical and melancholy attitude to landscape of the contemplative gentleman scholar, an attitude pervading the Canto:

> Behind hill the monk's bell
> borne on the wind.

'The dimension of stillness' is the special contribution of 49 to the *Cantos*, a Taoist preoccupation familiar from *Cathay*. Not that this fly is not tied to the line of the poem: 'by no man these verses' conceals an Odyssean wink.

Canto 49 is an oasis in the desert of Pound's politics—others are provided by the fly-tying section of 51 and the Chinese calendar of monthly activities in 52. These oases are the more notable in that they are followed by twenty solid Cantos of Chinese and American history which those who have traversed them usually report as arid. Hugh Kenner's 'Inventing Confucius' chapter in *The Pound Era*,[13] a most valuable part of that galactic work, demonstrates what one had sensed, how deeply infused with Taoism was Pound's neo-Confucianism, despite the anti-Taoism of his source for 52–61, de Mailla's *Histoire générale de la Chine* (1777–83). Kenner observes also that 'the *Cantos* by now had used up much of their capital'.[14] Cantos 53–72 appeared in 1940, only three years after the *Fifth Decad*, years when Pound was working desperately to prevent the U.S.A. from fighting Italy. These history Cantos can be read as a continuous commentary on the politics of the time.

Cantos 52–61 are based on de Mailla's work, itself based on a neo-Confucian interpretation of Chinese history. De Mailla apparently found the anti-Taoism of his sources congenial to his own Gibbonian scepticism towards the spiritual, and Pound also found the emphasis of firm enlightened rule consonant with his purposes. The corporate state, the desirability and efficacy of an Olympian style, distributist economics, mistrust of missionaries—these can naturally enough be supported from a survey of Chinese history in twelve volumes.

The reader is referred to Kenner for a proper opening up of the subject, which is beyond my competence. It is, however, evident that to attempt to summarize a 12-volume history of China in 84 pages, starting from scratch, is quite an enterprise even for Pound. It is as if Napoleon had decided to invade Russia not with the Grande Armée but with the sole help of Marshal Ney. To make things worse, Pound supported de Mailla with his own unsupported interpretations of Chinese characters. *Cathay* was a success, but Pound knew more about poetry than about Chinese history.

Of course, the Chinese Cantos are instructive and diverting; they fit coherently into the development of the *Cantos*, as an Enlightenment counter-example of a beneficent empire built upon humanism and nature rather than Protestantism and usury; they further develop earlier themes. They are frequently well written and epigrammatic; they alert us—and this is perhaps the best defence—to issues and subjects in which, as humanists, we ought to be interested.

It is surprising that Pound got as far as he did. But it is difficult to avoid the view that as an historical enterprise, an instant history of China from 2837 B.C. to A.D. 1735 was, for a non-sinologue, a project conceived in euphoria and executed with a gallantry which may be seen as heroic; it is certainly quixotic. It has been argued that Pound did not intend these Cantos as history, but this is special pleading. It can be argued that he produced something which though not history has useful historical lessons. Certainly the parallels are often provocative, but we have only Pound's word for them; there is no evidence, only paradigms. Besides, the lessons are all mythical:

> 'Yao and Chun have returned'
>   sang the farmers.

(53)

One does not have to be W. H. Auden to see this as open to parody.

Cantos 52–61 are the first major part of the poem that does not work. Yet from such a wreck much can be salvaged: let us have an inventory of effects. Canto 52 opens with an 'irrelevant' blast of brimstone which offers evidence, if required, of Pound's Fascist and anti-Semitic sympathies, and the less heinous crime of anglophobia. We pass immediately to the Book of Rites, which, like the early history in Canto 53, is well done because Hesiodic rather than historical. Cantos 54–61 I have often read with the interest of novelty, yet the reader will at times lose patience in a soup of names which can mean nothing to him. The names of dynasties and emperors pass like railway stations in the night. One is aware not so much of China as of Pound reading about China, and of his special interests: ceremonies, clever military tricks, local colour, just rulers, weak rulers, agriculture and crafts, money, Fascist parallels. One is also aware of his boredom:

> Han, Khitan, tartar wars, boredom of.
> Money and all that, stabilization, probably racket
> 1069

(55)

He can be detected in that refuge of the bored reader—reading to himself in funny voices:

> Now tarters in the murk night
> sent great numbers of sojers with anthorns
> which they held up very high
>   and thus spread light on proceedings
> causing great fear in Nanking.
>   so the last mingsters fled out by the Tchinkiang road.

(59)

Sometimes he talks to himself:

> so our lord KANG layed an embargo
> (a bit before Tommy Juffusun's)

(60)

This impersonation of the shrewd old savant nodding over his books is often put to sharper use:

> Et les Indiens disent que Boudha
> in the form of a white buck elephant
> slid into Queen Nana's bosom, she virgin,
> and after nine months ingestion
> emerged on the dexter side
>
> (54)

or: 'A Prince this was, but no Emperor, paladin, useless to rule' (55). This last is a nice discrimination, with a Confucian nuance not to be found in the early Cantos. Another example of a changed emphasis is:

> HAN sank and there were three kingdoms
> and booze in the bamboo grove
> where they sang: emptiness is the beginning of all things.
>
> (54)

A comparison with Kung's treatment of Tian in Canto 13 is revealing.

As I have indicated, it is here a question of salvaging good pieces from a wreck. Not that it is difficult to follow the *ideas* of the Chinese Cantos. Nothing could be easier: 'Kung rules, OK?' would be a fair slogan for much of them. Among the favourite dirty words are: tao, tartar, bhuddists (*sic*), boozers, girls, jews, highbrows and eunuchs. Chinese history is a Punch and Judy show where, when Kung rules, all *is* OK; when not, not. The downfall of the enemy is crowed over in a most un-epic way:

> Hochang, eunuchs, taoists and ballets
> night-clubs, gimcracks, debauchery
> Down, down! Han is down
> Sung is down
> Hochang, eunuchs, and taozers
> empresses' relatives, came then a founder
> saying nothing superfluous
> cleared out the taozers and grafters, gave grain
> opened the mountains. . . .
>
> (56)

So much for the Weimar Republic!

Of course, there is much of interest, like the treatment of Christians; and Pound has a good eye and a good ear. But even he reaches the end with relief:

                                    . . . And he wrote
                     a poem on the Beauties of Mougden
                  and condensed the Ming histories
                             literary kuss, and wuz Emperor
                  fer at least 40 years.
                             Perhaps you will look up his verses.

                                                                        (61)

A marvellous ending, like the best condensations in his own epistolary
criticism, getting it all in, leaving the question trailing on the air with all
the irony and poignancy one could wish. He recovers his poise. Yet, at
the end of 52–71, we can see why Pound prefixed to these 165 pages a
Table of the Contents of each Canto;[15] without it we might not have
been able to follow them. If he had, say, punctuated this last
Canto, or cited de Mailla even once, the reader's task might have been
easier.
    The Adams Cantos, 62–71, also have their contents listed in the Table.
These subject-headings, equally indispensable, are the titles of Pound's
ten-stage presentation of the career of John Adams, second President of
the United States, a subject with greater natural unity than any digest of
Chinese history, however consistent its ideology. The technique is similar
in that the Adams Cantos consist of selections and notes preponderantly
from one printed source, in this case *The Works of John Adams*, ed.
Charles Francis Adams, and a source written very much from one point
of view. The seventh decad of Cantos begins where the sixth left off, in
the year 1735, when Yong Tching died and John Adams was born.
Pound presents Adams as a Confucian ruler of the United States and a
founder of a dynasty, a conceit that had perhaps occurred to no one
before the author of *Jefferson and/or Mussolini*. The Confucianism is,
needless to say, in Pound's mind rather than Adams's, and the analogy
is not forced upon us; there are only three Chinese characters in the
Adams Cantos, each clearly glossed, and one is the character for Tea.
The use of this character is a witty if somewhat far-fetched link with
China, as is the date 1735. Pound's cross-references or 'rhymes' are often
thus arbitrary or ingenious—1766 B.C. 'rhymes' with 1766 A.D.; one does
not know how much to attach to them.
    The Boston Tea Party features early in the Adams section, and it is
as well at the outset to say that, for all the Confucian analogy and the
emphases of the 1930s, Pound's ancestor-worship is of a traditional
American kind. Reverence for the founding fathers is, or was, a *pietas*
inherent in American education, particularly before the mass arrival of
what Pound called 'melting-pot names', in much the same way as, in the

school histories that Winston Churchill grew up with, such English Worthies as Alfred, Drake and Chatham were once enshrined.

Adams is attractive to Pound as a comparative student of constitutions and the principles of government, as a leader of exemplary integrity and historical foresight, and as a champion of peace and of conservative fiscal policies. All except the last would be part of the traditional praise of John Adams. Pound cannot, however, keep himself out of this black-and-white history lesson:

> and as for Hamilton
> we may take it (my authority, ego scriptor cantilenae)
> that he was the Prime snot in ALL American history
> (11th Jan. 1938, from Rapallo)
> But for the clearest head in the congress
> 1774 and thereafter
> pater patriae
> the man who at certain points
> made us
> at certain points
> saved us
> by fairness, honesty and straight moving
> ARRIBA ADAMS

These lines concluding Canto 62 follow shortly after Adams's comment on Hamilton:

> wont to give to his conversation
> full impetus of vehement will. . . .

At no other time could Pound have been so blind to the effect of such juxtapositions. The Rapallo by-line is a gratuitous interruption, as is the earlier observation that Boston at the time of the Tea Party was 'about the size of Rapallo)/ scarce 16,000'. The opposition of heroes and villains is thus complicated by a troubling tension between author and hero. The reminder of Pound's political (not merely his personal) situation in Rapallo recalls other contemporary references in this Canto: 'Birth of a Nation' and 'Schicksal, sagt der Führer'. The effect is to enforce a bifocal view of the Adams example—as referring not only to the virtues needed in the late Thirties, specifically by the U.S.A., but alluding also, and equally specifically, to Italy and Mussolini, *pater patriae*, with Pound in a prophetic role, like Blake for the American and French Revolutions or Milton anathematizing the returning Charles II. Compared with these prophets, however, Pound is more reticent, confining himself to violent meaningful nudges.

In view of what we know, and what was known at the time, of Mussolini and Hitler, this political stance is profoundly disquieting. The artistic confusion of the Canto is similarly alarming. How could Pound condemn the 'vehement will' of Hamilton's conversation and immediately call him 'the Prime snot'? How can he so well exemplify the urbanely sardonic tones of Adams, thus:

> Routledge was elegant
> 'said nothing not hackneyed six months before'
> wrote J.A. to his wife

or thus:

> transferred to Adam Street in the Adelphi
> suspecting the post boy of humour in taking him there

and himself lapse into unconnected mutterings:

> force in fact of a right sez Chawles Fwancis
> at same time, and in Louses of Parleymoot. . .
> so fatal a precision of aim,
> sojers aiming??
> Gent standing in his doorway got 2 balls in the arm
> and five deaders 'never Cadmus. . .' etc.

Even if we restrict comment on the Adams Cantos to the artistic aspect, they give clear evidence, despite their virtues, of authorial confusion of attitude and of simple carelessness and incoherence in composition. They are often pointlessly difficult to follow.

The virtues spring from the vivid particularity with which Adams's career is specified. His *Works* are ransacked for their most telling material, and, though, as with Sigismundo Malatesta, the sequence of events and the identities of the dramatis personae are not clear, Adams's guiding principles and characteristic attitudes are very clear. The use of local colour is documentary and authentic: Adams's own impressions of Europe, or his captain's impressions of him aboard the *Boston*, lend more credibility than, say, Pound's views of the Palio procession in Siena, however picturesque, do to the Leopoldine Cantos. Thus Adams is firmly anchored to his background, and escapes the synthesizing process which affects some of Pound's more fleetingly cited heroes. A representative slice of Canto 64 will illustrate this:

punch wine bread cheese apples pipes and tobacco
Thursday oated at Martin's
when we saw five boxes of dollars
   going in a horse cart to Salem for Boston
FOR England, said to contain about $18,000
   lopping and trimming
walnut trees, and for felling of pines and savins
An irregular misshapen pine will darken
      the whole scene in some places
case between negro and owner. At same time a craving man
        (Hutchinson)
at Dr Tuft's where I found fine wild goose on the spit
    and cranberries in the skillet
to the White House in Brattle St.
office lucrative in itself but new statutes
   had been passed in Parliament
J.Q.A. born July eleventh
duty on glass incompatible
   with my ideas on right, justice and policy. . . .

The identity of Martin or Tuft is immaterial, and the passage survives one's not at this point divining the identities of Governor Hutchinson or of John Quincy Adams. The texture of the presentation suffices. The range of concerns in the lawyer's active life is rendered by these cross-cut excerpts with an economy that does no violence to the context of diary or letter. Adams's position on taxation without representation arises naturally out of the magisterial lucidity with which he characteristically regards the detail of life. His equitable tone, his 'norm of spirit', is what Pound wishes to secure, and he undoubtedly succeeds; he succeeds too in making it attractive. The Latinate irony we first found in *Ripostes* now makes itself felt quietly and pervasively:

   A statue of H.M. (His Majesty)
  very large
  on horseback
  solid lead gilded with gold
  on an high marble pedestal
          (65)

Such discreetly humorous examples of the natural object as the adequate symbol are found on every page. The delightful Canto 65 continues:

We then walked up Broadway
     magnificent building, cost 20,000 pounds
                       N.Y. currency
Ship
of 800 tons burden lest leveling spirit of New England
should propagate itself in New York
     whole charge of the Province
between 5 and 6 thousand pounds N. York money

The ship is to carry N.Y. money away to England, but Pound's implication of context can make it appropriate for 'Ship' to suggest to us Hampden's Ship Money, and loop us backwards in time to the taxation that
started the English Revolution (later linked by Adams with Magna
Charta). The lines of parallel and contrast intersect, articulate and give
relief to the cross-hatching of detail. The Adams Cantos offer sustained
proof that collage of secondary material can transcend scrappiness and
pastiche, to create significance and force.

    The Adams Cantos are, in general, didactic, and the lessons are many,
since the aim is to show a complete 'Renaissance' man, not a *philosophe*
but a leader whose aim in life was to 'be useful'. As well as studying
constitutions, defending Captain Preston, and nominating and succeeding
Washington, John Adams, as Pound stresses, did a great deal of hard
negotiating in Europe; and the balanced and detached accounts he gives
of London, Paris and Amsterdam suggest the attitudes Pound commends
to Adams's American successors. (They also, of course, reflect Pound's
own experience of Europe.)

    Among the medley of interesting material lit up by Adams's attention,
two considerations suggest themselves: one is the jurist's increasing
absorption in constitutional law, registered in Cantos 66 and 71, with
practical excurses into war debts etc., but resurfacing in the last, Odyssean
word of 71, κυβερνῶν. This gubernatorial emphasis is also to be found in
the other salient development, namely the piquant contrast now apparent
between the admirer of Sigismundo and the admirer of Adams. Sigismundo, it will be remembered, according to the Pope:

          . . . did among other things
    Empty the fonts of the chiexa of holy water
    And fill up the same full with ink
    That he might in God's dishonour
    Stand before the doors of the said chiexa
    Making mock of the inky faithful, they
    Issuing thence by the doors in the pale light of the sunrise

Which might be considered youthful levity
    but was really a profound indication. . .
                                                    (10)

Whereas Adams writes: 'I am a church-going animal' (71) and despite
the refreshingly dry urbanity of his outlook, he emerges, as indeed Pound
intends he should, as a man of uncompromising rectitude and integrity.
If George Washington could not tell a lie, John Adams, even as a boy,
seems to have been constitutionally incapable of stealing a cherry. Pound
renders this extreme virtue painless to behold, but this should not
conceal from the reader the difference between virtue and Machiavellian
virtù, nor the changes that took place in Pound in the Thirties.

Though Adams does not appear 'grave' (a grave sin in this book), his
tracing of *folcriht* from Ine to Runnymede to Coke is given to us with all
the seriousness at Pound's command. It is a reminder of the independence
due to every Anglo-Saxon by his hard-won chartered liberties, and
chimes with Pound's equal insistence on the plenitude of nature expressed
in the sentence: 'Nor has nature nor has art partitioned the sea into
empires'(71). While these convictions are cornerstones of Pound's view of
political rights, the most highly principled of readers of *Rock-Drill* and
Thrones will look back to Adams's painstaking establishment of the right
principles for the American Constitution with feelings torn between
morality and literature: it is an augury of excavations to come. However,
perhaps it is time to remind ourselves that we are dealing with an epic,
and that some *longueurs* must be allowed to epic inclusiveness and
ecumenism. The ideal of a humane and just society is to be mediated
through 'a sufficient phalanx of particulars', and, in the case of Adams
(and American independence), these particulars, if not always sufficiently
coherent, are sufficiently attractive and human. The sense of human
heroism is not so well communicated in the post-Pisan historical Cantos.

11. *The Pisan Cantos*

The *Pisan Cantos* begin:

The enormous tragedy of the dream in the peasant's bent shoulders

This line, following the exclusion of Cantos 72 and 73,[1] written in Italian, marks the crisis. The 'dream' is Pound's dream of social justice, a dream that, he believed, he shared with *contadino* and Duce. With this line the study of the *Cantos* comes to involve a study of the author's life and opinions: the *Pisan Cantos* are a directly autobiographical record of Pound's days in the Detention Training Center. They were written 'from the death cells in sight of Mt. Taishan @ Pisa' awaiting trial for treason, not only 'under discountenance' but in physical conditions both humiliating and cruel, if not, in 1945, unique.[2] Pound makes light of his situation, but, like Milton publishing 'The Ready and Easy Way to Establish a Free Commonwealth' in 1660, he makes no secret of his irreconcilable opinions. He immediately identifies himself as a follower to the last of 'Ben' Mussolini, 'the twice crucified', adding defiantly, 'yet say this to the Possum: a bang, not a whimper'.

Mussolini is reported in Canto 78 as having been interested by Pound's exposition of his fiscal theories:

> . . . Sd/ one wd/ have to think about that
> but was hang'd dead by the heels before his thought in proposito
>   came into action efficiently

There is also a memo to the master of the U.S.S.R.:

> and but one point needed for Stalin
> you need not, i.e. need not take over the means of production

(74)

In apologia for Pound's politics it is sometimes suggested that as his whole mode of thought, not only his political and economic thinking, is mythical and ideal—as he is an impractical visionary—he cannot be held responsible for his political mistakes. It is true that, after reminding his Anglican publisher that Mussolini, unlike Manes,[3] was 'twice crucified', he states his aim as 'To build the city of Dioce whose terraces are the colour of stars' (74). This just city, however, has low interest rates, though no drains. Once Italy was defeated, Pound transferred his hopes to an ideal realm, but even this realm, 'in proposito' until the end of *Thrones*, is supposed 'efficiently' to be realizable. Though Pound's idea of poetry has the ardour of Shelley's, his emphatically nonmetaphysical idealism insistently claims, unlike the visions of Yeats or Eliot, to be practicable. Only with *Drafts and Fragments* does he renounce the idea that the dream would actually work. His visions were not seen from an armchair but from the back of Rosinante: he wished to build his Hellenic Zion in a non-English green and pleasant land, but he was more than ready to tilt at real windmills in order to do so. His pen did not sleep in his hand.

To note that Pound's was not a passive kind of fantasy is not to deny that the value of his vision comes from its mythical nature. He sees himself in the *Pisan Cantos* not only as an individualist Odysseus who has sacked Troy but also as an Aeneas who has survived the ruin of Troy (or Rome) and is planning 'to build the city of Dioce': ' "I believe in the resurrection of Italy   quia impossibile est . . .' (74).

With the *Pisan Cantos*, however, the dream collides with public life in an unforeseen and tragic guise that must compel the attention of anyone who reflects upon the modern fate of poetry. We see the disciple of Adams facing a charge of treason. Yet as his crankiness stands revealed for what it is, his poetry achieves an emotional freedom and force, a fusion of mythical and actual, a psychological necessity, which it had perhaps never before possessed. The voice realizes the movement of the mind so perfectly that the reader can reach a stage when he is no longer bothered by Pound's deluded political judgement.

To take an example: 'Oh to be in England now that Winston's out' (80) can scarcely retain much power to offend the British reader accustomed to be told that he and Churchill helped to save Western Civilization, once he has read the next line but one: 'And the Bank may be the nation's'. The hope inspired in Pound by the result of the 1945 General Election was that the Labour Government, like the Fascist and Soviet dictators, might implement distributism. When Pound returns to his own situation his reflections have an altogether different kind of interest.

It is important to understand the radical nature of the change that now comes upon the poem. After the partisans had knocked on the door at Rapallo, nothing could ever be the same for the author of the *Cantos*. The irruption of actual events into Pound's political dream exposes once and for all the strong elements of fantasy, delusion and paranoia in his notions. Not that Pound surrenders his dream, though he sees that it has failed. It is rather that it is impossible any longer to take his active political judgement at all seriously. This knocks away one of the legs of the poem, and severely damages another, its judgement of history.

7

Another radical effect on the *Cantos* is that any strong semblance of overall architectural plan, and of a continuity beyond that provided by the author's life, now breaks down, though *Rock-Drill* and *Thrones* will make efforts to get the poem back on the road. A third effect is that the poem becomes for the first time openly autobiographical: it changes from a would-be objective presentation of ancient history to a private report on the author's actual situation and feelings: 'the drama is wholly subjective' (74). Finally, more important for the reader, the poem becomes henceforth a great deal more fragmentary and allusive, and this remains true even when, after Pisa, the 'objective' mode is resumed and we return for long spells to the quarries of history.

The fragmentariness and allusiveness and the simultaneous adoption of a subjective mode are inextricably associated, so that everything—even the hard history—in the hundreds of pages that remain, appears not as epic data but primarily as personal memory, perception, reflection and reading—as contingent phenomena of the shocked and distractable mind of Ezra Pound. Pound, however, was by now the author of the *Cantos* and in that sense a piece of objective history. The *Pisan Cantos* are thus a real part of the Second World War in a way that *Mauberley* was never part of the First.

The patterns of value and of reference built up earlier reassert themselves sufficiently for the poem to remain broadly intelligible, but the quality, accessibility and interest of the constituent items varies sharply, and the reader's confidence in a plan, if it has survived the Chinese history Cantos, also sags sharply, and with it the supposition that the *Cantos* are an integrated work. If the *Cantos* are now seen to be both uneven and unplanned, if inscrutable passages are no longer felt to be necessary to the design, then the character of the work is changed and no longer can it seem crucial to seek to understand such passages. Yet what the poem loses in one kind of interest, it gains in another, for the *Pisan Cantos* are not only its crisis but its climax.

The task of the critic alters correspondingly. Leaving explication to the explicator, he may pick and choose among the remaining Cantos, unburdened by any pressing sense that he may be missing the grand design. This is, in many ways, a relief, and allows the successful passages to stand on their own, and the unacceptable and the unintelligible to fall or to wait. If the *Cantos* change thus untidily from a work with a plan to a work that once had a plan, the inconvenience to our expectations is compensated for by the moving quality of much of what remains. Exercising the choice which this disintegration imposes on the reader, it becomes clear, I believe, that the forty-odd Cantos that follow Canto 74 are of two kinds—the poetry of memory, perception, reflection, of myth and vision; and the poetry of moral 'history'—and that these two kinds are respectively to be found, on the one hand, in the *Pisan Cantos* and *Drafts and Fragments*, and on the other, in *Rock-Drill* and *Thrones*, though the end of *Rock-Drill* is also visionary. The visions and the 'facts' are held together in a converging development offered in emulation of Dante's illumination and rapture in the *Paradiso*, and of the peace of Odysseus' homecoming. Yet they are at the same time infused with a sense of exhaustion, of having survived from 'prehistory'; this self-transcendence is at times agonizing, at times accepting. It often takes the form of asides which admit to a feeling of superannuation or fragmentation. Such moments of doubt, alternating with dogmatism, have a disintegrative effect. In so far as the *Cantos* remain an 'objective' epic, the post-Pisan sequences strive towards a thematic completion: in so far as they are autobiography, these later Cantos tell us what it feels like to be the author of such a gigantic and uncompleted enterprise, to have outlived not only two world wars and a great literary career, but also the prodigal ambition which sustained it.

Lest such a paradox should seem merely the hypothesis of a critic, I shall quote the author's considered retrospect in the last complete Canto, 116:

> I have brought the great ball of crystal;
> who can lift it?
> Can you enter the great acorn of light?
> But the beauty is not the madness
> Tho' my errors and wrecks lie about me.
> And I am not a demigod,
> I cannot make it cohere.

The crystal and the acorn are symbolic poles of the natural arcana towards which the paradisal Cantos have been leading us. 'I am not a demigod' refers to the climax of Pound's 1956 translation of Sophocles' *Women of Trachis*, where he has the dying hero Herakles exclaim: 'What splendour, it all coheres'.[4] In the retrospect of the late Sixties, Pound cannot 'make it cohere', where 'it' would primarily indicate the poem. Yet a few lines later he reaffirms the existence of Paradise, alluding to Dante's *riveder le stelle*, the final words of the *Inferno*:

> to "see again,"
> the verb is "see," not "walk on"
> i.e. it coheres all right
> even if my notes do not cohere.

And the Canto ends:

> A little light, like a rushlight
> to lead back to splendour.

These lines confirm that the argument between Truth and Calliope is now perceived as irreconcilable. It is difficult to avoid identifying the 'splendour' with Pound's imagination, and the 'errors and wrecks' with his history. However, it is also true that the argument or oscillation has been there from the beginning of Pound's work, and it continues to the end.

Confronting the *Pisan Cantos*, the critic may well feel like Satan facing Chaos in *Paradise Lost*:

> Into this wild abyss the wary Fiend
> Stood on the brink of hell and looked a while,
> Pondering his voyage; for no narrow frith
> He had to cross.
>
> (II, 917–20)[5]

Indeed, the undoubted quality of the *Pisan Cantos* cannot properly be illustrated in the space remaining, due to the intensified allusiveness, which calls for an amplified annotation. A general report may however be of some use.

The *Pisan Cantos* are composed, not of documentation of a case from reading, but of thoughts written, as Pound says at the outset, 'from the death cells in sight of Mt. Taishan @ Pisa'. They consist at first of agonized reflections upon the end of Pound's dream of Italy, and then of impressions of the life and landscape of the D.T.C., and of memories of old days, of London before the Great War, and also of America, Spain, France and Italy. There are political reflections and modern instances, but the staple of the *Pisan Cantos* is a continuous interaction of real and visionary landscape, literary allusion and personal memory. The references here, for example, are to Catullus, to the *Inferno* and to Provence:

> Butterflies, mint and Lesbia's sparrows,
> the voiceless with bumm drum and banners,
>   and the ideogram of the guard roosts
>   el triste pensier si volge
>   ad Ussel. A Ventadour
>   va il consire, el tempo rivolge
>
> (74)[6]

The poet's physical situation in the open-air metal cages:

> amid what was termed the a.h. of the army
> the guards holding opinion. . . .
>
> (74)

is at the centre of these Cantos. He was saved from despair by his conviction of his own integrity, by the charity of other prisoners, by observing the green world of lizards and ants; chiefly perhaps by his poetry of personal memory and visionary imagination.

This mythopoeia made him conceive himself as Odysseus in the Cyclops' cave, in Circe's swine sty or enduring shipwreck. This Odyssean identity is a raft provided by the poem. But the essentials of the situation were physical, and until the prisoner in the next cage made him a table, literally down to earth:

> and there was a smell of mint under the tent flaps
> especially after the rain
>   and a white ox on the road toward Pisa
>   as if facing the tower,
> dark sheep in the drill field and on wet days were clouds
> in the mountain as if under the guard roosts.
>   A lizard upheld me
>   the wild birds wd not eat the white bread
>   from Mt Taishan to the sunset
> From Carrara stone to the tower.
>
> (74)

On this physical basis visions—even Buddhist visions—appear:

> and this day the air was made open
> for Kuanon of all delights,
>
> (74)

but nature is always returned to, since it is always the source of Pound's supernature. He is now a nobody, like Odysseus *chez* Polyphemus, literally:

> ΟΫ ΤΙΣ
> a man on whom the sun has gone down.
>
> (74)

Canto 74 may be taken as a microcosm of the *Pisan Cantos*. It occupies 26 pages, more than twice as many as any previous Canto, and containing a vastly greater variety of material. And though the poet's habit of thinking of himself in Odyssean terms does not desert him, many other facets of his situation are equally apparent to him, *en ce bordel ou tenons nostre estat*. Villon making his testament, Ugolino in the tower at Pisa, the mad Tasso in prison, the wards of a slave ship, the dark night of the soul, all images for his condition. But the bulk of this Canto as of those which follow is not literary analogy but personal perception, imagination, and memory. The struggle is between the vigour and fullness of his mind and his present catastrophe, which most of the time he disdains to notice. When he does think about it he is preserved by holding on to physical facts; he mythologizes these facts, but returns to them. He sees a wasp carrying its infant, or a broken anthill, and thinks of Aeneas carrying his father from the ruins of Troy. Yet the basis of the *Pisan Cantos* is not in the analogies but in the facts, the actual situation of the author, the hills, clouds, guards, prisoners, passers-by, the moon, rain, insects and birds—and, amid them all, the author of *Hugh Selwyn Mauberley*.

This network of imagist perceptions holds a largely unacknowledged agony, a mute speaker, a man accustomed to analogy, allusion and indirection in the expression of emotion. The thoughts are chiselled, inscribed, distinct. But they float on a current of emotion which is chaotic, because Pound's picture of the world has collapsed, and though he does not concede, he knows.

> nor shall diamond die in the avalanche
> be it torn from its setting
> first must destroy himself ere other destroy him.

> (74)

This remarkable stoicism, this refusal to admit defeat, preserved Pound. But he continually reverts to the image of Odysseus' shipwreck, when 'the raft broke and the waters went over me' (80), and to images of water, flow and change. This water is real rain, the spring rains of 1945, but changes into a cycle of seasonal and mythological imagery, ultimately restorative. The pre-Socratic Thales derived the physical universe from the element of water, *Hudor*, and here water becomes an image of the Heraclitean flux of elements, of which the open-air world, to which Pound has forcibly been returned, is composed, and on which he meditates, also with restorative effect. The flux is also the flux of time, of events, of fortune, which has turned against him. And, more fundamentally and less consciously, it is an image of chaos, of irrepressible emotional surges, which have overset the raft of his cunning and threaten to drown him.

Death was indeed an imminent prospect, and like any man in the death cells:

> He passed the stages of his age and youth
> Entering the whirlpool.
>
> (*The Waste Land*, IV)

A hallucinatory recall of his whole life streams powerfully and irresistibly through the *Pisan Cantos*, and these memories have, for all their frequent humour and understatement, an effect of tragic pathos, for they are felt to be final. Pound keeps his balance, but he is reluctantly borne away on a Joycean tide of reminiscence, fragments of which—the vignettes of Yeats, for example—are the most immediately attractive things in the *Pisan Cantos*. The memories are sporadically marshalled into an epic roll-call of dead companions and of historical heroes; but the epic architecture is shattered, and it is their personal, not their representative, quality that makes them so diamond-like. The flood is ridden, yet the power is not that of the rational and selective mind which steers the raft, but of the protean sensibility beneath it, which, after its 'Confucian' suppression during the Thirties, imperiously demands expression.

No longer are we treated to ideological eclogues, 'voluntarist' readings in Chinese and American history. Without his books—he had only a copy of Legge's Confucius and a Chinese dictionary[7]—and past 'the Charybdis of action' (74), Pound is reduced to his most precious faculties, his eye, his ear, and his first gift, the making of images. His subject is his own situation, caught up in the mill-race of events, with the weir not far ahead. For the most part, the *Pisan Cantos* are, after the opening outcry, a sane, living and even joyful testament, which includes recognition of the author's own vanity and affirmations of that which 'is not vanity'; but despair, anguish and exhaustion are never far away. Hebrew repentance and Christian contrition are not to be looked for, but there are signs of human compunction, modesty and humility; and there are tears—*dakruon*—Greek tears, but none the less real for that. It is a testament as well as a work of art.

The fluid quality of the movement of the poet's mind throughout the *Pisan Cantos* makes them peculiarly difficult to summarize, as extensive quotation is required to give any idea of their texture, which is full of reprises, anaphora and self-quotation. Critics naturally cite and analyse such outstandingly consecutive passages as the end of 81, looked at in Chapter 2, or the picture of Yeats; the roll-call of dead companions or the 'libretto' to Lawes and Jenkins; the quatrains on England or the prayer to the lynxes of Zagreus. Marvellous as these are, they are not representative of the conversational unpredictability of these pages, distractable,

fragmentary, private, at times unintelligible, but never vague or un-
focused in sense, rhythm or visual quality. The *Pisan Cantos* are correctly
described as reverie, but they move like conversation rather than monologue, despite the absence of kindred spirits here alluded to—an absence
that had begun in 1920 and was to get very much worse.

>   on doit le temps ainsi prendre qu'il vient
>   or to write dialog because there is
>   no one to converse with
>   to take the sheep out to pasture
>   to bring your g.r. to the nutriment
>   gentle reader   to the gist of the discourse
>   to sort out the animals

(80)

There are, as the reference to nutriment suggests, saliences and strategies
within these Cantos, but the feline movement and improvisation has a
fascination of itself, to which the reader must surrender before he can
feel the enormous thematic tidal swells and artistic strategies of the *Pisan
Cantos*. And this surrender may be peculiarly difficult for the empirically-
minded critic, the intellectual analyst, the ideological watchdog or the
lover of consecutiveness. An unconditional response is required. As T. S.
Eliot once wrote to Stephen Spender, 'You don't really criticize any
author to whom you have never surrendered yourself.'[8] The ordering—if
that term may be used without begging the question—of the *Pisan
Cantos* defies most preconceptions thought respectable by practitioners
of literary criticism. Only among aesthetes, the young, or doctrinaire
informalists are such cautions entirely absent and even such adepts must,
if they wish to understand what they are reading at all, balk at the final
inconvenience to the 'gentle reader' of the *Pisan Cantos*, namely the
personal nature of their contents and their private style of reference.

Here the regular reader of Pound is at an incommunicable advantage.
The majority of the references in the *Pisan Cantos* have become intelligible
to me, for example, yet (without being conscious of any special laziness)
I am not desperate, at any one reading, to solve the remainder, or to
retrieve those that I have forgotten. The humane quality of the poetry
does not depend on this, though it does entail working out the meaning
of a key term such as *Hudor*. It is also reasonable to expect that the
reader bent on enjoying the *Pisan Cantos* should have read Cantos 1–71.

To the reader ignorant of previous Cantos, of Pound's prose, of modern
and ancient European literature, of Italy, of foreign languages, of mythology and of Pound's biography, the *Pisan Cantos*, though they constitute
Pound's strongest claim to greatness, will undoubtedly be obscure. Yet I

remember reading them with awe when I was ignorant of all but the earlier Cantos—an awed delight which has not lessened as my differences with Pound in his politics and philosophy have become more and more evident to me. His conversation—for such is the continuous primary effect of the *Pisan Cantos*—remains uniquely interesting, humorous, various, felicitous and spectacular; its themes emerge to the patient listener. If courage is 'grace under pressure', these Cantos are courageous; they have inflections of *hilaritas* and even *serenitas*.

> Thus march we playing to our latest jest,
> Only we die in earnest, that's no jest.

There is something of Raleigh's *sprezzatura* here, and what is 'in earnest' is equally laconic:

> but I will come out of this knowing no one
> neither they me
>
> (82)

or

> There is fatigue deep as the grave
>
> (83)

The balance between free improvisation and the moment of gravity is not unlike that in *Propertius*—for *humour* is an irrepressible part of Pound's natural temperament. The dogmatic intentions and the large blocks of historical material which increasingly occupied the Cantos of the Thirties disappear, and the responsibilities of the writer of epic are forgotten under the strain of mere survival; miraculously, the resilient tone of *Lustra* reappears.

The natural decorum, the automatic adjustment of tone to topic, of style and thought, creates an illusion of transparency even where the subject-matter is unrecognized and the remark is chucked over the shoulder:

> the queen stitched King Carolus' shirts or whatever
> while Erigena put greek tags in his excellent verses
> in fact an excellent poet, Paris
> toujours Pari'
>
> (Charles le Chauve)
>
> (83)

This encourages the reader to think—quite correctly—that if he knew a little more, he would understand the point perfectly. (In this case Pound is providing, with minimum context, a reminder of Scotus Erigena's 'Omnia quae sunt lumina sunt', one of the repeated links in his neo-Platonist underground tradition; nothing more complex is intended.)

Another result of the rigours of confinement and the trauma of disillusionment is that over-writing and preaching almost disappear; even the Ecclesiastes castigation of vanity is chiefly directed against himself. Not that Pound is ever without maxims; but they are personal, not soap-boxing:

> If deeds be not ensheaved and garnered in the heart
> there is inanition
>
> (83)

or

> the humane man has amity with the hills.
>
> (83)

One of the most famous of Confucian maxims introduces another passage which must serve as a final example of the alert movement of mind and the relaxed and varied talk that is the weave of the *Pisan Cantos*:

> To communicate and then stop, that is the
>   law of discourse
>   To go far and come to an end
> simplex munditiis, as the hair of Circe
> perhaps without the munditiis
> as the difference between the title page in old Legge
> and some of the elegant fancy work
>   I wonder what Tsu Tsze's calligraphy looked like
> they say she could draw down birds from the trees,
>   that indeed was imperial; but made hell in
> the palace
>
> (80)

One might discount this humorous ease as mere rambling, if there is felt to be no centre. The centre now is not the grand scheme of the poem, but the personality, history and beliefs of the poet. It could indeed be shown that Pound is here advocating a sub-Augustan style ('perhaps without the munditiis'), as Eliot advocates a more Virgilian style in *Four Quartets*. Later in Canto 80, we find:

and pass on the tradition
there can be honesty of mind
without overwhelming talent.

But such arguments will weigh little unless the reader does indeed feel that Pound is playing a game of digression: that the casualness is a deliberate gambit within a larger cohesiveness. Rapport cannot be demonstrated, it must be felt; Pound relies on it absolutely.

The reader who insists on his rights right away, who cannot proceed without identifying every reference, may, then, find the *Pisan Cantos* punishingly esoteric. They are not, however, themeless, as a brief list of their contents will show. The physical situation of the poet is the axis: he sees the hills and clouds and trees, the fauna, the prisoners and guards, and spins out of them mythological and moral elaborations, but these phenomena form the concrete centre of the meditations, literally holding him together 'in a sea of air strip', as he puts it in Canto 80. He had plenty of time for sitting and looking.

The main themes in the *Pisan Cantos* are the poet's attitude to his situation; his memories; and the mythology and morality arising from his perception of nature. Self-preservation is Pound's first reaction to the catastrophe, not without defiance, as we saw in Canto 74; obduracy is followed by Villon's prayer, 'que tous nous veuil absoudre'. The bleakness of 'a man on whom the sun has gone down' is followed by remorse, grudging at first: 'that had been a hard man in some ways'. The first entry of the theme of memory we have already cited: 'el triste pensier si volge/ad Ussel. A Ventadour. . . .' The sad thought returns to Ventadour, the home of the author of

> Quant ieu vey la' lauzeta mover
> De joi sas alas contral ray.

With this remembered joy come memories of youth, of *The Spirit of Romance*, of walking tours in France with his wife and T. S. Eliot. Other memories, of Basil Bunting, of a childhood tour with his aunt, are followed by the names of friends from his hey-day in London:

> Lordly men are to earth o'ergiven
> these the companions:
> Fordie that wrote of giants
> and William who dreamed of nobility
> and Jim the comedian singing
> "Blarrney castle me darlin'
> you're nothing now but a StOWne"

(74)

This river of reminiscence swells and sinks throughout the sequence, as Pound releases his (very varied) memories as a record for posterity. This is the best history in the *Cantos*.

As the *Pisan Cantos* proceed, the note of vindication sweetens and Pound draws sustenance both from these 'deeds ensheaved and garnered in the heart', of which he had a large stock, and from the action of his senses on the external world:

> When the mind swings by a grass-blade
> an ant's forefoot shall save you
> the clover leaf smells and tastes as its flower

(83)

The restorative effect is not merely organic, sensory, aesthetic—it is also moral. Pound, like the author of Proverbs, admires the industry of the ant, and like Bruce in his cave, the perseverance of the spider. Natural observation leads also to mythological as well as moral considerations, and in the most natural way:

> The infant has descended,
> from mud on the tent roof to Tellus,
> like to like colour he goes amid grass-blades
> greeting them that dwell under XTHONOS XΘONOΣ
> OI XΘONIOI;   to carry our news
> εἰς χθονίους   to them that dwell under the earth,
> begotten of air, that shall sing in the bower
> of Kore,   Περσεφόνεια
> and have speech with Tiresias, Thebae

(83)

Here we have a mending of the web of the whole poem: the infant ant enters the earth, and Pound thinks, grammatically, of Odysseus and Aeneas escaping from the shattered anthill of Troy and visiting the spirits of the dead and the bower of Persephone; and of himself surviving the wreckage of Europe. And he makes us think of these parallels by the gentlest of sequences, just as he had in 'Fan-Piece'. Some of the mythology is more arcane and more eloquent:

> Δρυάς, your eyes are like the clouds over Taishan
> When some of the rain has fallen
> and half remains yet to fall

    The roots go down to the river's edge
        and the hidden city moves upward
            white ivory under the bark

                                              (83)

The eyes of the Dryad are seen in a vision; I associate her with Dorothy
Pound. There are also references to Pound's daughter and to Olga Rudge
in the *Pisan Cantos*, but the Dryad, like the goddesses and nymphs who
appear to him elsewhere, is as much a spirit as a mortal woman.
  Some of the visionary experiences are mysterious and indeed arcane,
but most are embodiments of Pound's intuitions of natural numina, and
are never far from the light of common day:

        Dryad thy peace is like water
    There is September sun on the pools

    Plura diafana
        Heliads lift the mist from the young willows
    there is no base seen under Taishan
        But the brightness of '*udor*   ὕδωρ
    the poplar tips float in brightness
    only the stockade posts stand

    And now the ants seem to stagger
            as the dawn sun has trapped their shadows,
    this breath wholly covers the mountains

                                              (83)

There is a marvellous quality of light in the later *Pisan Cantos*, particularly
in 80 and 83, in which the elements of the composition, unfathomable as
some of them appear at first, mingle with a freedom and naturalness
which makes all credible and acceptable. The air of improvisation which
Yeats noted is now disciplined by the actual and humanized by the
suffering, which deepens even slight inflections. Though joy is never
extinguished, and indeed the positive progression of spirit through the
Pisan Cantos is important to recognize, each Canto ends sadly. More
telling than the avowed cultural import of the epic is the intrinsic value
of this drama of the heroic survival, and growth, of a unique mind.

12. After Pisa

The later *Cantos* show some specialization of creativity—a judgement anticipated by the account offered of the *Pisan Cantos* in the last chapter. Now for the first time the easy dismissal of the *Cantos* as a dogmatic desert with lyric oases, if a travesty, becomes at least recognizable. Only the dealings with nature, myth or with the poet's own life now show the old imagination; the rest—historical researches in a variety of neglected areas—will interest intensely only those convinced by Pound's thesis. There is much of interest to be gleaned from the history, and Pound's hand has not lost its cunning: it is rather that the thesis or theses advanced now wear an antiquarian aspect, and the note form is strangely sapless. Cantos 85–89, for instance, are the ghost of what might have been had not the *Pisan Cantos* intervened: further propaganda for a build-your-own political ethic combining Confucianism, imperial peacekeeping, and agrarian resistance to usury. The rear-guard action in *Thrones* to defend fiscal probity and guild standards of craft in Byzantium and mediaeval England is, again, a sermon preached only to the converted and to the archivist. The case against the effect of commercialism on life and art has already been powerfully made; this is a dossier of further evidence from less relevant periods.

Further evidence in a case for the defence is accompanied by further material for the paradisal conclusion of an epic: imagery of light becomes more prominent, Dionysus gives way to Athena, and her justice and wisdom give place to Amor, with a hint of Agape. The social chaos of the early *Cantos* and the social order of the middle *Cantos* give way to a mystical contemplation of nature, nature's gods and the priests of a religion of light. This attempt on the part of a humanist to fulfil the paradisal expections of a work modelled in part on the *Commedia* is not as unsuccessful as might have been expected; locally, it possesses a truly mystical quality.

The same success cannot be claimed for the universal history offered in the hope of substantiating the hunch about usury:

> This is not a work of fiction
>   nor yet of one man . . .
>
>   (99)

In so far as the 'history' can be seen as objective and impersonal it is

sadly lacking in the 'drama' of the *Pisan Cantos*, which, it will be remembered, was 'wholly subjective'.

The natural mysticism, which is at the apex of the analogy with the
Commedia, is implicit in Pound's deepest poetic impulse; it continues
the visionary experience of the *Pisan Cantos*, never disappearing from the
poem, and finally resurfacing at full strength. It forms a plenary exception
to any general negative account of the post-Pisan *Cantos*.

Rock-Drill and *Thrones* were written while Pound was in St. Elizabeth's,
Drafts and Fragments in Italy. It is inevitable that the volumes produced
in America under suspended threat of trial for treason should have a
defensive aspect; the 'old man ... serving small stones from a lath
racquet' at the D.T.C. obstinately kept his end up in the mental hospital.
When at long last he was released, it was no longer necessary to serve
stones, and he gradually relaxed the determination that if he fell he
would not fall on his knees.[1] He sat down and slowly abandoned
musketeering and the more imperial gestures that had sustained the epic
mandate since the fall of Mussolini. The commanding voice, will and
baton began to droop; he found a truer strength in what remained behind,
the more receptive qualities that had sustained him at Pisa.

Before examining the remaining *Cantos* in closer focus, the two translations of the period in St. Elizabeth's must be noticed briefly, *The Classic
Anthology Defined by Confucius* (1955) and *Women of Trachis* (1956).
These extraordinary productions will be considered in relation to the
author's confinement rather than in their own right. The cursory treatment offered here does not pretend to do them justice.

To translate the *Classic Anthology*, or Book of Odes as it is usually
called, would be a fair life's work for a scholar of the earliest Chinese
poetry, so Pound's effort may be saluted for its courage. It can be considered under a narrow aspect, for Pound had specific objectives in mind,
which dictated the resources he brought to the job. He wished his
version of the Odes to annex ancient Chinese tradition into English and
to spread his interpretation of Confucian thought, an interpretation which
limited the kind of English he was prepared to use. His Chinese was not
adequate to the task and it is doubtful whether the advances he made in
Washington, with the help of various scholars and scholarly aids, left him
in a better position for this task of much greater philological and historical
difficulty than he had had in producing *Cathay* from Fenollosa's glosses.

The best of Pound's pioneering work as a translator was produced not
only by his prodigious gifts of language and technique but also by his
generous sensibility and his startling critical intelligence. Both the *Classic*

Anthology and *Women of Trachis* show sensibility and awesome technique, but in places are weaker in critical intelligence and in their language. The decisiveness of instinct and the command of style which produced *Cathay* and Cantos 1, 13 and 49 deserted Pound in many pages of his two major late translations, though they returned with the delightful *Love Poems of Ancient Egypt* (1962), his last translation. The reasons must lie in his extreme personal isolation and the concomitant stubbornness of mind. His twelve years in the mental hospital did not silence him, but made what he produced there more idiosyncratic.

The *Classic Anthology* suffers from three disadvantages. (1) The ancient originals are often obscure as well as unfamiliar, and Pound adopts highly personal methods of haruspication to crack them. Hence the results are often doubly strange. (2) The concentration of the Chinese language, as against English, leads Pound into an excessively cryptic and laconic style of translation; he takes his *'dichten = condensare'* ideal of poetry[2] to extremes of knottiness, sacrificing on the altar of terseness all notions of decorum in diction. (3) The Odes are mostly either folk-songs or ceremonial and political; Pound takes his perception of these stylistic facts to extreme lengths, often forcing tone and idiom to fit his notion of 'Confucian' qualities, whether *folklorique* or ceremonial.

The results are sometimes beyond description. Part III, Book I, Ode x, the first three stanzas, may suggest something of this:

> Wang Hou Cheng Tsai
>
> Praise to King Wen for his horse-breeding,
> that he sought the people's tranquility
> and saw it brought into focus.
> > WEN! Avatar, how!
>
> 2
> Wen had the Decree and war-merit;
> when he carried the attack against Ch'ung
> he made Feng capital of the province.
> > Wen! avatar, how!
>
> 3
> He solidified the walls of its moat;
> He raised Feng on the pattern
> not hasting at whim, but in conformity, filial,
> > A sovran, avatar, how!

The last line of stanza 3 is characteristic of the 'Confucian' pigment which gets weirdly into the diction of the ceremonial Odes, mostly in the form of such French abstractions as amity, lucidity, felicity. The refrains, too, suggest that Pound's verbal energy has got out of touch with any sense of normal idiom or stylistic decorum: 'Big translatorese, how!' Again, 'brought into focus' in the first verse looks suspiciously like Pound riding a hobby-horse and importing his theories about light into a 'Confucian' reading of a character.[3]

Yet even out of context, this strange and factitious fragment also suggests that Pound's Odes are not lacking in force. Their vices of manner have corresponding virtues, particularly to be found in the first of the four parts of the anthology, where folk-songs and love-songs predominate. Two examples from the 'Songs of Wang':

v

Dry grass, in vale:
> 'alas!
'I met a man, I
> > met
> > > a man.

'Scorched, alas, ere it could grow.'
A lonely girl pours out her woe.

'Even in water-meadow, dry.'
Flow her tears abundantly,
> > Solitude 's no remedy.

vi

Rabbit goes soft-foot, pheasant's caught,
I began life with too much élan,
Troubles come to a bustling man.
> 'Down Oh, and give me a bed!'

Rabbit soft-foot, pheasant 's in trap,
I began life with a flip and flap,
Then a thousand troubles fell on my head,
> 'If I could only sleep like the dead!'

Rabbit goes soft-foot, pheasant gets caught.
A youngster was always rushin' round,
Troubles crush me to the ground.
> I wish I could sleep and not hear a sound.

The 'folk' quality shows in the strong American accent of many lines, and the firm handling of the rhythms. These simple lyrics are transposed

with decision 'into something'—a definite verse form and a strong idiom.
Pound's use of the repertory of traditional song-styles shows all his
virtuosity; and many of the best of the lyrics have a strongly personal
quality as well, like the two given above, or no. xvi of the 'Songs of
Cheng':

> 'As on the last day of the moon'
>
> Cold wind, and the rain,
> cock crow, he is come again,
>   my ease.
>
> Shrill wind and the rain
> and the cock crows and crows,
> I have seen him, shall it suffice
>   as the wind blows?
>
> Wind, rain and the dark
> as it were the dark of the moon,
> What of the wind, and the cock's never-ending cry;
> Together
> again
> he and I.

The best of the folk-songs are much better than, for instance, Pound's
early Provençal songs; if their vigour occasionally falls into a synthetic
or a crabbed idiom or a predictable rhyme, these are the faults of folk-
songs. On the whole, the *Classic Anthology* is, for all its weirdness and
unevenness, a proof of Pound's genius; it contains many authentic delights
and some remarkable feats of style. It also tells one a great deal about its
translator's state of mind, perhaps too much for it to be the classic
contribution intended.

The version of Sophocles' *Trachiniae* has little of the fascination of
style exerted by the *Classic Anthology* at its most perverse. The 'American'
vigour of speech is applied more radically than it is to the Chinese songs,
and even more eclectically:

> MESSENGER: All started when he had a letch for the girl,
> and when her pro-eh-Genitor 'Rytus wouldn't
>   let him put her to bed on the Q.T.
> Wasn't about Iphytz or Omphale
> he sacked the town, and killed 'Rytus to get her.
> He's not bringing her here as a slave. Too het up.
> So I thought I would be telling Your Majesty. . . .

Stage-American turns to stage-Irish in the last line; Bret Harte and
Mickey Spillane alternate with recherché dignities:

KHOROS: To hell with all double-crossers,
                they are the last of all dirtiness.

'Tudor' pastiche mingles entertainingly with gestures from a score of
other styles, achieving often a curious splendour. The best style in the
play is a plain starkness usually reserved to Herakles' speeches, but
evident too in these lines from the Nurse about Deianeira:

Terrible, you can believe me. She came in alone
and saw the boy in the hall preparing the hearse-litter
to fetch back his father.
She hid herself down back of the altar,
sank down there groaning because her brood had deserted her.
Then pitifully stroking the things she had used before,
went wandering through the best rooms—
didn't know I could see her, from a sort of kink in the wall—
drawing her hands over the things she was used to.

The impression the play makes, however, is not fundamentally to do
with its style, or lack of style, though this disqualifies it from being an
artistic success of any normal sort. The play is about the agony of Herakles
in the shirt of Nessus, sent to him by Deianeira as a love charm to win
back his love to her and away from Iole, whom Herakles wishes to share
their ménage. Deianeira kills herself on learning of her mistake; Herakles
makes his son Hyllos promise to carry him to the funeral pyre and, after
his death and apotheosis, to marry Iole. Pound tells us Herakles is Solar
Vitality, and the play offers some light on Pound's ideas of myth; but
its interest lies deeper. Pound has brought out a terrifying quality in the
original play with a ruthless violence that survives the strangeness and
corniness of his personal dialect (Herakles extends his hand to his son to
exact the final promise with the words 'Put her there'). Thus,

HERAKLES: Come ere the pain awake,
                O stubborn mind.
(*catches sight of* HYLLOS' *face and breaks off with*)
                And put some cement in your face,
                reinforced concrete, make a cheerful finish
                even if you don't want to.

This violence of emotion tears the academic veil from the Greek in a way that remains shocking, though it has since had its academic imitators; but the interest of *Women of Trachis* is not in its radically dissentient contribution to our awareness of Greek tragedy. It is rather that the Pound version manifests the horror of life, especially in Herakles' celebrated speech 'in the mask of divine agony', in a way not to be found anywhere else in his work. Leaving aside the conflicting love of the two women, the agony of Herakles is related to that of the author as obviously as is the agony of Milton's Samson. The neglected tragedy of Herakles Agonistes[4] unlocked something elemental in Pound, and the last scene, for all its brutality, has an awe-inspiring grandeur in the determination of Herakles and his son to accept and endure as something coherent 'the gods' great unreason': for 'all of this is from Zeus', and Herakles is the son of Zeus. Pound's intense identification with the great hero, both in his sense of his own divinity, and of his destiny in putting on the harness of necessity, is exceedingly strange but also terrible to witness: *Women of Trachis* is a jagged fragment containing perhaps the worst, certainly the most tasteless, writing in Pound's whole career, but also, in a realm beyond taste, some of the most compelling. For all their scholarly and aesthetic faults, these formidable late translations enlarge and deepen our idea of Pound; he was not an easy man to pin down, nor to keep down.

Rock-Drill, from the same period, is also conceived as a defensive manifesto, a vindication and defiance. Pound's early identification with the irreconcilables and outcasts of history, whether artists or men of affairs, had now come home to roost, and the itemized names and incidents which stud these pages are being rescued from undeserved neglect. Thus, in the first half of *Rock-Drill*, Van Buren, Benton, Randolph stood against usury before the Civil War; in the second, Jacques de Molay, Scotus Erigena and Apollonius of Tyana stood against restrictive orthodoxy and obscurantism. The memory of these honourable men has been suppressed by a conspiracy of mediocrity, corruption and usury. To read *Rock-Drill* as history, unaware of its purpose of personal vindication, would be to do less than justice to Pound's sense of indignation.

This section is called *Rock-Drill* because Pound, whom Wyndham Lewis likened to Epstein's bronze of that name, is drilling a way to the Thrones of Paradise, through public incomprehension and his own despair. The way is arduous, as Pound disarmingly warns: 'Yes, my Ondine, it is so god-damned dry on these rocks' (93). The poet drills out many chips of excellence, but the atmosphere is gritty, particularly in Cantos 85–89, where he throws behind him scraps of his readings in nineteenth-century history. Unless one has read Thomas Hart Benton's *Thirty Years' View: or a History of the Working of the American Government 1820–1850* (New York, 1854–6) many of these research suggestions are not merely hard going, they are rubble. Even the glorious figure of John Randolph of Roanoke, a new Sigismundo, does not emerge clearly. For Pound is no longer presenting but referring; and the refining of such nuggets as there are is left too much to us. There is also the question of balance: Pound tends now to present his suggestions as essentials rather than as corrections to the normal views of educated people; and since many of those who will be induced to study him will not have a historical grounding in humane studies the consequences may be perilous.

Canto 90 marks a transformation of mood and subject, a breakthrough from the darkness of the liberal age of usury into the light of the Dark Ages. The paradox is not fanciful, for the light that comes to Pound comes from occult sources:

> Sibylla
>> from under the rubble heap
>>> m'elevasti
>> from the dulled edge beyond pain,
>>> m'elevasti
>> out of Erebus, the deep-lying

What Pound sees by the new light vouchsafed him is extremely mysterious. Much of it is identical with the visions of the gods and heroes familiar from his earlier escape from Hell after Canto 14, though with a larger zoomorphic cast of cats, birds and trees. There are also the essences of light and water distilled in the *Pisan Cantos*, images mediated by feminine presences, like the Sibyl or the Muses of Castalia:

> Grove hath its altar
>> under elms, in that temple, in silence
> a lone nymph by the pool.
>
>>>>> (90)

If Pound's vision has narrowed it has also taken on a pellucid intensity. Perhaps no English poet has produced images of such simple and refined beauty.

The dreams of fair women which rescue Pound from his deep-lying depression include encounters similar to those of Odysseus and visions not unlike those Dante has of Beatrice. They also include, in Canto 91 alone, Ondine, Helen of Tyre, Theodora, Miss Tudor (Elizabeth I), the

Princess Ra-Set, the wives of Egyptian peasants, Artemis, Diana, Merlin's mother, the daughter of Cadmus, the water-nymphs of Porphyrius, Leucothea, la Pinella, Joan of Arc and the reigning goddess of the heaven of love, Cytherea, 'che 'l terzo ciel movete'.

It becomes clear that the inveterately fragmentary nature of allusion and reference of these Cantos is no mannerism, but reflects Pound's experience:

> Le Paradis n'est pas artificiel
>   but is jagged,
> For a flash,
>   for an hour.
> Then agony,
>   then an hour,
>   then agony
> Hilary stumbles, but the Divine Mind is abundant
>   unceasing
>   *improvisatore*

(92)

The last word refers to the Divine Mind, not the author's, though they are intermittently in touch, since for Pound the poet at the moment of loving perception is divinely inspired. Apollonius of Tyana is used in Canto 92 as an example of the marvels available to a pagan sensibility informed with a sense of wonder and a kind of neo-Platonic pantheism. After which we have had two thousand years of 'desensitization'—

> & a little light from the borders:
> Erigena,
> Avicenna, Richardus.
> Hilary looked at an oak leaf

—thus demonstrating his kinship with Pythagoras, John Heydon and the Selloi (the priests of the oak grove of Zeus at Dodona). . . .

At such points it is difficult to ignore the sense of isolation, or to acquit Pound of eclecticism, escapism and fantasy, though it is equally difficult to deny either the strong glamour of his vision or the sense of calm coherence which informs some of the fragments. In so far as the vision is natural and mythopoeic, it is poetic; in so far as it enlists authorities, it is fanciful pedantry, sometimes offered quite seriously.

Sometimes, however, it is not so serious. In Canto 95 Pound considers:

```
I suppose St. Hilary looked at an oak-leaf.
(vine-leaf? San Denys,
        (spelled Dionisio)
Dionisio et Eleutherio.
Dionisio et Eleutherio
        "the brace of 'em
that Calvin never blacked out
                        en L'Isle.)
```

The suppositiousness here is pretty marked. Though it may well be true that free love is commoner in Paris than in Geneva, this is not a consequence of the etymology of the names of Saints Hilary and Denis; nor is it easy to see how Calvin could have been able to black it out. . . . In this mood, Pound might have been just as happy to play with the names of Calvin and Charles le Chauve. The passage is a harmless example of playful free association yet suggests a weakness for seeing historical significance in convenient verbal coincidence. There is no reason to suppose St. Hilary of Poitiers was particularly cheerful or particularly sensitive to nature, pleasant though it is to think that he was.

This passage is followed by the conclusion of *Rock-Drill*:

```
That the wave crashed, whirling the raft, then
Tearing the oar from his hand,
                        broke mast and yard-arm
And he was drawn down under wave,
        The wind tossing,
Notus, Boreas,
                as it were thistle-down.
Then Leucothea had pity,
                        "mortal once
Who now is a sea-god:
                        νόστου
γαίης Φαιήκων, . . ."
```

This is a concentrated and powerful allusion to *Odyssey*, v, where Odysseus is rescued by Ino, daughter of Cadmus, who comes to a rock by his raft in the form of a seagull, and lends him her veil to keep him afloat. Pound calls her Leucothea, and we have just heard her say—in the accents of Lauren Bacall'—My bikini is worth yr/ raft'. The mortal who became a sea god is Glaucus, an apotheosis described in Book XIII of Ovid's *Metamorphoses*, as Leucothea's was in Book IV. The rescue of the shipwrecked Pound by human and natural powers is to be carried further in 'the land of the Phaeacians' by the providential and equally attractive Nausicaa.

The mysterious process of restoration experienced by Pound, not unlike that in Shakespeare's *Pericles*, is cast in this mythical and syncretic form because he thinks of himself as like Odysseus, and because those influences which did restore him in real life were natural, human and feminine. The moving power of these passages in the later *Rock-Drill*— and despite their encoded forms they are fresh and moving—seems to me neither epic, nor even like incidents in a Greek romance, but personal, even private. But if the effect is un-Homeric, it is even more un-Dantescan, despite the gestures and the name-lists of the blessed. Far from graduating through the circles of Paradise according to a programme philosophically informed, Pound is, rather, feeling more sanguine than he had in Cantos 85–89: 'And there is something decent in the universe', he writes before introducing St. Hilary. The reason for his mysteriously feeling better must be physical, for his paradise is real, well treed and well watered. Though it may seem a rather idealized garden, Pound emphasizes that Paradise is neither artificial nor metaphysical. He sees no need for metaphysics.

> Do not Hindoos
> > lust after vacuity?
> With the Gardasee at our disposition.
>
> > > > (95)

Despite the visionary nature of his arcana, Pound insists that his paradise—like that of Catullus—is earthly; and this, though simple enough, is scarcely escapist.

Thrones (1958) begins with some interesting if cryptic extracts from the history of Paulus Diaconus; from the Book of Leo the Eparch; and from the nummulary researches of Del Mar.[5] The purpose is to exhibit societies where monetary justice was observed; but the flavour remains antiquarian, despite occasional curses on the head of Roosevelt and his 'Spew Deal'. Chinese characters are interspersed through the text, as are asides referring to earlier subjects, and some resonant new *sententiae:* 'The temple is holy, because it is not for sale' (97). But the buzzing of the bees in the Ezratic bonnet is indulged, sometimes humorously:

> May 4th Interruption
> > mid dope-dolls an' duchesses
> > > tho' orften I roam,
> > some gals is better,
> > > > some wusser
> > > > > than some.

> But that the free-born run wode into slavery
> this is not good;
>> run wode in job hunting,
>> this is NOT good.
>>>   (97)

The queen bee remains Usura:

>> And Byzance lasted longer than Manchu
>> because of an (%) interest-rate.
>>>   (98)

The rage, however, has died down; Pound has become more amiably crusty: 'And not to lose life for bad temper.' This, the ending to Canto 98, is one of the Confucian precepts which dominate 97–99, crustily enough at times:

> And if your kids don't study, that's your fault.
> Tell 'em. Don't kid yourself, and don't lie.
> In statement, answer; in conversation
>> not with sissified fussiness (chiao[1])
>> always want your own way.
> Let 'em ask before taking action;
> That there be no slovenly sloppiness
>> between goodman & wife.
>>>   (99)

> Dress 'em in folderols
>> and feed 'em with dainties,
> In the end they will sell out the homestead.
>>   (99)

The purpose of *Thrones*, in the analogy with the *Commedia*, is to honour civic courage and principle, so it has an administrative and imperial bias. True to his Enlightenment heritage, Pound provides thrones for Antoninus and Julian the Apostate. The scrappiness of the presentations, however, does not allow the reader to get more than a general impression of the virtues and persons in question; whole pages degenerate into chat or even into notes and diary entries. At such points one might recall Sir Philip Sidney's comment on the poets of his day: 'Our matter is *quodlibet* indeed, though wrongly performing Ovid's verse, *Quicquid conabor dicere versus erit*, never marshalling it into any assured rank, that almost the readers cannot tell where to find themselves.'[6] The dominance of the contingent is admitted by the end of Canto 100 (Dante's round number), where Pound signs off with a date, 1 January 1958. This was to be the year of his release.

Confucianism appeals to Pound because it begins in nature and in human nature, and its supernatural aspect is mysterious but organic, without being, like Christianity, Buddhism, Taoism and Hinduism, otherworldly. It is therefore possible to harmonize it with his syncretic paganism, his religious awe before nature and his 'neo-Platonic' mysticism about light as the principle of divine intelligence. This simple trust in natural reality gives him the confidence to defy his peers; he had (in Italy) seen polytheism, and knew that it worked.

> But the lot of 'em, Yeats, Possum, Old Wyndham
> had no ground to stand on
> Black shawls still worn for Demeter
> in Venice,
> in my time,
> my young time
> (102)

In this confidence he continues his animadversions on the inside history of Europe in the sixth or the nineteenth century, in a succession of *obiter dicta*, of which the most telling are to do with his exile in his own country: 'Winter in Pontus distressing' (103). The others are never lacking in Attic salt, especially when fanaticism is in question:

> "Puteum de testiculis impleam clericorum"
> dixit Alchis
> would fill full a well with priests' balls,
> heretics', naturally
> (103)

Indeed, when explicit enough, the individual items rarely lack interest, especially when they are first-hand:

> Luigi in hill paths
> chews wheat at sunrise,
> that grain, his communion
> (104)

Yet there is a persistent sense of the poet having too many things to say, rearranging his memories, referring by means of a word to an earlier Canto, interweaving reminiscences, but finding no way of putting them all in any particular order. Canto 105 begins:

Feb. 1956
Is this a divagation

whereas Canto 100 had ended '1 Jan '58'. The order, then, is not chronological, but according to some loose-leaf filing system, the plan of which
may be cyclical or spiral but is not clear. A justification for such
inclusiveness ('You cannot leave these things out') is offered in the
middle of a more than usually coherent Canto about the values of St.
Anselm:

> Fragmentary:
>   (Maverick repeating this queery dogmaticly.
>   mosaic? any mosaic.
> You cannot leave these things out.
>   οὐ θέλει ἔην εἰς κόσμον
> but from at least here is the Charta Magna
> I shall have to learn a little greek to keep up with this
>   but so will you, drratt you.
> "They want to bust out of the kosmos"
>
>   (105)

There is an upward movement in *Thrones*, as in *Rock-Drill*, particularly
in the second half. Canto 106 notably is a celebration of Artemis at her
temple:

> By Circeo, the stone eyes looking seaward
>   Nor could you enter her eyes by probing.
>   The temple shook with Apollo
> As with leopards by mount's edge,
>   light blazed behind her;
>   trees open, their minds stand before them
> As in Carrara is whiteness:
>   Xoroi. At Sulmona are lion heads.
>   Gold light, in veined phylotaxis.
> By hundred blue-gray over their rock-pool,
>   Or the king-wings in migration
>   And in thy mind beauty, O Artemis
> Over asphodel, over broom-plant,
>   faun's ear a-level that blossom.

It ends on a note of exaltation in praise of light and perception:

Selena, foam on the wave-swirl
      Out of gold light flooding the peristyle
          Trees open in Paros,
              White feet as Carrara's whiteness
in Xoroi.
      God's eye art 'ou.
          The columns gleam as if cloisonné,
            The sky is leaded with elm boughs.

Here the jungle does indeed become a temple.

The remainder of *Thrones* deals with the ethos of mediaeval England shown through its laws, an ethos which allowed the sort of precise verbal awareness manifested in Anselm's doctrine of Mary's Immaculacy, or the rights laid down in Magna Charta. This world of principle and clear definition ended with the accession of 'Jimmy Stewart', vituperatively memorialized thus:

> Flaccus' translator wore the crown
> The jew and the buggar dragged it down:
> "Devil in dung-cart" Gondemar
> And Raleigh's head on King James' platter."

                                                    (107)

The author of *The History of the World* was, naturally, one of Pound's heroes; at this time, equally naturally, the poet, deemed unfit to stand trial, had an interest in the law of *habeas corpus*, foreshadowed in Magna Charta, and in jury trial. The end of *Thrones* is perhaps a fair sample to represent its splintered beauty. Every phrase is illuminated by other phrases immediately preceding this passage:

                      Jury trial was in Athens
Who for bridges
          reparando
For every new cottage   4 acres
            Stat de 31 Eliz.
                Angliae amor
And false stone not to be set in true gold
to the king onely to put value
          and to make price of the quantity
auxy soit signe teste leopard
Clear deep off Taormina
          high cliff and azure beneath it

form is cut in the lute's neck, tone is from the bowl
Oak boughs alone over Selloi
        This wing, colour of feldspar
                phyllotaxis
Over wicket gate
        INO Ινώ Kadmeia
Erigena, Anselm,
           the fight thru Herbert and Rémusat
Helios,
      Καλλίαστράγαλος Ino Kadmeia,
San Domenico, Santa Sabina,
                Sta Maria Trastevere
                  in Cosmedin
Le chapeau melon de St Pierre
      You in the dinghy (piccioletta) astern there!
                              (109)

Drafts and Fragments of Cantos CX–CXVII (1970) are the last of the *Cantos*. Whatever may come out of Yale, this was clearly intended as the valedictory volume, though it must be said that the *Cantos* come to an end rather than that Pound finished them. As *Drafts and Fragments* has only recently been incorporated in the volume of collected *Cantos*, it is not sufficiently known. I give some account of the contents, considering these Cantos as of the greatest interest and importance, both intrinsically and as modifying the final effect of the work.

Cantos 110, 113, 114 and 116 are given complete, with notes for 111, 112 and 115. After two fragments written in 1941, for inclusion earlier in the poem, there follow 'Notes for Cantos CXVII *et seq.*'. The volume is not much concerned with history, nor is its purpose self-vindication. On the contrary, it contains expressions of doubt about the *Cantos* and implies second thoughts about some of the poet's youthful asperities. Indeed, malicious satisfaction has been taken by some in finding in the the final Canto (116) such phrases as 'a tangle of works unfinished', 'I cannot make it cohere', and references to errors, wrecks and madness. (Frank as always, Pound gave interviews at this time regretting his anti-Semitism, his superficial study of economics, and his insufficient attention to questions of structure; he disarmingly described the *Cantos* as 'a botch', and to an Italian journalist, as *brutto*.[7]) But if *Drafts and Fragments* are not an apologia, neither are they an apology, still less a confession of failure or despair. They are, not surprisingly, rather more complex: each of the phrases cited above, for example, is immediately qualified by

something more affirmative, and the tone of this dialectic of memory and
meditation, though chastened, is quietly affirmative—quietly, and also
modestly, for the affirmations concern the universe rather than the poet's
own doings, a paradox memorably expressed in:

> A blown husk that is finished
> but the light sings eternal.
>
> (115)

In the sequence of Cantos 110–116, the prevailing note is suggested by
such phrases as 'thy quiet house', *compassione*, *serenitas*, and 'I hate no-
one'. The last word of 116 is 'splendour' and the last line of the last
fragment is 'To be men not destroyers'.

The volume is dedicated to Olga Rudge, the companion of the poet's
middle and last years, and begins in Venice:

> Thy quiet house
> The crozier's curve runs in the wall,
> The harl, feather-white, as a dolphin on sea-brink
>
> I am all for Verkehr without tyranny
>   —wake exultant
>   in caracole
> Hast 'ou seen boat's wake on sea-wall,
>   how crests it?
> What panache?
>   paw-flap, wave-tap,
>   that is gaiety . . .
>
> (110)

Quietness and gaiety are prominent in these last Cantos.

Calling on Pound in 1962 at Miss Rudge's small house at Sant'
Ambrogio, in the olive groves above the bay at Rapallo, I remarked how
very quiet and peaceful it was, to which the poet, who had received me in
his bedroom, replied with marked emphasis, 'Quiet . . . and peace . . . do
not mean the same thing.' It was mid-morning, a little early to call on an
old man recovering from an operation, and it proved a time for silence
rather than for talking; but the gnomic remark had a general as well as a
particular application. The 'serenity' of these last Cantos was rare and
hard-won, and, despite the supreme lyric quality of Canto 110 and of the
'nice quiet paradise' generally, there is a fragility and a sense of threat:

A wind of darkness hurls against forest
the candle flickers
is faint

(110)

or

Out of dark, thou, Father Helios, leadest,
but the mind as Ixion, unstill, ever turning.

(113)

The serenity is not untroubled, nor was all passion spent.
There seems little bitterness, however, except perhaps towards another intervention:

And 600 more dead at Quemoy
they call it political.

(111)

The values he stresses are love, compassion, charity, as well as the old courage and perception:

Wyndham Lewis chose blindness
rather than have his mind stop

(115)

The homage to heroes is still there in the recording of names.

But these had thrones,
and in my mind were still, uncontending—

(114)

The effort to create a pantheon fades; the emphasis is on 'still' and 'uncontending'; on the naturally existing *paradiso terrestre*, the singing of the light; and on humane equivalents of the theology of Dante's *Paradiso*. In Canto 94 we were told: 'beyond civic order:/l'AMOR', yet the 'thrones' were still subordinate to Justice; by Canto 111 love is associated with *compassione*, and even pity.

The most important consideration, both poetically and personally, is that in the last Cantos Pound finds again the qualities of *Lustra*, *Cathay* and 'For the seven lakes', though their expression is more fragmented, complex and refined. The visions are once more rooted in natural perception.

And in thy mind beauty, O Artemis,
                as of mountain lakes in the dawn,
Foam and silk are thy fingers,
                Kuanon,
and the long suavity of her moving,
                willow and olive reflected,
Brook-water idles,
                topaz against pallor of under-leaf
The lake waves Canaletto'd
                under blue paler than heaven,
the rock-layers arc'd as with a compass,
                this rock is magnesia,
Cozzaglio, Dino Martinazzi made the road here (Gardesana)

                                                (110)

Back in Italy, Pound's sharpness of eye, ear and mind return to their accustomed objects of contemplation, refined but also humanized, as in the *Pisan Cantos*. There is less strain to complete the epic design, and the mysticism is largely implicit. It is this unforced quality that is so welcome. The climate is balmier, the intimations gentler:

The kindness, infinite, of her hands.
        Sea, blue under cliffs, or
William murmuring: "Sligo in heaven" when the mist came
        to Tigullio. And that the truth is in kindness.

                                              (114)

We hear no more of the misgivings of 103 that love is a marshmallow rather than a fulcrum for getting things done. There are still the cavalry charges; and the cavalier oversimplifications: 'Disney against the metaphysicals' (the philosophers not the poets), and the incorrigible

As to sin, they invented it—eh?
                        to implement domination
      eh? largely.
                There remains grumpiness,
                    malvagità

                                              (113)

But the humour in the voice shows he is more his old self. An intimate quietness prevails:

> but about that terzo
> > third heaven,
> > > that Venere,
> again is all "paradiso"
> > a nice quiet paradise
> > > over the shambles
>
>   (116)

or

> Twilit sky leaded with elm boughs.
>
>   (117)

The homecoming to Penelope passes almost unnoticed: 'if love be not in the house. . .' (116).

The last fragment in the volume, however, though it too retains the intimate and particular quality of Pound's mind, reminds us that it was a mind not only humane and wonderfully accurate in articulation but, like Li Po's, unique, the mind of a visionary:

> Two mice and moth my guides—
> To have heard the farfalla gasping
> > as toward a bridge over worlds.

What to say of a dedicated life? In seeking to make an estimate of Pound's poetic achievements, Pound's own career is itself a warning not to rush to conclusions. To take only the last of its transformations for example, *Drafts and Fragments* significantly softens the impression left by *Rock-Drill* and *Thrones*, and by the *Cantos* as a whole; it has a reintegrative effect on the reader's experience of the poem. The shape the *Cantos* will assume in the minds of poets and readers of the future cannot be predicted, though it is already clear that whereas in the past it has been asked to stand as sponsor at many an unlikely font, in the future it risks becoming a semi-academic institution, at least in the U.S.A. The account given here does not do justice to the overall design of the poem, especially in the later stages, for which much evidence is being produced.[8] It will remain true, however, that this plan is often lost to view, and that for many readers it will be the variety of the *Cantos*, its picaresque explorations and reclamations, that strike and hold the mind. Little heed has been paid here to the various prospectuses to the enterprise; likewise the poet's own later doubts are only part of the story. Asked about the continuing progress of the poem in 1962, he replied: 'I have lots of fragments. I can't make much sense of them, and I don't suppose anyone else will.'[9] But it is not necessarily the best artists who remain confident about the value of their work until the end. Pound was well aware he had been 'hard as youth sixty years'; or, as he put it to Robert Lowell, 'To begin with a swelled head and end with swelled feet.'[10] Old men ought to be explorers, according to Eliot.[11] It can only deepen one's respect for *il miglior fabbro* that in old age he came to think of his artistic achievement as inadequate.

This realization of the limits of art dates back to the Pisan experience: 'Learn of the green world what can be thy place' (81). And the poetry of the Pisan experience entails dissent from any view that Pound's poetry shows 'a tragic decline'; any decline was halted by Pisa. The tragedy that struck Capaneus rescued the humanity of his poem. Who is to say, in view of this, that the epic ambition was mistaken? Despite the quixotic gestures along the way, despite the confusions, despite 'that nonsense about Jews on Rome wireless'[12] and in the poem, the ardours and ex-actions of the epic form confer on it a grandeur and elevation not easily available except from 'the saddle Homer rode'. Yeats's 'brilliant im-provisator' undoubtedly had 'more style than form'[13] and there are many moments, not only in the decades of the Thirties and the Fifties, when the 'inclusion' of history did not meet up to the requirements of epic. I have suggested that the poem became consciously autobiographical, a romantic sequel to the *Odyssey*; the objective ambitions represented by the 'real' history and the moral authority aspired to in emulation of Dante or Confucius are not attained. The moral authority of the poem has little to do with Dante or Confucius, though the Odyssean analogy was more natural and useful to Pound, and accommodated his chaotic Ovidian mythopoeia better than the deep symmetries of Dante. About the learning and elliptical nature of the *Cantos*' expository method, enough has been said; to see the poem, as Pound intended, as an ideogram as large as a galaxy would be possible only if we had world enough and time.

The greatness of the *Cantos* is concentrated in the *Pisan Cantos*, though it is liberally scattered elsewhere. Only in the *Pisan Cantos* do the unerring rightness of style and the refinement of phrase have a great job to accomplish, namely the survival of the author's mind, with its extra-ordinary freight. Not that Pound becomes confessional or emotional—the pathos is largely inadvertent—it is simply that he has so much to tell us and himself, and a great number of interesting things going through his head, as he watches the guards, the clouds and the insects. It is often his lightest observations that give the clearest proof of his genius: 'grass nowhere out of place', or:

> beyond the eastern barbed wire
> a sow with nine boneen
> matronly as any duchess at Claridge's

(80)

or:

> and if her green elegance
> remains on this side of my rain ditch
> puss lizard will lunch on some other T-bone.

(80)

This last is followed, however, by 'sunset grand couturier', a typically original Poundian combination of image and word-play. It resumes the whole 'vanity' theme of the later *Pisan Cantos*, where the 'green world' and the elements of nature rebuke heroic human vaingloriousness and the 'pride of life' to which Pound has paid such splendid homage. But the image suggests not only the borrowed robes of men and the gorgeous colours of the sunset, but also cultural professions other than that of *haute couture*. Here the nice calculation of effect serves a grand idea, which is not usually the case in the poem, for its organization is aesthetic and instinctive rather than intellectual. Indeed its conscious ideas and theories are fitful and inconsistent, though its wisdom can be simple and profound. One of the many paradoxes of Pound is that he is just as happy in discovering that 'Brother Wasp' is really 'Madame La Vespa' as at any grander cultural discovery. The elegist of restaurants is also, disarmingly, the amateur of Joel Chandler Harris, and the inventor of animal nicknames for his friends.

In *The Pound Era* Hugh Kenner presents the break-up of the Vortex in 1914 as the nemesis of the men who made the modern arts, casting them into exile. Certainly his residence in Rapallo and his devotion to the *Cantos* took Pound away from the English language and from the modern world, possibly to his (and their) detriment. Who is to say, however, that the *Cantos*—though a long way round—were a misuse of his gifts, since they clearly remain 'the most important long poem of the century'?[14] For all their wrong-headed politics and confusing form, they present simultaneously an heroic imaginative openness to actual living and to nature, and also to cultural and ideal worlds more various, larger and deeper. This double vision may prove a precious legacy in an age when our own historical culture is becoming alien to us; already, the London, Paris and Provence he knew have gone, and with them certain cultural possibilities that cannot be reproduced. The distinctness and concentration of Pound's mind will not be easily emulated; nor his skills of free-verse composition. But enough has been said here to show that Pound has more than an eye and an ear.

The tendentiousness and unevenness of some of Pound's achievement make it difficult to settle squarely on a tolerable generalization about his place among the poets; he is perhaps the greatest of the moderns, since that term does not exactly fit Yeats, nor the Eliot of *Four Quartets*. However, his Promethean gifts are so original that the process of comparison with others does not seem very productive; perhaps he should not be placed among others. Eliot entitled his first article on Pound 'Isolated Superiority'.[15]

Unlike many of his readers, I do not exclude any period of Pound's work as without good poetry, from 'The Tree' to the last sybilline leaf of the *Cantos*; nor do I see significant and decisive developments which lead to radical positive or negative judgements about his career, either in its modernization in *Lustra*, its sophistication in *Mauberley*, its grandiose epic ambitions or its later fragmentation. Like many readers, I do not find the Chinese history fruitful, and find that many of the fragments of politics and history stick in my throat, just as other fragments stick in my head. I share Pound's 'coherent idea'—the idea around which, he said in 1962, his 'muddles accumulated'—that 'European culture ought to survive'; in this enterprise the *Cantos* are perhaps the biggest single effort made by an individual of this century; and may well prove the most valuable.[16] Unlike many readers, I cannot discard the idea that the *Cantos* do form a unity and do record a moral progress both in their content (by design) and in the author. It follows too that I see Pound's whole poetic output as a unity.

Leaving aside the translations, themselves a fresh and distinct adjunct to any bouquet for the Muses, the best of the original work seems to come from six periods: *Lustra* and *Cathay*; *Propertius* and *Mauberley*; the first seventeen *Cantos*; the *Fifth Decad of Cantos*; the *Pisan Cantos*; and *Drafts and Fragments*. *Cathay* seems to me the most underrated of his volumes, and I would repeat the suggestion that if the British want to make a fresh start on Pound (and it is about time they did) they could begin with the disciplined free verse of *Lustra* and *Cathay*. 'We will leave it as a test: when anyone has studied Mr. Pound's poems in *chronological* order, and has mastered *Lustra* and *Cathay*, he is prepared for the *Cantos*—but not till then. If the reader then fails to like them, he has probably omitted some step in his progress, and had better go back and retrace the journey.'[17]

Notes

Quotations from Pound's verse are taken from the 1973 reprint of the *Collected Shorter Poems* (London, 1952), or from the *Collected Early Poems*, ed. M. J. King (London, 1977), in the case of poems not in the *Collected Shorter Poems*; and from *The Cantos of Ezra Pound* (London, 1975), all published by Faber and Faber. The 1975 collected edition of *The Cantos* is the first edition to include *Drafts and Fragments of Cantos 110-117*, and is virtually complete, except for the Italian Cantos 72 and 73. The text is taken from the American (New Directions) edition and, for practical purposes, failing a properly edited text, it supersedes all previous editions of the *Cantos*, including previous British (Faber) editions; these differed in many textual details from the New Directions editions.

Bibliographical references in the notes list the date of first publication where appropriate. If quotation is made from a subsequent edition, the date of that edition is given as well.

Full bibliographical data will be found in the Select Bibliography for those works cited below in short form. For works cited frequently in the notes, the following abbreviations are used:

Gallup   Donald Gallup, *A Bibliography of Ezra Pound* (London, 1963; 2nd edn., 1969)
CSP   *Collected Shorter Poems*
CEP   *Collected Early Poems*
SR   *The Spirit of Romance*, rev. edn. (London, 1952)
LE   *Literary Essays of Ezra Pound*, ed. T. S. Eliot (London, 1954)
Letters *Letters of Ezra Pound 1907-1941*, ed. D. D. Paige (London, 1951)

Preface

1 See bibliography. Of Pound's prose I find particularly stimulating *The Spirit of Romance* (1910; rev. edn., 1952); *ABC of Reading* (1934); the *Literary Essays*, ed. T. S. Eliot (1954); and the *Letters*, ed. D. D. Paige (1951). Among the writings on Pound listed in the bibliography, those of Eliot and Yeats impress themselves most deeply. I am very largely indebted, like all students of Pound, to the scholarship and insight of Hugh Kenner, to the bibliography of Donald Gallup and the criticism of Donald Davie.
2 From the last line of the opening 'Ode' of *Hugh Selwyn Mauberley* (henceforward referred to as *Mauberley*).
3 See bibliography.
4 T. S. Eliot dedicated *The Waste Land*

to Pound as *il miglior fabbro*, a tribute taken from Dante's *Purgatorio*, XXVI, 117.

Chapter 1. Introductory

1 See bibliography. General works include Hugh Kenner, *The Pound Era* (1971); Noel Stock, *The Life of Ezra Pound* (1970; rev. edn., 1974); Donald Davie, *Pound* (1975). American developments are indicated by the number of recent academic studies; by the bibliographical care expended on the *CEP*, which is only the first fruit of the Ezra Pound Archive (the bulk of his papers) at Yale; and by *Paideuma: A journal devoted to Ezra Pound Scholarship*, published from the University of Maine, Orono, since 1972.

2 *The Times,* 2 Nov. 1972; Cyril
Connolly, *Sunday Times,* 5 Nov.;
A. Alvarez, *Observer,* 5 Nov.; Donald
Davie, *Guardian,* 9 Nov.
3 See Pound's note to *Mauberley* in
*Personae: The Collected Poems of Ezra
Pound* (New York, 1926), p. 185.
4 T. S. Eliot, Introduction to *Selected
Poems* (1928), p. 20.
5 Ford Madox Ford, *Return to Yester-
day* (1931), p. 388.
6 *Observer,* 5 Nov. 1972.
7 See Julien Cornell, *The Trial of Ezra
Pound* (1966); also *Pound/Joyce,* ed.
Forrest Read (1968), pp. 269 ff.
8 Hugh Kenner, *The Poetry of Ezra
Pound* (1951) and *The Pound Era.*
9 *A Lume Spento* (1908), *A Quinzaine
for This Yule* (1908), *Personae* (1909),
Exultations (1909), *Canzoni* (1911),
Ripostes (1912) are collected in *CEP.*
Personae (1908, 1909, 1910), *Ripostes*
(1912), *Lustra, Cathay,* Poems from
Blast (1914), Poems from *Lustra* (1915),
*Miscellaneous Poems, Homage to Sextus
Propertius* (1917), and *Hugh Selwyn
Mauberley* (1920) are collected in *CSP.*
10 'that great forty-year epic': see
'Scriptor Ignotus', *CEP,* p. 24.
11 'scaled invention' and 'true artistry':
see extract from Canto 81 on p. 39.
America's attention: see note 1 to this
chapter.

Chapter 2. Examples

1 Quoted in Canto 53.
2 A slightly different version appears in
Stock, *Life,* p. 4.
3 *The Life and Letters of John Donne,*
ed. E. Gosse (London, 1899), vol. I,
p. 291.
4 The lines quoted are the first in
W. B. Yeats, *Collected Poems* (1950) and
T. S. Eliot, *Complete Poems and Plays*
(1969). For Pound's dismissal, see Fore-
word to 1964 reissue of *A Lume Spento*
(*CEP,* p. 314).
5 See Ovid's *Metamorphoses,* I (Daphne)
and VIII (Philemon and Baucis), in, e.g.,
the Loeb edn., trans. F. J. Miller

(Cambridge, Mass. and London, 1916,
1921), vol. I.
6 H. A. Giles, *A History of Chinese
Literature* (1901), p. 101, gives a ten-line
version of the same poem.
7 'A Few Don'ts', *Poetry,* vol. I, no. 6
(March 1913); *LE,* p. 5.
8 John Milton, *Of Education* (1644), in
Milton's Prose Writings, ed. K. M.
Burton (London, 1958), p. 326.
9 In Canto 81. See p. 38.
10 ibid.
11 In 'Hugues Salel', *The Egoist,* vol. V,
no. 7 (August 1918); quoted from 'Early
Translators of Homer', *LE,* p. 250.
12 *The Poems of Alexander Pope,* ed.
John Butt (London, 1963; rev. edn.,
1968), p. 424.
13 *Iliad,* III, 243-4. John Ruskin, 'Of
the Pathetic Fallacy', *Modern Painters*
(1856), vol. III, ch. 12; quoted from
2nd edn. 'in complete form' (London,
1900), vol. III, p. 167.
14 'gists and piths': see *ABC of
Reading,* p. 92.
15 Based on the *Ta Hio* of Confucius,
translated by Pound as *The Great
Learning* (1928). See Kenner, *Pound Era,*
pp. 445-7.
16 Pound's version, *The Classic
Anthology Defined by Confucius* (1954),
is discussed on pp. 207-10.
17 See Kenner, *Pound Era,* pp. 460-95.
18 'Ed ascoltando . . .' (Pound's Italian;
not a quotation) might be rendered:
'and listening to the light murmur'. The
Greek word means 'knowing'. Paquin
is a Parisian dress designer. Wilfrid
Scawen Blunt (1840-1922), poet and
radical independent, was visited by
Pound (Stock, *Life,* pp. 187-8); the 'fine
old eye' is his.

Chapter 3. Personae

1 Eliot, Introduction, p. 20.
2 F. R. Leavis, *New Bearings in English
Poetry* (1932; 2nd edn., 1950, 1972),
p. 105.
3 Eliot, Introduction, p. 19.
4 These paragraphs are indebted to

Stock, *Life*, pp. 1–66, the most recent account.
5 Ford, *Return to Yesterday*, p. 370.
6 Matthew Arnold, 'The Function of Criticism at the Present Time', *Essays in Criticism, First Series* (1865), ed. Kenneth Allott (London, 1964), p. 19.
7 See John Heath-Stubbs, 'The Last Humanist', in *Ezra Pound: A Collection of Essays*, ed. Peter Russell (1950), pp. 249–56.
8 For example, the works of T. H. Jackson and Hugh Witemeyer; see bibliography.
9 'A Retrospect' (1918); *LE*, p. 3.
10 T. S. Eliot, *The Use of Poetry and the Use of Criticism* (1933), chs. 4 and 5.
11 *Mauberley*, 'E.P. Ode'.
12 To be distinguished from *Personae: Collected Shorter Poems (1926)* (New York, 1926).
13 See Christine Brooke-Rose, *A ZBC of Ezra Pound* (1971), pp. 213 ff.
14 T. S. Eliot, 'Macavity: the Mystery Cat', *Old Possum's Book of Practical Cats* (London, 1939); in *Complete Poems and Plays*, p. 226.
15 'Vorticism', *Fortnightly Review*, vol. XCVI, no. 573 (1 Sept. 1914), pp. 463–4; quoted from K. K. Ruthven, *A Guide to Ezra Pound's 'Personae' (1926)* (1969), pp. 7–8.
16 *T.P.'s Weekly* (6 June 1913), p. 707; quoted from Ruthven, p. 218.
17 *SR*, p. 87, where Pound states that 'This chapter was first published in G. R. S. Mead's *The Quest*, about 1916'.
18 F. Hueffer, *The Troubadours* (London, 1878). Ford's 'On Heaven' appears in *Confucius to Cummings*, ed. Ezra Pound and Marcella Spann (1964), pp. 290–302; Pound's comment quoted from Ruthven, p. 250.
19 *SR*, p. 41.
20 See *The Oxford Book of Mediaeval English Verse*, ed. C. and K. Sisam (Oxford, 1970), nos. 43 and 188.
21 *The Oxford Book of Italian Verse*, ed. St. John Lucas, 2nd edn. rev. C. Dionisotti (Oxford, 1952), p. 40.
22 See T. S. Eliot, *Ezra Pound: His Metric and Poetry* (1917), extracted in *Ezra Pound: A Critical Anthology*, ed. J. P. Sullivan (1970), pp. 67–80.

23 Reprinted in *CEP*, pp. 36, 43, 71 ('Histrion' appeared in 1908; see *CEP*, p. 299).
24 Uncollected adaptation: *CEP*, p. 125. For the Vidal poem, see *SR*, p. 49. The refrain is from 'En un vergier', quoted in Ruthven, pp. 166–7.
25 Recalled in Canto 76.
26 *SR*, pp. 96–7.

Chapter 4. Ripostes

1 Eliot, Introduction, p. 12.
2 See Chapter 3, note 10.
3 See Davie, *Pound*, Introduction, for discussion and references; also Daniel Cory, 'Ezra Pound: A Memoir', *Encounter*, vol. XXX, no. 5 (1968), extracted in Sullivan, *Critical Anthology*, pp. 374–6.
4 'Praise of Ysolt', *CSP*, p. 29.
5 'Fratres Minores', *CSP*, p. 168.
6 John Masefield, 'Cargoes', *Poems*, rev. edn. (London, 1946), p. 906. Compare Pound's 'Idols and ambergris and rare inlays' with Masefield's 'Firewood, iron-ware, and cheap tin trays'.
7 T. S. Eliot, 'Portrait of a Lady', *Complete Poems and Plays*, p. 20.
8 Translated by Peter Whigham, *The Poems of Catullus* (1966), pp. 53–4.
9 See Charlton T. Lewis and Charles Short, *A Latin Dictionary* (New York, 1879). See also J. P. Sullivan, *Ezra Pound and Sextus Propertius* (Austin, Texas, 1964), on Alexandrianism (pp. 39–41) and on *logopoeia* (pp. 64 ff.).
10 Ruthven, p. 1.
11 Samuel Johnson, 'Life of Pope', *Lives of the English Poets* (1779–81), ed. L. Archer-Hind (London, 1925), vol. II, p. 222.
12 Robert Frost, quoted in *The Poem Itself*, ed. Stanley Burnshaw (Harmondsworth, 1964), p. xi.
13 *CSP*, p. 54. See Ruthven, pp. 207–8.
14 Pope, 'An Essay on Criticism', l. 298, in *Poems*, ed. Butt, p. 153.
15 ibid., ll. 130–5. Samuel Johnson, *Preface to Shakespeare* (1765), in *Johnson on Shakespeare*, ed. W. Raleigh, rev. edn. (Oxford, 1925), p. 11.

16 Claude Lévi-Strauss, 'The Structural Study of Myth', in *Myth: A Symposium*, ed. Thomas A. Sebeok (Bloomington, Ind., 1955), pp. 81–106.

17 In *'Dubliners* and Mr James Joyce', *The Egoist*, vol. I, no. 14 (15 July 1914), pp. 399–402; quoted from *Pound/Joyce*, ed. F. Read, p. 28.

18 Phrases quoted from *The New Age* (14 Nov. 1912), p. 33, and *Umbra* (London, 1920), p. 128; see Ruthven, pp. 212, 214.

19 Pound's 'Philological note' accompanying first publication, *The New Age*, vol. X, no. 5 (30 Nov. 1911), pp. 213–14; *CEP*, p. 311.

20 'We would write nothing that we might not say actually in life—under emotion'—Preface, *The Poetical Works of Lionel Johnson* (1915), p. vi.

21 Eliot, Introduction, p. 12.

22 J. R. R. Tolkien, 'Prefatory Remarks' in *Beowulf and the Finnesburg Fragment*, trans. J. Clark Hall and C. L. Wrenn, rev. edn. (London, 1950), p. xx.

23 W. P. Ker, *Mediaeval English Literature* (London, 1912), p. 42. Compare: 'Until the 17th century, nearly all English translations were good, perhaps because scholars were more often educated'—David Hawkes, 'Translating from the Chinese', *Encounter* (July 1955), pp. 83–6.

24 Thomas Jefferson, *An Essay Towards Facilitating Instruction in the Anglo-Saxon Dialect* . . . (Charlottesville, Va., 1851).

25 See note 19 above. The current edition of *Sweet's Anglo-Saxon Reader*, rev. D. Whitelock (1970), omits ll. 109–24 as 'very corrupt', p. 227. But see *The Seafarer*, ed. I. L. Gordon (1960), p.11.

26 Wordsworth's letter of 1 May 1805, quoted in *The Prelude* (1805), ed. E. de Selincourt, rev. H. Darbishire (Oxford, 1960), p. xii.

27 *The New Age* (15 Feb. 1912), p. 369; quoted from Ruthven, p. 213.

28 See K. Sisam, 'Mr. Pound and "The Seafarer",' *Times Literary Supplement*, no. 2734 (25 June 1954), p. 409.

29 See note 18 above. 'At the Heart o' Me', *CEP*, p. 81.

30 With the Revd. J. D. 'Bib' Ibbotson. See Stock, *Life*, pp. 22–5. Kenner, *Pound Era*, p. 354, quotes an unpublished letter at Yale in which Pound says: 'the CANTOS started in a talk with "BIB".'

31 ' "The sublime" ': *Mauberley*, 'E. P. Ode'.

32 Eliot, Introduction, pp. 13, 14.

33 ibid., p. 17.

34 *Fortnightly Review* (1 Sept. 1914), p. 464; quoted from Ruthven, p. 204.

35 Pound's doctrine: *LE*, p. 9. W. C. Williams's principles: see his *Paterson: Books I–V* (London, 1964), p. 18; and 'Asphodel, that Greeny Flower', *Pictures from Breughel* (London, 1963), p. 179.

Chapter 5. Lustra

1 *'Cui dono* . . .' ('To whom shall I present my neat little new book') opens the *Carmina Catulli*.

2 See Kenner, *Pound Era*, pp. 138–44.

3 Eliot, Introduction, p. 13.

4 From the last line of 'A Girl', *CSP*, p. 75.

5 Eliot, *Ezra Pound: His Metric and Poetry*; quoted from Sullivan, *Critical Anthology*, p. 76.

6 Pope, *Poems*, ed. Butt, p. 598. Horace's nine-year counsel: *Ars poetica*, l. 388.

7 *Letters*, p. 35.

8 See *Pound/Joyce*, ed. Read, p. 146.

9 Eliot, Introduction, p. 19. Absence of Christianity: see Noel Stock, *Reading the Cantos* (1965).

10. A. C. Swinburne, 'Hymn to Proserpine', *Poems* (London, 1909), vol. I, p. 67.

11 For example, see *Guide to Kulchur* (1938), p. 77.

12 See Canto 77.

13 Also the poems listed on p. 82.

14 Leavis, *New Bearings*, p. 117.

15 See *Confucius to Cummings*, Appendix 1; and Davie, *Pound*, pp. 46–51.

16 From 'Histrion', *CEP*, p. 299.

17 See *LE*, pp. 3, 9.

18 ibid.

19 *Fortnightly Review* (1 Sept. 1914), pp. 465, 467; quoted from Ruthven, p. 153.
20 John Donne, *The Complete English Poems*, ed. A. J. Smith (Harmondsworth, 1971), pp. 41, 84, 54.
21 'A Few Don'ts', *LE*, p. 4.
22 W. B. Yeats, Introduction to *The Oxford Book of Modern Verse* (1936), p. xxvi.
23 Donne, *Complete English Poems*, ed. Smith, p. 60.
24 Robert Herrick, 'Upon Julia's Clothes', *Poetical Works*, ed. L. S. Martin (Oxford, 1956), p. 261; Donne, 'Elegy 4', *Complete English Poems*, ed. Smith, p. 100.
25 'The Beautiful Toilet', *CSP*, p. 138.
26 'High are the mountains and the valleys dark': *Le Chanson de Roland*, ed. F. Whitehead (Oxford, 1942), l. 814.

however, uses syllabic metres with striking success.
10 Nadezhda Mandelstam, *Hope Against Hope*, trans. M. Hayward (London, 1971), p. 246.
11 Eliot, Introduction, p. 15.
12 ibid.
13 See Cooper, *passim*.
14 Pound preferred the early Yeats. See *Confucius to Cummings*, pp. 287–9.
15 See Kenner, loc. cit., and Donald Davie, *Ezra Pound: Poet as Sculptor* (1964), pp. 41–6.
16 Kenner, op. cit., pp. 212–13.
17 Arthur Waley, *The Poetry and Career of Li Po* (London, 1950), p. 11.
18 *Cathay* (London, 1915), p. 32. In it he speaks of 'the personal hatred in which I am held by many'.

Chapter 6. Cathay

1 For details of further complications, see Kenner, *Pound Era*, pp. 192–222.
2 *Cathay* (1915) was followed by Arthur Waley's *Chinese Poems* (London, 1916) and *170 Chinese Poems* (London, 1918). See Wai-lim Yip, *Ezra Pound's 'Cathay'* (1969), for discussion and references. Compare A. C. Graham, *Poems of the Late T'ang* (1965); David Hawkes, *A Little Primer of Tu Fu* (1967); and Arthur Cooper, *Li Po and Tu Fu* (1973).
3 Fenollosa's 'Essay on the Chinese Written Character' appeared in Pound's *Instigations* (1920). See Cooper, *Li Po and Tu Fu*, pp. 84–6.
4 'A Retrospect' *LE*, pp. 3–5.
5 Bentley: 'A pretty poem, Mr. Pope; but you must not call it *Homer*' (James Boswell, *Life of Samuel Johnson, LL.D.*, ed. G. B. Hill, rev. L. F. Powell (Oxford, 1934–6), vol. III, pp. 256–7). For the comment on Pope's Greek, see Johnson, 'Life of Pope', *Lives of the English Poets*, ed. Archer-Hind, vol. II, p. 158.
6 See Yip and Kenner, as above.
7 Johnson, op. cit., p. 154.
8 Yip, pp. 88, 163.
9 Eliot, Introduction, p. 14. Cooper,
8*

Chapter 7. Propertius and *Mauberley*

1 Kenner, *Pound Era*, p. 143.
2 But see G. S. Fraser, *Ezra Pound* (1960), pp. 48–52.
3 Alluded to in Canto 80.
4 For a much amplified version of the Noh plays, with introduction by Pound, see *The Translations of Ezra Pound*, ed. Hugh Kenner (1953), pp. 213–360.
5 Letter (31 March 1921) quoted and discussed, Davie, *Pound*, pp. 46–52.
6 Johnson, Preface to Shakespeare, in *Johnson on Shakespeare*, ed. Raleigh, pp. 35–6.
7 *Catulli Tibulli Propertii Carmina* recensuit Lucianus Mueller, Lipsiae, 1892, was Pound's text; see Sullivan, *Ezra Pound and Sextus Propertius*, p. 111. The lines quoted are Book II, Elegy 32, ll. 65–6 in Mueller.
8 *The Elegies of Propertius*, trans. P. J. F. Gantillon (1912). Pound refers to this Bohn edition twice; Sullivan, op. cit., pp. 8, 11.
9 Sullivan, op. cit., p. 111, gives a selection.
10 Gantillon, p. 131.
11 Gilbert Highet, *Poets in a Landscape* (1957; 1959), pp. 91, 92.

12 'Ride to Lanuvium', Sullivan, op. cit., pp. 8, 11.
13 Gantillon, p. 79.
14 Highet, in *Horizon* (January 1961); quoted in Sullivan, op. cit., p. ix.
15 Highet, *Poets in a Landscape*, p. 87.
16 Sullivan, op. cit., p. 5, discusses Pound's attitude to such minutiae. Sullivan suggested some emendations, of which Pound sanctioned a few but rejected others (p. 109). Thus all but one of the idiosyncrasies exemplified here from section i of the *Homage* are retained in the critical text Sullivan prints.
17 Fraser, *Ezra Pound*, p. 66.
18 Letter to Iris Barry (27 July 1916), *Letters*, p. 142.
19 J. J. Espey, *Ezra Pound's 'Mauberley': A Study in Composition* (1955), provides a scholarly foundation. See also, apart from Eliot, Introduction, and Leavis, *New Bearings*, Hugh Kenner, *The Poetry of Ezra Pound* (1951), pp. 169 ff., and discussions by Davie (*Pound*, pp. 52–5, for references and revisions).
20 Kenner, *The Poetry of Ezra Pound*, p. 170.
21 Espey, Ch. 2, especially p. 36.
22 Sullivan, *Critical Anthology*, p. 333.
23 Leavis, *New Bearings*, p. 110.
24 Espey, p. 70.
25 ibid., p. 98.
26 Quoted from Davie, *Pound*, p. 51.

Chapter 8. The Cantos

1 All bibliographical information drawn from Gallup.
2 See '*Ulysses*, Order and Myth', *The Dial*, November 1923; quoted from *Selected Prose of T. S. Eliot*, ed. Frank Kermode (1975), pp. 175–8.
3 The letter to Homer L. Pound of 11 April 1927 is enlightening:
Dear Dad: —/—/ Afraid the whole damn poem is rather obscure, especially in fragments. Have I ever given you outline of main scheme ::: or whatever it is?
  1. Rather like, or unlike subject and response and counter subject in fugue.

A. A. Live man goes down into world of Dead
C. B. The "repeat in history"
B. C. The "magic moment" or moment of metamorphosis, bust thru from quotidien into "divine or permanent world". Gods, etc.
Letters, pp. 284–5; see also ibid., p. 386. Also Yeats, *A Packet for Ezra Pound* (1928), pp. 1–4; *Oxford Book of Modern Verse*, pp. xxiii–xxv.
4 Davie, *Pound*, p. 73.
5 Johnson, 'Life of Milton', *Lives of the English Poets*, vol. I, p. 108.
6 Eliot, Introduction, p. 12.
7 Pound, 'Date Line', *Make It New* (1934); *LE*, p. 86.
8 Yeats: 'Form must be full, sphere-like, single', *Oxford Book of Modern Verse*, p. xxv. Yvor Winters, *The Anatomy of Nonsense* (1943); quoted from Sullivan, *Critical Anthology*, p. 198.
9 Augustine, *On Christian Doctrine*: 'What is attended with difficulty in the seeking gives greater pleasure in the finding'; *The Works of Aurelius Augustinus*, ed. M. Dods (London, 1873), vol. IX, p. 38.
10 W. C. Williams: see, e.g., 'Marianne Moore', *Selected Essays* (1954), p. 125.
11 Pound, *Impact: Essays on Ignorance and the Decline of American Civilization*, ed. Noel Stock (1960), p. 177.
12 *Letters*, loc. cit.
13 *Guide to Kulchur* (1938), p. 194.
14 T. S. Eliot, *After Strange Gods: A Primer of Modern Heresy* (1934); quoted from Sullivan, *Critical Anthology*, p. 182.
15 *Selected Cantos*, p. 9.
16 Personal conversation.
17 *Selected Cantos*, p. 9.
18 'a butterfly': Cooper, *Li Po and Tu Fu*, p. 36; the 'Old Poem', p. 141.
19 Yeats, *Oxford Book of Modern Verse*, p. xxiii.
20 'If we never write anything save what is already understood, the field of understanding will never be extended' (Canto 96). ' "You damn sadist!" said mr. cummings,/"you try to make people think" ' (Canto 89). 'I shall have to learn a little greek to keep up with this/ but so will you, drratt you' (Canto 105).
21 See Forrest Read, review of *Ezra*

Pound: Selected Prose 1909–1945, ed.
William Cookson, in Paideuma, vol. III,
no. 1 (1974), pp. 125–8.

Literary Supplement of 28 Aug. 1970
(p. 951) and 11 Sept. 1970 (p. 998).

Chapter 9. Cantos 1–17

1 'Andreas Divus', The Egoist, vol. V,
nos. 8 (September 1918) and 9 (October
1918); now Part II of 'Early Translators
of Homer', LE, pp. 259–67.
2 See Kenner, Pound Era, especially
p. 361.
3 See discussions in Daniel D. Pearlman,
The Barb of Time: On the Unity of
Pound's 'Cantos' (1969); Christine
Brooke-Rose, A ZBC of Ezra Pound
(1971). On sources, see Eva Hesse,
'Books behind the Cantos, I: Cantos
1–30', Paideuma, vol. I, no. 2 (1972),
pp. 137–51.
4 T. S. Eliot, 'Burbank with a Baedeker
. . .', Complete Poems and Plays,
pp. 40–1.
5 Pope, The Dunciad, IV, 307–8; Poems,
ed. Butt, p. 782:

But chief her shrine where naked
   Venus keeps
And Cupids ride the Lyon of the
   Deeps.

6 See Bernetta M. Quinn, 'The
Metamorphoses of Ezra Pound', in
Motive and Method in 'The Cantos' of
Ezra Pound, ed. Lewis Leary (1964),
pp. 60–100.
7 A common formula in the Iliad, as in
Book I, where Achilles walks by 'the
much-roaring sea'.
8 The Commentaries of Pope Pius II,
Book 2, trans. F. Gragg, ed. L. Gabel
(Northampton, Mass., 1937); quoted
from The Portable Medieval Reader, ed.
J. B. Ross and M. M. McLaughlin
(1949), pp. 288–9.
9 Jacob Burckhardt, The Civilisation of
the Renaissance in Italy (1860), trans.
S. G. C. Middlemore (1945).
10 See Dante, Inferno, V.
11 Walter Savage Landor, The Complete
Works, ed. T. E. Welby and S. Wheeler
(1927–36), vol. XV, p. 376.
12 Guide to Kulchur, p. 113.
13 F. R. Leavis, letters to the Times

Chapter 10. Cantos 18–71

1 Eliot, Introduction, p. 11.
2 Letters, p. 285.
3 See discussion in Kenner, Pound Era,
pp. 110–20.
4 Jane Harrison, Ancient Art and Ritual
(1927).
5 See Kenner, Pound Era, p. 354.
6 Pound explained the allusions in the
letter to his father (Letters, pp. 284–5).
See also discussions in Pearlman, pp. 98
ff., and Brooke-Rose, pp. 211–12.
7 Dante, Inferno, V.
8 Compare W. S. Landor's Imaginary
Conversation, Boccaccio and Petrarca,
Complete Works, ed. Welby and Wheeler,
vol. II, pp. 234–42.
9 W. B. Yeats, A Packet for Ezra Pound,
pp. 4–5.
10 In earlier British editions, Cantos
52–71 are instead followed by Notes to
similar effect.
11 Found only in earlier British editions.
12 See Forrest Read, 'A Man of No
Fortune', in Motive and Method, ed.
Leary, pp. 101–23.
13 See Kenner, Pound Era, pp. 445–59,
and Pearlman, Appendix B.
14 Kenner, op. cit., p. 433.
15 See note 10 above.

Chapter 11. The Pisan Cantos

1 See Stock, Life, p. 516.
2 See Kenner, Pound Era, pp. 460–95.
3 'Manes' (Mani), a Persian of the third
century B.C., founder of the Manichaean
religion. 'Dioce' is Deioces the Mede,
surnamed the Just, of the sixth century
B.C., founder of Ecbatana, a wonderful
city described by Herodotus; mentioned
in Cantos 4 and 5.
4 Women of Trachis (1956), p. 50.
5 John Milton, Poetical Works, ed.
D. Bush (Oxford, 1969), p. 252.
6 Carmina Catulli, 2, 'Passer, deliciae

meae puellae'. The impression of the *Inferno* is more general, but see Canto III, l. 52. Pound's Italian might be rendered: 'And the sad thought turns to Ussel. To Ventadour goes my grieving mind, and that time returns.'

7 Kenner, op. cit. Pound later acquired a verse anthology and a Bible.

8 Stephen Spender, 'Remembering Eliot', in *T. S. Eliot: The Man and his Work*, ed. Allen Tate (1967), pp. 55–6.

Chapter 12. After Pisa

1 'lath racquet', Canto 74; 'non casco in ginocchion' ', Canto 77.

2 See *ABC of Reading*, p. 36.

3 See Kenner, *Pound Era*, pp. 449–53.

4 See H. A. Mason, 'The *Women of Trachis* and Creative Translation', *Arion*, vol. II, 1963; in Sullivan, *Critical Anthology*, pp. 279–310.

5 See Stock, *Reading the Cantos*, pp. 106 ff., and *Paideuma*, e.g., vol. II, no. 2 (Fall 1973), on Leo the Eparch.

6 Sir Philip Sidney, *Defence of Poetry*, in *Miscellaneous Prose*, ed. K. Duncan-Jones and J. van Dorsten (Oxford, 1973), p. 112.

7 Comments on economics and structure: personal conversation. 'Botch' and '*brutto*' (ugly, badly made): see Davie, *Pound*, pp. 9–12.

8 E.g., J. J. Wilhelm, *The Later Cantos of Ezra Pound* (New York, 1977).

9 Personal conversation.

10 Robert Lowell, 'Ezra Pound', *History* (London, 1973), p. 140.

11 Eliot, 'East Coker', v, *Complete Poems and Plays*, p. 182.

12 Lowell, 'Ezra Pound', loc. cit.

13 Yeats, *Oxford Book of Modern Verse*, pp. xxv–xxvi.

14 An Eliotic phrase on jackets of Faber editions of the *Cantos*.

15 See also W. P. Ker as quoted in Eliot, *The Use of Poetry*, pp. 22–3.

16 Ezra Pound to Donald Hall, *Paris Review*, no. 28 (1962); quoted in Sullivan, *Critical Anthology*, p. 278.

17 T. S. Eliot, *Ezra Pound: His Metric and Poetry*; quoted from Sullivan, op. cit., pp. 79–80.

Select Bibliography

For works published in more than one country, the first British editions only are given.

WORKS BY EZRA POUND

VERSE

Pound's verse is now collected in the three standard editions cited below. Individual volumes of the early poems, and instalments of the *Cantos*, are mentioned in the Notes. Full details may be found in Donald Gallup, *A Bibliography of Ezra Pound*, London, 1963, 1969.

> *Collected Early Poems*, ed. M. J. King, London, 1977
> *Collected Shorter Poems*, London, 1952; 2nd edn., 1968
> *The Cantos of Ezra Pound*, London, 1975
> *Selected Poems*, ed. T. S. Eliot, London, 1928
> *Selected Cantos*, London, 1967
> *Selected Poems 1908–1959*, London, 1975

PROSE

A list of main works cited in the text and Notes.

> *The Spirit of Romance*, London, 1910; rev. edn., 1952
> *Gaudier-Brzeska*, London, 1916
> *Instigations*, New York, 1920
> *Indiscretions*, Paris, 1923
> *ABC of Reading*, London, 1934
> *Make it New*, London, 1934
> *Jefferson and/or Mussolini*, London, 1935
> *Guide to Kulchur*, London, 1938
> *The Letters of Ezra Pound 1907–1941*, ed. D. D. Paige, London, 1951
> *Literary Essays*, ed. T. S. Eliot, London, 1954
> *Impact: Essays on Ignorance and the Decline of American Civilization*, ed. Noel Stock, Chicago, 1960
> *Pound/Joyce, The Letters of Ezra Pound to James Joyce, with Pound's Essays on Joyce*, ed. Forrest Read, London, 1968
> *Selected Prose 1909–1965*, ed. William Cookson, London, 1973

TRANSLATIONS

> *The Translations of Ezra Pound*, ed. Hugh Kenner, London, 1953; rev. edn., 1970
> *The Classic Anthology Defined by Confucius*, London, 1955
> *Sophocles: Women of Trachis*, London, 1956

Certain Noble Plays of Japan, Dundrum, 1916
Ta Hio: The Great Learning, Seattle, Wash., 1928
Confucius: The Great Digest and the Unwobbling Pivot, London, 1952

ANTHOLOGIES, EDITIONS, etc.

Poetical Works of Lionel Johnson, with a Preface by Ezra Pound, London, 1915
Guido Cavalcanti Rime . . . , ed. Ezra Pound, Genoa, 1932
The Chinese Written Character as a Medium for Poetry, London, 1936
Confucius to Cummings: An Anthology of Poetry, ed. Ezra Pound and Marcella
    Spann, New York, 1964

WORKS ABOUT POUND

A list of works cited in the text and Notes, with a selection of other studies.

BIOGRAPHICAL

Cornell, Julien, *The Trial of Ezra Pound*, London, 1967
de Rachewiltz, Mary, *Discretions*, London, 1971
Hutchins, Patricia, *Ezra Pound's Kensington*, London, 1965
Norman, Charles, *Ezra Pound*, London, 1960; 2nd edn., 1969
Stock, Noel, *The Life of Ezra Pound*, London, 1970; 2nd edn., Harmonds-
    worth, 1974

CRITICAL

Agenda, vol. IV, no. 2 (1965) and vol. VIII, nos. 3–4 (1970), ed. William
    Cookson, London, 1960–
Brooke-Rose, Christine, *A ZBC of Ezra Pound*, London, 1971
Davie, Donald, *Ezra Pound: Poet as Sculptor*, London, 1964
—— *Pound*, London, 1975
Dekker, George, *Sailing After Knowledge: The Cantos of Ezra Pound*,
    London, 1963
Dembo, L. S., *The Confucian Odes of Ezra Pound*, London, 1963
Edwards, J. H., and Vasse, W. W., *The Annotated Index to the Cantos of
    Ezra Pound I–LXXXIV*, Berkeley, Calif., 1957
Eliot, T. S., *Ezra Pound: His Metric and Poetry*, Chicago, 1917
—— Introduction to *Selected Poems of Ezra Pound*, London, 1928
Emery, Clark, *Ideas into Action: A Study of Pound's Cantos*, Coral Gables,
    Fla., 1958
Espey, J. J., *Ezra Pound's 'Mauberley': A Study in Composition*, Berkeley,
    Calif., 1955
Fraser, G. S., *Ezra Pound*, Edinburgh, 1960
Gallup, Donald, *A Bibliography of Ezra Pound*, London, 1963; 2nd edn., 1969
Hesse, Eva (ed.), *New Approaches to Ezra Pound*, London, 1969
Homberger, Eric (ed.), *Ezra Pound: The Critical Heritage*, London, 1972
Jackson, Thomas H., *The Early Poetry of Ezra Pound*, Cambridge, Mass.,
    1969

Select Bibliography   239

Kenner, Hugh, *The Poetry of Ezra Pound*, London, 1951
—— *The Pound Era*, London, 1971
Leary, Lewis (ed.), *Motive and Method in 'The Cantos' of Ezra Pound*, New York, 1964
Leavis, F. R., *New Bearings in English Poetry*, London, 1932; 2nd edn., 1950
Paideuma: A journal devoted to Ezra Pound Scholarship, ed. Carroll F. Terrell, Orono, Maine, 1972–
Pearlman, Daniel D., *The Barb of Time: On the Unity of Pound's 'Cantos'*, Oxford, 1969
Rosenthal, M. L., *A Primer of Ezra Pound*, New York, 1960
Russell, Peter (ed.), *Ezra Pound: A Collection of Essays*, London, 1950
Ruthven, K. K., *A Guide to Ezra Pound's 'Personae' (1926)*, Berkeley, Calif., 1969
Stock, Noel, *Reading the Cantos*, London, 1965
Sullivan, J. P., *Ezra Pound and Sextus Propertius: A Study in Creative Translation*, London, 1965
—— (ed.), *Ezra Pound: A Critical Anthology*, Harmondsworth, 1970
Witemeyer, Hugh, *The Poetry of Ezra Pound: Forms and Renewals 1908–1920*, Berkeley, Calif., 1969
Yeats, W. B., *A Packet for Ezra Pound*, Dublin, 1928. Reprinted in *A Vision*, Dundrum, 1962
—— Introduction to *The Oxford Book of Modern Verse*, Oxford, 1936
Yip, Wai-lim, *Ezra Pound's 'Cathay'*, Princeton, N.J., 1969

PRINCIPAL OTHER WORKS CITED

A selection of general works cited in the text and Notes. Bibliographical details of other works cited in passing will be found at the appropriate place in the Notes.

Benton, Thomas Hart, *Thirty Years View; or, A History of the Working of the American Government for Thirty Years, 1820–1850*, New York, 1854–6
Burckhardt, Jacob, *The Civilisation of the Renaissance in Italy*, Basel, 1860; trans. S. G. C. Middlemore, Oxford and London, 1945
Cooper, Arthur, *Li Po and Tu Fu*, Harmondsworth, 1973
Del Mar, Alexander, *Barbara Villiers; or, A History of Monetary Crimes*, New York, 1899
de Mailla, J.-A. M. Moyriac, *Histoire générale de la Chine*, 12 vols., 1777–83
Eliot, T. S., *After Strange Gods: A Primer of Modern Heresy*, London, 1934
—— *Complete Poems and Plays*, London, 1969
—— *Selected Prose*, ed. Frank Kermode, London, 1975
—— *The Use of Poetry and the Use of Criticism*, London, 1933
Ford, Ford Madox, *Provence*, London, 1938
—— *Return to Yesterday*, London, 1931
Gantillon, P. J. F. (trans.), *The Elegies of Propertius*, London, 1912
Giles, H. A., *A History of Chinese Literature*, London, 1901
Gordon, I. L. (ed.), *The Seafarer*, London, 1960
Graham, A. C., *Poems of the Late T'ang*, Harmondsworth, 1965
Harrison, Jane, *Ancient Art and Ritual*, London, 1927

Hawkes, David, *A Little Primer of Tu Fu*, Oxford, 1967

Highet, Gilbert, *Poets in a Landscape*, London, 1957; Harmondsworth, 1959

Landor, Walter Savage, *Complete Works*, ed. T. E. Welby and S. Wheeler, 16 vols., London, 1927–36

Mueller, L. (ed.), *Catulli Tibulli Propertii Carmina*, Leipzig, 1892

Ross, J. B. and McLaughlin, M. M., *The Portable Medieval Reader*, New York, 1949

Tate, Allen (ed.), *T. S. Eliot: The Man and His Work*, Harmondsworth, 1967

Whigham, Peter, *The Poems of Catullus*, Harmondsworth, 1966

Whitelock, D. (ed.), *Sweet's Anglo–Saxon Reader*, Oxford, 1970

Williams, William Carlos, *Selected Essays*, New York, 1954

Winters, Yvor, *The Anatomy of Nonsense*, New York, 1943

Yeats, W. B., *Collected Poems*, London, 1950

Index

305.5   Gilbert, Charlene.
GIL
          Homecoming.

DATE		

305.5 GIL 2000

Gilbert, Charlene.
Homecoming : the story of
African-American farmers.

HOMECOMING

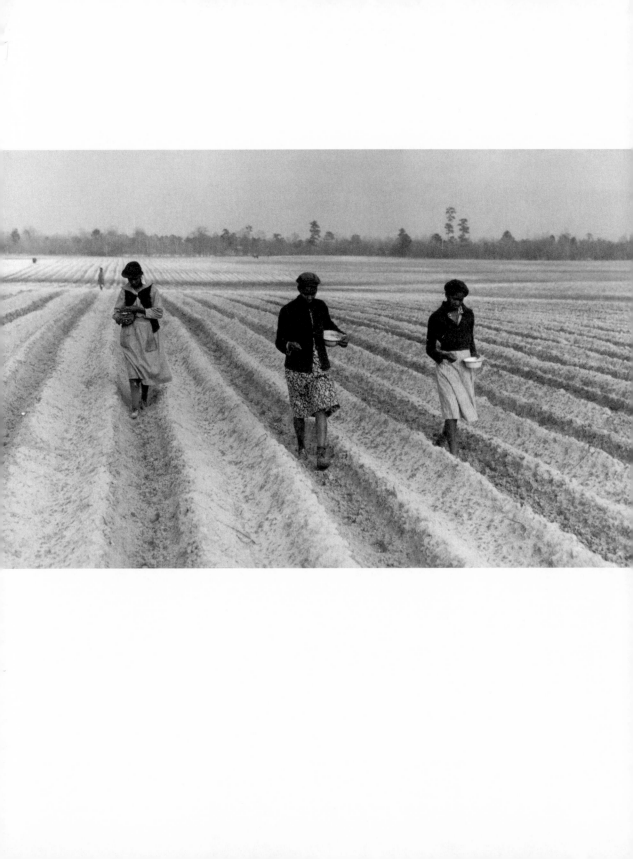

Charlene Gilbert and Quinn Eli

HOMECOMING

THE STORY OF AFRICAN-AMERICAN FARMERS

Beacon Press : : BOSTON

FOR MR. FRED H. MATHIS SR.,

10.13.1904 – 8.16.1983

BEACON PRESS

25 Beacon Street Boston, Massachusetts

02108-2892 *www.beacon.org*

Beacon Press books are published under the auspices
of the Unitarian Universalist Association of Congregations.

Based on the film *Homecoming,* produced for the Independent Television Service
with funding provided by the Corporation for Public Broadcasting.

Grateful acknowledgment is made to Furthermore, the publication program of the
J. M. Kaplan Fund, whose generous bequest to Beacon Press helped make the publication
of this book possible.

05 04 03 02 01 00   8 7 6 5 4 3 2 1

This book is printed on acid-free paper that meets the uncoated paper
ANSI/NISO specifications for permanence as revised in 1992.

Composition by Wilsted & Taylor Publishing Services   Design by Lucinda Hitchcock

LIBRARY OF CONGRESS CATALOGING-IN-PUBLICATION DATA
Gilbert, Charlene.   Homecoming : the story of African-American farmers / Charlene
Gilbert and Quinn Eli. p. cm.   Includes bibliographical references and index.
ISBN 0-8070-0962-8 (hardcover : alk. paper) 1. Freedmen – Southern States – Economic
conditions. 2. Afro-American farmers – Southern States – Economic conditions.
 3. Afro-Americans – Southern States – Land tenure – History. 4. Freedmen –
Southern States – Social conditions. 5. Afro-American farmers – Southern States –
Social conditions. 6. Southern States – Economic conditions. 7. Land tenure – Southern States –
History. 8. Southern States – Race relations. I. Eli, Quinn. II. Title. E185.8 .G52 2000
305.5'63'08996073075 – DC21   00-008995

CONTENTS

PHOTOGRAPHS

PLATE 1

PLATE 2

PLATE 3

PLATE 4

PLATE 6

PLATE 7

PLATE 8

PLATE 9

PLATE 10

PLATE 11

PLATE 12

PLATE 13

PLATE 14

PLATE 15

PLATE 16

PLATE 17

PLATE 18

PLATE 19

PLATE 20

PLATE 21

PLATE 22

PLATE 23

PLATE 24

PLATE 26

PLATE 27

PLATE 28

PLATE 29

PLATE 30

PLATE 31

HOMECOMING

I began Homecoming, *a personal documentary film on African-American farmers in the southern United States, the day I discovered that my uncle Leroy James Sr. was about to lose his life's work and land. This particular moment coincided with my discovery that thousands of African-American rural communities were under siege, struggling against a systematic effort to remove black farmers from their land and their livelihood.* Homecoming *began as a historical investigation and evolved into a personal journey. On that journey I discovered the power of community, family, and tradition.*

For all of us who have never toiled in hundred-degree sun with a six-year-old child at our knees, the South can be a romanticized dream of family or a nightmare of burned bodies hanging from trees. What I discovered in the telling of this history was the importance of the land to those who continue to work it and in working it honor those who spilled their blood to escape it. I shot the documentary Homecoming *in Montezuma, Georgia, on the same land that held up the world for the young "smart Negro" children of the fifties and sixties who dreamed of lives off the farm, who dreamed of labor free of sweat, and who dreamed of giving their sons and daughters a world of choices beyond forty acres and a mule. As the granddaughter of a farmer who offered up his land so that his daughter, my mother, might discover new dreams beyond those that ended in rows of cotton, so that his granddaughter might never know the smell of exhaustion, I offer my film,* Homecoming, *for Fred H. Mathis Sr. And now, with the help of a brilliant writer, Quinn Eli, I offer more of this compelling history in a companion volume to the film. I hope together the film and book tell a powerful story of land, love, and loss.*

— C.G.

Whatever the Civil War accomplished – or failed to accomplish – its aftermath changed the world of the white Southern farmer beyond recognition. His identity as slaveholder, his membership in the Southern wing
of the Whig Party – which contained gentleman farmers and yeoman
farmers alike – and the very fabric of the land that stretched before him
had disintegrated. For these reasons, then, the word *reconstruction* can
be taken quite literally. Reconstruction refers to the era (generally 1865
through 1877) when the American political, social, and economic system
had been all but blown apart, and the American people were forced to
design, build, and establish a new system to replace the one that had
been destroyed.

More than a dozen years passed before the country's efforts at reconstruction began to cohere in 1877, and even then the continued loss
of life and the unrelenting human suffering left an indelible mark on the
country's future. During the course of this difficult and painful process
an African-American body politic was shaped – if only in answer to the

question of where four million freed slaves would fit into this new, reconstructed union of states. Having worked the land and contributed to its growth with their own lives, enslaved Africans had been promised freedom and land of their own during the Civil War — on the condition that they side with the Union and take up arms against the Confederates. In time, of course, these promises made by the Union would prove unreliable, and the massive disfranchisement of freed slaves by legal means (through many court decisions and amendments to state constitutions) as well as by more violent methods would shape the destiny of African-Americans in the South.

That these men and women managed to accumulate land at all throughout Reconstruction, however, is testament to their strength, tenacity, and faith. That so much of the land was taken from them is certainly criminal. That their legacy is still very much alive remains an indisputable fact. This legacy exists in the soil itself and in the memories of their children and grandchildren who can tell a story that is rarely told . . . a story that grew out of the land.

part one

THE PROMISE OF LAND :: 1850–1899

1.

TAKING ROOT :: The Civil War and Reconstruction

My great-great-grandfather William Mathis is sort of a mystery in my family. Our family
history begins with his life. He was the first freedman in my maternal family line. There are
lots of stories about him but none that are ever told in the official family record. The story I
constructed as a child was that he was a light-skinned teacher who came to the South just after
the Civil War. Another story is that his father was white, which perhaps is why there is no
paternal history beyond this point — or at least none that we choose to pursue.

I like my story of the schoolteacher best. I like to think that William Mathis was a free
man from Philadelphia or Boston, that he came to start a school in a small rural farm
community, that he joined with others to build a free, educated, land-owning "Negro"
community that still stands to this day in south-central Georgia. This is the story of a place
where with every breath, every newborn child, and every chosen name, the descendants of
enslaved Africans, the descendants of William Mathis, live and celebrate freedom every day.

My great-great-grandparents William and Alice had one child together, Bill Mathis.

For some reason William Mathis left Montezuma, Georgia, and his small family sometime in the late nineteenth century and was never heard from again. Alice went on to have thirteen other children. One of the youngest of those children is my great-great-uncle A. B. Brown, who still lives in a modest farmhouse in Montezuma. I have asked my uncle A.B. if he knows what happened to William, who he was and where he was from, but Uncle A.B. doesn't have much to say on the subject, just nods and says he "can't really say," which is a long way from "I don't know." My uncle J. W. Mathis says that sometimes old folks hold secrets for us that we don't need to know. He figures that Uncle A.B. has his reasons for knowing but not telling and we should respect that. I guess some stories we leave behind: in the wind, in the land, or in the shadows of our memories. So I can't really say too much about how our story begins, but I can say: "Once upon a time there was a man named William Mathis. I am his great-great-granddaughter and this is my family story."

NO ONE had any idea where to go, what to do, or how even to live.

Long after the Civil War had ended and victory had been declared by the Union army, even President Abraham Lincoln wondered aloud what to do with the newly emancipated slaves. To his closest advisers and friends, the president conceded that he could see no way to accommodate them successfully in the country's wounded, hostile, and racially charged atmosphere. There seemed no way for these freed black Americans to live prosperously in such convulsive times.

Predictably, every interested party on either side of the Mason-Dixon had an opinion on the subject. There were those who wanted the slaves freed all at once, and others who felt that a slow integration into society was the best course of action. This last suggestion was made by the most prudent of the abolitionist groups, but even their temperate approach was rejected by those white landowners who vowed to continue fighting – sometimes killing their slaves, one by one – rather than accede to what they considered Lincoln's unacceptable demand that all slaves be emancipated.

Taken together, these voices must have sounded like a continuous buzz in the president's head, a clamor that would not desist, even in sleep. At last, in 1865, Lincoln approached Massachusetts statesman and former Union general Ben Butler and asked him to come up with a plan. The president had in mind a plan of voluntary deportation. He wanted Butler to evaluate the logistics of deporting the recently freed slaves to Africa or some other horizon distant from American shores. Butler didn't have to deliberate on the logistics for very long, however. Within days, as quoted in historian Lerone Bennett's *Before the Mayflower: A History of Black America,* Butler reported to Lincoln that even if the president mobilized "all . . . naval vessels and all the merchant marines fit to cross the sea with safety, it will be impossible [to export all the Negroes of the South] . . . to the nearest place . . . half as fast as Negro children will be born here." In effect, Butler's answer was no different than what the abolitionist Frederick Douglass had been saying all along: the Negro was now a fixture on the American horizon, no more likely to disappear than the horizon itself.

No one had any idea where to go, what to do, or how even to live.

Like a person resentful of being spoken about in the third person while standing in the same room – "What shall we *do* about him?" – Douglass took offense at the heady discussion in newspapers, white households, and the executive office about the fate of the Negro. He insisted that the Negroes should decide for themselves their own next step – an approach, Douglass argued, that was already long overdue and the only possible solution to the crime of having denied black Americans their inalienable rights for so long. "Do nothing with the Negro," said

Douglass, also quoted in *Before the Mayflower,* in his bold baritone that thrilled as well as frightened those around him. "Your *doing* with [Negroes] is their greatest misfortune. . . . The Negro should have been let alone in Africa . . . let alone when the pirates and robbers offered him for sale in our Christian slave markets . . . let alone by the courts, judges, politicians and slave drivers." To the question that seemed to hover at everyone's lips — what is to be done about the Negro? — Douglass answered boldly and definitively: Nothing. "If you see [the Negro] on his way to school, with spelling book, geography and arithmetic in his hand — let him alone. . . . If he has a ballot in his hand, and is on his way to the ballot-box to deposit his vote for the man whom he thinks will most justly and wisely administer the Government which has the power of life and death over him, as well as others — let him alone."

Of all the occupations that might be assumed by American blacks — occupations that they should be allowed to pursue without the burden of some politically motivated intervention — Douglass reserved his most emphatic plea on behalf of black families who chose to make a life for themselves by cultivating land: "If you see [the Negro] plowing in the open field, leveling the forest, at work with a spade, a rake, a hoe, a pick-axe, or a bill — *let him alone!* He has a right to work." These words must have resonated clearly, because not long afterward Pennsylvania congressman Thaddeus Stevens took a cue from Douglass's remarks and added to it his own suggestion: give the Negro forty acres of land and a mule.

It was not exactly a new idea. In the South there was no greater currency than land, and during the Civil War, Union soldiers often attempted to secure the loyalty of blacks by making implicit — some say explicit — promises of land. This powerful incentive resulted in African-Americans offering their services to the Union soldiers as they marched across an unfamiliar landscape. As part of Sherman's plan to move through the South with as few supplies as possible – in order to move more quickly – Sherman enlisted the service of local African-Americans for information about the location of smokehouses and wells where food and water could be obtained. Occasionally he enlisted them to fight as well. Although Sherman could not pay the African-Americans directly for their help, he offered to reimburse them with land in the event of a Union victory. He also offered the promise that the Union would swiftly overturn the Dred Scott decision of 1857 (and the simultaneous decision of the U.S. Land Office to deny African-Americans public land grants), which would ensure that blacks could easily obtain land even after the Union army had departed the South.

Similarly, the Confederate army made a few promises of their own. Even more amenable to blacks fighting in the war than was the Union army – which had debated the issue for months – the Confederates installed a policy by which a slave who showed "particular valor" would be given freedom and allowed to work locally. Given that the biggest local industry was agriculture, this suggested an implicit promise of land. When the war was over, however, the Confederates were in no position to honor their promises. And the victors, the Union army, proved unreliable: in the end they had proven more interested in promising land than in delivering that land into the hands of blacks who could have used it to build new and better lives.

The Reverend Garrison Frazier no doubt chose his own first name. He was an ex-slave who purchased his and his wife's freedom in 1859 for $1,000. The money had been accumulated over the years, the sum total of a life of diving for stray pennies in the dust and accepting secret gifts from freed relations who had made it to paying jobs in the North. In addition to their modest gifts, Frazier's freed relations told him often of a great abolitionist named William Lloyd Garrison.

Long before Frazier knew how to read or write, he prided himself on his ability to listen, and eventually it occurred to him that he had listened so often to stories about Garrison that he felt as though he knew the man personally. It also occurred to him that such a great friend to blacks deserved a namesake of African descent – someone to promote the interests of enslaved Africans in Georgia, as Garrison did in every corner of the country. So the Reverend Garrison Frazier was born.

His freedom secured, Frazier knew instantly that true freedom would be his only if he could purchase land and work it for profit and as a means of keeping his family self-reliant. Turning his faith to God – and learning to read the Bible so that he might share its stories with others – Frazier acquired enough land to make a start for himself, even as those around him continued to struggle in bondage.

Frazier's first opportunity to speak on behalf of his people arrived on Christmas Day 1864, shortly after Union general William Tecumseh Sherman and his forces arrived in Savannah, Georgia. Sherman was greeted by whites with bitter animosity – many left the city entirely to avoid a skirmish – but blacks perceived the Union army as agents of liberation and lined the streets to greet them. Before the general's arrival, Secretary of War Edwin McMasters Stanton had arranged a meeting between black leaders and Sherman to discuss some of the charges and rumors of brutality inflicted on blacks by rogue Union soldiers. Frazier was at that meeting and served as the group's spokesperson. By now, Sherman had become almost giddy with the scent of triumph, and indeed his long "March to the Sea" through Georgia was considered by many whites to be a cruel and vindictive parade, meant to rub salt in the wounds of the deteriorating Confederacy. Sherman did not have a clear sense at this point of what the Negro might need, and probably he was not concerned with these matters. He saw himself as deliverer – as an angel of retribution – and many blacks shared that perspective.

Frazier was less romantic and more pragmatic about Sherman, however; the Reverend felt that the Union army's job was not yet complete. In addition to helping secure the freedom of blacks, Frazier believed that the Union was now mandated – on moral grounds – to play some role in helping the newly freed blacks to become self-sufficient. The way African-Americans can best take care of themselves is to have land, Frazier expressed to Sherman, and turn it and till it by their own labor. He explained that blacks want to be placed on land until they are able to buy it and make it their own. Frazier no doubt reminded Sherman that most Southerners gained their livelihood from the land, and if the newly emancipated slaves were to become full members of Georgian society, they too would be most likely to make their living as farmers. Furthermore, Frazier understood – and apparently was able to convey – the way in which a person could recapture a sense of dignity and pride from having yielded from the earth its own sweet rewards, by honest labor and persistent faith.

This was a message that Sherman needed to hear. Thirty miles outside of Savannah, in Liberty County, he had previously stripped all landowners of their property in 1864, even though many of these landowners were black. Liberty County had been founded years before by Puritan Congregationalists and therefore had a much less stringent system of slavery than did the rest of the state. Here black family members were rarely separated, and many slaves had been allowed to accumulate property. Restoring the land that had been taken from blacks in Liberty County was the first order of business, and if Frazier had his way, all blacks throughout Georgia would participate in landownership by the time the Union juggernaut had completed its blistering journey across the South. Frazier, though insightful and ambitious, perhaps let his enthusiasm get the best of him in that meeting with Sherman, however. It would take until 1871 to reimburse those Liberty County landowners – both black and white –

whose land had been confiscated by the Union army. It took even longer for blacks throughout Georgia to learn what it meant to plant seeds in their own land, to assure their own futures rather than to fatten the purses of white landowners.

Georgia stood apart from other Southern states in its determination to hold fast to the traditions of slavery and white supremacy long after the Civil War. Despite the federal government's best efforts to encourage Georgia to honor the Thirteenth Amendment, which had emancipated the slaves in 1865, white Georgians became especially talented at finding ways to circumvent the law and to maintain a strict social hierarchy that positioned them on top. Maintaining that it was outside the purview of the federal government to dictate the legislation of local race relations, for example, the Georgia legislature met that year to ratify a new constitution. This document resembled almost to the letter the state's pre–Civil War constitution. Although the new one conceded to the existence of the Thirteenth Amendment, it took the teeth out of that amendment by making it unlawful for blacks to vote, to sit on juries, or to hold any social advantages equal to those of whites. These "advantages" that the legislature was determined to keep out of the hands of blacks had everything to do with land.

Throughout the South, and in Georgia in particular, the issue of land tenure was a volatile one for many whites, who would not stand for perceived insolence from blacks, particularly if this involved blacks suddenly having equal access to the land. For example, Frazier heard stories in 1865 of white planters telling the blacks on their plantations that they were still slaves and that they should behave accordingly and ignore the "rumors" of freedom. He traveled throughout Georgia in the months after the war accompanied by another black religious figure, the Reverend James Lynch (who would eventually rise to prominence in Mississippi). They discovered innumerable blacks who either did not know they were free or who were terrified of discussing the subject. It took until 1867, when U.S. Congressman Thaddeus Stevens introduced a bill to give each African-American forty acres and a mule – a bill that was eventually defeated – for most blacks to get word of the shift that had occurred in their destinies. In the meantime, Frazier made efforts to spread word of the Emancipation Proclamation to blacks throughout Georgia and to help them cobble a vision of landownership and prosperity – a vision in which they could now all share.

In 1865 land seemed to be the only thing on anyone's mind, especially in the South. Blacks who got word of the vision that Frazier had outlined to Sherman came to believe that in time every black family would be given a plot of land and the tools needed to work the soil. This did not seem entirely a pipe dream. Vaguely they knew that in the colonial era, land had been awarded to indentured servants who in some instances had only worked the fields of others for periods of three to five years. Thus it didn't seem impossible that slaves who had devoted entire generations to the tilling of other people's property would be granted a similar reward once slavery was ended.

But African-Americans faced mighty obstacles. For one thing, in the last days of the Civil War, the Confederate forces had attempted to rouse their withering forces by insisting that the Northern aggression was actually a plot to turn the entirety of Southern landholdings over to the slaves. With this in mind, the beleaguered Confederate soldiers did not fight with any greater possibility of success, but they became inspired to hold on even more determinedly to their property once the war was over. Fortunately, the freed slaves had such leaders as Frazier on their side, who watched these developments with a close eye and managed somehow to stay out of harm's way. Helping to advance Frazier's vision was the creation by Congress in March 1865 of the Bureau of Refugees, Freedmen, and Abandoned Lands. Soon to be called simply the Freedmen's Bureau, this government-sanctioned agency was primarily interested in confiscating "abandoned" land and distributing it to freed black families.

On the heels of these developments, the promise of land spread among communities as quickly as wildfire. One persistent rumor insisted that the federal government would make a general land distribution to blacks on Christmas Day of 1865. Frazier got wind of the rumor and even encountered a black Georgian who was so convinced that the Union would play Santa Claus and distribute land grants like Christmas candy that this man had offered to sell part of his own booty back to his former master. Such developments alarmed Frazier, who traveled along the red dirt of Georgia and learned firsthand of the delirium that had started to grip both blacks and whites around the issue of land redistribution. He wondered if in some way he had played a role in promoting this hysteria. After all, Frazier had brought to the Union's attention the necessity of ensuring that blacks had land to farm.

Frazier knew he hadn't gone as far in his fervor as had his friend Abalod Shigg, a self-appointed black leader who had become fixated on the promise of black Georgians acquiring land. Early in 1865, Sherman responded definitively to the meetings he had had with Frazier and others in Savannah. He issued Field Order Number 15, which set aside a portion of the Sea Islands region of Georgia and made it available in forty-acre plots to black families. Needless to say, this was a cause for celebration among black families, any three of whom could gather together and petition for a license to establish a settlement. Furthermore, according to Sherman, no white ownership would be allowed in this region, which he claimed exclusively for blacks. Even under Sherman's direct orders, however, the Freedmen's Bureau was slow to act. Shigg and others took matters into their own hands and seized two plantations along the Savannah

River on the assumption that these lands would eventually become part of the general distribution.

Frazier warned Shigg against making such a bold stroke, but Shigg would not listen. Instead, he solicited others to join him, and soon a group of congregants under the leadership of another black pastor, Ulysses L. Houston, was poised to take advantage of Sherman's order by assuming control of a remote area called Skidway Island. The plan, though, failed. In the end, as Frazier feared, the hope for land that had been built up in the hearts of blacks in Georgia was abruptly dashed. By now Lincoln had been assassinated and his successor, President Andrew Johnson, immediately began to restore the status quo in the South. Unlike Lincoln, Johnson saw no reason to further antagonize the planter aristocracy. Furthermore, Johnson fancied himself a champion of the little guy – that is, the little guy who was white – and he even resisted giving blacks the power to vote on the basis that such power might be used to usurp poor whites. Although Johnson was at first reluctant to return the white aristocracy in the South to power – they too, he believed, might conspire against poor whites – eventually, for reasons still not clear, he became champion to many whites throughout the South, regardless of their economic status. In doing so, he all but demolished the rights to citizenry upon which so many blacks were depending. When the Georgia legislature met in 1866, according to historian Donald L. Grant, their first order of business was to pass a resolution that cited Johnson as a "wise and patriotic statesman."

The treachery, the lost hope, and the broken promises left Frazier sick to his stomach. He despaired how easily a dream could become thwarted by deception and ill intent. Already the Georgia legislature had begun taking apart the Thirteenth Amendment piece by piece, by establishing something called "Black Codes," which regulated black labor.

Rather than owning land of their own, African-Americans were expected to work as "servants" – the word *slave* was not to be spoken – on the farms of whites and to abide by a series of new laws on labor contracts, which all but drove blacks back to agricultural work that paid them a slave's wage. According to these labor-contract regulations, the hours of labor would extend from dawn to sundown, excluding Sundays. In addition, there were provisions that allowed a white planter to fire a black servant for any reason – a loophole that was employed near the end of every growing season in 1865 and 1866, which made it possible for the white planters to avoid paying the blacks any wages at all.

Frazier's friend Henry McNeil Turner told Frazier that although true contracts existed between white planters and their black "servants," the terms of these contracts were often misrepresented to the African-Americans, who were largely illiterate. Turner was at the time one of the few African-American agents working for the Freedmen's Bureau of Georgia. According to Turner, although the Freedmen's Bureau recommended that $144 plus allowances for food and shelter be paid to servants, most white planters paid out only about $50 a year – often even less. Somehow, though, Frazier was heartened when he learned that so many recently freed blacks saw any opportunity to work for a wage as a measure of progress, thus seeking to make the best out of a dismal situation. In this context working close to the land, black men and women saw a new opportunity to build a foundation for the black family, which at the very least was no longer as vulnerable to violent dissolution as it had been during slavery. Even while struggling under cruel conditions, African-Americans interpreted their freedom as a signal that rather than devote themselves to white families, they could now devote themselves – at long last – to their own families. The land would provide the sustenance and framework for those black families, and farming would be the proud legacy inherited by each new generation.

From time to time during these years black families gathered at Frazier's home or at his tiny church, looking for inspiration. That so many were illiterate did not keep them from understanding that they had been the victims of a scam: in good faith, Sherman had promised them land of their own, but Johnson had swooped down like a merciless hawk and snatched that land away. By pardoning Southern whites for crimes against the Union, Johnson reinstated their citizenship and restored to them full license to all available land. Even with the strength of family to sustain them, some African-Americans who gathered at Frazier's house would shake with rage, despair, and bitterness at this unspeakable and despicable turn of events.

One night, long after sundown, a group of black women and men met at Frazier's church, their bones aching from the strain of a day's work. The Reverend looked out at their faces and could think of nothing to say that might ease their frustration or lift their spirits. Having no words to speak, he lifted his voice and sang a hymn, a quiet melody of faith in the face of adversity. Frazier could hardly finish the song, however, because he was moved to tears. He was overwhelmed with the desire to make right what had gone so horribly wrong. But even his best efforts would for a while be in vain. Without land of their own, without tools and equipment, the newly freed African-Americans were without the resources they needed most to prosper. Without mules or lines of credit, they stood at the beginning of a cycle that was already in full bloom, a form of peonage that would ensnare black farmers for years: the sharecropping system.

2.

My great-grandfather, Bill Mathis, was born on February 2, 1881, in Dooly County, Georgia.
He grew up with his mother Alice Haugabrook and his maternal grandmother, Indiana,
a Native American woman from the Cherokee tribe, on a small farm in one of the most
tumultuous periods in American history. This was the era of Reconstruction, the white
plantation owner backlash, Black Codes, and a great deal of violence against the recently freed
Africans who remained in the South. Alice probably didn't have the economic means to leave
the region, and with small children she probably just decided to plant herself and hold on.

My great-great-great-grandmother, Indiana, is unique in my family history in that she
is the only Native American mentioned. I always wonder about this part of our story. I wonder
about the truth of this family history. It seems as if one can often find references to Cherokees in
most African-American family lines. I am usually suspect of claims to Native American
ancestry, as I am sure are many Native Americans. These claims are usually to romanticized
fantasies of strong "Indians" with long black hair who mysteriously just disappeared

from the American landscape. The truth, unfortunately, is far more brutal. Millions were forced off their land and marched through the dead of winter to Oklahoma, with vultures following the march as thousands of sick or elderly men, women, and children died along the way.

However Indiana came to be part of my family story is probably not as important as what she and other Native American ancestors represent in family histories. This part of Georgia, where my family began its American nightmare / dream, was the land of the Creek Indians and the Cherokee Confederation. Historical maps show that there were numerous communities in the area now known as Macon County, and the city of Montezuma got its name from its original inhabitants. Indiana marks my family history with the reminder that this land that we hold dear belonged to a nation of people long before the Africans arrived and added their blood to the red Georgia dirt.

WE MIGHT WAKE UP AT DAWN AND SEE
THE LAND STRETCHING BEFORE US AND
KNOW IN OUR HEARTS THAT IT BELONGS
NOT TO US OR TO ANY MAN, BUT TO GOD.
—GARRISON FRAZIER

THE REVEREND Garrison Frazier turned the words over in his head. They had come to him in the night, fragmented and hushed, like a song he only half-remembered. And now he let the words roll from his lips to see if they could survive in the world. They seemed to him so delicate somehow — as fragile as snow — that he imagined the words might come apart as soon as they made contact with the air. When finally Frazier was able to say the words aloud a few times — in scarcely more than a whisper — it increased his confidence. He felt ready to see if they would make as strong an impression on someone else as they had made on him, so he called to his wife and asked her to join him in the front room of their tiny house.

A thin woman with enormously large hands that moved about restlessly when she talked — traveling through the tight curls of her almond-
color hair or smoothing out the wrinkles of her faded linen dress — Susie
Frazier came in carrying a make-shift version of a tea tray and placed it
down on a table that sat in the center of the room. For years it had been
Frazier's habit to practice his sermons with his wife before he took them
to the pulpit, but on this occasion he had no sermon — just words. The
words were about land and people, and together they sounded to him like
a song, a mournful song of all the freed Africans who had been thwarted
in their efforts to purchase land of their own. At the same time Frazier
hoped the words would make clear to his parishioners that it didn't matter
how strenuously the white planters of Georgia conspired to keep land out
of black hands. In the end the land was God's to give or to take away.
When at last God chose to bestow an abundance of land on black women
and men, no one — no planters, no legislators, no marauding terrorists
dressed in white hoods and robes — would be able to change the course of
God's will.

After Frazier had shared some tea with his wife, he cleared his
throat. His wife placed her hand on his arm. Frazier stood up and by the
pale light of a candle, he read to his wife the words that had come to him
in the night. "We might wake up at dawn," he whispered, "and see the
land stretching before us and know in our hearts that it belongs not to us
or to any man, but to God."

Susie Frazier's eyes remained closed while her husband spoke.
When she looked at him at last, he seemed in the grip of something wonderful and strange. She asked him if anything was wrong, and Frazier
shook his head. He was just fine, he said, sitting down beside her. With
the echo of the words still hovering over the room, the couple talked and
talked through the night, until the entirety of the Reverend's next ser-

mon came more clearly into focus. With his wife's help, he knew he had finally come up with something to say to his parishioners that might bring some measure of comfort to their hearts.

Frazier was well aware that very few of the women and men around him shared his good fortune. He had relatives — other freed blacks, many of them in business for themselves up North — who had helped him gather the capital to purchase his freedom, his wife's, and a small portion of land. After the emancipation of the slaves, however, and despite all the promises to make them equal partners in the South's farming industries, most blacks without financial resources found the door to opportunity slammed in their faces. There were any number of obstacles to the dream the freed Africans shared of owning land. In addition to the bitter even hateful outlook of some whites — who in certain areas of Georgia, for example, refused even to acknowledge the repeal of slavery — there were commercial considerations. Many white planters resented the loss of the cheap labor that had been the lynchpin of their economic success.

There were social pressures as well. Frazier heard stories of whites who became victims of violence and social expulsion for selling land to blacks. This threat of violence in particular served as an effective deterrent to many African-American families. At best, those who managed to secure property for themselves would suffer a nighttime visit from the Ku Klux Klan — a visit that was designed to intimidate the family so ruthlessly that they would feel they had no choice but to flee. If that tactic didn't achieve the desired result, however, the Klan had other methods at their disposal. The most violent of these methods was tacitly encouraged by white farmers, many of whom intended to strip blacks of both their land and their independence.

Arriving on horseback in the stillness of night to a black family farm, Klan members would draw their white hoods over their heads and stampede forward, the legs of their horses breaking down the family's front door. Once inside, all property would be set aflame – the meager furniture that filled the house, the family's ragged clothes, and the few precious heirlooms that had somehow survived from one generation to the next. The family might hover in its rooms, holding on to each other tightly, praying aloud that the fiery damage might be limited to mere property. Invariably, however, some family members were sacrificed to the Klan's fury. Frazier was sometimes summoned afterward to these tragic scenes, and he witnessed firsthand the bitter remains: A daughter, no more than ten, who had been raped and beaten beyond recognition. A son who had been castrated and left to bleed to death in the deep red soil of the family's own land. With the threat of such violence hovering over the heads of recently freed blacks, and with so few resources available to them, many returned to their prewar position as cheap agricultural laborers who served at the whim of white planters.

This problem was not a secret in the North, and word came back regularly of the atrocities being endured by Southern blacks. Even the unsympathetic President Andrew Johnson dispatched an emissary on a fact-finding mission to make an assessment. The emissary, General Carl Shurz, traveled throughout the Southern states, and he confirmed for Johnson that the rumors of blacks being terrorized in the South were indeed true. Shurz heard firsthand accounts of the brutality when he arrived in Georgia, where Frazier was likely among the black men and women who gathered to give testimony. Truthfully, though, no such gathering was necessary. According to historian Lerone Bennett Jr., Shurz could see with his own eyes that, in his words, "some planters held back their former slaves on the plantations by brute force. A reign of terror prevailed."

Such activities continued well into the 1870s – years after the Civil War – and Frazier was no doubt instrumental in getting word to Shurz that the murdered bodies of Negroes could be found at the bottom of swamps and lakes or discarded haphazardly in pits. Shurz also noted that the burning of black schools and churches had become commonplace. Having seen for himself the malevolence inflicted upon blacks at the hands of whites — and having gathered evidence of the unspeakable crimes that made it impossible for African-Americans to enjoy a truly free existence in the South — Shurz filed his report with the president. As cited in Bennett's *Before the Mayflower,* Shurz wrote:

> Although the freedman is no longer considered the property of an individual master, he is considered the slave of society. Wherever I go . . . I hear the [white] people talk in such a way as to indicate that they are yet unable to conceive of the Negro as possessing any rights at all. Men who are honorable in their dealings with their white neighbors will cheat a Negro without feeling a single twinge of that honor. To kill a Negro, they do not deem murder . . . to take property away from a Negro, they do not consider robbery.

Of course, as the report Shurz filed makes clear, taking property away from blacks was in fact robbery, and it had reached epidemic proportions. In this volatile atmosphere the system of sharecropping was born. In the years after the war, an abundance of white planters found themselves strapped for cash, and in their reduced circumstances they put freed black men to work in the fields and paid them a "share" of the crop they harvested. The terms, though, were awful. The share offered the freedmen was hardly enough to feed and support a family. What's more, the white planters often drove the freedmen into even further debt by charging them for use of tools or for access to basic necessities, such as food, clothing, and a place to sleep. Many felt the Freedmen's Bureau was to blame for insisting that recently freed blacks sign labor contracts with white landowners — contracts that ensured black people would be once again under the authority of whites. However, the Bureau was feeling enormous pressure from the federal government to appease the white landowners, whom President Jackson favored. To this end, contracts between white landowners and black laborers were both unequal and unregulated, which meant a white landowner was rarely obligated to honor even the most basic terms of the contract. As historian Darlene Clark Hines points out in *The African-American Odyssey,*

> There were no wages. Freedmen worked land as families (including women and children) and not under direct white supervision. When the landowner provided seeds, tools, fertilizer and work animals (mules, horses, oxen), the black family received one third of the crop. There were many variations on these arrangements, and frequently black families were cheated out of their fair share of the crop.

For all these reasons the sharecropping system quickly became corrupted. In truth, it was a corrupt system from the start. Many whites reneged on their agreements or instituted loopholes by which they could get rid of the black laborers just shortly before the harvesting of crops. Banished from the land before the crops were harvested and sold, these blacks were robbed of an opportunity to use the proceeds of their labor to build equity of their own.

Frazier saw despair everywhere he turned. When word of the emancipation of the slaves had first been delivered, he had envisioned a Georgia that would embrace its black children, giving them no more or no less than what was necessary for survival—food, clothes, and land to work, land that would provide any hardworking family with resources for self-sufficiency. He had dimly imagined the sight of black farmers and white farmers working side by side, perhaps not as friends but at least as colleagues, working together to achieve that which was in both their best interests—the full economic development of the land.

Instead, matters seemed to have gone from bad to worse. In the years since the repeal of slavery, blacks in Georgia and throughout the South still toiled land that was not their own. Hunched over and picking crops by hand, their spines grew brittle from the hard labor. Their spirits faltered. Frazier knew that if there had ever been any hope in his followers' eyes, it was extinguished now, left vacant and gray, like a flame that has been doused by water and reduced to smoke and ash. Touring the countryside, Frazier saw bodies—dark and emaciated—piled on top of one another, left unburied for want of a grave. There were other corpses too, beaten so badly they were disfigured, or partially devoured by rats, or left naked and violated like a bizarre attraction—a warning to blacks that any transgression, real or perceived, would be met with swift and violent action by those who previously had been their masters.

The situation worsened in 1867. The Freedmen's Bureau had begun making diligent efforts to give black farmers an increased portion of the crops they harvested for white planters. Because of these efforts, black sharecroppers were deemed entitled to at least one-quarter of the harvested crops, and gradually the allotted portion increased to one-half. But white planters bitterly resisted the change, and they registered their sentiments by violent means. There were also many fair-minded white planters who saw no future in continued aggression. They struck honest and equitable deals with black farmers and often arranged to turn over a portion of the land to the black farmers after a given period of time. Frazier, having been informed of such opportunities, began steering his followers to the farms of white planters with reputations for fairness. Such farms weren't few and far between, but neither were they the majority, so the struggle to find amiable working conditions was fierce. Furthermore, many black sharecroppers who went looking for a better deal were appre-

hended by the white planters whose farms they had fled, punished severely, and put back to work under threat of death.

By 1890, according to some scholars, a full 90 percent of all black
farmers were sharecroppers. Few other arrangements were available at
the time, however. Some farmers received cash wages instead of a share
of the harvest, a system that was as rife with corruption as sharecropping.
Others, called tenant farmers, paid an annual cash rent to white planters
and kept the proceeds of whatever they harvested. In many ways most
freedmen preferred this system. It reduced the likelihood of being
cheated out of their settlement at the end of harvesting season. Best of all,
tenant farming meant there was no "boss" hovering over the freedmen
from dusk till dawn monitoring their work.

However, there was a steep downside. Because he had to supply his
own farming equipment — tools, seed, fertilizers, and a mule — the tenant
farmer would often find himself in enormous debt to local merchants for
the cost of this equipment. Moreover, it was difficult to support oneself
from one harvesting season to the next. Still, by all reports, the black
farmers who successfully navigated these pitfalls were nearly as prosperous as those who owned their own land. But there numbers were few.
Failed attempts to buy land or to survive as tenant farmers led to the
steady increase of black sharecroppers in the South in the years after the
repeal of slavery. Although few black farmers had a thorough knowledge
of economics, it was clear that white resistance to black advancement
kept much of the South — especially Georgia — in the throes of economic
hardship. The sharecropping system, the preference of white planters,
had effectively created a culture of poverty among black farmers, one that
would last well into the twentieth century.

Having been denied the promise of landownership, black farmers
felt little incentive to produce any more than was necessary to survive.
This lack of incentive did two things: First, it promoted the perception

of African-Americans as shiftless and lazy, a stereotype invented by whites to obscure their own role in depriving blacks of real opportunities to advance. Second, with wages low and opportunities scarce, many blacks eventually fled the South, leaving behind the fertile land that had blossomed at their hardworking touch. Their migration to Northern cities caused a shortage of available labor, and soon an agricultural depression took hold, one that persisted until the First World War. Crop diversification in the early 1900s began to pull Georgia out of its dire agricultural straits, but by then the die had been cast. White Planters had squandered their economic potential by turning the land into a site of racial conflict and by making hatred the primary harvest for too many seasons.

Forty years after the Civil War had ended, now in the early twentieth century, Frazier was in his seventies. Although he had seen improvement in the lives of many African-Americans around him, there remained in his mouth the bitter taste of lost opportunities, broken promises, and patterns of racial hatred that had driven away so many black farmers. It had long been his dream that the sons and daughters of his generation would see the land as their birthright, claim it as their own, and derive from it the prosperity and pride that had eluded their ancestors.

Instead, the new century seemed to hold even less hope for the black farmer, so Frazier closed his eyes and slept, finding comfort only when he dreamed.

part two

THE CALM BEFORE THE STORM :: 1900–1928

3.

World War I and the Peak of Black Landownership

My great-grandparents, Bill Mathis and Viccie Brunson, married in 1900 in Macon County, Georgia, at the Phillip Primitive Baptist Church, in an area known as Four Points. I know the area well, because as a little girl I would take the long walk down the only paved road near my grandfather's house, to the general store at Four Points. I, my brother, and our same-age cousins would walk on a hot summer day for nearly a mile for the small joy of Nehi soda and Now and Later candy.

In traditional West African culture the meeting of two roads, the crossroads, is a powerful symbol, the meeting of the spirit world with the here and now. I never thought about who had walked those country roads before me or who would walk them when I was gone. All I thought about was the sweat on my brow as I skipped, laughed, and talked my way down the road to the combination candy store / gas station / food shop / supply store, standing all alone at the intersection of two paved roads in the middle of Macon County.

I am sure that Viccie and Bill had no way of knowing what their union would produce at the beginning of the twentieth century. They had nothing but their freedom, love, and faith. Behind them were generations of enslaved Africans who had endured nameless atrocities and had somehow managed to survive. Before them was unknown possibility. For some reason, despite the waves of people leaving the South, they decided, there at the crossroads, to stay and build a life. They settled in Macon County, where between 1901 and 1924 my great-grandmother gave birth to fourteen children. In between giving birth, Viccie helped her husband farm rented land in both Dooly and Macon Counties. They rented the land from Leon Harrison, a local white landowner. He also sold a group of black farmers land for a small church, which they built and named Harrison Chapel. Harrison Chapel still stands to this day. My great-grandfather and grandfather were deacons in that church and my aunt and cousin continue to be members.

Having the opportunity to rent some land rather than only sharecropping it made the difference for Bill and Viccie. By 1926 they had saved enough money to buy their own two-hundred-acre farm in the southern part of Macon County, in an area known as Blue Ruen. It took twenty-six years, but they did it. They became the first in their families to own the land they worked. It was a small farm, a small act, in a small place, but it changed the lives of their children and their children's children. The Blue Ruen farm has been gone for a while, but the legacy is found in the faces of the children who gather every other year to give thanks, honor, and respect to the beautiful young couple who stood at the crossroads and entered the twentieth century as sharecroppers: one step removed from slavery, hoping for land, praying for justice and holding onto dreams, planted in red dirt, white cotton, and yellow peaches.

CALL IT A MIRACLE, an act of God, or simply the result of persistence, stamina, and determination, but by 1910 some two hundred thousand African-Americans had managed to acquire land. The number is staggering. The circumstances conspiring against black ownership were numerous and deeply embedded in Southern law and legislature, so that such a substantive number of blacks managed to make lives for themselves on what amounted to just more than fifteen million acres of land is all but inconceivable.

BY ALL ESTIMATES AND EVALUATIONS, THE ACHIEVEMENT OF BLACK PEOPLE BY 1910 IN THEIR OWNERSHIP OF JUST OVER 15 MILLION ACRES OF LAND IS REMARKABLE. HISTORIANS TELL A STORY OF THE LATE-NINETEENTH-CENTURY RECONSTRUCTION AS A PERIOD OF TRAGEDY, BETRAYAL, AND DISAPPOINTMENT FOR BLACK PEOPLE, BUT IT WAS ALSO A TIME OF ASPIRATION, HOPE, AND HARD WORK.
—MARSHA DARLING

Somehow, though, the acquisitions slowly and steadily took place and many African-Americans cultivated prosperous and abundant farms. From one season to the next, however, there were no guarantees that a black farmer's good fortune would last. It is true of course that any farmer faces the threat each year of the cruelty of the elements, which can undermine his best efforts to raise a bumper crop. But whereas many white farmers had banks, insurers, and the goodwill of their neighbors to sustain them in difficult times, black farmers had few such resources. A bad year in the fields could mean a quick and complete dissolution of the black family farm.

With the Reverend Garrison Frazier long deceased by the start of the twentieth century, a new and powerful voice was needed to speak on behalf of Southern black farmers, especially in Georgia, where African-Americans were routinely subjected to the violent intimidation of the Ku Klux Klan. For a long time, however, such a voice was difficult to hear—muted by the threats of hostile whites or made indistinct by too many voices speaking at once about the fate of the black farmer. Among these voices was that of the minister J. W. Carter, who had started in 1889 a Colored Farmers' Alliance, which continued to thrive into the twentieth century. The Alliance was a black version of similar organizations that whites had established in the South since the end of the Civil War. For example, the Patrons of Husbandry—or the Grange, as they were more commonly known—was created by white farmers in 1872 and immediately succeeded in regulating the cost of farming supplies by encouraging cooperative buying among its members.

The Grange was not explicitly a whites-only organization, but as the group grew throughout the South, each state's local branches were allowed to decide for themselves whether or not to offer membership to black farmers. In Georgia, where landownership was an explosively racial issue, few blacks were invited to join the Grange. For this reason a parallel organization of black farmers was established. A precursor to Carter's Colored Farmers' Alliance, the Council of Laborers began in 1875 to welcome the black farmers who had been turned away by the Grange.

Despite the tensions that existed between white and black farmers during the late nineteenth century, they shared in common many of the same goals—specifically, finding a means to redress what they saw as their exploitation by profit-hungry businesses and financial institutions. Starting in 1870, the goods needed by Southern farmers to survive steadily went up in cost, while the prices for the goods they sold declined. This shared sense of outrage unified farmers across the color line, but it was an uneasy union, and black farmers continually found themselves segregated from larger farming organizations.

Eager to find more militant ways to redress their grievances, white farmers in Texas gathered together several statewide groups in 1884 under a single banner: the Farmers' Alliance. Branches of the Alliance soon popped up all over the South, and Carter emulated this model when he formed the Colored Farmers' Alliance. More than an organization, these black and white chapters of the Farmers' Alliance were actually a *move-*

ment – a political and economic uprising that had quickly spread throughout the nation's Southern states. By 1889 there were 240 chapters of the Colored Farmers' Alliance in Georgia alone – which would have included Eatonton, Macon, Marshallville, and Washington Counties – and their numbers continued to grow. The movement saw impressive gains in these final years of the nineteenth century, gains that were shared by white and black farmers alike. For example, according to historian Donald L. Grant the predominantly white Farmers' Alliance – which grew each year in size, power, and influence – was able to reduce the markups of farming supply from 50 percent to 25 percent, a reduction that gave economically strapped black farmers a reason to rejoice. Although they were still kept at a distance by their white counterparts, these black farmers immediately recognized the value of the Alliance movement. As the new century approached, there were reportedly more than eighty thousand members of Georgia's Colored Farmers' Alliance.

As the Colored Farmers' Alliance blossomed, members were occasionally made welcome at meetings of the National Farmers' Alliance, although such occasions were rare and usually marked by strife. In 1889, however, Georgia's Colored Farmers' Alliance was invited to send delegates to St. Louis, Missouri, to attend the National Farmers Alliance annual meeting. So riled up were participants with a militant fervor to improve the circumstances of farmers throughout the South, blacks and whites were said to have hugged openly at the meeting, calling each other "comrade" and extolling the virtues of "brotherhood." By the following year, however, the honeymoon had ended, and at the 1890 conference, held in Florida, white farmers and black farmers met separately.

Still, these attempts at some measure of racial reconciliation had enduring and largely positive effects on black farmers. So intent were farmers of all races to improve their circumstances that they forgot, at least for the moment, the animosity that existed between them and focused instead on doing what they could, either separately or together, to ensure that the agricultural industry did not become a thing of the past. African-Americans, who were just beginning to enjoy some modicum of success as planters, were keenly aware that if farming were to fall to the bottom of the country's list of priorities, black farmers might suffer the most, given that African-Americans were already at the bottom of the country's social hierarchy.

Soon the Colored Farmers' Alliance in Georgia had followed the example of the National Farmers Alliance and opened a number of cooperative general stores. These stores bought large assortments of farming supply in bulk, and the savings they experienced were passed along to Alliance members. By 1891 an estimated ninety thousand black farmers in Georgia (1.2 million nationally) were members, and as their numbers grew, so did their sense of independence, pride, and self-determination. These traits soon began to offend many whites, however, who felt the black farmers had forgotten their "place." Racial tension began to heat up again, with white members of the Farmers Alliance insisting at a national meeting that blacks continue as sharecroppers rather than as independent land-owning farmers. Black delegates at that meeting balked at the idea, threatening to pull out of the Alliance rather than subject themselves to such exploitation.

By the 1890s an increasing number of African-Americans in the South had managed to break free of the sharecropping system, and each such success story served as an inspiration to other black farmers. In addition to hard work, cooperation, perseverance, and faith, these role models played an important part in the gradual acquisition of more and more land by black farmers. Just one prosperous African-American in an agrarian community could simultaneously provoke considerable rage among his white counterparts and profound hope among his black brethren. This hope was often translated into a determination to succeed at all costs, and by 1900 the number of successful black farmers in Georgia had started to increase significantly.

Perhaps the most inspiring story was that of the Hubert family, three brothers from Hancock County, a small farming community in Georgia. Their story exemplifies the ways by which an African-American family managed to achieve landownership. The Hubert family had been slaves, but after the Civil War their owners freed them and bestowed on them a bale of cotton. The brothers—Zach, Floyd, and David—quickly became renters on a distant plantation, but the cotton they brought along made them an uncommonly well-supplied family of renters.

By 1871 their devotion to discipline and hard work had attracted the attention of a white lawyer named Burke (no first name is recorded), who was new to Hancock County. The lawyer had moved to the area when he saw an opportunity to exploit the resources of local farms that had been abandoned by or seized from their impoverished owners. No farmer himself, Burke was happy to sell a rocky and undeveloped section of his newly acquired holdings to the Hubert brothers when they approached the lawyer during his first weeks in town. Burke inflated the value of the inferior land, however, and the brothers were forced to accept an unfavorable agreement—a quick three-year payment schedule. If they fell behind on payments, they would face instant eviction; but if they kept up with the payments, Burke would sign over to the Huberts the deed on the property at the end of the three-year period.

After building a log cabin for themselves, the brothers worked steadily to clear the land, starting at sunrise each day and continuing well into the night. Somehow they managed to incur no additional debt during this period and lived exclusively on what they were able to grow. Anything that remained was sold, and that income was used to pay off their debt to Burke. Working tirelessly and cooperatively with one another, the brothers kept to the payment schedule, and in three years time they had raised the necessary funds to purchase the property outright. Burke reneged on the agreement, however — a common practice of the time — and refused to turn over the deed. Flummoxed by the brothers' success, he argued that because the contract between the two parties had been signed without a witness present, it was null and void. Shaken and defeated, the brothers were left with no choice but to *rent* the land they had already purchased. This went on for years.

Eventually, the Hubert brothers managed to secure the service of another white lawyer, who agreed to help them fight Burke in court. During this time the Grange and other farming collectives were gaining the kind of political influence that often led to farming disputes being settled by the courts in the farmers' favor. Burke was aware of these developments, so he had little interest in trying the case before a judge; at the same time the brothers' lawyer felt that even though the tide of change was rising in favor of farmers, the case of three black farmers against a white landowner wasn't likely to get a fair hearing in a Georgia courtroom. Finding Burke at home one night — who may well have been bleary-headed at the time from drink or plain exhaustion — the Huberts's lawyer badgered, cajoled, and bedazzled his adversary until Burke finally agreed to turn over the deed to Zach, Floyd, and David.

The brothers divided the 165 acres into thirds, each man taking 55 acres for himself. Having achieved ownership of the land together, they now set out to work it as individual farmers. Their efforts succeeded beyond anyone's wildest dreams, and in time Zach had expanded his holdings to more than a thousand acres of land. According to historians, this was the first and most sizable black landholding in Georgia. When the brothers married and started families, their individual holdings continued to grow, as each new generation of Huberts acquired additional land. By 1940 the family collectively owned almost thirty thousand acres, making it the largest private landowner in the South at that time. Their prosperity allowed family members to pursue other occupations as well, and two of Zach's sons – Benjamin Franklin Hubert and Zachary Taylor Hubert – became well-known scholars and presidents of Georgia State Industrial College in Savannah and Langston University in Langston, Oklahoma, respectively.

Although few farming families – black or white – enjoyed such vast success, a number of other African-Americans followed a similar path to landownership. The prominent writer and scholar W. E. B. Du Bois became fascinated by independent black farmers who thrived in the wake of slavery. During his early years as a teacher at Atlanta University (from 1897 until 1910), Du Bois familiarized himself with the stories of a number of such farmers, sometimes even traveling a distance to meet them in person. For example, Issac Miller, born a slave in Georgia in 1856, inherited a portion of the land in Fort Valley that his former owner had given Miller's father during Reconstruction. Though Miller's father's success with the land was modest, Miller devoted all his time, energy, and meager resources to cultivating and expanding the property. By 1910 he had become a successful landowner of some fifteen hundred acres. Similarly, a black landowner named Deal Jackson had followed the example of his white counterparts and installed both black and white tenants on his property, all of whom apparently worked together to give Jackson one of the most successful harvests of the 1912 season.

Du Bois was most impressed with an African-American farmer named Bartow F. Powell, whose career Du Bois studied from 1900 until Powell's death in 1918. Born in 1865, one of the gray years between slavery and Reconstruction, Powell grew up in a family that managed to acquire a small plot of land that was either a gift or a throwaway from a white family. Where others saw limited opportunities for what this land might yield, Powell immediately began looking for ways to turn his modest holdings into something bigger. Eventually he won a few government dredging contracts, which proved to be very lucrative. By the time he died, Powell was said to have parlayed the proceeds from these contracts into holdings of more than ten thousand acres. He had had five hundred people in his employ and, as a result, sold about a thousand bales of cotton a year.

Just as all the stories of black farmers who never acquired land of their own have several elements in common – the violent resistance of their white counterparts; the corrupt and discriminatory practices of local and state government; the cycle of debt and impoverishment caused by greedy landowners and the exorbitant prices of farming supplies – the stories of black farmers who managed to successfully navigate these pitfalls have many elements in common as well. First, the African-American most likely to achieve independence as a landowner was the one who joined or formed alliances – either with other black farmers or with members of his own family. Certainly no Hubert brother alone could have paid off in three years the cost of a large piece of land, but all three brothers working together made such a payment possible. Furthermore, even though the Huberts found themselves at first denied the property that was rightfully theirs, they managed to remain self-sufficient as renters because of the goods they harvested and sold as a team.

Second, black farmers were largely better off trying to buy marginal, undeveloped, or unwanted pieces of land, the kind of acreage a white owner would happily sell off. Although there were no guarantees that such property would prove to be fertile, often the property was simply in need of the kind of hard work and attention that a black farmer would be willing to devote to achieve some degree of self-sufficiency. Also, land that was isolated or off the beaten track was less likely to come under the scrutiny of intolerant white landowners or violent white supremacists. Banished to the margins of an agricultural landscape, a black farmer would often be left alone to cultivate his property in peace.

Finally, the support and approval of a white benefactor often served as the foundation of a black farmer's prosperity. Many of the most successful African-American farmers started off with either land or resources their former masters had given them. Unfortunately, such gifts were particularly vulnerable to attack; white planters would simply confiscate the property, for example, arguing that any land formerly owned by whites should remain in the hands of whites. When those gifts were left undisturbed, however, they provided for the black farmer a leg up, one that brought a greater chance of achieving financial self-sufficiency.

Similarly, given the legal and legislative barriers constructed to inhibit black landownership, the support of a white patron often ensured that African-American families were apprised of their rights and armed with the information they needed to hurdle the obstacles forthcoming. Again, the example of the Hubert family illustrates this point. Having been defrauded by a white lawyer, the brothers turned to another white lawyer for help. To be sure, this was a risk but clearly the brothers bet that the two men spoke the same language and had access to the same resources, thereby making a fight between them infinitely more fair than one between Burke and the Huberts.

These were the tools by which African-American farmers moved into the twentieth century with a significant amount of their own land. By now, of course, a good many black farmers had left, driven from the South by the lack of opportunity and the continual threat of violence. Those who remained, however — regardless of whether they prospered — sustained themselves with the lessons they had accumulated over a lifetime of working the land. From their religious leaders — like Garrison Frazier and J. W. Carter — they learned to give over their hearts to faith, to trust that their own prayers could move mountains and change the course of their lives. From the example of white farmers who established such cooperative groups as the Grange and the Farmers Alliance, black farmers learned to harness their energy and pool their resources toward the singular goal of acquiring the land to support their families. From the example of the African-American families who found prosperity as farmers, black farmers learned their dreams were perhaps no longer as elusive as they had seemed during the bitter days of Reconstruction. Relying on the collective power of family was a proud tradition that could be traced back to the black farmer's ancestors in Africa. This tradition would figure prominently in the cultural survival of a people.

Looking back, African-American farmers were reminded that there had been no "forty acres and a mule" and no homesteads like those that had been pledged by General William Sherman. In fact, no such promises were ever fulfilled to improve the lives of freed black men and women. Unable to trust in the assistance of the Union army, African-Americans turned to one another for strength and support and founded among themselves a vision of the future to which they were faithful to the end. Along the way they were forced to make countless compromises – settling on land that others rejected and soliciting the support of whites whose cooperation and endorsement often determined whether a black family might be allowed to own property at all. Eventually, however, these compromises – like the land itself – began to bear fruit. In truth, this didn't happen all the time, and for every Hubert family there were countless others who found themselves debt-ridden and impoverished, either unable to acquire property or to hold onto it for long. Still, that so many black families managed to survive and prosper during this era is arguably one of the most important economic achievements of the twentieth century. If nothing else, this feat provides an enduring example of the power of faith, determination, and hard work in the face of adversity.

The example resonates even today, lingering in the blood and bones of all black children born in the South. They know in some unutterable way of the sacrifices made by their ancestors, but chances are that only a small portion of the truth is actually known. More than the immediate threat of violence or poverty, black farmers at the turn of the century had to confront political forces that began to renew all at once a strict racial hierarchy, one that continued to keep African-Americans at the bottom.

There were other forces to contend with as well. The new nonagrarian industries of the North offered blacks a promise of prosperity that was difficult to ignore. These industries would eventually drain from the South the best of its African-American farmers. The process was slow, however, drifting across the Southern landscape as lazily as smoke from the factories. At the same time a variety of voices began whispering into the ears of black farmers – that of Booker T. Washington and W. E. B. Du Bois, for example – and the sound of it was dizzying. Whereas farming had seemed for so long the only possible career for Southern blacks, other options had suddenly come into view, and it was difficult to know which way to turn or where any of these new roads might lead.

4.

The second child born to Viccie Brunson and Bill Mathis was my grandfather, Fred Mathis. Born on October 13, 1904, he grew up working: children were labor; women were labor; men were labor. They were a family of sharecroppers trapped in a system designed to bind families to land that was not their own. While great minds struggled over ideas, resources, and the leadership of the new "colored" America, Viccie and Bill made their own small plan. They worked toward buying land. This was the sharecropper's dream: land of one's own. It was an immense dream that they held close and somehow managed to shape in the red clay and dirt roads of Macon County, Georgia. And then, somewhere along the way, they discovered that the future held more possibilities than just owning land. Education became another kind of freedom dream. Fort Valley State College had opened its doors in 1895, fewer than twenty miles from Montezuma, to educate young black children. It was just close enough for a few farmers to see the future. Bill and Viccie saw that future: not for themselves, and not for all of their children, but maybe just for one.

It must have seemed like an easy choice. My grandfather, Fred, was a strong and hard worker. His younger brother, Bennie Lee, was a little smaller, a bit sickly, and not quite as strong as his older brother Fred. So when Viccie and Bill decided to send one of their youngest sons to college at Fort Valley, it made sense that Bennie Lee was the one who left the field for the classroom. Left behind was Fred, yearning for an education but stuck in a hot field, asked to do the work of two because he was strong and healthy. This was not the choice of Du Bois's "talented tenth." This was the economic Solomon's choice that poor people have made for centuries. This was the economic rationale of a poor black farming family making the only choice they could.

Fred Mathis never forgot this choice, a choice he vowed never to make for his own children. He would give all of his children the chance to leave the field. He would give them all what he didn't have. Viccie and Bill had set their sights on the land, and their son Fred had set his on education.

WHEN W. E. B. DU BOIS spoke these words within the first decade of the twentieth century, they seemed to blaze across the Southern sky like lightning. Or, perhaps more accurately, they drew a kind of metaphorical line in the sand, signaling a sharp divide between two camps of thinkers. On one side of the line stood Booker T. Washington and on the other stood Du Bois. The debate between these men was more than just a war of words, however. Instead, it was an emotional and spiritual fight to determine which direction Negroes should take in the years ahead to secure freedom and self-determination for themselves and their families.

SO FAR AS MR. [BOOKER T.] WASHINGTON PREACHES THRIFT, PATIENCE, AND INDUSTRIAL TRAINING FOR THE MASSES, WE MUST HOLD UP HIS HANDS AND STRIVE WITH HIM, REJOICING IN HIS HONORS AND GLORYING IN THE STRENGTH OF THIS JOSHUA CALLED OF GOD AND OF MAN TO LEAD THE HEADLESS HOST. BUT SO FAR AS MR. WASHINGTON APOLOGIZES FOR INJUSTICES, NORTH OR SOUTH, DOES NOT RIGHTLY VALUE THE PRIVILEGES AND DUTY OF VOTING, BELITTLES THE EMASCULATING EFFECTS OF CASTE DISTINC-TIONS, AND OPPOSES THE HIGHER TRAINING AND AMBITION OF OUR BRIGHTER MINDS, – SO FAR AS HE, THE SOUTH, OR THE NATION, DOES THIS, – WE MUST UNCEASINGLY AND FIRMLY OPPOSE THEM. —W. E. B. DU BOIS

This debate had specific implications for black farmers, who in many ways served as the catalyst for the fight. Both Washington and Du Bois knew the majority of African-Americans either lived in the South or hailed from Southern states and that farming was as integral to these people's lives as the air they breathed. Washington felt strongly that successful cultivation of the land was the African-American's greatest defense against those who questioned his discipline, his industry, his very existence. According to Washington and others of similar mind, if there had been a positive outcome to slavery – which itself seems a contradiction in terms – it was that black women and men emerged from the "peculiar institution" with an incomparable knowledge of the soil, of the land, of farming. Washington felt that blacks should apply this knowledge vigorously, developing the land in a way that would contribute to the overall prosperity and economic stability of the United States.

This kind of hard work and diligence would be rewarded, Washington believed, when recognition was made at last of African-Americans' valuable contribution to the country. Such recognition would in turn diffuse the hate and hostility of intolerant whites, thereby removing any lingering prejudice that prevents blacks from becoming fully integrated into mainstream society or gaining access to the privileges enjoyed by all U.S. citizens. "Nowhere is there afforded us such business opportunities" as in the South, said Washington, all but dictating a Declaration of Principles that was adopted by a group of black farmers, mechanics, ministers, and others at the Tuskegee Negro Conference in 1892. According to Washington and others at the conference, owning and cultivating farms in the South would endow black Americans with an increased level of self-respect, one that was guaranteed to "bring us many rights now denied us." The document, reprinted in Louis R. Harlan's *Booker T. Washington: The Making of a Black Leader, 1856–1901,* indicated that diligently working the land was necessary to a life of prosperity, social advancement, and self-improvement:

> We urge all to buy land and to cultivate it thoroughly; to raise more food supply; to build houses with more than one room; to tax themselves to build better school houses, and to extend the school term to at least six months; to give more attention to the character of their leaders, especially ministers and teachers; to keep out of debt; to avoid lawsuits; to treat our women better; and that conferences similar to this one be held in every community where practicable.

Alternatively, Du Bois did not feel that the prospects of the American Negro should be limited to cultivating the land, although he expressed a healthy amount of respect for those black farmers who managed to pursue these goals with integrity and success. For every black farmer, however, Du Bois wanted to ensure there was a black scholar as well, and a black politician, and a black person among all the industries and occupations that had traditionally been available only to whites. In many ways the differences between Du Bois and Washington reflected the differences in their upbringing. Whereas Washington had been born into slavery in 1856 and raised among Southern plantations – where he remained for the duration of his life and achieved his greatest personal and professional successes – Du Bois was almost the embodiment of Northern sensibilities. Born in Great Barrington, Massachusetts, in 1868, Du Bois's family had been long free. He grew up in a traditional New England setting, where education and an appreciation for art, culture, history, and the political process were emphasized.

Unlike Washington, Du Bois likely encountered little overt racial hatred in his childhood, so when he first entered the South in 1885 to attend Fisk University in Nashville, Tennessee, the degradation of black life deeply offended and shocked him. At the same time he observed such degradation with a critical distance that Washington did not possess, because Washington, after all, had been at its front lines his entire life. Soon after arriving at Fisk, Du Bois dedicated himself to a campaign of improving the lives of African-Americans, beginning in the South, where the plight of black farmers in particular saddened and outraged him. He believed that the black farmer's greatest enemy in the South was political disfranchisement. Without the right to vote, to participate actively in the political process, and to assert his view at the polling booth, the black farmer would never achieve social equality with his white counterparts. The lack of equality would be reflected in inferior schooling and fewer economic prospects, which would ultimately condition blacks to believe they were inherently inferior to whites.

By contrast, Washington dissuaded his followers from protesting for civil rights or seeking political redress to their grievances. Instead, in public at least, he advocated a policy of racial accommodation. In his famous 1895 speech known as the Atlanta Compromise address – delivered at the Cotton States and International Exposition – and on many other occasions as well, Washington encouraged blacks to "cast down [their] buckets where [they] stood." This accommodationism called for African-Americans to remain in the South, to avail themselves of the economic progress that would come as a result of working to develop the land, and most of all to "[make] friends in every manly way" with their white neighbors. After reminding whites that their own economic fortunes would be jeopardized if they disregarded or chased away the Negro workforce, Washington ended his speech on a dramatic note that would haunt him the rest of his days. Deferring to the desire of Southern whites to maintain segregation at any cost, Washington said, "In all things that are purely social, we can be as separate as the fingers, yet one as the hand in all things essential to mutual progress."

Perhaps making specific reference to Du Bois – or, more likely, to William Monroe Trotter, another well-educated, black New Englander, who wrote extensively on Washington and took every opportunity in the black press to disparage the so-called Tuskegee Machine – Washington added to his speech a final thought on the topic of segregation: "The wisest among my race understand that the agitation of questions of social equality is the extremist folly, and that progress in the enjoyment of all the privileges that will come to us must be the result of severe and constant struggle rather than an artificial forcing." Washington's message of accommodation had an economic premise. Clearly, his words indicate a belief that no race of man that made a solid, consistent, and undeniable contribution to the economic prosperity of a nation would continue to be ostracized or oppressed. In sharp contrast to this approach, Du Bois called for blacks in the South and elsewhere to begin "ceaseless agitation and insistent demand for equality [which must include] the use of force of every sort: moral [per]suasion, propaganda and where possible even physical resistance."

To speak of Washington and Du Bois as polar opposites, however, debases the complexity of their differences. This approach fails to take into consideration the traits the two men shared in common and the true nature of their struggle. More often than not, this struggle is defined as one of industrial education versus higher education. It is probably more accurate to say that Washington and Du Bois struggled to define the nature and direction of black leadership. The two men shared in common a belief that American blacks needed a leader to defend them and articulate their views to the world at large. Their true difference, suggests historian Lerone Bennett, lay in deciding the qualities such a leader should possess.

On the one hand, Washington – so close to the land and to Southern blacks – felt strongly that a leader (modeled, no doubt, after himself) would emerge from the modest circumstances of the farming community. Such a leader would arrive at his power "through the back door," so to speak, accumulating it slowly and surely, until whites had no choice but to acknowledge that power and welcome both the black leader and his followers into the larger social order. It is likely that in Washington's mind only a Southerner, a black farmer whose life had been spent cultivating the land, would possess the qualities necessary to cultivate his people. On the other hand, Du Bois would settle for nothing less than the immediate integration of blacks into the country's social and political order. He argued that no such advancement could be made unless a portion of the black population, whom he dubbed the "talented tenth," were allowed to pursue higher education. Whereas Washington believed a Negro leader would emerge from the fields, Du Bois believed that person would emerge from the halls of academia but only if he were allowed to move freely through those halls.

Du Bois's principle objection to Washington's emphasis on industrial education was specific. He did not object to the Tuskegee curriculum in its entirety, as some historians have suggested, and indeed he saw enormous value in Washington's goal of promoting thrift, morality, and economic self-sufficiency among blacks. However, Du Bois bemoaned what he perceived as Washington's failure to equip his students with a greater awareness of modern politics and culture. Bereft of this awareness, blacks would be forced "to accept white leadership." According to Lerone Bennett in *Before the Mayflower,* Du Bois believed that "such leadership could not always be trusted to guide the Negro group into self-realization and to its highest cultural possibilities."

Just as Du Bois encouraged blacks to explore options beyond farming while at the same time singing the praises of those Southern black farmers who achieved success, so too did Washington have contradictions. In 1900, for instance, he founded the National Negro Business League, an organization that promoted black entrepreneurship, not only among farmers but among educated professionals. Through this organization Washington also encouraged the rank-and-file members of the black community – the very African-American farmers to whom he had advocated a policy of accommodation – to patronize black entrepreneurs and, when necessary, to seek the services of the black doctors and lawyers whose offices could be found in Southern cities like Atlanta and Savannah, Georgia.

Similarly, Washington eventually developed a secret practice of making anonymous financial contributions to black groups that advocated a more militant position than the one he assumed in public. That he might demonstrate contradictory impulses helps to underscore the divergent roads that had come into view for the black farmer. Washington, whose formative life experience was similar to that of countless African-Americans with ties to Southern farming communities, felt as keenly as any of his constituents the force of changing times. For all his talk of patience – of working and waiting – he wasn't blind to the fact that violence against blacks in the South was escalating. Although there were a number of African-Americans who enjoyed the middle-class success in the South that Washington had predicted, he could also see that even among his Tuskegee graduates there were a host of farmers who lived poor and desperate lives. The degradation that Du Bois had observed in the South and complained of bitterly to the world was not out of Washington's purview; he simply tried to moderate his concern and channel it toward an integrationist policy that he believed – or forced himself to believe – would eventually lead to the economic salvation and social advancement of black people.

No doubt a number of black farmers embraced Washington's strategy. Until his death in 1915, Washington remained one of the most influential men in America, dearly beloved by a large number of African-Americans. Nonetheless, in their deepest hearts the black farmers knew as surely as Washington did that the rights won for blacks during Reconstruction were being increasingly denied. As a result, like Washington himself, a number of black farmers began to consider, if only briefly, the allure of other options, other voices. Some black leaders throughout the country were urging the "scorned dark children of the South" to return to the Motherland, to Africa. For example, Henry M. Turner, a bishop in the African Methodist Episcopal (AME) church, shared with black farmers a common heritage, and when he spoke to them of returning to Africa, his words had a distinct resonance.

Born to free parents in South Carolina in 1834, Turner was exposed at an early age to the ravages of slavery and racial intolerance. At the time of his youth, South Carolina was still reeling from the slave uprisings of Nat Turner and Denmark Vesey, so local white planters had committed themselves to constraining the movement of slaves and freedmen alike. Although Bishop Turner received an advanced education, he maintained a strong sense of kinship to other blacks, regardless of whether they were freed or slaves. This kinship may have been a result of his belief that he was descended from African royalty on his mother's side. In any event this conviction triggered Turner's lifelong interest in Africa and his unwavering perception that blacks had been stripped of their proud African heritage by the European slave trade.

Ordained a minister in the AME church in 1853, Turner was commissioned by President Abraham Lincoln to serve as chaplain to the First Regiment, U.S. Colored Troops, making him the first African-American U.S. Army chaplain. Eventually Turner ended up in Georgia, where he worked for the Freedmen's Bureau, established a number of AME churches and organizations, and served for a time in the Georgia legislature — before Georgia refused in 1868 to ratify the Fifteenth Amendment and in the process negated the rights of blacks to vote or serve in local government. The amendment, of course, was ratified in 1870.

Turner became president of Morris Brown University, while remaining quite active in the AME church. After becoming a bishop in 1868, he used the AME pulpit with increasing frequency to decry the disfranchisement of blacks in Georgia. By the mid-1870s, Turner was beginning to show sympathy to factions that believed black Americans could only regain a sense of self-respect and self-sufficiency by returning to Africa. In 1876 he wrote, as cited in *Before the Mayflower,* "There is no instance mentioned in history where an enslaved people of an alien race rose to respectability upon the same territory of their enslavement and in the presence of their enslavers, without losing their identity or individuality by amalgamation. Can any result be hoped for the Negro in the United States? I think not." Turner directed his message at black farmers in particular, whom he felt should practice their skills at cultivating the land in an environment where they would not be treated as second-class citizens. The bishop was especially outraged by Booker T. Washington and his emphasis on accommodation and compromise. Soon after Washington's famous address in Atlanta in 1895, Turner worried openly that

Washington's remarks about social equality would be used by whites, as quoted in Harlan's *Booker T. Washington,* "to prove that the Negro race is satisfied with being degraded." These concerns led him to declare from the pulpit that Washington would "have to live a long time to undo the harm he has done to our race."

More pessimistic and cynical than even Du Bois about the likelihood of blacks achieving social equality in the United States, Turner directed the thousands of African-Americans he reached through the AME church to think of themselves as a separate nation, one that should return to its homeland. As the AME church grew in size and influence, Turner and his ideas enjoyed wider renown and circulation. He remained virtually unknown to whites, however, which gave him ever greater freedom to speak his mind. Unlike Washington and Du Bois, Turner spoke in the language of the common person, and black farmers in particular responded to his message, his "African dream." By the thousands black farmers affiliated with the AME church donated large amounts of money to various projects that promised to help them emigrate to Africa.

Unfortunately, Turner couldn't control the operation, and a number of swindlers took advantage of his many followers. A number of the Back to Africa initiatives proved to be elaborate confidence games, and the ones that were legitimate or authorized by Turner were often woefully mismanaged. Of the few hundred American blacks who reached Liberia in response to Turner's message, the vast majority were black farmers. More often than not, however, these farmers died from tropical diseases shortly after arriving in Africa, or else they returned to America, penniless and disenchanted. Still, the fact that so many black farmers took an interest in the Back to Africa movement is significant. It points to their growing awareness of the range of opportunities they might pursue. Furthermore, it suggests an increasing frustration with the second-class citizenship that crippled black farmers economically and psychologically in the South. To make an attempt to emigrate to Africa – even a failed attempt – was a potent, symbolic protest against a way of life that had begun to seem more and more fruitless and obsolete.

In Washington's call for economic self-sufficiency among blacks, Du Bois's demand for the full integration of blacks into the intellectual, cultural, and political life of the country, and Turner's insistence that blacks be considered a separate nation, beholden to no one but themselves, the seeds of a new kind of black consciousness were sown. It is not a coincidence that these seeds were handled first by farmers, who comprised the majority of the black population at the turn of the century. Without the emotional commitment of black farmers, no ideological movement among African-Americans could have hoped to succeed. For this reason the prominent voices in the larger black community addressed their messages first to black farmers, a fact that may have initially overwhelmed the farmers, so insistent were the various voices that were suddenly bellowing in their ears. Eventually, however, it seems that black farmers became adept at synthesizing the various elements of each new point of view, and in that synthesis they developed a prototype for black nationalism – a broadening political awareness that confirmed that the farmers' worth as human beings was undeniable, no matter how often it was denied by whites.

Moving into the 1920s – when the promise of economic empowerment began to seem less dim – this heightened sense of self-worth was imparted to the children of black farmers, even those children who left the South. The message would be passed down from one generation to the next, establishing a clear and direct line between the first impulses among blacks at self-determination in the wake of the Civil War and the Civil Rights Movement, which would bring such impulses to spectacular fruition in the 1950s and 1960s.

part three

HARVEST TIME :: 1929–1979

5.

THE THICKENING SHADOWS :: Black Migration to the North

My mother had an uncle Rose whom she saw only once in her entire life. He died in Chicago, Illinois, and she always wondered how he ended up so far from home. He was my grandfather's oldest brother. He left when he was very young and never returned. Maybe every generation has those who leave. My great-great uncle left, my mother left, my father left, and in some ways so have an entire generation of my cousins.

Some of us have to leave and should leave. As a little girl, I wondered why my parents or any black people for that matter had stayed in this country. I discovered my world through history books and biographies, and I was deeply disturbed by the horror of U.S. history as it related to me and generations of Africans. I would often think that if someone kidnapped me and eventually freed me, that I would go running back to my mother and father. So when I read about the great migrations and the occasional "back to Africa" movements, I wondered why my forebears did not just buy a ticket and walk away from this place that held our worst nightmares.

As an adult, I grew to understand the courage it took for many of those early Africans and their descendants to choose to live and then choose to stay here. Despite the difficult memories and the de facto segregation that was alive and well in Montezuma, Georgia, throughout my childhood, I continue to return to Georgia every chance I get. I find solace in this place. I find community, memory, and faith. But I also have family that have never visited Montezuma, Georgia.

I am sure most of my relatives never had childhood fantasies of family and blood on distant shores. I on the other hand remember my romantic imaginings of a young woman who laughed like me, walked like me, and occasionally looked across the Atlantic wondering about some cousin or great-great aunt she would never know. A part of her existed in a place that was barely spoken of and only remembered as being from a time of shame, fear, and loss. I would imagine that this African woman was waiting for us to return and wondering what was taking us so long to find our way back.

Whenever I go home, my family asks about those who have been gone a long time. They want to know how the missing kinfolk are doing and when they will be coming for a visit. I would like to tell them that this place of warm earth and weeping willows is not everyone's home. I would like to tell them that some of us choose to stay and some of us have to leave. Many of the people in our family won't be coming back anytime soon. They will make their homes in new places, places without bad memories or haunting spirits; places where the dead rest and the living create a new world. And while they and many others take a new and hopeful journey, there will always be those of us who will take the long walk between the homes we remember and the places we have come to know.

THEY LEFT in droves.

From the time of Reconstruction to the mid-twentieth century, blacks in the South were perhaps more keenly aware than blacks in any other part of the country of the failure of America's promise to provide liberty and justice for all. In the years after the Civil War a systematic attempt to strip African-Americans of the entitlements bestowed upon them in 1865 by the Emancipation Proclamation left many blacks in positions of poverty and servitude that resembled exactly the circumstances they had endured as slaves. For this reason a good many of them fled the South. They left in droves. Despite the fact that the Thirteenth Amendment ended slavery and the Fourteenth Amendment mandated that all persons born in the United States were to enjoy full citizenship and equal rights before the law, many Southern states refused to acknowledge these laws, thereby forcing a number of African-Americans to look elsewhere for a better quality of life.

Congress, aware of this problem, passed the Civil Rights Act of 1866 to compel recalcitrant states to obey the law. The act stipulated that all persons born in the United States had the right to make contracts, sue, buy or lease property, marry, and testify in court – all of which were rights that had been routinely and often arbitrarily deprived of Southern blacks in the aftermath of the Civil War. Although many states agreed to this new legislation, they removed its teeth by enacting strict "vagrancy" laws, which were enforced almost exclusively against blacks. These laws were simply an extension of the old Black Laws or "Black Codes." Such a law might require an African-American to carry with him at all times proof of his employment. If he was stopped and could not produce the necessary documentation, he would be prosecuted for vagrancy. By these means and others the former slaves were retained as cheap agricultural labor.

A similar Civil Rights Act was passed in 1875, again for the purpose

of enforcing the Thirteenth Amendment. Because federal troops had remained stationed in the South in the wake of the Civil War, enforcement
of civil rights statutes was not always an exercise in futility. However, in
1877 the newly elected President Rutherford B. Hayes withdrew from
the South all remaining federal troops, thereby removing any chance of
civil rights enforcement. Soon afterward, each of the Southern states began in earnest a new plan to disfranchise African-Americans from the voting process. Poll taxes, literacy tests, and grandfather clauses were some
of the methods by which the black vote was suppressed. In addition, the
Ku Klux Klan began asserting more of a presence at polling places, which
served to frighten and intimidate would-be black voters.

At the same time strict segregation laws were introduced throughout the South. According to these laws, blacks and whites were to walk a
separate path in all social affairs. The interpretation of these laws was
often broad, but their lunacy and hatefulness was quite specific. In one
Southern state, for example, it was against the law for white doctors to
treat black patients. In another state no textbook handled by black schoolchildren could be passed into the hands of white schoolchildren. This approach to segregation allowed whites to scrutinize, patrol, and legislate
the activities of blacks, controlling and dictating the behavior of the former slaves as though they were still in bondage.

These so-called Jim Crow laws were strengthened in 1896, when
the U.S. Supreme Court handed down its decision on *Plessy v. Ferguson,*
which upheld Louisiana's right to segregate racially "separate but equal"
facilities of passenger trains. A French-speaking lawyer named Homer
Plessy had attempted to sit in a whites-only passenger car. Although
Plessy had only one-eighth African blood, that qualified him as a Negro in
the eyes of Southern law. When he refused to move to the "black" car,
he was arrested. After being convicted by a Louisiana state court, Plessy
appealed to the Supreme Court, where his case was eventually heard and

the conviction upheld. The Court insisted that separate-but-equal facilities for blacks was not a violation of their constitutional rights, so long as these facilities were comparable in all substantial ways. With only one dissent – from Associate Justice John Marshall Harlan, the son of a Kentucky slaveowner – the Court insisted that such laws actually served the public by providing fewer opportunities for racial disharmony. Added the Court, "The object of the Fourteenth Amendment was undoubtedly to enforce absolute equality of the two races before the law, but in the nature of things it could not have been intended to abolish distinctions based on color, or to enforce social, as distinguished from political equality, or a commingling of the two races upon terms unsatisfactory to either."

Whereas Jim Crow laws had appeared intermittently throughout the South in the years before *Plessy v. Ferguson* – for example, only Georgia had instituted separate seating on streetcars before 1900 – every Southern state interpreted the decision as license to continue banishing blacks to the margins of society. Black farmers felt the sting of these measures most directly, because they represented the majority of Southern blacks. The flood of such laws moved so quickly and destructively across the Southern landscape, black farmers looked in vain for some reasonable course of action, something that would stem the tide of further humiliation.

The reckless disregard by whites of the Civil Rights Acts of 1866 and 1875, the withdrawal of federal troops from the South in 1877, the various political disfranchisement activities of the early 1890s, and the *Plessy v. Ferguson* decision of 1896 cumulatively and profoundly affected the lives of black farmers. Each new setback seemed to do more damage than the one before, and eventually all the setbacks began to feel like a hard, swift, single blow to the heart of every Southern black farmer. Unlike the fighter Jack Johnson – who, in approximately this same era, managed to withstand the blows of countless white opponents – black farmers began to lose their footing. Even though African-Americans operated about 937,000 farms in the South by 1913, a decline in the number of new farms was becoming increasingly steep. Many of the old farms were being abandoned — sold off quickly to pay debts or absorbed by white farmers who had started a campaign to "reclaim" the land now owned by African-Americans.

It was against this backdrop of racism and lack of opportunity that many black farmers set their sights on the North. The exodus began slowly, but it picked up momentum quickly. Between 1910 and 1920 a relatively small number of 300,000 blacks departed the South. This initial migration gave rise to a larger one, and between 1920 and 1930 a wave of 1,300,000 African-Americans flooded into such cities as Chicago, Detroit, New York, Philadelphia, and Pittsburgh. The migration continued in the 1930s, when a total of 1,500,000 blacks arrived in the North. Finally, in the 1940s the sustained migration reached its peak, culminating with the departure of some 2,500,000 African-Americans from Southern farming communities.

By the 1920s African-Americans in the South who did not own their own farms were working in the agricultural industry for wages that were deplorable. For example, those who worked for large manufacturers made on average about $1.10 a day, which was equal that received by whites in similar "unskilled" positions. In the wake of Jim Crow, however, it became increasingly easy for an employer to insist that even his hardest-working black employees were not pulling their weight, thereby justifying a reduction in their wages.

Few African-Americans were spared this humiliation, as it struck women as well as men, children as well as adults. Since the days of sharecropping, farming among African-Americans had been a family endeavor, and indeed there is evidence to suggest that family members working in such close proximity to each other strengthened the familial bond, even if the circumstances of their work lives were dismal. Black families who worked together on farms tended to be better informed of local affairs than many of their white counterparts, and more likely to pursue schooling or to be involved in the church. As a result, when the black family farm became increasingly jeopardized and many left the farms for the industrialized North or were forced to take menial jobs as agricultural laborers, the integrity of the black family itself was threatened. Eventually a widespread moral and emotional crisis befell the black families of the rural South in the 1920s, and no African-American man, woman, or child wasn't scarred by the effects of the crisis.

Predictably, some Southern politicians argued that the political and economic degradation of blacks would lead to a restoration of the traditional Southern social order. In some instances, for example, blacks were deliberately refused jobs to make them vulnerable to vagrancy laws or else to condemn them in the Northern press as inherently lazy and unwilling to work. Conviction on a vagrancy charge, bolstered by the persistent rumor that blacks were "shiftless," pushed many a black farmer into the ranks of expendable, cheap labor.

For years many whites waged a campaign to drive blacks entirely out of the South. African-American farmers were not only cheated and threatened, they were also closed out of the marketplace, where their crops — usually cotton or soy — would have fetched top dollar and led to an improvement in their circumstances. Such improvement would have made them less susceptible to the authority of whites, and a good many whites were determined to maintain their authority at all costs. Lynchings became an integral part of the campaign to both reduce the number of blacks in the South and to maintain control over the blacks who remained. In addition, in places like Georgia it wasn't enough to simply drive blacks away; as early as 1865, representatives in the Georgia legislature were introducing bills that would "prevent persons of African descent from coming into the state." Somehow these white Georgians failed to anticipate the labor shortage that a black exodus would cause, however. When that shortage arrived, they were caught off-guard, and immediately efforts were made to replace the African-American workforce.

They were not so easy to replace, however. First, most black Southerners were familiar with the temperament and texture of the land, making them uniquely qualified to grow and harvest its crops. Second, white laborers from Europe or from other parts of the country demanded higher wages than those that Southern white employers had paid their black employees. Furthermore, European laborers in particular wanted the same things their black counterparts had wanted – that is, equal access to landownership. Although many of these laborers had been hired to further drive down the cost of black labor – apparently a common slogan of the time was "Work Nigger, or starve" – their demands went unanswered by their employers, and soon the European labor force fled the South as well.

Well into the 1920s, then, the struggle to replace the scorned black workers was ongoing in the South. When things didn't work out with the European immigrants, employers set their sights on China. Enormous efforts were made to obtain Chinese laborers, who at the time were rumored to be pliant, docile, and extremely easy to train. The stereotype of Chinese laborers as obedient and agreeable was so prevalent, white planters hoped to pay them even less than they had paid blacks. However, not only did the Chinese laborers have trouble adapting to the South's particular farming techniques, they also violated the expectations of their employers by demanding fair treatment and a livable wage. When news of the shabby treatment of the Chinese began to spread, Asian-American advocacy groups in California and elsewhere alerted their constituents to avoid the American South at all costs.

Efforts to get blacks to return to the South were largely unsuccessful, except in the years immediately following the Civil War. In Georgia especially the economic impact of the migration was severe. More than sixty thousand African-Americans left the state between 1915 and 1917, and the majority of these were able-bodied men in their teens and twenties. A number of whites tried to close their eyes to the problem, but soon the mass exodus had become a crisis that could not be ignored. There simply weren't enough laborers, farmers, or black workers of any kind to keep the Georgia economy intact. A reporter in the *Macon Telegraph* wrote in 1915, "Everybody seems to be asleep about what is going on under our noses, that is, everybody but those farmers who have wakened up on mornings recently to find every male Negro over 21 on [the] place gone — to Cleveland, to Pittsburgh, to Chicago, to Indianapolis."

Many white Georgians were slow to respond to the impending labor crisis for an obvious reason: they did not want to acknowledge that their own treachery and racial intolerance had created the problem. Defensively, they insisted that Jim Crow laws and similar initiatives weren't to blame for the black migration. Instead, they argued, various acts of God had driven the black farmers away: floods, lousy crop prices, and especially the boll weevil. But blacks had started leaving the South even before floods had caused the price of various crops to drop in 1914. And even after the prices stabilized, the migration continued. Moreover, the boll weevil had done its least damage in 1916 — during the peak of the black migration — and it did its worst damage in the mid-1920s, when migration numbers were beginning to slacken. After having considered legislation to keep blacks out of the state, white Georgians were now looking for ways to bar blacks from *leaving* the state. In the meantime, the threat to the economic stability of Georgia and other Southern states made whites more likely to respond to the demands of African-Americans. Chastened by the hard lessons of potential economic disaster, white officials realized, for example, that if they condemned lynchings and violence against blacks, the likelihood of blacks remaining in the area would increase dramatically.

By 1917 groups of white and black farmers huddled together to address the crisis, and the cooperation among them was unprecedented, albeit a little tense. In these meetings agreements were made to increase wages and improve working conditions for black laborers, to punish whites who incited mob violence against blacks, and to promote land-ownership among African-Americans. Still, the migration continued well into the 1920s. For many folks the efforts of white Georgians to reconcile with the black labor force was a classic example of too little, too late. After so many years of persecution, few blacks wanted to return to or remain on a landscape that was soaked with so much African-American blood. Even as some black clergymen preached against the migration – arguing, like Booker T. Washington had, that business opportunities would now abound for blacks – their parishioners continued to strike out on their own.

Although no amount of white conciliation could slow the black migration – by 1918 for example, various influential white women's groups issued a call to condemn lynchings in the South – there were a number of African-American farmers and laborers who chose not to leave. Those who remained began, slowly but surely and in very specific circumstances, to fare a bit better than their ancestors had fared since Reconstruction to the late 1890s. If he was willing to go about his business quietly, abiding by the South's hateful and outdated social protocols, a black farmer or laborer might have experienced from 1910 to 1920 an unprecedented level of success. The psychic cost was high, however, and it is no coincidence that his more militant, outspoken black neighbors might have suffered considerable hardship during this same period.

Nonetheless, as the 1920s wore on Georgia and other Southern states found themselves all but crippled by the continued Northern migration of blacks. As a result, these states were in particularly vulnerable positions when the Great Depression of the 1930s befell the country. For many in the South the first indications of the Depression were felt in the mid-1920s, and as with all economic downturns, the black farmer would be hit the hardest. In the meantime, though, that same farmer saw for the first time a glimmer of the social equality and economic empowerment that Washington, Du Bois, and so many others had predicted. Because of the South's recognition of the value of the black workforce, and because of the country's debt to the many African-American soldiers who fought bravely and heroically in World War I, a dramatic shift in the social landscape could be felt under the black farmer's feet. The shift didn't undermine his equilibrium – he had been preparing for it for years – and in fact it seemed to make him even stronger for the new, long, and difficult struggle that lay ahead in the 1920s.

6.

*My great-great-uncle A. B. Brown and my great-uncle Willie B. Mathis still live in
Montezuma, Georgia. Willie B. chose to be a minister, while A.B. chose to farm. My uncle
A.B. is a soft-spoken man whose eyes slowly fill with tears when he speaks of the old days.
The days before I was born, the days before Martin and Malcolm, the days before "civil rights."
Those days during the Depression were hard times for everyone, but they were particularly
difficult for poor black folks in rural Georgia. Although my uncle A.B. remembers the poor
wages — men, forty cents a day; women, thirty cents — what he remembers even more clearly is
the fear, the fear that white landowners and their hooded operatives had instilled in black
workers. If you complained, you could disappear the next day and never be seen again.
Lynchings were the "strange fruit" left out occasionally. More often than not, an outspoken
farm worker could be murdered, buried, and never heard from again, simply for complaining
about low wages and harsh conditions. So folks learned to speak softly and wait. Some
waited for the opportunity to leave at night and head for one of the "up-south" cities, with*

factories and rumors of better days. My uncle A.B. lost a brother this way, a brother who moved
to Newark, New Jersey, and never came back. Uncle A.B., like my grandfather, decided to wait
on his faith to deliver him and his, a faith that remains strong today, despite all that he has
seen and all that he knows.

Uncle A.B. thinks things are better now, but he remembers the wagons filled with white
children going to school while black children worked in the fields. He remembers well the
faces of the young white men and women, now community elders, who reaped the benefits of
paying black folks low wages and instilling in them fear and suffering. This is why he seems a
little skeptical sometimes about the changes in the South. Conditions in the South may be
better today, but I leave my conversation with Uncle A.B. with the feeling that it would be best
to talk softly and keep my eyes open, just in case they (the Klan and all their kind) come again.
He wouldn't want me to disappear in the night because somehow I had been misled to think
that everything was all right.

TIMES ARE NOT WHAT THEY USED TO BE. THERE IS NO USE SHUTTING OUR EYES TO THIS FACT. PROSPERITY HAS GONE INTO RETIREMENT. OUR ADVICE IS FOR EVERYONE TO GET SOMETHING, AND HOLD ONTO IT. GET IT IN THE CITY IF POSSIBLE, BUT, FAILING THIS, START TOWARD THE FARM BEFORE THE SNOW FLIES.
—EDITORIAL [ROBERT ABBOTT] IN *CHICAGO DEFENDER*

THAT A RENOWNED African-American newspaper, the *Chicago Defender*, urged its newly arrived urban readership in 1930 to consider returning to living as farmers in the South is a remarkable thing. Having been a vocal member of the chorus of voices that insisted black farmers pursue their dreams of prosperity in the North, the *Defender*'s sudden plea that the most impoverished blacks living in cities "start toward the farm before the snow flies" is an indication of just how fully the Great Depression ravaged the lives of all Americans, particularly those who had so little to begin with.

Equally noteworthy is the *Defender*'s assertion that "times are not what they used to be." Truer words were never spoken. Between 1923 and 1929 there had been a postwar boom in the American economy, one that seemed to expand precariously beyond anyone's wildest imaginings. In the Southern states, however, farmers in general – and black farmers in particular – could read the handwriting on the wall. They were the last to realize the rewards of this boom – the rise in profits for landowners and the availability of work for agricultural laborers – but they were also the first to feel the pinch of the impending Depression. The labor shortage that followed the Northern migration, which all but emptied the South of its black labor force, also put considerable strain on Northern economic resources. An intense economic strain was not only limited to the North, however, or even to the United States. The various capitalist systems of the world had been slowly heading for trouble for quite some time, in part because of an international crisis of overproduction, various industrial shutdowns, and the explosion of mass layoffs that followed. The United States was inexorably tied to the rhythms of the world's economy, despite the smug position taken by many bankers and others that the U.S. economy was invulnerable. When a crash occurred in other capitalist countries, the extended run of prosperity Americans had enjoyed came to a halt.

African-American farmers felt the pinch almost immediately. From 1929 through 1933, $160 billion in stock market values were lost in the United States, the output of factories was reduced by 50 percent, nearly six thousand banks were ruined, and the value of farm products took an enormous drop, from $8.5 billion to $4 billion. Similar events took place all over the world, where production in other capitalist countries dropped by more than 40 percent and foreign trade plummeted to roughly 65 percent. On Southern farms, however, the trouble had started much sooner. During the mid-1920s economic developments in Georgia in particular exemplified the financial crisis that was taking shape across the Southern landscape.

Perhaps most important is the issue of the declining black workforce, an issue that cannot be emphasized enough in relation to its impact on the Southern economy. During the 1920s, Georgia's African-American population declined by nearly 150,000. By the beginning of the Great Depression, blacks comprised less than 40 percent of the state's total population – roughly the same low percentage as in the early 1790s, when the legalization of slavery in Georgia was only a few decades old and the number of African slaves in the state was still far from its peak of 462,198 in 1860. The departure of 150,000 African-Americans from Georgia in the 1920s left 70,000 jobs unfilled. At the same time these rural black Southerners were flooding into both Northern and Southern cities at a rate that even a booming economy could hardly accommodate. That so many blacks who left the South had been farmers was verified by the U.S. Department of Agriculture (USDA), which reported that between 1920 and 1925, only 84,000 black farmers remained in Georgia, from a previous high of 130,000. The bulk of these farmers left in 1922, abandoning 46,000 farms and leading the USDA to conclude that "the situation in Georgia is much worse than realized."

With nearly a third of the black farms abandoned, the remaining two-thirds enjoyed notable prosperity but only for a short time. By 1925 a second significant development destabilized the Georgian economy. A plague of boll weevil had descended on the state with such force that cotton yields were cut in half. Black farmers who had been slow to achieve some measure of financial gain saw much of it lost to the boll weevil crisis, and even those who managed to survive the crisis were brought to the edge of bankruptcy. The tide slowly changed, and by 1929 cotton was much more abundant, selling for eighteen cents a pound. By 1933, however, in the throes of the Great Depression, the price had dropped to a meager six cents a pound.

So Southern farmers, particularly those who were black, had been on an economic roller coaster for nearly a decade by the time the Depression hit. While the diminishing labor force hit white farmers especially hard, and both white and black farmers suffered the boll weevil crisis, there was an additional development that had far-reaching and specific ramifications for black farmers. With cotton values still slow to recover toward the end of the 1920s, black farmers who had been either wiped out entirely or brought to the brink of financial ruin were unable to pay back the operating loans they had received during this period. This is significant because it was primarily the African-American banks of Southern cities like Atlanta that had made the loans, so when a large number of black farmers were unable to make their repayments, the banks suffered a devastating blow – one that was exacerbated by the stock market crash of 1929.

The failure of banks is always a sign of an impending economic crisis. The failure of a number of Negro banks before the Great Depression served as a signal of the grim days ahead, and it is likely that black farmers recognized that signal immediately. By this time African-Americans had already endured a long and often tense relationship with Negro banks. Although many powerful church groups such as the AME and a number of black fraternal organizations had operated banks since the late 1870s – at first in the North but then increasingly in the South – it had taken a while for these institutions to win the trust and respect of other African-Americans, who had themselves fallen victim to the stereotype of blacks as unreliable. Subjected for so long to the racial hostility that was a fundamental element of Southern culture, blacks in the South experienced a collective sense of self-loathing, one so palpable that it caused them to believe their modest, hard-earned savings would somehow be safer in the hands of whites than in the vaults of a black-owned bank.

When Booker T. Washington and others encouraged African-American farmers in the late 1800s to invest their trust and their money in Negro businesses, some of the tensions were alleviated. A number of black farmers perhaps still remembered vividly the Freedmen's Savings Bank, a post-Reconstruction banking institution allegedly aimed at and run by Southern African-Americans. When the bank suffered a spectacular failure – literally closing overnight and losing all the assets of its African-American depositors – black farmers came to regard such institutions with increased wariness. After it was pointed out that the Freedmen's Savings Bank had been managed (or, rather, carelessly mismanaged) by whites for blacks, however, some faith in black-owned banks was restored. Between 1900 and 1914 nearly eighty Negro banks were established, primarily in the South, and their relationships with black farmers grew and strengthened over the years.

As a result, it was these very banks that black farmers turned to for loans, and more often than not, these loans were granted, even if the investment didn't appear especially sound on paper. Although Negro banks were in business to make money, they often felt their primary mandate was to encourage thrift, economic self-sufficiency, and a feeling of shared responsibility among their black clientele. This positive, socially oriented approach to banking took its toll long before the cotton crisis of the 1920s. For example, in 1916 there were nearly fifty Negro banks nationwide, but by 1930, after years of significant losses, there were only half that amount. The setbacks black farmers endured in that bitter period of the mid-1920s threatened to wipe out entirely the Negro banking industry.

Because of this, even farmers who somehow managed to steadily repay their operating loans were often thrown a financial curve. Crippled by the combination of diminishing funds and the stock market crash of 1929, a Negro bank might lose all its deposits, which was often comprised of the entire life savings of its black clientele. Of the 8,812 banks to fail nationwide between 1930 and 1933, 12 were black, according to the *Encyclopedia of Black America,* edited by W. Augustus Low and Virgil A. Clift. In the spring of 1933, when President Franklin Delano Roosevelt attempted to suspend economic chaos by declaring a four-day bank holiday – that is, a closing of U.S. banks by executive order – only 11 black banks survived. In the South these included the Citizens Trust Company of Atlanta, Georgia; Citizens Savings Bank and Trust Company of Nashville, Tennessee; and the Tuskegee Institute Savings Bank of Tuskegee, Alabama. Set adrift from their one consistent financial resource, black farmers entered the 1930s with a great sense of impending doom and disillusionment. Whatever financial advances they had made seemed to be receding now, fading as steadily as a dream. "When Hoover was president," said one farmer, Rev. Willie B. Mathis, "everything went to the bottom. By that I mean there was no money. . . . [Some] black people . . . would go to church with shoes tied up with string and [they would] wire the soles to the tops of the shoes 'cause they didn't have any."

For most Americans suffering through the ravages of the Great Depression, President Herbert Hoover was the focal point of their frustration. Blacks in particular had reason to feel abandoned by Hoover. His Republican Party, "the Party of Lincoln," had tried for years to shed the reputation of being friendly to blacks, a reputation left over from the days of the Emancipation Proclamation. Hoover perceived African-Americans as a political liability, and he and many other Republicans now distanced themselves from racial issues to curry favor with white voters. Nonetheless, even though a number of prominent African-Americans spoke out against Hoover during the 1928 election, many black voters in the North and in select provinces in the South continued to feel a strong sense of loyalty to Lincoln's memory. As a result, at ballot time these Republican loyalists cast their vote for Hoover. Hoover's cruel indifference to the plight of poor blacks soon became apparent, however; he would become the last Republican in history to win a majority of the black vote.

Not unlike some contemporary political figures, Hoover subscribed to a trickle-down theory of economics. Accordingly, he responded to the financial crisis that gripped the country by focusing his attention on the needs of prominent corporations. He believed that if the fortunes of those on top were made stable by government assistance, this stability would eventually trickle down to poorer Americans and improve their economic prospects. With this objective in mind, Hoover's administration founded the Reconstruction Finance Corporation to breathe life into companies that had been hit hard by the stock market crash of 1929. From the perspective of many poor Americans, however, Hoover was simply giving handouts to fat cats while ignoring everyone else.

Southern black farmers had a specific relationship to Hoover, one that dated back to 1927, when he was Secretary of Commerce. In that year a devastating flood hit the Mississippi Valley, and Hoover led the relief efforts. To this end, he pulled from black farms all available able-bodied men and pressed them into compulsory service. They simply were not at liberty to refuse, even though many of these men did not have experience with levee work. The dismal work conditions Hoover authorized were akin to those of slavery. In the 1928 election, however, this experience was not enough to turn Southern blacks en masse against Hoover. Oddly, though, in the minds of many white voters, his time in the Mississippi Valley somehow suggested a connection with blacks. Many whites didn't remember that Hoover had mistreated the African-Americans in his charge; they remembered only that he had spent considerable time among blacks. This was not the sort of reputation that Hoover wanted in circulation, so in time he made it a habit to express as little interest as possible in the affairs and well-being of African-Americans.

Although Hoover's apparent indifference to Southern blacks did not cause them to turn against him entirely, this attitude did seem to galvanize them politically in a way that hadn't been seen since the early days of Reconstruction. Unrest among African-American voters had been brewing since 1912, when Woodrow Wilson had been elected president. Almost immediately after taking office, Wilson seemed to go out of his way to alienate black voters. In quick succession he broke a long-standing tradition of appointing prominent African-American political figures as consulates to Haiti and Santo Domingo; he publicly dismissed a proposal for a National Race Commission to study the status of blacks in the United States; and he began segregating blacks and whites in government offices.

Wilson had been a Democrat, and his indifference and even hostility toward blacks seemed no less pronounced than current president Hoover's, a Republican. With no apparent friends in either of the two major parties, African-Americans became vulnerable to the overtures of alternative political movements, many of which existed outside the mainstream of American life. These movements hoped to capture the hearts, minds, and imaginations of all African-Americans, starting with those on the bottom rung – the black farmer in the rural South. Even though their political strength was limited and their ranks were dwindling, farmers remained at the frontlines of African-American political unrest, and no ideological movement stood a chance of succeeding without their support.

Various political activists descended on African-American farmers as aggressively as had Washington and Du Bois in earlier years. This time the "savior" they promised was a radical one, a system of government the activists said would eliminate poverty and social injustice in one fell swoop. "It was the god that failed," the author Richard Wright and others would eventually comment. But now, in the desperate economic and political climate of the 1930s, Communism must have seemed a more attractive god than capitalism, which had turned its back on the black farmer for so long, he no longer knew where to turn.

As though it were 1890 again, the Great Depression brought back with a vengeance the ugly system of sharecropping. This is not to say that sharecropping had ever gone away. In the previous forty years white planters had continued to put African-American farmers to work in the fields and to pay those farmers a "share" of the crop they harvested. The work was back-breaking — conducted seven days a week, from sunup to sundown — and just as certainly as the ferocity of lynching had, the degrading system of sharecropping also caused many blacks to flee the South. With so few blacks remaining in the South, however, the sharecropping system seemed for a while to go into a temporary remission. Because of the labor shortage in the early 1900s through the 1920s, many black farmers could demand better terms from their employers. Often these terms were lucrative enough to allow a farmer to eventually purchase his own land. Even those black farmers who had continued as sharecroppers were subjected to a touch less indignity in those days, if only because their white employers couldn't afford to lose any more labor from the fields.

Unfortunately, in the 1930s an already exploitative system took a turn for the worse. The northern migration had finally slowed down, which meant there was now less of a labor shortage in the South. With fewer African-Americans leaving for the North — and more unemployed white laborers competing with blacks for even the most meager jobs — the treatment of African-American sharecroppers became as cruel as it had ever been in the past. The number of sharecroppers began to increase as more black families found themselves unable to maintain farms of their own during the Depression. For these families sharecropping now seemed the only way to make a living in the South. But unlike sharecroppers of the nineteenth century, whose political impulses had been stymied, the black sharecroppers in the 1930s had a heightened political awareness that made them keenly aware of the extent to which they were being exploited.

The number of African-American tenant farmers also saw a dramatic increase during the Depression. Again, though, the terms of their arrangements with white planters were rarely in the farmers' favor. As the economic crisis of the 1930s persisted, many black farmers found it increasingly difficult to continue paying a cash rent to white planters, which meant the black farmers were obligated to turn over the proceeds of whatever they harvested. As a result, they became stuck in a financial rut that made it impossible to get ahead. In time many of these tenant farmers fell into such tremendous debt, they were forced into a position that was really no different from sharecropping. Many black farmers began to feel they were back at square one. Whatever modest economic progress they had started to make was halted by the Depression, and some families found themselves in conditions that were far worse than any they had ever known. Levels of frustration grew higher as the 1930s wore on, and none of the old consolations seemed to make much of a difference any more – the soothing refrains of the Bible or the promise of a bright future that preachers and politicians had been trotting out for years.

Convinced that Hoover's economic reforms had passed them by entirely, Southern blacks looked for a more radical solution to their hardships. The National Association for the Advancement of Colored People (NAACP), a political organization that had been formed by Du Bois and others in 1909 to advocate on behalf of all black Americans, had become highly centralized in Northern cities, which put the group at a distance from black farmers who faced particular adversity in the South. The cruelest example of this adversity was lynching. In 1930 there were thirty reported lynchings of blacks in Southern states, almost four times the number reported in 1929, before the stock market crash. In addition to struggling with their own poverty, then, African-Americans in the South had become the target of increased violent hostility from whites who needed someone to blame for the economic crisis that had ravaged their lives.

Into this fray came the Communist Party, which had been growing steadily in the South since the 1924 presidential election. Hoping to capitalize on the NAACP's failure to assert more of a presence in the rural South, the Communist Party increased its efforts in the late 1920s to recruit black farmers and laborers. The position they took on lynching was central to these efforts, and they publicly chastised the NAACP for treating lynching as, as quoted in Donald L. Grant's *The Way It Was in the South,* "an isolated phenomenon, the terrible sport of lawless uneducated whites." Speaking specifically to Southern blacks who spent every day living in fear of lynching, the Communists promised a more aggressive attack against such violence. They called lynching "one of the weapons with which the white ruling class enforces its national oppression of the Negro people."

At every possible opportunity the Communists appeared to take a harder line against lynching than did the NAACP. More important, they always spoke of a clear relationship between such violence and the bitter economic circumstances Southern blacks endured. Nearly drowning in these circumstances, and living in fear of mob violence that was often arbitrary and unprovoked, African-American farmers in Georgia and elsewhere could not help but pay attention to the Communists' platform. Neither could they help but be impressed by the Communists' efforts to end lynching in the South. In 1934, for example, when Congress began deliberating an antilynching bill, Communists opposed the bill on the basis that it did not get to the heart of the problem — the social and economic oppression of the Negro — and also because the bill did not make it mandatory to impose the death penalty on the leaders of mob violence. The NAACP, consumed by various internal struggles about its leadership, stood by as the bill died in Congress.

Upon arriving in the South, however, the Communist Party tended first to the plight of the black sharecropper. Many years had passed since the dissolution of the Colored Farmers' Alliance — indeed, of the entire Alliance movement — and no recent efforts had been made in the South to organize black sharecroppers, tenant farmers, and laborers. Although the national farming organizations continued to exist, advocating on behalf of its exclusively white membership, it would take until 1934 for the Southern Tenant Farmers' Union to emerge on behalf of all struggling farmers throughout the South. In the meantime, beginning in 1931, the Communist Party helped to spearhead the Sharecroppers Union in Tallapoosa and Lee Counties in Alabama.

The Sharecroppers Union conducted a number of strikes against particularly unscrupulous white planters, who deprived black sharecroppers of the proceeds due them at the end of each harvesting season or found ways to drive the tenant farmers into so much debt that they would be forced to become sharecroppers themselves. A number of demonstrations turned violent, but small gains were made, and eventually branches of the Sharecroppers Union were established in a number of other Southern states. By 1935 the Union reported a membership of twelve thousand members — an inflated number, perhaps, but a clear indication of the growing credibility of the Communist Party among Southern black farmers.

Continuing to present themselves as an alternative not only to the two mainstream political parties but also to the NAACP, the Communists remained a highly organized and visible force on the Southern landscape, taking up the most radical causes that others chose to avoid. To black farmers in particular, the reputation of the Communists was probably enhanced most of all by their involvement in what would become known as the case of the "Scottsboro boys."

According to *Timelines of African-American History: Five-Hundred Years of Black Achievement,* police in Scottsboro, Alabama, arrested nine African-American men in the spring of 1931 for allegedly raping two white women who were riding, like the men, onboard a freight train. Eventually the case became the most well-known civil rights case of its time, tying into knots a number of trials, retrials, and appeals that were not fully untangled until 1950. The nine African-American young men on the train — ranging in age from thirteen to twenty-one — fell into an argument with some white hoboes. Two white women riding in a different car were somehow coerced into saying that the black men had raped them. All nine black men were subjected to a speedy trial, found guilty by an all-white jury, and then sentenced to death. Although the NAACP and a number of other liberal organizations became involved in the case, providing a legal defense fund and such, the most consistent champion of the men's cause was the International Labor Defense, the legal arm of the Communist Party.

Fighting in court on behalf of the defendants, winning a retrial and then an appeal after the men were found guilty by the Alabama Supreme Court, veteran lawyers Joseph Brodskey and Samuel Leibowitz kept the case alive in the public imagination. More than that, he and the Communist Party brought the case worldwide attention and publicity, condemning the blatant racism in the South and appealing the guilty verdict all the way to the U.S. Supreme Court. In the end the executions were prevented and charges were dropped against four defendants; the other five were sentenced to long prison terms – one remained in prison until 1950. Through its involvement with the Scottsboro case, the Communist Party achieved for itself more credibility with Southern blacks than it had ever enjoyed before.

Despite these efforts, however, the Communists never managed to make bona fide party members of most Southern blacks. Although membership nationwide hovered at about two hundred in the 1920s and exploded to more than two thousand during the 1930s, the African-Americans who were most likely to become party members lived in Northern cities. For all their rage and frustration, black farmers remained somewhat conservative, preferring to align themselves with traditional political parties in the 1932 presidential election. They wanted nothing less than to see Hoover expelled, and they were willing to shift their allegiance from the Republicans to the Democrats to bar Hoover from a second term in the White House.

Although some Northern black voters continued to drag their feet – still believing, no matter how reluctantly, that "the Republican Party is the deck and all outside is the sea," to quote historian Lerone Bennett in *Before the Mayflower* – African-American farmers and laborers had more at stake, it seemed, given how badly they had been crushed by the weight of Hoover's economic policies during the Depression. For them a switch in political allegiances wasn't a philosophical issue: it was a matter of life and death. So when a choice was given to them at last, they shrugged off the old ways of the party of Lincoln and embraced a New Deal.

7.

Black Agricultural Workers and the Promise of Roosevelt's New Deal

My grandfather Fred Mathis was the second oldest child of Bill and Viccie Mathis. By the time
he bought his farm in 1937, he had spent his entire life working the land. He was able to
acquire the farm on Flint River Road as part of the short-lived federal Resettlement Program,
which provided small farms for sharecroppers. The Flint River Resettlement Project became
one of the most successful sites in the nation, and Fred became one of the most successful
farmers in Macon County. In 1955 he became the first black Georgia Merit Farmer to be
recognized and honored by the local paper, the Macon Telegraph and News.

Fred Mathis, his wife, Janie, and their young family, including my mother, who was
only a year old when they moved in, transformed their 192-acre farm into a legacy. The
government provided the land and the farmhouse, but he built the small plot into a productive
and envied farm. He cleared a lot of land by hand, adding new acres that could be farmed; he

built his own type of irrigation system, long before irrigation became common; he dug trenches and laid hoses to deliver water to his cattle; and he never sold the land.

All of his children worked on the farm. Everyone who could walk, no matter how young, had a job. My mother's job was to carry my grandfather's midday meal down the dirt road leading to the field. He would meet her halfway and eat the food while it was still hot. As she grew older, my mother would find herself working in the fields, but as a small child, this job was just enough.

I wonder if my grandfather, when he saw his young daughter walking from the distance, knew that the days of the family farm would end with him? Did he know that his dream of education for all of his children would mean that they would eventually leave and find other ways to live and other places to call home? Did he know that some of his children would leave the farm and stay gone, only returning to bury him and say a final good-bye? Could he have known how different a "better" life would be in just one generation?

BECAUSE A FAMILIAR enemy often seems preferable to an unfamiliar friend, it makes sense that even as the Republican Party continued to turn its back on the African-American body politic, there remained in 1932 a number of blacks who felt almost physically unable to cast their vote for a Democrat in that year's presidential election. The great nineteenth-century abolitionist Frederick Douglass had been a Republican, and his endorsement of Lincoln and the Party of Lincoln still resonated in the collective memory of many African-Americans. What little political stability they had known over the years had been provided by the Republican Party, and even though that stability had long ago been snatched like a rug from under their feet, blacks understood that their rights as voters were so tenuous that they could not afford to burn any political bridges.

So 1932 was a threshold year for black voters. Their strong sense of history all but obligated them to vote for the Republican candidate, Herbert Hoover, whom they knew to be no friend to blacks in particular or to the poor in general. Further muddying the water was the Communist Party. The party had overwhelmingly chosen African-American James W. Ford as its vice presidential nominee. (He would be chosen again in 1936 and 1940.) This, too, seemed to challenge black voters' sense of loyalty: Wasn't a black candidate, even a Communist one, more deserving of the black vote than the lily-white candidates who usually dominated politics?

In Georgia, and some other Southern states, then New York governor Franklin Delano Roosevelt had a reputation that seemed to transcend politics. The polio-stricken New Yorker had been taking treatments for his condition since the early 1920s at various Southern locations, particularly Warm Springs, Georgia. During these treatments he had become familiar with the degradation suffered by so many black families in the South. Roosevelt's firsthand observations of poverty, bigotry, and racial violence did not exactly make him an outspoken advocate of civil rights, but it did convince him of the need for Democrats to build a broad base of support in the South by distancing themselves from white supremacists and other racial extremists.

Like any politician looking to broaden, expand, and improve his profile in the South, Roosevelt recognized immediately that he would have to win the support of black farmers. These farmers were not an especially important political force, and already their numbers had dwindled too low to make them a unified constituency. But so many blacks in Northern cities traced their ancestry to Southern farms, and it was the imagination of these Northern blacks – and their Southern kin – that Roosevelt would need to capture if he expected to take the White House. He understood that the poor and downtrodden would be most willing to take a chance on his candidacy.

When Roosevelt took office in March 1933, as the country flailed and floundered through the Depression, he immediately rewarded the reluctant minority of black voters who had supported him by bringing several prominent African-Americans into government to serve as part of his so-called Black Cabinet. This loosely defined cohort of advisers worked hard to bring the new president up to speed on the needs of black Americans, and they included such important national figures as Mary McLeod Bethune, the educator and civil rights activist who had founded in 1904 the Daytona (Florida) Normal and Industrial Institute for girls, which merged in 1923 with the Cookman Institute to form the coeducational Bethune-Cookman College. The daughter of black agricultural workers and former slaves in South Carolina, Bethune left the cotton fields of her childhood to pursue her education, but she never forgot her modest beginnings. Roosevelt named her director of the Division of Negro Affairs. Her membership in the Black Cabinet gave her a highly visible forum from which to advocate for black farmers.

The various relief and recovery programs Roosevelt instituted as part of his New Deal appealed to impoverished blacks in both the North and the South. The decline in the number of Southern black farmers had not always corresponded to the number of black *hired* farmers in those states. As these individuals continued to get the short end of the stick from the intolerant white planters who employed them, they saw greater value in Roosevelt's plan to improve the national economy by improving the various industries that drove the economy.

One of the first New Deal programs to have direct bearing on the lives of black farmers and agricultural workers in the South was the National Industrial Recovery Act (NIRA), which was governed by the National Recovery Administration (NRA). African-Americans working in the Southern agricultural industry hoped the NRA would work to close the wage differential that existed between them and their white counterparts. In Georgia, for example, where many rural families relied on government assistance to supplement their meager salaries, the average black family's income without assistance was less than 50 percent of the average white family's income. To add insult to injury, a greater percentage of whites than blacks received federal relief, according to a study conducted at the time by the Federal Emergency Relief Act. (Such data would later be used by some of Roosevelt's African-American detractors, who pointed to a racial bias in how New Deal relief packages were administered.)

According to historian Donald L. Grant, author of *The Way It Was in the South: The Black Experience in Georgia,* the work of the NIRA started off as well-intentioned. In time, however, its execution had distressing ramifications for Southern blacks who made their living in the agricultural industry. Grant explains:

> The NIRA permitted business representatives to gather in Washington and write the codes and regulations that would cover their particular industries. These codes fixed prices, set wages, and regulated hours of work. The first code approved was for cotton textiles. It provided for wages of twelve dollars a week in the South and thirteen dollars in the North. In the South, three-fourths of the industry's fourteen thousand cleaners, outside crewmen, and yardsmen were black. These codes did not cover these jobs; therefore, [blacks] were paid even less. Many thought the NRA minimum wage was too much for blacks and if it had to be paid, whites should get it. Consequently, many blacks in "covered" jobs who held their positions thanks to the wage differential lost their jobs to whites.

The U.S. Supreme Court eventually declared the NIRA unconstitutional, and no one (particularly black farmers) seemed especially sorry to see it go.

Other New Deal initiatives similarly failed to successfully address the plight of black farmers and agricultural workers. These programs failed to take into consideration the fact that racism might undermine the successful dissemination of New Deal programs in the South. Although the government might attempt in good faith to counter the impact of a drop in cotton prices by paying white planters to keep their farms idle, these same planters might not give any warning to their black sharecroppers, tenant farmers, and farm workers that the land was being idled, which would in turn lead to the blacks being evicted from the land. In such circumstances no "share" of the harvest could be paid to a black farmer because now there were no harvests. Without a harvest tenant farmers couldn't earn the wages they needed to secure their place on the white planter's property. Furthermore, black farm workers were summarily fired, on the basis of a lack of work, although many whites in the agricultural industry managed to retain their jobs.

Still, New Deal programs continued to make their way through the South. One such program was the Agricultural Adjustment Administration (AAA), to be administered by federal agents and local planters working in cooperation. As part of this effort to provide relief to farmers, a crop reduction program was instituted by the AAA to give farmers cash benefits for the crops that economically strapped Americans weren't inclined to consume. Farmers were in effect paid to plow under their cotton and wheat crops and to slaughter their hogs. This program became a bastion of white privilege, however. The amount of the cash benefits rose into the millions, but the funds intended for black farmers rarely reached their destination. So even as the AAA appeared on paper to serve the needs of all tenant farmers on a fair basis, the actual practices were anything but fair. Grant clarifies:

> Under 1934 revisions in the AAA law, tenants were to receive half of the government payments when cotton fields were plowed up, but one study showed that landlords used force on 22 percent of the white and [almost 60] percent of the black tenants to get them to give up their share. Often force was necessary, for there were many ways that the landlord could apply pressure. One landlord refused to supply fertilizer because the tenant's son had taken a job at a quarry rather than stay and help work the land. In accordance with the "company store" tradition, government checks intended for tenants were often confiscated by landlords to pay debts inflated by usurious interest rates. Black farmers seldom received any cash.

Grant goes on to write in *The Way It Was in the South* that because the vast majority of government payments intended for black tenants went instead to their white landlords, the average white-owned farm actually grew during the Depression, while the average black-owned farm remained small, usually no more than a hundred acres. Like Hoover's trickle-down approach to economic revitalization, Roosevelt's New Deal program rarely seemed to extend its reach to the black farmer, although perhaps not for lack of trying. Fundamentally strong programs were corrupted by racial bias, and when that bias was coupled with the economic hardship so many Americans endured during this period, black farmers were stretched beyond their capacity.

In this atmosphere, when food was scarce and families of six or more lived in a single room, unable to work or to harvest crops that would bring them any return on the marketplace, black farmers who had acquired their property in more prosperous times were forced to sell their farms and work instead as tenant farmers. But this shift brought little relief. As tenant farmers they qualified for government allotments administered by the AAA, but because of the racially biased way in which these allotments were distributed, these black farmers rarely saw a dime. With white landlords taking for themselves more than 90 percent of the subsidies intended for tenants, one black tenant farmer after another was forced to admit defeat.

Those who had been landowners were now tenants, and those who had been tenants were now sharecroppers. In some situations an independent black farmowner might be reduced to sharecropping in a single season, missing entirely the "opportunity" to work as a tenant farmer. To some, it appeared as though reducing all black agricultural workers to the level of sharecropper or cheap laborer had been the intention of white planters all along. Indeed, when some blacks traveled to Southern cities at the start of the Depression to apply to the Red Cross for relief, they found their efforts thwarted by white planters back home. The planters complained to the Red Cross that providing relief during harvest time reduced a Negro's incentive to work and thus diminished the availability of cheap labor. The Red Cross eventually sided with the planters.

For African-Americans who had previously owned land, the slide to sharecropping or even tenant farming was certainly a steep one, but for those who had never found the means or support to ascend from the sharecropping system, the brutal degradation of living a life at the very bottom of the economic ladder had become inscribed on their skin. Unlike those who had been tenants or landowners, these long-term sharecroppers and farm workers were deprived even of the memory of better days. For them the economic hardship of the Depression was just another part of the landscape, a dark cloud that passed over everyone at some point or another, but which seemed to hover over black farmers for life. Nothing about their lives reflected any of the societal advances that had been made since the days of slavery. As late as 1940, for example, African-Americans who lived at the bottom of rural life in the South rarely had electricity or running water in their homes.

Black farmers were increasingly drifting again toward the Alliance movement that had served them fairly well in the late 1870s. For the time being, however, they continued to place their faith in the promise of the New Deal. Indeed, some of them were rewarded for their patience and faith. For example, the short-lived Tenant Purchase Program, administered by the Farm Security Administration, allowed farmer Fred Mathis and his family to purchase a farm in 1937. To this day members of the Mathis family continue to farm that modest property, where the slivers of red soil and blue cotton seeds underneath one's fingernails seem never to be washed away.

In addition to the Tenant Purchase Program, other New Deal efforts gained some momentum among black farmers, though only in fits and starts. Toward the end of the 1930s, for example, after a number of thwarted beginnings, an agricultural program called the Resettlement Administration (RA) was established, which was intended to help return to farming those unemployed agricultural workers who had fled to Northern and Southern cities. The Farm Security Administration's nexus, meanwhile, was in Macon County, Georgia, on an enormous consolidation of property called Flint River Farms, which boasted almost eleven thousand acres. A number of black families were brought to Flint River Farms to start a new life for themselves, and by and large, according to Grant, the program was a success:

> Each of the 106 black families settling there were provided with about one hundred acres. They prospered under federal guidance at first and almost quadrupled their average net worth the first year. They developed good

kitchen gardens, preserved and canned food, diversified their crops, and developed cooperative marketing, a health center, and a school under the management of Cozy L. Ellison, later chairman of the Agricultural Division of Fort Valley State College. . . . the Flint River Project proved that blacks' "former positions as tenants and croppers were not the result of some innate inferiority, but the product of [Georgia's] economy and certain definite attitudes about their color." Flint River Farms was the RA's most successful project and the first to be attacked by Georgia's congressmen and senators.

Despite resistance from white legislators, the Resettlement Administration (RA) continued to flourish. According to Robert Zabawa, author of "The Black Farmer and the Land in South Central Alabama, from 1818 to the New Deal," the RA's contribution to black landownership, black community, and black farming throughout the South during the 1930s is considerable. Established in 1935 and funded by the Federal Emergency Relief Act (FERA), the RA had three functions: the resettlement of "destitute or low income" families; the administration of programs dealing with erosion, pollution, reforestation, and flood control; and the management of farm ownership and operating loans. At Flint River Farms in Georgia, Prairie Farms in Alabama, and other farms a number of African-Americans who had been living on the margins of the rural South were brought into the agricultural industry's mainstream. Although life in these communities was centered around farming, considerable emphasis was also placed on educational and social activities. To this end, each community developed by the RA usually included schools as well as health and community centers. As a result, something happened in these communities that was rare. Zabawa writes: "African American farmers were given the opportunity to own land, to educate their children, to form communities. . . . Some farmers succeeded; many failed. Many of the communities that developed from these endeavors are still there. Perhaps the only real failure would have been never to have tried."

The resistance to such programs by white politicians and white supremacists alike ensured that sharecropping and tenant farming would remain the status quo for African-Americans in the South. That blacks might achieve success on their own as farmers was a notion that tore at the fabric of the racist culture that had been sustained for so long across the Southern landscape. Those who objected to such efforts seemed to take comfort in reducing the circumstances of black farmers to the lowest depths imaginable. Increasingly, reporters from the North descended on such states as Georgia and wired back stories that told of the terrible conditions endured by sharecroppers in particular. These stories rarely led to any meaningful improvement in the black farmer's prospects, however.

Furthermore, the threat of violence hung constantly in the air, symbolized by the Night Riders who descended on African-Americans who attempted to leave their situations or complained about working conditions. "I had been sharecropping for three or four years," said Mathis family member A. B. Brown of the Depression era. "It was rough. From sunup, to sundown. Men making forty cents and women making thirty. Two dollars and twenty cents for five and a half days' work . . . and we had to do just as they say do. We was working *for* them, you know. They couldn't treat a dog any worse. And you couldn't say — you couldn't talk much about it. The black folks couldn't talk . . . much about it. You'd [end up] missing and nobody won't know where."

From the misappropriated funds of the AAA to the threats of violence heaped on any black farmer or agricultural worker who sought a better life for himself and his family, the pressure put on African-Americans in the South to endure these conditions reached a boiling point in 1936. After years of complaining to Washington about such crippling conditions — complaints that frequently went unheeded — a group of black and white tenant farmers and sharecroppers in Arkansas started the Southern Tenant Farmers Union. Working successfully together toward a shared goal, they consolidated their efforts to initiate the kinds of work stoppages and collective lobbying efforts that might cause Washington to at last lend a helping hand.

White planters immediately reacted to the union with violence. They began a series of systematized beatings and lynchings to intimidate the black union members, and they made explicit appeals to racial prejudice to forge a divide between white and black farmers. Yet somehow in this explosive and dangerous atmosphere, the union grew throughout the South, much as the Alliance movement had done more than fifty years before. The union eventually acquired thirty thousand members in six Southern states. Their influence was short-lived, however. The Roosevelt administration all but ignored the union, although at first there were a few changes in the ways in which certain New Deal agricultural efforts were conducted. For example, changes were made to the AAA so that cash benefits would be paid directly to tenants rather than to landowners, but this amendment was easily corrupted: white landowners would simply evict the tenants farmers from the land and pocket the benefit checks when they arrived in the mail.

According to historian Pete Daniel, without more consistent support from the Roosevelt administration, the Southern Tenant Farmers Union was increasingly undermined by white planters. The planters ultimately prevailed, and the union simply faded away. The erasure of the union from the Southern landscape mirrored that of the black landowner, who by the end of the 1930s seemed to be a relic, a faded memory from another time and place. At the outset of the decade there had been almost 900,000 black farmers throughout the South, constituting 14 percent of all farm operators in the country, at a time when African-Americans comprised less than 10 percent of the population. At the start of the

1940s, however, things had changed irrevocably. Now the number of black farmers had fallen to 682,000, and each day saw the failure of another black farm, stolen from its owner by deception, intimidation, manipulation, or else abandoned by those whose only harvest seemed to be poverty and fear of racial violence. Black farmers had seen their best days come and go, although they would achieve in the years ahead a new and better way of existing in the world, despite their slim numbers. In the meantime, however, with the 1930s behind them, black farmers looked toward something on the horizon—not exactly a better day, but a less dim one. This vision, however, was corrupted by an impending war that would forever alter the face of the nation.

8.

World War II and the Call for Southern Change

By the time my mother, Earlene Mathis Gilbert, was twelve she had her own dreams for the future. She dreamed of leaving the field. She wanted to escape the cotton rows, open fields, and hot days. She wasn't the best worker. Her sisters helped her meet her quota. She could get a beating for coming in with under one hundred pounds of cotton at the end of the day. All she could think about was how to get out. Then one day her uncle's wife came to pick him up from the field. She drove her own car, had a big pretty hat, and sat in the shade of the car listening to the radio while the farm workers finished their day. That was the first time my mother had seen a black woman doing something other than cooking or picking cotton. When she found out that her aunt was a teacher, my mother had found herself a new dream: she wanted to go to college and become a teacher, because teachers didn't pick cotton.

Before my mother could get to college, she endured many more harvests. On one of those harvest days she made the mistake of openly venting her contempt for the farm. It was a hot afternoon and she saw a dog lying underneath the shade of a tree. The shade looked good and my bone-weary mother just wanted to lie down and rest, so she turned to her brother and said, "Sometimes I wish I were a dog." My mother got in a lot of trouble that day. My grandfather had heard these words, which must have cut deep. After all, this was all he had, the best life he could give her, the life that would eventually allow her to go to college. Despite what was to come, in that moment my grandfather's baby daughter had preferred the life of a dog over the only life he knew how to provide.

When my mother finished high school, she applied to Tuskegee Institute in Tuskegee, Alabama, to study teaching. My grandfather went to the bank to plead for a loan to send her to college. He offered his land to back the loan — in those days a quick way to lose one's land to unscrupulous bankers — but even that was not enough. The local banker couldn't stand the thought of black children going to college; he did everything he could to keep black families from sending their children to school, but somehow they managed to find the money and send them off one by one. Those educated black children who came back would change the South forever. My mother was one of the many children who chose not to return. She left when she was seventeen and only came back for one month in 1965, so that I, her only daughter, could be born in Montezuma — the only place we both call home.

IN 1940, the year in which the U.S. Supreme Court rendered the historic decision making it unlawful to restrict blacks from buying homes in white neighborhoods, the U.S. Postal Service issued the Booker T. Washington postage stamp, the first stamp to honor a black American. Meanwhile, in the Southern states that had been Washington's province, only 5 percent of the region's African-American population was registered to vote. African-American writer Richard Wright received great acclaim for his novel *Native Son,* while the life expectancy of blacks lagged behind that of whites by ten years or more. The social, economic, and political advances of African-Americans were indisputable, but the progress was slow, and the momentum seemed founded on something no more sturdy than a butterfly's wing. This was especially true in the South, where African-American farmers wondered if they might ever realize the potential for economic independence that had seemed within their reach, if only for a moment, during the 1920s. With each passing year, the chances of liberating themselves from the bitter chokehold of poverty, sharecropping, tenant farming, and menial agricultural labor appeared to be drifting further away.

The 1930s had clearly been a devastating time for black farmers, as it had been for so many Americans. Even when the promise of economic salvation began to appear on the horizon, it did not eclipse the racial intolerance that had added to black farmers' burdens during the Depression. Night Riders still roamed the countryside, ensuring by dint of violence that no black family in the rural South would achieve a quality of life that too closely resembled that of a successful white family. Apparently such a sight offended the sensibilities of those whites who believed

WE WERE A LAND-BASED AGRARIAN PEOPLE FROM AFRICA. WE WERE UPROOTED FROM AFRICA AND SPENT TWO HUNDRED YEARS DEVELOPING OUR CULTURE AS BLACK AMERICANS, AND THEN WE LEFT THE SOUTH. WE UPROOTED OURSELVES AND ATTEMPTED TO TRANSPLANT THIS CULTURE TO THE PAVEMENTS OF THE INDUSTRIALIZED NORTH. IT WAS A TRANSPLANT THAT DID NOT TAKE. I THINK IF WE HAD STAYED IN THE SOUTH, WE WOULD HAVE BEEN A STRONGER PEOPLE. AND BECAUSE [OUR] CONNECTION [TO] THE SOUTH OF THE TWENTIES, THIRTIES, AND FORTIES HAS BEEN BROKEN, IT'S VERY DIFFICULT TO UNDERSTAND WHO WE ARE.
—AUGUST WILSON

themselves placed by God at the top of the social hierarchy. These people did not seem to wonder why a social arrangement ordained by God would require the violent force of humans to sustain. Still, some modicum of pride must have swelled in the hearts of those black Americans who stood on the brink of a new decade and recognized that somehow they had managed to make it to that point alive. Even as so many African-Americans hurried away under cover of night to find better lives in industrialized cities, a number of black families stayed in the rural South. Convinced that their ancestors had given their blood to the land, they were determined to follow in that proud tradition.

Roosevelt's New Deal efforts were still a comfort to many blacks, and like all Americans they joined in a common prayer for prosperity. In this way African-American farmers were fully invested members of the American body politic. Even though these women and men who worked in the fields from sunup to sundown were marginalized and isolated from mainstream society, they understood that their fates were inextricably tied to the rest of the country's: that which threatened the country in general might inflict particular harm on individual black farmers, as the Depression had proved, so they became more determined than ever in the 1940s to work in the country's best interest.

For this reason, then, when Adolf Hitler's activities in Central Europe were recognized in 1939 as a danger to U.S. interests, and the country began laying the groundwork for entry into a European war, thousands of blacks from the South and elsewhere attempted to join the U.S. Armed Forces. But their enthusiasm was met with resistance. Many white military officials believed that African-Americans were too physically lazy and intellectually inferior to be effective in combat. Nonetheless, a series of military events made it necessary to call on the assistance of African-Americans. When Japanese carrier planes surprised and crippled the U.S. fleet at Pearl Harbor on December 7, 1941, Congress de-

clared war on Japan the very next day. A few days later, the Roosevelt administration responded to declarations from Italy and Germany – who
were allied to Japan by treaties – and the United States found itself at war.
This necessitated a complete reorganization and expansion of the Army
and Navy, which led to fuller inclusion of African-Americans in the war
effort.

Having been elected in 1940 to an unprecedented third term as
president, Franklin Delano Roosevelt spoke of America at this time as an
"arsenal for democracy." In this way he appealed to Americans to bridge
their racial differences in the interest of national unity. In June 1941 he
issued Executive Order 8802, which banned discrimination in war industries – or in any businesses working on government contracts. The effect
of the order on the lives of African-Americans was profound. Gearing up
for war had all but transformed the U.S. economy, and employment was
increasing in leaps and bounds as defense plants and other war-related industries thrived. Many of these industries refused to hire blacks, however. What's more, with the economy finally beginning to boom, other
industries that had bottomed out during the Depression now experienced
a resurgence, but they too hired only whites, or at least limited access to
the better-paying jobs to whites.

Because of this refusal to hire African-Americans, Roosevelt issued
Executive Order 8802. In *The Way It Was in the South: The Black Experience in Georgia,* historian Donald L. Grant further explains: "In 1940 the
national jobless rate for blacks was 29% (19% for men and 36% for
women), twice that of white unemployment. Ten years earlier, the black
rate was only 50% higher. This widening gap reflected the growth in job
discrimination during the Depression. Blacks grew increasingly restive;
equal opportunity in the workplace became a top priority on the black
agenda."

When military industries refused to hire blacks before the war, and when the military discriminated against blacks during the war, the seeds of the Civil Rights Movement were sown. Black farmers in particular were caught up in the tide of these changing times. For example, as it became increasingly necessary to bring all Americans together to assist in the war effort, individuals in all walks of life began to recognize the counterproductivity of turning a blind eye toward a disfranchised black populace. Not only did the violence inflicted on blacks in the South undermine the country's assertion that it could be a moral leader for peace in the world, it also raised the possibility that influential black activists might encourage their followers to engage in acts of civil disobedience – the kind that might keep the government from devoting its full attention to winning the war. Government leaders called for a greater spirit of racial cooperation, and a concrete result of this cooperation was a lack of tolerance for unbridled racial violence in the South.

For one thing such violence simply didn't look good for the country's reputation internationally. Reports of lynchings made the United States vulnerable to the charge that its policies weren't democratic at all, but rather, consistent with the mandates of racial purity advocated by the Nazis. For the first time in the national memory instigators of violence against blacks in the South were actively pursued by authorities, charged, tried, and sometimes even convicted. Aside from being keenly sensitive to how America was perceived in the larger world, many government officials understood that racial violence could diminish the loyalty of blacks at a time when the country had no time to attend to domestic unrest. The country's fate rested on the loyalty and support of its citizens, regardless of whether those citizens were black or white. Although the assistance of blacks in the war effort was accepted without enthusiasm or gratitude, such assistance was necessary. No matter how much the military tried to limit the involvement of black soldiers, African-Americans joined the army in large numbers and played a crucial role in the eventual triumph of the Allied forces over Germany and Japan. According to the *African-American Encyclopedia,* edited by Michael W. Williams, approximately one million African-Americans served in the various branches of the armed forces, including several thousand women in the Women's Auxiliary Army Corps (WACS). Although blacks served primarily in the service corps – as quartermasters, cooks, engineers, or drivers – nearly five hundred thousand African-Americans saw combat overseas.

The scale at which the war activities occurred was nothing short of operatic, and significant shifts in race relations took place as part of larger, more sweeping patterns of social change. Strong feelings of every kind ran high during the war, and often these feelings conflicted with each other, leading to a near explosion of emotions from the North to the South. In vain, patriotism tried to coexist with racial intolerance, and an economic boom tried to coexist with discriminatory hiring practices. The United States was in effect waging two wars at once – the one overseas, which was based on asserting America's democratic ideals on those who would challenge them, and the war at home, which pushed Americans to act according to those ideals in all areas of life. Is it any wonder, then, that in 1942 a deadly riot erupted in Detroit when twelve hundred whites carrying weapons attempted to prevent three black families from moving into the new two hundred–unit Sojourner Truth Settlement, which had been designated as black housing by the U.S. Housing Authority? Is it any wonder that in that same year the Department of Justice threatened to sue several prominent African-American newspapers for sedition because they had attacked the government's racial policies in the military?

As General Douglas MacArthur was named commander in chief of American efforts in the Far East, presumably to promote peace and freedom abroad, domestic legislation in 1942 sanctioned the internment of more than one hundred thousand Japanese-Americans in "relocation camps" in California and elsewhere. These camps struck few in the federal government as an affront to U.S. democratic ideals. In the following year, a riot occurred in Mobile, Alabama, when white welders at a shipyard were asked to work alongside black welders. A riot also erupted in Harlem after a white police officer shot an unarmed black soldier, in much the same manner that more than fifty-five years later a cadre of police would fire forty-one bullets at an unarmed African immigrant named Amadou Diallo. During the Harlem riot five other African-Americans were killed and hundreds were wounded. Yet another riot took place in 1943 in Detroit, this time in reaction to blacks being denied access to civilian defense-related jobs.

The operatic strains of discontent on the homefront continued to provide a kind of musical accompaniment to the world war being waged overseas. Gradually, even lynching came back into vogue, escalating from an all-time reported low of three in 1943 to seven in 1945. Then in 1945 a similarly atrocious act of violence occurred as part of the American war effort against Japan: the United States dropped atomic bombs on the Japanese cities of Hiroshima and Nagasaki, killing or wounding more than two hundred thousand.

In this atmosphere of sustained and unparalleled violence, African-American farmers were also caught up in the fervor of the times. Like Japanese-Americans, however, they found themselves victims of the sort of racial aggression that the war seemed to condone. Many farmers wanted badly to leave behind the red dirt of the South that now seemed to choke them as surely as the lyncher's rope had. Sensing the opportunity for prosperity at war-related factory jobs in the North, many sharecroppers and tenant farmers wanted to throw off the agricultural peonage that continued to pay them Depression-era wages long after the Depression had ended. At the same time, however, those who wanted to remain on their farms also felt an impulse to serve their country in the war effort. These dueling impulses – to leave for better jobs, to fight overseas, or else to stay in the South and maintain the agrarian traditions they had inherited over the generations – defined the dilemma of many African-Americans. Their loyalty to the traditions that seemed to them uniquely "black" was sometimes put into direct conflict with the loyalty they felt simply as Americans.

What further stirred the pot for them was the attitude of many intolerant whites who resented the idea of blacks feeling as though they had any rights, privileges, or choices at all. Unwittingly, however, these very same whites helped expedite the rise of the black Civil Rights Movement by imposing exorbitant poll taxes to keep African-Americans from voting in the South; by appealing to Washington to keep Northern black "instigators" in the army from doing their basic training at military bases in the South; and most of all, by using whatever means at their disposal to keep unemployment high and the standard of living low among rural blacks. Just as white landowners had done in the 1920s, during the war years they effectively drove away their primary supply of cheap labor by making conditions all but unlivable for African-Americans. Similarly, they fostered in blacks an ever-increasing commitment toward achieving civil rights. As Grant clarifies:

> Everyone was needed to work or fight as the military's needs grew and industry fully converted to war production. This induced the greatest migration ever of blacks out of Georgia [and other Southern states] during the war years. For the first time, great numbers went to the West Coast. They found jobs there, although the pay was not great. In 1941, 80 percent of defense workers averaged less than thirty dollars a week – but it beat picking cotton for fifty cents a day. As new opportunities opened up, blacks left their posi-

tions as . . . agricultural serfs. As this occurred, white anger grew, and [the South] saw a repeat of the World War I atmosphere of white resentment and fear of blacks' newfound economic independence and increased militancy.

From 1940 to 1945 the potential for economic independence for blacks had become something more than a pipe dream in both the North and South. Evidence that the economic ravages of the Depression were now a thing of the past was everywhere, and real jobs awaited African-Americans in wartime industry—if only they could access those jobs. There were also possibilities of serving America's war efforts too, if only blacks were allowed such a chance. Because of the twists and changes in the cultural fabric caused by the war—the abundance of jobs and the sense that the world was undergoing a profound reordering—African-Americans moved more stridently toward a social equality based on something more than just the promises of the New Deal. This vision was based on the hierarchical shifts taking place on the international stage.

Black farmers, who had seen their numbers reduced to a precious few by the mid-1940s, waited with bated breath for the changes they knew would soon flood the South. After all, not even the most institutionalized forces of white supremacy could survive a complete overhaul of the world order. When the changes finally came to their concern of the world—as dramatic and divine as Moses parting the Red Sea—these farmers would be there to bear witness. For the first time in history, they weren't kept waiting for long.

In the fall of 1944, Franklin Delano Roosevelt was elected president for a staggering fourth time. By the spring of 1945, however, he was dead. When sixty-year-old Harry Truman assumed the office, he had served as vice president for little more than eighty days. Now, with a bitter war waging overseas and the flames of racial discontent raging at home, Truman stepped into the shoes of the man who had guided the country with a singularity of focus for more than a decade. It apparently both thrilled and humbled Truman to take his turn at bat.

From the beginning, there was considerable speculation about how the new president would react to the various racial tensions that had been brewing since the end of the Depression, particularly those tensions related to hiring practices in the North and civil rights in the South. At the time Southern Democrats controlled the Senate, and they felt confident that Truman would see eye to eye with them on racial affairs. Their confidence was based on the fact that Truman had been one of their own – a senator for ten years and a Southerner at heart (his grandparents had been loyal Confederates from Kentucky, although Truman himself was from Missouri). In Senate chambers, it was rumored, Truman was known to crack a racial joke or in some manner assure his colleagues from Dixie that he took their side on all matters racial. So the senators felt confident that Roosevelt's death would mean a rebirth of the old status quo, the one that put blacks at the bottom and didn't brook any new laws or executive orders aimed at equality.

In the first years of peace after World War II, things went exactly as these Southerners had hoped. A bipartisan coalition of Southern Democrats and Northern Republicans in the Congress and the Senate exacted their revenge on the New Deal policies that Roosevelt had imposed on them. With swift fury they dismantled as many New Deal economic and social policies as they could, and they rejected the authority of the Fair Employment Practices Committee (FEPC) launched by Roosevelt as part of Executive Order 8802. They also saw to it that all anti–poll tax legislation was killed.

What these politicians failed to notice, however, was that the war had significantly changed the mood of African-Americans, in both the North and South. No longer willing to protest for change and wait patiently to be heard, blacks now seemed more committed than ever to effect change for themselves. During these years NAACP membership grew astronomically, and accordingly so did the group's influence. These new members had shed blood overseas or participated in the war effort at home with diligence and honor, and their sense of themselves as full U.S. citizens – entitled to all the rights and privileges thereof – was now in full bloom. This sense had been carefully cultivated over the course of many years, and now black Americans were harvesting and claiming their citizenship in much the same way that black farmers had for countless decades cultivated and harvested land in the South.

As part of this new wave of energy and fresh mandate from its members, the NAACP submitted in 1947 to the newly formed United Nations an unusual document. Called "A Statement on the Denial of Human Rights to Minorities in the Case of Citizens of Negro Descent in the United States," the report outlined the social and civil injustices American blacks endured and implored the U.N. to intervene, exactly as the body would if famine or drought or some other disaster threatened the lives and well-being of people overseas.

Although the U.N. was slow to respond, Truman saw the handwriting on the wall. To the consternation and indignation of his Southern supporters, Truman appointed a civil rights committee to address the issues raised by the NAACP in their report to the U.N. When the committee eventually made its report, however, there was no follow-up action by the Truman administration. In response, the leader of the Brotherhood of Sleeping Car Porters, A. Philip Randolph – who in mid-1941 had motivated Roosevelt to issue Executive Order 8002 and form the FEPC – threatened to "lead a civil disobedience movement against the peacetime draft," according to historian Lerone Bennett. Bennett continues in *Before the Mayflower: A History of Black America*:

Faced with this threat, President Truman backtracked, issuing on July 26, 1948, two executive orders which created an FEPC board to eliminate racial discrimination in federal employment and a President's Committee of Equal Treatment and Opportunity in the armed services. The Truman response was apparently a function of conviction, but it also stemmed from material and political convictions. First . . . the war had internalized the race problem. . . . Secondly, President Truman was besieged by disgruntled democrats who were organizing a new party, the Progressive party, which rejected the token approach of both the Democratic and Republican parties and called for basic changes in the lives of both black and white Americans.

Confronted by these developments, Truman compelled his party to take a more decisive stand on civil rights issues in its 1948 nominating convention. Not surprisingly, white Southern Democrats believed that Truman their friend had fled the party. But their white supremacist attitudes were already beginning to seem antiquated in postwar society, so they failed to defeat Truman. He won the 1948 election and carried most of the African-American vote.

Among Truman's most ardent supporters were black farmers. His antilynching stance in particular secured their support, despite the fact that poll taxes continued to make it impossible for so many black farmers to vote. Still, the farmers were caught up in the mood of rapid change that had gripped blacks in the North, and Truman was clearly helping to foster some of that change. His efforts to enforce equality in the military, for example, opened up another employment possibility for blacks who continued to feel humiliated and drained by farming life in the South.

As always, the problem wasn't with farming itself, which continued to have an important symbolic hold on the African-American consciousness. Even after so many years of struggle, the land still seemed to whisper its sweet promises into the black farmer's ear as insistently as the voices of his ancestors. But the financial rewards of such a life remained elusive, particularly in comparison to the economic gains made by blacks who had fled to other parts of the country. Between 1941 and 1945 more than fifty thousand African-Americans had migrated from the South to Detroit, Michigan, alone. Although such migration led to the racial tensions that eventually erupted in the form of riots in that city and others, a number of these African-Americans would by the late 1940s enter college, buy their own homes, and ride a modest crest of prosperity in the 1950s that would continue to evade Southern blacks.

This doesn't mean, however, that the changes black farmers expected to blow into their corner of the world never arrived. On the contrary, the postwar economy had transformed the country, and the South was no exception. The changes arrived quickly, with great pomp and circumstances, but unfortunately they weren't entirely social. Rather, these changes were mostly technological. In the 1940s most farms in the South were still powered by mules. According to historian John Egerton in *Speak Now against the Day: The Generation before the Civil Rights Movement in the South,* there were more than three million in the fields, compared with fewer than 150,000 tractors, but such labor methods would soon be in decline. A mechanical revolution in farming took place after the war, and although the South was slow to respond to this revolution, it arrived eventually and brought with it not only tractors but new devices for seeding and irrigation. As a result, the tens of thousands of laboring women and men in the fields were no longer necessary by the end of the 1940s. What's more, the cost of maintaining a competitive farm increased enormously, as farmers now looked for loans to buy expensive irrigation systems, rather than to buy a few mules and some harvesting tools. This increase in the expense of doing business made it even more difficult for black farmers to strike out on their own. Rather than improving life for black farmers, such technological advances only led to less work, more layoffs, and the subsequent racial tension that always follows a dip in financial fortunes. For this reason, according to Egerton, "two million more blacks moved out of the South than into it during the 1940's."

By 1950, there seemed fewer compelling reasons than ever for black farmers to remain in the South. At least during the Depression, efforts had been made by the government to improve the farmers' fortunes, and even if such efforts failed, a poor black farmer knew the rest of the country was struggling too. In the 1940s, however, as the U.S. economy recovered, stabilized, and then grew massively because of the war, black farmers found themselves negotiating a level of poverty that was now comparatively lower than anywhere else in the country. They could no longer attribute their troubles to some abstract economic phenomenon; instead, it now appeared their poverty was endemic to the lives they had chosen. Either that, or it was a symptom of the racial disparities that still gripped the South, although this seemed less likely, because many white agricultural workers also suffered.

In any event black farmers knew such poverty would only serve as an impediment to achieving the kind of social equality that was becoming increasingly the first order of the day for black folks throughout the country. The refrains of "We Shall Overcome" weren't yet on everyone's lips, but this song would become louder and more insistent in the years ahead, as the Civil Rights Movement came into full bloom. For black farmers the song would have particular relevance, as they would have to overcome in the 1950s and 1960s more than the sting of racism and poverty. They would have to decide if there was even a place for the black family farm in postwar America.

9.

My mother, Earlene Mathis, arrived in Tuskegee, Alabama, in 1955 with a high school

diploma from the Flint River Farm School, which she had achieved over the years in between

the harvest and planting season. Shortly before enrolling at Tuskegee, she was politely

stripped of one dream and offered in its stead a "more appropriate" vocation. Her high school

principal informed my mother that she could not speak English well enough to be a teacher,

but she was a good cook, so she should pursue dietetics. My mother accepted this advice,

because her only real dream had been to leave Montezuma, Georgia, so anything that kept her

out of cotton was fine by her. In between working in the cafeteria to help pay her school fees

and going to classes, she met my father, Charles Wesley Gilbert, from Sparta, Georgia. Like

my mother, he never looked back when he left Georgia, and both had plans to stay gone. They

would eventually marry, have two children, and live in nine different Northern cities.

When my mother graduated from Tuskegee in 1960, the Reverend Martin Luther King

Jr. spoke at the commencement ceremony. By this time young black folks were embracing a new

*attitude and coming into their own. It was the beginning of the Civil Rights Movement,
and the young people would lead the way. Some of that energy got confused with arrogance,
however, and when graduation day came, students found themselves laughing at their
"country" parents who had arrived in their finest overalls in freshly washed pickups and a few
on tractors to see their children graduate. King apparently noticed the snickering and chastised
the students. He asked them to remember that it was their parents who had made that joyous
and proud day a possibility.*

*My mother remembers the speech, and when she tells the story, I can almost feel the
warmth of the day and see the pickups lining the edge of the horizon. My grandfather and
grandmother were there that day. For my grandfather this was the day that made all the others
bearable. He had not only sent his daughter to college, he had managed to keep her there
and see her graduate. It was a proud moment for my grandfather. That night he made it back
to Montezuma just in time to rise at dawn the next day and plow one more field. He still
had forty acres to plant and nine children to send to college.*

THE POLITICAL disfranchisement of African-Americans in the South had become a matter of public record after World War II. No matter the advances made by blacks serving in the military or living in cities — and to be sure these advances were modest — the fact remained that those blacks still living in the South and toiling on farms and in agricultural industries existed on the margins of the American political system. Without equal access to the polling booths, African-Americans in the South would continue to have no say in the legislative affairs that had the most direct impact on their lives.

SINCE RACIAL DISCRIMINATION WAS MOST INTENSE IN THE SOUTH, WE FELT THAT SOME OF THE NEGROES WHO HAD RECEIVED A PORTION OF THEIR TRAINING IN OTHER SECTIONS OF THE COUNTRY SHOULD RETURN TO SHARE THEIR BROADER CONTACTS AND EDUCATIONAL EXPERIENCE IN ITS SOLUTION. MOREOVER, DESPITE HAVING TO SACRIFICE MUCH OF THE CULTURAL LIFE WE LOVED, DESPITE THE EXISTENCE OF JIM CROW, WHICH KEPT REMINDING US AT ALL TIMES OF THE COLOR OF OUR SKIN, WE HAD THE FEELING THAT SOMETHING REMARKABLE WAS UNFOLDING IN THE SOUTH, AND WE WANTED TO BE ON HAND TO WITNESS IT.
—MARTIN LUTHER KING JR.

Black farmers deprived of the right to vote were at a particular disadvantage. Since the Civil War and Reconstruction, the issue of land tenure had been the site at which the battles for black equality and freedom were fought. Political legislation in the South had historically been used to secure entitlements for affluent white landowners while making it impossible for African-Americans and the poor to enjoy equal access to such entitlements. Just as the Founding Fathers had considered listing "life, liberty, and the pursuit of *property*" as the three inalienable rights to which every free person should have access, government officials in the South regarded the pursuit of property as integral to a life of true freedom and prosperity. So limiting African Americans' access to property was in effect limiting their access to freedom. Furthermore, because Southern law favored the pursuit of property, it was important to deny African-Americans the right to participate in the creation of such laws, or else they might also achieve the attendant freedom, power, and influence bestowed on white landowners.

In Georgia one long-standing device for denying blacks the right to vote was the all-white primary system. Historian Donald L. Grant writes in *The Way It Was in the South: The Black Experience in Georgia:*

> The adoption of the primary election to select [a] party's candidates for the general election was considered a democratizing step. Primaries did away with the old convention system that kept the power to nominate in the hands of a caucus of the few in the fabled "smoke-filled" back rooms. Ironically, along with the poll tax, primary elections became the most effective disenfranchising tool by the turn of the century. Local primaries in which blacks could vote were first used by Democrats in 1874, but Georgia soon found a way to turn the new method against blacks by ruling that only whites could vote in primary elections. With the state's political power concentrated in the Democratic party, the Democratic primaries became the only meaningful elections. When blacks were excluded, they were effectively disenfranchised for all practical purposes, even if they paid their poll taxes and met residency requirements. The effect of the white primary on black political power was devastating.

The white primary had become an institution in Georgia by World War II, one that continued to devastate and neutralize the political power of African-Americans. However, in 1947 the white primary system was challenged successfully in court, making it possible for Georgians of African descent to participate more actively in the voting process.

At first, though, there was no grand rush to the polls. Many African-Americans feared reprisals from whites who objected to what they considered to be a blatant assertion of political power. Their fear was reasonable. The renewed attempts by African-Americans to vote had caused a wave of violence across the South, particularly in Georgia, where NAACP president D. V. Carter was beaten in 1948 in Montgomery,

Alabama, for leading a group of black farmers and others to the polls. Similarly, in Vidalia County, Georgia, African-American Richard Mallard was lynched for attempting to vote. And in Tougaloo, Mississippi, at Tougaloo College, student William Bender was held prisoner at gunpoint to prevent him from voting. Given this atmosphere, it is not surprising that the Southern Regional Council (SRC) reported in 1946 that only 12 percent (about six hundred thousand) of African-Americans living in the South were eligible to vote. The SRC began monitoring such activities in 1944, according to Donald L. Grant. Organized primarily by Atlanta University president Rufus Clement and Atlanta *Constitution* editor Ralph McGill, the SRC was an interracial watchdog group that alerted state and federal governments to the prevalence of lynching. In such states as Alabama, Louisiana, and Mississippi, statistics from this period show that not even 3 percent of blacks were eligible.

This pattern of violence and intimidation continued through the end of the 1940s. By 1947 all but one of the nation's reported lynchings took place in rural Georgia, as more and more African-Americans attempted either to register to vote or to actually cast a ballot during gubernatorial elections. The leading candidate for Georgia's governor in 1946, Eugene Talmadge, encouraged the violence by asserting throughout his campaign that maintaining white supremacy at any cost was his top priority. He courted supremacist groups and openly warned blacks that voting might prove a hazard to their health. Although he won the election, Talmadge died of cirrhosis of the liver before inauguration, which many black Georgians perceived as a kind of divine retribution.

By 1949, Talmadge's son Herman was governor of Georgia, and he introduced into the legislature a "Four-Point White Supremacy Program" designed to keep the majority of the state's African-Americans from voting en masse. In the metropolitan areas such efforts did not go very far, however, and indeed Atlanta was recognized nationwide as a leader in ensuring and maintaining black voting rights. At first, these advances in big Southern cities made little difference in the lives of rural African-Americans – that is, the farmers and agricultural workers who continued to suffer at the front lines of the most violent battles for white supremacy. Such battles were fought in the area of public education as well. Indeed, there was no area of life in the 1940s that was not touched by racial discord. For African-Americans, explains Grant, "inequality in income and medical care and discrimination throughout [Southern] society would remain significant obstacles."

For every push made against African-Americans, however, there seemed to be a push forward, accomplished in most instances by the unrelenting drive of such civil rights organizations as the National Association for the Advancement of Colored People (NAACP); its autonomous legal arm, the NAACP Legal Defense and Educational Fund; and the Congress of Racial Equality (CORE). Although black farmers weren't always at the forefront of these growing civil rights initiatives, they served as a kind of shadowing influence: the discrimination they suffered in the South was a symbol of the horrific lengths to which racial bigotry and hate might extend if allowed unchecked. Their efforts to maintain dignity on their Southern farms no doubt resonated with every African-American who could trace his or her ancestry to those very farms. Lynching by the Ku Klux Klan and other groups, the constant efforts created to keep blacks from voting, the inferior education and unlivable wages – these were the specific conditions that the civil rights activists sought to improve. All of these conditions were endemic to the black farmer's life.

African-Americans in Northern and Southern cities tangled with racism, to be sure, and they suffered keenly its ill effects, but for them at least there was always the prospect of hope. They saw in these urban centers the way in which the world had been transformed after World War II, and already the wave of change had carried these urban African-

Americans to better jobs and living conditions and a greater sense of impending social equality than they had ever known before. African-Americans in the rural hinterlands of the South, however, were largely isolated from the full impact of such social advances, which cut them off even from hope. As long as they continued to endure abject poverty, political disfranchisement, and social degradation, their condition was a reminder to other blacks of how easily they might be returned to such a rueful existence. In this way Southern black farmers were an inspiration to civil rights workers, many of whom made it a priority to ensure that *all* blacks had the right to vote. If even one African-American remained a slave to the South's discriminatory policies, it follows that the entire black population was effectively enslaved — vulnerable to the ire of certain white legislators who might just as easily turn their hateful gaze from the lowliest African-American on the farm to the most accomplished African-American in the city.

So the pioneering civil rights groups of the 1940s marched into the next decade by way of Southern farms. Often they would stop along the way to take food and shelter at the homes of the few remaining black landowners and to remind themselves as they marched through the rural blight of just how much was at stake for Africans-Americans everywhere. In quick succession these activists brought the world's attention to the prevalence of racial hatred in the South by sending missives back home to the Northern black press, by enlisting the support of a growing number of sympathetic whites, and by fighting continually in court for an end to the legacy of racism that had been passed down over the years. These civil rights activists no longer wanted unfair conditions to be improved; they wanted them *changed*.

In the courts civil rights lawyers enjoyed unprecedented success in the 1950s. Before 1950, appeals courts, federal courts, and even the Supreme Court had shown little interest in considering the civil rights of

African-Americans. Before World War II even the term *civil rights* had not yet achieved the connotation it is ascribed today, and courts heard such cases only sporadically, at the behest of injured individuals rather than as part of a systematized effort by a number of various parties to improve the living conditions of blacks, the poor, or anyone else struggling under chronic social duress. The efforts made in the nineteenth century by Frederick Douglass, Ida B. Wells, Booker T. Washington, and others had involved arguing on moral grounds to the nation or to government leaders the need to bestow on newly freed African-Americans the same rights and privileges of citizenship that were enjoyed by all Americans under the U.S. Constitution. By 1950, however, the strategy had changed.

Civil rights organizations began petitioning the courts on a regular basis, arguing for a systemic change in American racial policy, thus ushering in the Civil Rights Movement. Like African-American social activists had done before, legal experts at various civil rights organizations continued to make arguments on moral grounds, but they were ultimately more interested in demonstrating to the courts the way in which the social degradation of African-Americans and others violated constitutional law. This strategy strengthened their cause and helped to change the implications of the term civil rights. Americans have always been keenly sensitive to the issue of "inalienable rights" — that is, the universal rights of freedom to which all human beings are entitled simply by virtue of being human. By attaching the cause of disfranchised blacks to the time-honored American concept of inalienable rights, African-American social activists managed to conflate *human* rights with *civil* rights in a way that continues to be significant.

In other words, before World War II there had been a long tradition in the United States of protecting the sanctity of civil rights, which were understood to be those rights bestowed on humans by God and protected by the Constitution. After the war, however, because of the way civil rights organizations drew on this constitutional tradition to argue in court against social injustice, the term civil rights slowly came to refer to any violation of – or claim to – equal treatment under the law by members of minority groups. This shift in the meaning of the term initially caused some ambiguity about its usage, according to the *Encyclopedia of Civil Rights in America*. The editors, David Bradley and Shelly Fisher Fishkin, explain:

> Sometimes ["civil rights"] is used to refer to all rights guaranteed to the individual by the U.S. Constitution. At other times it is used to refer to the rights of equality, especially those which protect racial and ethnic minorities from discrimination. Constitutional commentators have often differentiated between civil liberties and civil rights to maintain this distinction. This ambiguity is understandable, however, because both uses grow out of the overlapping guarantees of the Fourteenth Amendment. Moreover, equality rights and other liberties ultimately converge because people rarely demand equality in the abstract, but instead seek equal respect for rights they consider fundamental. In the American tradition, they are summed up in [seventeenth-century English philosopher] John Locke's phrase "life, liberty, and property" – a phrase repeated in the Fourteenth Amendment.

For civil rights activists the pursuit of property did not only apply to those urban blacks who were looking to buy their own homes. It also applied to African-Americans in the rural South who were deprived ownership of the very land they had been tilling for generations. For many black activists – who could no doubt trace their own ancestry to the fields of Georgia, Mississippi, South Carolina, and elsewhere – there must have been a particular incentive to argue in court for those African-Americans whose "lives" and "liberty" were as connected to "the pursuit of property" as that of the Founding Fathers. From this perspective, in fact, the cause of black farmers was the quintessential American cause: an inexhaustible impulse to achieve freedom from tyranny, poverty, and the prolonged violation of one's inalienable rights by some distant and intractable government.

Armed with this inspiration, civil rights workers returned to court repeatedly and often traveled through Southern farming communities to gather supporters, register new voters, and spread news of their efforts to African-Americans who may not have received word. In this way every visit was a kind of homecoming. Like all committed social activists, the civil rights workers were not demanding equality in the abstract; instead, they were demanding equality for the very real women and men they encountered on their trips across the forgotten dirt roads of the South.

There were other sources of inspiration as well. Jackie Robinson signed in 1947 a professional baseball contract, making him the first African-American to play for a major league club. The sound of the ball smacking against his bat the first time he entered the field would resonate for years to come in the minds and hearts of every African-American. Gwendolyn Brooks became in 1950 the first African-American to win the Pulitzer Prize in poetry for her book of verse, *Annie Allen*. In that same year Ralph Bunche became the first African-American to win the Nobel Prize for peace, granted because of his achievement as a United Nations mediator in Palestine.

Whether word of these events made its ways to the black families of the rural South is impossible to know; many such families were still removed from mainstream culture, living without electricity and running water, much less radio and telephones. However, the news of successful court cases seemed to travel as quickly as rumors of freedom had spread among enslaved Africans in the final days of the Civil War. Such news was frequent and often had clear relevance to their lives. For example, in addition to the outlawing of white primaries in Georgia in the mid-

1940s, a federal district court ruled in 1948 that the Democratic Party of South Carolina could not require members to take an oath upholding segregation and denouncing the Fair Employment Practices Committee. The oath had in effect prevented African-Americans from joining the party for years. In 1949 the Supreme Court ruled that the University of Kentucky was obligated by law to admit African-Americans into its graduate school. And in 1950, as North Korean forces launched a campaign against South Korea – thus initiating the Korean War – the Supreme Court ruled in *Henderson v. United States* that dining cars on interstate trains could not be segregated. Additional cases brought by civil rights attorneys compelled the University of Texas, the University of Virginia, and Louisiana State University to admit African-American students.

Meanwhile, because of Truman's 1948 executive order banning segregation in the military, many African-Americans were again departing the South and elsewhere to fight in the Korean War. Although these soldiers were barred from 198 of the army's 490 so-called specialty divisions, African-Americans asserted a strong and successful presence for themselves in the military. Indeed, black troops of the army's Twenty-fourth Infantry Regiment helped recapture Yechon in South Korea in 1950, the first major victory of the war.

In 1952, through various legal actions, the NAACP managed to desegregate a wide range of public facilities in the South, including a golf course in Louisville, Kentucky, and Ford's Theater in Baltimore, Maryland. Despite these successes, which often triggered violent responses from so-called White Citizens' Councils and other supremacist groups, the Tuskegee Institute reported no known lynchings of African-Americans in 1952. It was the first time the school was able to make such a report in the seventy-one years that it had been keeping a record of lynchings. A wave of race-related bombings soon flooded the country, however, killing countless civil rights activists in its wake. The election that year of Dwight D. Eisenhower, who had opposed Truman's efforts to integrate the military, felt like a step backward to many black Americans who were attempting steadily to move ahead.

In 1953, as the Korean War was coming to an end, the NAACP continued to use the courts to attack the remaining Southern school districts that had refused to integrate their elementary and secondary schools. African-Americans watched these developments with particular attention, regardless of whether they worked in the South's agricultural industry or the North's automotive industry. From the farms to the cities African-Americans understood that any sustained social advancement would require having equal access to the same educational opportunities as whites.

In 1954 the most important step toward that advancement was achieved at last. It had been a long time in the making. In 1952 the Supreme Court had decided to hear and combine five separate cases related to segregated public education. The school districts under fire were in Delaware, the District of Columbia, Kansas, South Carolina, and Virginia. The Kansas school board had attracted particular attention in 1950 when Topeka minister Oliver Brown attempted to enroll his eight-year-old daughter, Linda, in the local elementary school, which was just a few blocks from the Brown home. Unfortunately, the local public school was for white children only, and Linda was forced to walk across town every day to attend the nearest school for black children. When the school board refused Brown's request — invoking the Kansas state law that mandated segregation in public education — Brown took his case to court.

Grouped together under *Brown v. Board of Education of Topeka,* all five cases sought to challenge the 1896 *Plessy v. Ferguson* decision, which held that separate-but-equal facilities were all that was needed under constitutional law for a state to ensure it wasn't discriminating against its black citizens. More pointedly, the court had argued in 1896 that restricting African-Americans to separate facilities and accommodations had caused them "no badge of inferiority." Bolstered by this court decision, many Southern states had adopted a sweeping separate-but-equal policy that they imposed on all areas of everyday life. Before long, however, the separate facilities reserved for blacks became markedly inferior, thereby confirming to the world in general and to African-Americans in particular that they were second-class citizens. Already in 1952 the NAACP Legal Defense and Educational Fund had challenged the legality of *Plessy* in a number of cases related to dining facilities, train travel, even golf courses. Now, however, the objective was to dismantle the *Plessy* decision entirely, so that black children could access the same educational opportunities as their white counterparts.

After deliberating for nearly two years – in which time the Chief Justice Fred Vinson died and was replaced by Earl Warren – the Supreme Court struck down the separate-but-equal mandate of *Plessy* and in the process handed down perhaps the most significant and far-reaching constitutional decision of the twentieth century. According to the *Encyclopedia of Civil Rights in America,* the justices barred in one fell swoop the age-old practice of imposing racial segregation in public schools:

> Chief Justice Warren, writing the unanimous opinion, stated there was "no place" for segregation in education. The ruling further argued that separate schools were "inherently unequal" and therefore denied black children the equal protection guaranteed by the Fourteenth Amendment. . . . Looking at segregation as a sociological issue, the Court cited several social science publications and declared the dual educational system generated among black children a "feeling of inferiority" as to their status in the community that may affect their hearts and minds in a way unlikely to ever be undone.

Although it would be years before the full impact of the *Brown* decision would be felt in all corners of the country – and it was necessary in 1955 for the Court to revisit the issue in *Green v. County School Board* (known as *Brown II*) to address issues related to enforcement – the proverbial die was cast. Whereas so many earlier civil rights decisions had a direct impact on those African-Americans already enjoying some modest measure of equality in Northern cities, where access to education and a livable wage were understood to be fundamental elements of life, the *Brown* decision would also make a difference in the lives of African-Americans in Southern farming communities. True, it would take a long time for black children in these areas to enjoy the spoils of an integrated school system; nonetheless, the Court's insistence on integration was the most concrete example of productive change that many Southern African-Americans had seen for years. For them it seemed that equal access to public education might possibly lead to the availability of other opportunities, which might in turn keep young African-Americans from believing it was necessary to flee the South to achieve a better way of life. Ultimately, it might even encourage blacks who had migrated to the North to consider coming home at last to the land of their ancestors.

In the meantime, however, it was clear that such changes would not occur overnight. In the years immediately following *Brown,* the South became a dangerous and inhospitable place for African-Americans. According to historian Pete Daniel, author of *Breaking the Land: The Transformation of Cotton, Tobacco, and Rice Culture since 1880,* many whites feared they would be displaced by blacks and that any African-American advancement would come at the expense of whites. Daniel continues:

> When *Brown v. Board* came down in the countryside, a lot of [black] farmers who needed credit found out that they couldn't get credit anymore. The Farmers Home Administration would say, "Well, you can't get credit this

year." And the banks would say, "We don't want your money." These were people who only belonged to the NAACP maybe – that was their only crime. Or they tried to register to vote. Or they tried . . . to sign a petition so that their children could go to integrated schools. And if you did that, chances are you weren't going to be able to find the money to farm.

All this was part of an ongoing system of white domination in the rural South that had become intensified because of the *Brown* decision. The number of black-owned farms had been steadily decreasing after World War II, and the size of the few remaining farms was small, so the effect of cutting off an African-American farmer's access to loans was devastating. Without these resources farmers were unable to purchase labor-saving technology or increase the size of their property. Indeed, during the 1950s in Georgia and other Southern states, land auctions would often begin with a pronouncement from the auctioneer that only whites could participate in the bidding.

Presumably, the Farmers Home Administration (FmHA) was supposed to ensure that all farmers had equal access to the resources that could help them grow and cultivate their property. An offshoot of the New Deal's Resettlement Program, the FmHA was created to provide loans to farmers who had exhausted all other options. Unfortunately, writes Grant, "loan decisions were made by committees of local, mostly white, farmers. Racism and discrimination were rampant in local FmHA offices." These offices were the first to shut the doors on black farmers in violent response to the *Brown* decision.

So the question of whether the black family farm could survive in postwar America seemed to be answered by a strange collision of political advancements and technological ones. One the one hand, black farmers could celebrate with all African-Americans the *Brown* decision, which made plain at last that a separate-but-equal policy of race relations led to inferior facilities and services for blacks and served to convince black children that they were somehow inferior to their white counterparts. On the other hand, as these farmers rejoiced, the whites around them responded with particular cruelty to the decision. Because of their own prejudices that had been reinforced over the years by white Southern culture, many whites in rural communities felt deeply threatened by the Civil Rights Movement, and they attempted to stave off the advances of blacks by any possible means.

All of this occurred at a time when farming itself was undergoing a transition, and technology was changing the way in which crops were grown and harvested. Already the use of tractors, mechanical harvesters, and chemical weed control had reduced the amount of work available to African-American laborers in the Southern agricultural industry. By 1960 more than half of most U.S. crops were picked by machine, according to Grant, and this trend increased in the years ahead. More pointedly, however, many black farmers weren't able to purchase this new technology because the *Brown* decision had made bigoted banks and local government agencies less likely than ever to help black farmers improve their fortunes.

Recognizing the handwriting on the wall, more African-American farmers than ever encouraged their older children to take advantage of desegregation laws by attending college. It was a selfless gesture – after all, the likelihood of these children returning to the farming life was slim, and the expense of sending a child to college was considerable. And a white Southern bank that had already denied loans to black farmers for the purchase of tools and equipment was even less disposed to loan them money to send their children to college. Nonetheless, the spirit of the Civil Rights Movement seemed to engender a spirit of selflessness in many African-Americans, who had been instructed by the Reverend Martin Luther King Jr. to meet hatred with love. Accordingly, black farmers opened their hearts and their doors, allowing their children to pursue opportunities elsewhere and making room in their homes for civil rights activists, who always found safe haven on black-owned farms.

By the end of the 1950s, the soul of the black farmer seemed at rest, even if the times remained turbulent. No amount of hostility, violence, poverty, or injustice had passed over rural black communities since the end of slavery, and somehow African-Americans endured it all. There was hardly anything left to fight over as the 1960s dawned, and so few black farmers remained in the South that they perhaps accepted their diminished numbers as the will of God. Perhaps they expected, as they looked over how much they had accomplished on the land in the face of so much adversity, that if the black family farm did not survive the second half of the twentieth century, at least the land itself would always contain something of the black farmer's blood.

In the absence of any redress for the chronic injustice endured by African-American farmers, the land itself would have to be both their reward and their legacy. The soil, more than any physical structure, was the home to which their children might return. And although acknowledgment of all that had gone wrong in the past might be long overdue, what mattered most now was the idea that the land would endure, along with the memories of that land carried in the hearts of the black farmer's descendants. Toward the mid-1960s, however, the long overdue acknowledgment was made. There was even some compensation for past grievances. Although these belated efforts did not necessarily revitalize the black family farm, they assured that the struggles that took place on these Southern farms were neither forgotten nor buried beneath layers of earth.

10.

Four days before I was born, Malcolm X was assassinated on February 21, 1965. My mother
was pregnant and alone in Temple, Texas, while my father was serving in the U.S. Army.
My mother went back to Montezuma, Georgia, to be with family when she gave birth in a small
hospital in Americus, Georgia, about thirty miles from Montezuma. She stayed in Montezuma
for a month while she adjusted to being a new mother. After that, the only time I spent in
Montezuma was during our family summer vacations.

    My brother and I dreaded the thought of Montezuma. After all, in a child's mind it was
a place with bad TV reception, only two channels, no air-conditioning in my grandparents'
house, no ice-cream trucks to chase, and lots of people asking us questions we never had to
answer back in our own home in New Jersey or in Washington, D.C., Colorado, or wherever else
we had happened to come from that particular summer. Questions like "Who your folks be?"
We often stood silent and perplexed until an uncle or a cousin would answer for us. "These are
Fred Mathis's grandchildren" or "Aunt Bernice's niece" or "Aunt El's nephew." It was those

cousins, aunts, uncles, and grandparents that always made us forget our dread and fears. They would help us find our place in those short visits with long days. Eventually, we would find ourselves playing games in the red dirt, running from the chickens, and laughing at the hogs. The farm became the best kind of playground. My grandfather even taught me and my cousin Elaine to drive the pickup truck. We landed in a gully, but we always remembered his joy in getting us there.

As I got older and read more about the Civil Rights Movement, I began to understand the ghosts that lingered in the South. I read about a man who had been shot in the back in Mississippi for going in the whites-only bathroom the year I was born. I heard the stories of U.S. apartheid and realized that these stories were those of my parents and grandparents. They had lived through some of the most repressive times in the twentieth century, had seen the whites-only water fountains and used the "colored" faucets. I realized that I owed a great debt, that my life of choices had been bought at a high price. The South then became something more to me. That small farm on Flint River Road is a sacred place with a long memory and a short history. It is my home, and it is the place where this story began.

THE NATIONAL EVENTS from 1960 to 1963 made it more plain than ever to African-Americans in general — and particularly to those in the South — that the cost of freedom was high. Asserting one's beliefs, pursuing racial uplift, participating in the democratic process, raising one's voice to protest injustice — these activities came at no small cost to African-Americans as they moved into the second half of the twentieth century.

I CAN REMEMBER WHEN PEOPLE WOULD COME BACK—FAMILIES WOULD GATHER—BACK ON THE LAND FOR HOMECOMING.... ALL THAT WAS HOOKED TO THE LAND, BECAUSE IT WAS A SENSE OF OWNERSHIP, A SENSE OF BEING, A SENSE OF CONNECTION.... I COULD GO TO A FAMILY REUNION OR A HOMECOMING AND GET A CHANCE TO SEE EVERYBODY. YOU CAN'T DO THAT ANYMORE. THAT'S LOST. THAT'S PART OF OUR CULTURE, AND IT'S LOST NOW.
—RALPH PAIGE

As President Dwight D. Eisenhower was signing the Civil Rights Act of 1960 to make the federal government more responsive to civil rights demands, a peaceful demonstration against segregation in Jacksonville, Florida, erupted into sustained and horrifying violence. A group of black and white protesters had gathered to stage a sit-in at a public facility, and before long a group of white police officers arrived to end the protest. They were joined by various members of Jacksonville's white community. Using a staggering amount of force, police and civilians slapped, beat, and kicked the protesters until the pavement was covered with blood. Newspaper photographers rushed to the site and took numerous pictures, which were published nationwide the next day. The photographs highlighted the fact that rather than helping to implement civil rights laws, certain police officers in Southern states were violating such laws. Confronted with these photos, many whites were stripped of their complacency about the extent to which other whites might resist the tide of black empowerment. The photos also served to remind many blacks that their safety, their well-being, and even their lives might be sacrificed in the quest for social equality.

Such events confirmed for Eisenhower that his new civil rights legislation was necessary. It was intended as an extension to the Civil Rights

Act of 1957, the first significant civil rights legislation since 1875. Unfortunately, the teeth had been taken out of the 1957 act by determined Southern senators, who slowed the bill's process and deleted from it many strongly worded provisions for public school integration. Similarly, Southern lawmakers undermined the bill's enforcement provisions by insisting that any white voting official who violated an African-American's access to the polls should be tried by a *local* jury, which in the South meant a predominantly white jury that would no doubt rubber-stamp an acquittal. If nothing else, however, the Civil Rights Act of 1957 gave birth to the U.S. Civil Rights Commission and authorized the president to appoint (with the consent of the Senate) an assistant attorney general for civil rights in the Department of Justice. Still, with good reason, the NAACP was unhappy with the 1957 act and over the years applied increasing pressure on the White House to revisit its stance on civil rights legislation. By 1960 they got their wish, although the new legislation fell short in many ways as well.

Eisenhower's objective was to further strengthen voting rights protections for African-Americans and to make the federal government more accountable in cases of civil rights violations. The bill's most compelling feature was a proposal to appoint federal registrars to monitor elections. These registrars would work with the Civil Rights Commission to investigate charges that state registrars had refused to register qualified voters on the basis of race, color, religion, or national origin. However, the proposal was shot down by Senator Herman Talmadge, former governor of Georgia. He argued that federal registrars, who were appointed by the president and thus owed him their allegiance, would be untrustworthy as monitors of free elections. Talmadge supported a proposal for local, court-appointed "voting referees." In the end his proposal won the day.

Faced now with two important but vague and often toothless civil rights acts, the NAACP, CORE, and other groups rallied for even more stringent provisions in civil rights legislation. From this foundation the sit-in was born. Starting with a group of college students in Greensboro, North Carolina, who refused to move from a Woolworth's lunch counter when they were told they wouldn't be served, African-Americans throughout the South staged sit-ins at a wide range of public facilities where blacks were refused equal service. Encouraged in particular by James Farmer, the leader of CORE, who had initiated similar activities in the 1940s, the sit-in became the most visible and well-known method of passive resistance to emerge from the Civil Rights Movement. This tactic inspired a host of other such actions – including "stand-ins," "sing-ins," and on the steps of churches that refused to segregate, "kneel-ins" – and attracted the attention and participation of whites and blacks alike. Such multiracial and peaceful gatherings were often met with violence – as had occurred in Jacksonville – but they served as visible and frequent reminders to government officials of the far-reaching extent of the campaign for civil rights.

In the South, African-American farmers paid close attention to the initiatives related to voting rights. By now the rural South was hemorrhaging its African-American population. For the first time in history, more than 50 percent of the nation's blacks lived outside the South, and the few who remained behind – on farms or in other industries – held firm to the belief that an improvement in voting rights was the last, best thing they might ever see before their numbers dwindled entirely. The black farmer's faith was nurtured not only by the accomplishments in the North of civil rights workers but also by local churches. Working quietly and often surreptitiously, these churches sometimes served as touchstones for the Civil Rights Movement in African-American farming communities. They would disseminate information, hold prayer vigils for protesters, and spiritually support those local black families who felt beaten down by poverty, backbreaking work, and the constant threat of racial violence. In this way the African-American church served its traditional dual mission — partly political, partly spiritual — to show the relationship between social justice and Christian ideals. No black community was likely to have a strong, unifying identity without the presence of a church, and many rural African-American communities throughout the South could indeed boast that their small local church was built from the timber of a black farmer's land.

These black churches were often delicate structures, which made them especially vulnerable to acts of terrorism by white supremacists in the South. Arson, bombings, or bricks thrown through a stained-glass window were some of the types of violence inflicted on black churches in rural communities whenever those churches were thought to be promoting the cause of civil rights. The congregants were also vulnerable because so many of them gathered together inside these tiny houses of worship. Corrupt white law enforcement officials who wanted to track down visiting civil rights activists would often swoop into a crowded black church on a Sunday with guns drawn to search for "agitators."

In time, the increasing role of the black church in civil rights activities put a strain between white and black clergy. Many denominations still practiced segregation, and white churches that allowed blacks in at all would often put them in separate pews, as was common among Presbyterians in the rural South, for example. Like the rest of the segregated South, these white churches perceived civil rights activists as troublemakers and hoodlums, and they saw no reason to change the existing social order in such a sweeping, dramatic fashion. In this way, surprisingly, their attitudes reflected that of some conservative black ministers, who also found themselves at odds with the methods and leaders of the Civil Rights Movement. As historian Donald L. Grant illustrates in *The Way It Was in the South: The Black Experience in Georgia:*

> The civil rights movement created a strain not only between black and white churches but also within the black Baptist community. The Progressive National Baptist Convention was formed by the more trained and forward looking clergy following a schism within the National Baptist Convention USA in 1961. Progressives favored a limited-tenure presidency and supported Dr. Martin Luther King, Jr., more than the older group, which was headed by an avowed enemy of King's, the Rev. Joseph H. Jackson of Chicago's Mount Olive Baptist Church. King's efforts to influence the National Baptist Convention failed, and Jackson, an entrenched conservative, did not support the civil rights movement.

Generally, however, the African-American church was central to advancements made by the movement, and although black churches in farming communities rarely made the national news, their efforts on behalf of the families they served remained a continuing source of strength, guidance, and comfort to black farmers. In Georgia's rural communities—most notably Albany and Leesburg—a feverish wave of violence often followed the arrival of civil rights activists, most of whom were part of voter registration drives and campaigns against segregation. Somehow, although such violence might serve to intimidate African-American farmers and keep them from the polls, it did not prevent them from inviting the activists into their churches and homes. For example, Ralph Paige, executive director of the Federation of Southern Cooperatives, recalls "during the civil rights days on Highway 80 during the march from Selma to Montgomery, a lot of the land where people stopped along the way to rest . . . was owned by black families. The churches, the land – all that [was] connected together. There were cases when black landowners were able to go down and sign a bond and bail people out. You know, that was *power*."

Offering land as a refuge to civil rights workers was thus a form of power black farmers exercised with increasing frequency in the early 1960s, and these acts of hospitality and kindness proved as vital to the movement's success as any sit-in, speech, demonstration, or march. Many a photograph from the time depicts weary marchers and protesters, fallen to the ground in exhaustion, pouring soothing water onto their feet from the well of a black landowner. The contribution of African-American farmers to the struggle was not limited to hospitality, however. Many of them, caught up in the spirit of the era, risked violent retribution by registering to vote. In doing so, they sent a clear signal to white Southerners that there was truly no turning back the tide of change. Admittedly, there was no mass descent on registration offices; in fact, in a typical Southern rural community such as Fayette County, Georgia, there were approximately 1,255 African-Americans of voting age, according to Grant, but only 25 were registered voters, as opposed to nearly all of the county's 3,500 white adults.

Nonetheless, even twenty-five voters was better than none, and those who dared to register were part of a growing phenomenon among black farmers. As their numbers continued to grow smaller – and their resources dwindled even further – African-Americans who remained on farms often felt they had nothing to lose by supporting civil rights initiatives. By this time it didn't seem likely that the black family farm would even survive the 1960s, but the threat of losing the land did not mean these rural families had to lose their dignity as well. Registering to vote was a way of asserting their dignity, in a spiritual sense, but there were practical concerns as well. After decades of enduring the benign neglect of the federal government, farmers may have hoped to use the power of the ballot box to call the government's attention to the plight of African-Americans in the Southern agricultural industry.

No one expected a miracle. Exercising the power to vote was likely to prove difficult in the end, because the Ku Klux Klan often stationed themselves outside of polling stations to identify and terrorize black voters. But the arrival of civil rights activists to such rural areas as Albany, Georgia, had already captured the attention of the nation and the federal government. Media coverage of these activists allowed the entire world to glimpse on TV the dilapidated housing, tattered clothing, and obscene levels of poverty and illiteracy that seemed to mark the lives of poor blacks in the Southern countryside. The sight of them caused embarrassment to President John F. Kennedy, who had been elected in 1960 with a large percentage of the African-American vote, but who had been dragging his feet on the civil rights issue. The outrage that often followed the news appearance of rural blacks living in abject poverty or being beaten by whites who resisted segregation seemed to stir the Kennedy administration into action. In 1963 the president declared that segregation was morally wrong, the strongest statement ever made on the subject by a president. Soon after, however, Kennedy was assassinated, and for a time it looked as though support from Washington on civil rights initiatives would no longer be forthcoming. Fortunately, Kennedy's successor, Lyndon B. Johnson, took up the cause, and his administration addressed the plight of the black farmer in a way that had not been seen since the days of the New Deal.

"You get up to 1964, and you've had a number of years of the civil rights movement," notes historian Pete Daniel, author of *Breaking the Land: The Transformation of Cotton, Tobacco, and Rice Culture since 1880,* "and finally under the Johnson Administration, they do a study, studying the Department of Agriculture. In every agency, they found out, there'd been discrimination. But not just discrimination – there'd never been, in the South, an African American elected to an agricultural committee in a county. And it went on from there: In every level, whether it was borrowing money or trying to get more land to farm or whatever, there was discrimination." Such discriminatory practices had been in place since African-Americans first attempted to buy land and build farms of their own after the Civil War. As a result, the discrimination had become fully institutionalized, and each new federal effort only deepened the corruption that kept black farmers at a permanent disadvantage. The government's failure to keep its promise to provide forty acres and a mule to recently freed Africans in the 1860s had established a precedent that determined the course and tenor of relations between black farmers and the government for the next hundred years. In all that time, as agricultural studies in the 1960s made clear, black farmers had been playing against impossible odds. A cruel and long-standing pattern of racial discrimination had turned the farming industry into a game that they were expected to lose.

A wave of interest in African-American farmers followed the announcement of the Johnson administration's study in the mid-1960s. Outraged blacks and whites alike wanted to know how the Department of Agriculture idly had stood by as black farmers were all but driven into extinction. The U.S. Department of Agriculture (USDA) had been formed at the very height of Reconstruction, in the 1860s, and started out as "an outgrowth of the Patent Office, which was in the Department of the Interior, where it remained until the early 1890's," according to professor of agriculture R. Grant Seals, author of "The Formation of Agricultural and Rural Development Policy with Emphasis on African Americans." "The duties of the department were not glamorous. They primarily involved collecting and disseminating data on agriculture and performing agricultural research."

In time, however, legislation related to land grants and the funding of agricultural colleges in various state universities was initiated by the USDA, which brought the agency into the political arena. Because land had historically been the basis for so much racial tension in the South, whites in Congress and the Senate insisted that any bills related to landownership and property be worded in a way that was not likely to benefit African-Americans, and the USDA expressed no objection. From this point on, the USDA remained a passive participant in the slow, perilous decline of black farmers. By 1964 the agency's failure to intervene when, for example, it was evident that a pattern of corruption had allowed white landowners to easily swindle, withhold, or otherwise usurp government funds from African-American farmers became a source of considerable embarrassment for the USDA. In the years after such allegations came to light, the USDA felt pressure to make some kind of public amends.

Secretary of Agriculture Clifford Hardin, the USDA director from 1969 to 1971, spoke clearly to the point and attempted to establish a policy of nondiscrimination in the South. "Our goal," he expressed, "is to ensure equal access and opportunity in all aspects of our programs without regard to race, color, or national origin, to the full extent of the law. The policy is clear: Any discrimination in our programs and activities must cease." Years of discrimination are impossible to undo in one fell swoop, however, and by the time Hardin made his comments, many local USDA officials in the Deep South were continuing to resist any efforts to allow black farmers to participate as equals in agricultural policy. This kind of resistance to equal rights was becoming more and more difficult to sustain. Segregation was slowly dying a fitful death, and the national prominence of the NAACP, CORE, and Dr. Martin Luther King's Southern Christian Leadership Conference (SCLC) ensured that civil rights issues were placed at the forefront of the national agenda, rather than banished to the margins. Although white supremacists and even the FBI made concerted attempts to discredit civil rights leaders – in both the national and international press – these endeavors were not especially successful. Furthermore, the entry of U.S. combat troops into the Vietnam War in 1965, and the ongoing displays of racial violence at home, made it increasingly difficult for the United States to assert itself as the world's moral leader.

To improve the country's quickly tarnishing global image, and to ensure the international community that the United States was qualified to promote stability abroad because of the stability its citizens enjoyed at home, Kennedy and Johnson had put into a motion a series of actions to strengthen the cause of civil rights. In 1962, for example, Kennedy pushed for an amendment to the Constitution that would outlaw poll taxes, the last remaining tool by which the right to vote had been systematically withheld from African-Americans. Many civil rights leaders felt a constitutional amendment was in many ways an admission of defeat, a sad acknowledgment that all the branches of government had been unable to agree on a more direct, concrete method for eliminating abuses of voting laws. Still, in the Deep South, where the poll tax had made the cost of registering to vote prohibitive for many black farmers, the ratification of the Twenty-fourth Amendment, which abolished the use of poll taxes in all local, primary, and general elections, was embraced by African-Americans, if not by local white authorities.

With Kennedy's assassination in November 1963, the entire nation held its breath. When at last Americans dared to exhale, they did so mournfully. For a while all major civil rights measures were simply put on hold. In time, however, Johnson pushed the measures forward with even more vigor than had his predecessor, culminating in the passage of the Civil Rights Act of 1964. According to the editors of the *Encyclopedia of Civil Rights in America,*

> With much prompting from . . . Johnson, Congress passed the most far-reaching civil rights legislation since the reconstruction [*sic*] era. Among other things, the Civil Rights Act of 1964 contained new provisions to help guarantee African Americans the right to vote, guaranteed access to public accommodations such as hotels, motels, restaurants and places of amusement, and prohibited discrimination in employment on the basis of race, color, religion, sex, or national origin.

Despite a few shortcomings, the act could not have dealt a more devastating blow to discriminatory policies and practices if the NAACP itself had written the document. To this day, the landmark act is considered the Magna Carta of racial minorities, according to the *African-American Encyclopedia,* edited by Michael Williams, and there is no doubt that in a sweeping fashion it fulfilled many of the earliest and most basic ambitions of the Civil Rights Movement.

As always, there was difficulty with enforcement, however, which Johnson had perhaps failed to anticipate. In *Marching toward Freedom, 1957–1965: From the Founding of the Southern Christian Leadership Conference to the Assassination of Malcolm X,* author Robert Weisbrot writes that on the very same day that Johnson signed the Civil Rights Act of 1964, thus making it a law, the president told Martin Luther King Jr. that because the new law "secured" Negro rights, "any future civil rights actions might be 'unnecessary' and possibly even self-defeating." Apparently King demurred and the conversation went no further, but that summer the evidence that further action was necessary came vividly and horribly into view.

The Council of Federated Organizations – comprised of the Student Non-Violent Coordinating Committee (SNCC), CORE, the NAACP, and King's SCLC – decided in 1964 to sponsor an event called the Mississippi Summer Project. Their objective was to send representatives into the most rural and depressed areas of the Mississippi countryside to help African-American farmers and other black agricultural workers register to vote. At the time Mississippi was perhaps the Southern state most resistant to granting civil rights to blacks, and all previous attempts to promote voting rights among African-Americans had ended in violence. For example, according to Weisbrot, shortly before the Mississippi Summer Project in McComb County, "a state legislator warned a black resident not to register to vote." But "the [black] man registered anyway, and the legislator shot him dead in broad daylight." Although the white legislator was tried, and the jury acknowledged he was responsible for the black man's death, the jury nonetheless acquitted him. Such was the value often placed on African-American life in the rural South during this tumultuous era.

Because of such cases as this, the Council of Federated Organizations felt it was crucial to continue its efforts to register black voters, despite the hanging threat of violence. So in the hottest months of the year, not very long after Johnson suggested that civil rights demonstrations were no longer necessary, more than one thousand black and white volunteers fanned out through rural Mississippi. Three such volunteers – two white men and a black man, named Andrew Goodman, Michael Henry Schwerner, and James Earl Chaney, respectively – headed out for Philadelphia, Mississippi. Within days, all three men were murdered. Among the suspects was the sheriff of the county in which the murders took place, and although several arrests were made in relation to the crime, no one was ever convicted.

The murders of Goodman, Schwerner, and Chaney dampened the enthusiasm that many rural African-Americans had experienced at the passing of the Civil Rights Act of 1964. Further, it squashed the morale of many volunteers who were attempting to register black voters during the Mississippi Summer project. Weisbrot continues:

> Weighed down by a sense of constant danger and lack of support by the federal government, the volunteers threw themselves into the work of organizing local blacks. But this, too, had its discouraging side. Many volunteers had expected a rush of eager black sharecroppers to the nearest registration office, but it did not work out that way. Black Mississippians greeted their visitors politely but often remained unwilling to disobey the local authorities by registering to vote. They knew any political act might cost them their jobs, their homes, even their lives.

Volunteers continued to find that African-American farmers would open their doors to them, providing them with a place to relax and rest awhile. But for a time after the slayings of the three volunteers in Mississippi, registering to vote seemed a more dangerous proposition than ever. In Georgia especially the majority of African-Americans declined to register, although Atlanta appeared to have more registered black voters than any other city in the South. But in the city the threat of Klansmen was considerably more remote than it was in the countryside, so while urban folks continued to direct their attention at desegregation and voting rights, African-Americans in rural communities returned to the issue of land.

As the 1960s wore on, there was still considerable talk about the documented cases of racial discrimination in the policies and practices of the Department of Agriculture. No farmer was foolish enough to believe that such a long history of injustice might be reversed overnight, but the documentation of those injustices suggested that perhaps the last days of the black farmer were not imminent after all. The civil rights cases all over the country seemed to have touched on every issue but landowner-ship, and now that the issue was on the table at last, many rural African-Americans wanted to pursue it closely, if only to understand what had gone wrong in the past and what might be improved for the future.

In this effort, they received some help from civil rights activists. SNCC communications director Julian Bond, activist and farmer Fannie Lou Hamer, historian Vincent Harding, and others, as part of the Task Force on the Southern Land Bank (organized by the Black Economic Development Conference), ran an advertisement in the *New York Times* on Sunday, April 26, 1970, to promote interest in the issue of African-American landownership. In the years after the ad ran, the group pre-pared a report called *Only Six Million Acres: The Decline of Black-Owned Land in the Rural South* that charted the decline of black landownership since its peak in 1910. This was the first documented evidence to support the idea that self-sufficient black farmers had almost become "extinct." The find-ings were a wake-up call, a reminder to the civil rights community that a people dispossessed of its land is destined to wander endlessly, lost and fragmented, without a foundation – a home – from which to expand and grow.

Although it was too late to recuperate all of the land that had been lost, abandoned, or stolen from black farmers, civil rights activists in the late 1960s made an effort to recover what little they could by attending auctions and tax sales where previously black-owned property was offered on the open market and by encouraging black farmers still in possession of their land to draw up wills and deeds of ownership. The activists were not very successful in getting the farmers to draw up wills—farmers assumed that their children would understand that the land was their inheritance and would tend to it accordingly—but there was some modest success in reclaiming lost property and helping farmers to protect their land. Robert Browne, founder of the Emergency Land Fund (ELF), recalls in the documentary film *Homecoming,*

> The Black Economic Research Center asked one of its staff members, who was stationed in Mississippi, to take some money—we sent him $2500, if I remember correctly—to take it into the tax sale of September of that year [1970] and to see what he could do. . . . And so he identified some blacks whose land would be up for sale that September, and he and his assistant went into the tax sale. Well, one of the first things he said happened was that one of the people in the room shouted, "What are these niggras doin' here?" Apparently it was one of the first times a black person had ever thought—or dared, I don't know which—to come to a tax sale. And another guy replied, "Oh, well, some folks from New York sent a big check down here the other day, I don't know if it has anything to do with this or not." Well, they did it—they saved a little land that day.

Out of such efforts the ELF was born. More useful than the Farmers Home Administration, which is principally charged with getting impoverished farmers out of century-old shacks and placed in modern, modest housing, the ELF not only helped black farmers recover land; they also developed training to keep farmers from losing their land in the first place. Recalling her days as a researcher in the rural South, Georgetown University professor Marsha Darling says in the film *Homecoming,* "I remember traveling around and meeting farmers whose land had been saved—from some measure of adversity or duress—by the Emergency Land Fund. It was crucial."

What made the ELF so crucial was its understanding that more often than not, black landowners had been or were stripped of their property by what Browne calls "chicanery." Using methods that were not exactly illegal—but, as Browne adds, "only marginally legal"—an intolerant white landowner or a greedy developer might exploit various loopholes in landownership laws to acquire the black farmer's property. For example, when a farmer died, his land would be passed down, by a commonly recognized "heirs" statute, to his wife and children; when they died, the land would pass to the next set of heirs, the grandchildren. Within two or three generations, explains attorney C. Scott Graber in "A Blight Hits Black Farmers: Cloud on the Title," an article appearing in a 1978 issue of *Civil Rights Digest,* a hundred people could be part owners of this tiny strip of property. This means that ownership is "scattered" or has a "cloud" over it, and thus cannot be mortgaged or used as collateral to buy farm equipment or to secure credit. Graber continues: "A person bent on acquisition can purchase the interest of any single heir—any fractional interest—then demand that 'his' interest be partitioned from the tract. If the land cannot be easily subdivided, and very often that cannot be done equitably, the court will order a sale of the land and a division of the proceeds. It is not uncommon for the person triggering the sale to purchase the entire tract, that having been the plan."

Donald L. Grant further clarifies this point, explaining,

> Lack of education made unsophisticated black landowners easy prey to trickery by lawyers, land speculators, and officials operating through tax sales, partition sales, and foreclosures to gain title to land. The historical distrust of the legal system kept nine out of ten Southern black landowners

from drawing up wills, [according to] the Emergency Land Fund. The result was often a partition sale that was forced when any heir asked for his or her share of the estate.

Although the heirs may have been scattered throughout the country, they were considered by law to own the property jointly. Therefore, if even one heir could not be traced, the result was that the black farmer who inhabited the property did not have a "clear" title, which made him vulnerable to predatory developers, who needed only entice one heir to sell a small piece of the property. In this way the inhabitant's grasp on the property was weakened and often the land slipped through his hands.

The full extent of the methods by which black farmers were stripped of their land did not come to light until the turbulent 1960s had ended, clearing the way for the 1970s. One decade would follow another, but no matter the Herculean effort made by such agencies as the ELF, the damage that had been done to the black family farm had been so consistent and so deeply woven into the social and legal fabric of the South that trying to fix the problem was not much different than trying to empty the sky of all its stars. Had it simply been racists to blame – combing the countryside at night, terrorizing black farmers from their homes – perhaps the advances of the Civil Rights Movement would have been enough to make things right. Acquiring the right to vote would have meant installing new officials in local government, men and women who were not too blinded by racial hatred to lend black farmers a hand. Similarly, segregation might have given black farmers access to the resources and opportunities that would have allowed their farms to flourish.

Unfortunately, a lot more than voters rights and integrated schools was needed to redress the particular humiliation black farmers had endured over the years. This is not to say that such advances did not eventually serve farmers well, allowing them to claim at last the "inalienable rights" that had been denied them for so long. But they faced particularly ugly challenges on the road to acquiring these rights, and these challenges very often posed a direct threat to their lives. During the Civil Rights Movement Southern black farmers simply tried to catch up to a standard of living that many Northern blacks had already obtained. Electricity, running water, a livable wage – these things were outside black farmers' purview in the first half of the twentieth century. Meeting such needs must have seemed far more pressing than achieving the right to swim alongside whites in a public pool.

Unlike African-Americans in Northern and Southern cities, who could sometimes glimpse a withering away of old-fashioned racial bigotry, black farmers were faced with such bigotry every day of their lives in the first half of the twentieth century, and the long-term effects of continued exposure to hatred and contempt had both strengthened and weakened them in countless ways. Suffering under the benign neglect of the USDA – "one of the last Federal agencies to integrate," according to USDA publications, "and perhaps the very last to include women and minorities in leadership positions" – black farmers' livelihood was always under assault, often from the very agency that had been assigned to protect them. With white supremacists preying on them at night and bureaucracies preying on them by day, African-American farmers somehow managed to cultivate the land, to raise families, and to grow things of sustenance and beauty at no small cost to their self-respect.

In the end, more often than not, that which was cultivated and grown was taken away, stolen by developers and legislators whom, it appears, argued to keep rural blacks from pursuing an education because a degree might make them less easy to exploit. There were heroes among these African-American farmers, women and men who refused to be trampled, bullied, killed, or forgotten. But there were tragedies among them too, women and men who suffered and died on the land they loved, the victims of someone's hateful whim.

Our job, then, is to celebrate the heroes and the tragedies alike. To sing their praises, to learn from their stories, and to carry in our hearts their affection for the land. Even now we can hear them, if we listen closely enough, a gathering of ancestors in the South, calling us back home.

African-American farmers, whose ancestors contributed so much to the vitality of Southern agriculture, have continued to diminish in number over the years. At one time nearly a million of them derived a living from farming. In 1920, African-American farmers owned fifteen million acres of land, but even then, when their numbers were high, the land was slipping through their fingers because of a combination of factors. The demise of Southern cotton production, the abandonment of the sharecropping system, and the obstacles placed in front of blacks who attempted to either purchase or rent viable farm land all led to the so-called Northern Migration — the exodus of so many African-Americans from Southern farms. By the time the exodus ended, countless black family farms had been lost; the ones that remained were often in precarious shape, teetering along on the brink of extinction.

The elements posed a constant threat, as they did to all farmers, but because black family farms were generally smaller than white-owned farms, even a modest amount of poor weather could do extensive damage. Similarly, by the 1960s and 1970s black farmers as a group had grown older than their white counterparts and received less formal education; as a result, they were vulnerable to younger, better educated whites looking to expand their own holdings by any means, even those that fell just marginally within the law. Finally, because African-American farmers often had only modest capital to invest in their farms, sold less than their white counterparts, concentrated primarily in tobacco and cotton crops, and diversified slowly into livestock and poultry operations, they continued to find themselves at a disadvantage in the marketplace in the last half of the twentieth century.

In the end, however, what distinguished the struggles of black family farms from those of small farms owned and operated by white families was racial bias, which made it consistently harder for African-American farmers to acquire training in farm management and, most important, to secure equal access to loans and other forms of financial assistance. In the absence of such assistance, many black family farmers had no resources to defend themselves against the economic forces that drove small farms out of business and, according to Ralph Paige, president of the Federation of Southern Cooperatives/Land Assistance Fund, replaced them with massive agribusiness operations. "This isn't just another black farmer going out of business," Paige has commented in response to the decline of one black-owned farm or another. "It is our community losing a piece of the country."

By 1960, according to a 1992 article in the *New York Times,* 11 percent of Americans owning farms were black, which is roughly the same proportion of blacks in the general population; and while the number of Americans who worked as farmers fell steadily in the next few decades, the number of black farmers plummeted to 1.5 percent in 1990, or about sixty-nine thousand of the nation's farmers. The handwriting had long been on the wall, however. In 1982 the U.S. Commission on Civil Rights found that farm displacement and land loss among black farmers was two and a half times the rate of that among white farmers. Predicting that the rate of attrition would remain unchanged, commission officials reported to the *New York Times* that "there will be virtually no blacks operating farms in this country by the year 2000."

Perhaps the only thing that has kept the commission's prediction from coming to pass is the determination of black farmers themselves. They have been up against incredible odds, including a chronic lack of response from the government in general and the U.S. Department of Agriculture (USDA) in particular. Indeed, according to Paige, the prediction that black farms would become extinct in 2000 was something of a "self-fulfilling prophecy on the part of the government," because no action was immediately taken to interrupt the black farmer's slide into extinction. For this reason, in increasing numbers, black farmers began to take matters into their own hands. Their actions were often coordinated under the auspices of one of several important organizations, including the Coordinating Council of Black Farm Groups, a council of black farmers' organizations that serves to build unity and to coordinate issues relevant to black farmers; the Land Loss Prevention Program, a nonprofit, public interest law firm created by the North Carolina Association of Black Lawyers to use legal expertise, community education, and advocacy skills to help landowners who face legal, economic, and environmental challenges; or the Federation of Southern Cooperatives/Land Assistance Fund, which offers technical assistance to small farmers, most of whom are black.

The activities of these groups and the individuals they serve have often been tireless. In February 1980, for example, a group called North Carolina Black Farmers filed a discrimination suit against the Farmers Home Administration, which administered loans to farmers who could not get them elsewhere. Pointing out in their suit that most decisions about such loans were made by predominantly white committees of local farmers – many of whom allowed racial bias to influence their decisions – the North Carolina Black Farmers attracted the attention of the Office of Equal Opportunity's Compliance Branch, which conducted a special investigation to determine the validity of the allegations. Writing in the *New Pittsburgh Courier,* journalist Raynicka Wilder covered the proceedings: "The investigations found discrepancies in the real estate appraisal of farmland owned by African Americans. According to the findings, African Americans did not receive deferred loan payment schedules. They were also required to agree to voluntary liquidation of their property should they default on their loans. Disparities were also found in the number and amount of emergency loans made to African Americans."

Because none of these findings were reported to the complainants, they filed another lawsuit the following year, and eventually their efforts were integrated into an even larger series of events, one that began to gain momentum in the early 1990s. First, there was the appointment – and subsequent resignation – of Mike Espy, the twenty-fifth U.S. Agricultural Secretary, the first African-American to hold that position. Described as a "workhorse" member of the Clinton Cabinet, Espy, the son of a Tuskegee Institute–trained federal farm agent, was perceived by black farmers as a godsend. During the Reagan and Bush administrations of the 1980s, efforts to dismantle the social welfare programs that had been created in the days of the New Deal had been especially hard on black farmers, and the neglect of small farmers in general by the Republican Party had been long and severe. Espy immediately began to reverse this tide by dispensing money to community-based groups in the rural South and developing long-term programming to serve small, minority, or otherwise disadvantaged family farmers. This was great news not only to many rural and civil rights groups but also to women's groups, because women had recently started to represent a growing proportion of black and other minority farmers.

In October 1994, however, Espy became the target of a criminal investigation. He was charged with relaxing poultry regulations and providing other favors for Tyson Foods. The company had provided football game tickets, lodging, and a plane ride for Espy and his girlfriend, Pat Dempsey. (Espy had reimbursed the company for the costs, however.) Many critics saw in the charges a politically motivated effort to further discredit the Clinton administration; others felt it was a vindictive attempt by the meat industry to punish Espy for ordering new labeling requirements and stepping up inspections of both meat and poultry plants. In any event, when Espy resigned on December 31, 1994, he took with him the hopes of black farmers who had believed that someone in the nation's capital was finally on their side, looking out for their interests. To this day, Espy has never been convicted of any wrongdoing, and no other African-American has achieved as influential a position in the administration of U.S. agricultural policy.

During this time black farmers continued to see their numbers drop. Between 1982 and 1992, for example, the number of all farmers decreased by 14 percent, but the number of black farmers dropped by 43 percent — from 33,250 to 18,816. It was almost as if a clock was ticking, counting off the hours until black farmers would finally be extinct. Those who managed to remain farming fought even harder against what seemed an inevitable end. By December 1997, African-American farmers from Louisiana, Mississippi, North Carolina, Texas, and Virginia marched in front of the USDA to protest loss of farms and farmlands as well as the agency's policies. "This event will bring national attention to the rights of denied black farmers in this country," said John W. Boyd, president of the National Black Farmers Association (NBFA). "The department [USDA] has acknowledged discrimination, but they have not paid anyone to compensate for it. They have not settled any of the cases."

Also in 1997, a number of African-American farmers consolidated their claims of racial discrimination in farm lending and benefit programs into one class-action suit against the USDA, *Pigford v. Glickman.* The class is defined as all African-Americans who farmed, or attempted to farm, between January 1, 1981, and December 31, 1996, applied to the USDA during that time for participation in a federal farm credit or benefit program, and believed they were discriminated against on the basis of race in the USDA's response to that application. Discrimination complaints had to be filed on or before July 1, 1997, regarding USDA's treatment of the farmer's credit or benefit application. Despite the rigid parameters of these dates, however, the suit in many ways asked the USDA to make a symbolic gesture toward all African-American farmers who had been denied by local and federal officials a fair share of the pie that white farmers had enjoyed for so long.

In late 1998, Agricultural Secretary Daniel Glickman and the USDA settled with plaintiffs in the multimillion-dollar case, which alleged that the department regularly denied loans and other help to black farmers. For many it was a joyous day – a day in which the sins of the past were finally acknowledged and the playing field could be made more level at last. According to J. L. Chestnut, the lead attorney in the class-action lawsuit, too many black farmers – about 40 percent – were denied compensation in the federal settlement, however. "The fight is not over," said Chestnut, a refrain that has become increasingly familiar to black farmers.

The fight is not over. Under the settlement farmers who can show evidence of discrimination are entitled to $50,000 each and to have outstanding loans forgiven. About eighteen thousand farmers filed claims under the settlement, and checks began being issued in November 1999. But Chestnut said that more than 40 percent of the claims had been rejected. To farmers who waited so long to escape from under the weight of debt and racial bias, the slowness of the process was disheartening.

"The only thing you can credit the Agriculture Department for is . . . the fact that they admitted something happened and had the guts to look at this," said NBFA president Boyd. "That's the only progress we've made."

The fight is not over. According to a report filed in spring 2000 by the USDA, about eighteen thousand farmers filed claims under the settlement. Although many cases remain pending, many more have been approved and payments of $50,000 awarded to each of the proper recipients. "From hiring practices to program outreach to accountability and disciplinary action, we have taken strong steps to ensure that all USDA employees and customers are treated with the fairness, dignity, and respect that they deserve," wrote Agriculture Secretary Glickman in the report's preface.

The deepest wounds, however, are often the slowest to heal. African-American farmers are slowly recovering from a long and painful history, but what lies ahead may well be the fulfillment of the desire they have held for a long time – a desire to build something enduring for their families, even if they have to build it one acre at a time.

1. Hoe culture, Eutaw, Alabama, July 1936. U.S. Department of Agriculture, Farm Security Administration. *Photograph by Dorothea Lange.*
2. Tenant farmer LeRoy Dunn, White Plains, Georgia, June 1941. U.S. Department of Agriculture, Farm Security Administration. *Photograph by Jack Delano.*
3. Fred H. Mathis, farmer, (Charlene Gilbert's grandfather) displaying his goods at the Macon County Fairgrounds, Montezuma, Georgia, c. 1954.
4. A Flint River Farms family and their wagon, near Montezuma, Georgia, May 1939. FSA-OWI Collection. *Photograph by Marion Post Wolcott.*
5. Farmer holding infant, c. 1939. Library of Congress.
6. Woman hoeing cotton, Mississippi, June 1937. *Photograph by Dorothea Lange.*
7. Man in front of chicken house, Thomasville, Georgia, c. 1905. Georgia Department of Archives and History.
8. Community cotton gin owned and operated by African-Americans, Hadison County, Alabama, c. 1940. U.S. Department of Agriculture.
9. Woman sorting tobacco on porch, Douglas, Georgia, July 1938. U.S. Department of Agriculture, Farm Security Administration. *Photograph by Dorothea Lange.*
10. Descendants of former slaves of the Pettway Plantation, Gee's Bend,

Alabama, February 1937. U.S. Department of Agriculture, Farm Security Administration. *Photograph by Arthur Rothstein.*

11. Hands of Henry Brooks, former Georgia slave, Greene County, 1941. Library of Congress. *Photograph by Jack Delano.*

12. Agricultural workers waiting to leave Belcross, North Carolina, for Onley, Virginia, July 1940. FSA-OWI Collection. *Photograph by Jack Delano.*

13. African-American sharecropper and his wife, Pulaski County, Arkansas, October 1935. U.S. Department of Agriculture, Farm Security Administration. *Photograph by Ben Shahn.*

14. St. Landry Small Farmers' School, March 1969. Amistad Research Center, Ronnie Moore Collection, Tulane University.

15. A meeting of Farm Security Administration borrowers held in a church, Woodville, Georgia, May 1941. U.S. Department of Agriculture, Farm Security Administration. *Photograph by Jack Delano.*

16. African-American farmer dissatisfied with the offering price, taking his samples to another buyer, Clarksdale, Mississippi, November 1939. U.S. Department of Agriculture, Farm Security Administration. *Photograph by Marion Post Wolcott.*

17. Children dumping cotton, Troup County, Georgia, 1939.

18. Women planting corn, Moncks Corner, South Carolina, March 1941. U.S. Department of Agriculture, Farm Security Administration. *Photograph by Jack Delano.*

19. Woman and children taking a rest from hoeing cotton on the Allen Plantation, a Farm Security Administration cooperative, Natchitoches, Louisiana, July 1940. U.S. Department of Agriculture, Farm Security Administration. *Photograph by Marion Post Wolcott.*

20. Cotton porter, Savannah, Georgia, c. 1900. Leib Image Archives.

21. Mississippi flood refugees waiting for boat, April 17, 1897. Library of Congress Prints & Photographs Collection. *Photograph by Carroll's Art Gallery.*

22. Farmer, White Plains, Georgia, June 1941. FSA-OWI Collection. *Photograph by Jack Delano.*

23. Agricultural worker holding the handles of a cultivator on the Allen Plantation, a Farm Security Administration cooperative, Natchitoches, Louisiana, August 1940. FSA-OWI Collection. *Photograph by Marion Post Wolcott.*

24. Men loading furniture, c. 1939. Library of Congress. U.S. Department of Agriculture, Farm Security Administration. *Photograph by Arthur Rothstein.*

25. Field workers at the Bayou Bourbeaux Plantation, a Farm Security Administration cooperative, Natchitoches, Louisiana, August 1940. U.S. Department of Agriculture, Farm Security Administration. *Photograph by Marion Post Wolcott.*

26. Civil rights worker Carol Prejean attempts to register an Alabama farmer to vote, c. 1960. Amistad Research Center, Tulane University.

27. Lake Dick Arkansas (a Farm Security Administration project, Phillips County), September 1938. U.S. Department of Agriculture, Farm Security Administration. *Photograph by Russell Lee.*

28. Men working in brickyard, Macon County, Georgia. The Harriet Tubman Museum.

29. Man next to bale of cotton, probably in Alabama, c. 1960. Amistad Research Center, Tulane University.

30. Warren James (Charlene Gilbert's cousin), kneeling on his land, Montezuma, Georgia, 1997. *Photograph by Marcel Reedus.*

31. A. B. Brown (Charlene Gilbert's great-uncle), a sharecropper in the 1930s, Montezuma, Georgia. *Photograph by Vickie A. Smith.*

BIBLIOGRAPHY

"AFRICAN American Farmers Organize against 'Freedom to Farm' Bill."
   In Motion: An Online Publication about Democracy. (March 1996). Available on-line
   at http://www.inmotionmagazine.com/paige.html.
BANKS, Vera J. *Rural Development Research Report No. 59: Black Farmers and Their
   Farms.* Washington, D.C.: U.S. Department of Agriculture, 1986.
BENNETT, Lerone, Jr. *Before the Mayflower: A History of Black America.* 5th ed.
   Chicago: Johnson Publishing Company, 1982.
BERRY, Mary Frances, and John W. Blassingame. *Long Memory: The Black
   Experience in America.* New York: Oxford University Press, 1982.
BILLINGSLEY, Andrew. *Climbing Jacob's Ladder: The Enduring Legacy of African
   American Families.* New York: Simon & Schuster, 1992.
"BLACK Farmers Being Denied Claims." National Brief. *Charlotte Observer,*
   14 February 2000, p. 6A.
BRADLEY, David, and Shelley Fisher Fishkin, eds. *The Encyclopedia of Civil Rights in
   America.* Armonk, N.Y.: Sharpe Reference, 1998.
BRASHER, Philip. "Black Farmers Say USDA Isn't Doing Enough on Civil Rights."
   [Columbia, S.C.] *The State,* 16 April 2000, p. A4.
BROWNE, Robert S., et al. *Only Six Million Acres: The Decline of Black-Owned Land in*

the *Rural South.* Atlanta, Ga.: Black Economic Research Center and Rockefeller Bros. Fund, 1973.

COTTON, Barbara. *The 1890 Land-Grant Colleges: A Centennial Review.* Washington, D.C.: Agricultural History Society, 1992.

COWAN, Tom, and Jack Maguire, eds. *Timelines of African-American History: Five Hundred Years of Black Achievement.* New York: Berkeley Publishing Group, 1994.

DANIEL, Pete. *Breaking the Land: The Transformation of Cotton, Tobacco, and Rice Culture since 1880.* Urbana: University of Illinois Press, 1985.

————. *Standing at the Crossroads: Southern Life since 1900.* New York: Hill and Wang, 1986.

DRNFELD, Margaret. *The Turning Tide, 1948–1956: From the Desegregation of the Armed Forces to the Montgomery Bus Boycott.* New York: Chelsea House Publishers, 1995.

EGERTON, John. *Speak Now against the Day: The Generation before the Civil Rights Movement in the South.* New York: Alfred A. Knopf, 1994.

FLYNN, Charles L., Jr. *White Land, Black Labor: Caste and Class in Late Nineteenth-Century Georgia.* Baton Rouge: Louisiana State University Press, 1983.

FOSTER, William Z. *The Negro People in American History.* 3d ed. New York: International Publishers, 1973.

FRANKLIN, John Hope. *From Slavery to Freedom: A History of the American Negro.* 3d ed. New York: Alfred A. Knopf, 1967.

GRABER, C. Scott. "A Blight Hits Black Farmers: Cloud on the Title." *Civil Rights Digest* 10 (1978): 21–30.

GRANT, Donald L. *The Way It Was in the South: The Black Experience in Georgia.* New York: Birch Lane Press, 1993.

HALL, Robert L., and Carol B. Stack, eds. *Holding on to the Land and the Lord: Kinship, Ritual, Land Tenure, and Social Policy in the Rural South.* Athens: University of Georgia Press, 1982.

HARDING, Vincent. *There Is a River: The Black Struggle for Freedom in America.* New York: Vintage Books, 1983.

HARLAN, Louis R. *Booker T. Washington: The Making of a Black Leader, 1856–1901.* New York: Oxford University Press, 1972.

HINE, Darlene Clark, William C. Hine, and Stanley Harrold, eds. *The African-American Odyssey.* Upper Saddle River, N.J.: Prentice Hall, 2000.

HOLMES, William F. "The Demise of the Colored Farmers' Alliance." *Journal of Southern History* 41 (2): 187–200.

INSCOE, John C. *Georgia in Black and White: Explorations in the Race Relations of a Southern State, 1865–1950*. Athens: University of Georgia Press, 1994.

JACKSON, Bernice Powell. "Congress' Threat to Black Farmers." *Oakland Post,* 6 December 1995, p. 4.

JAYNE, Gerald David. *Branches without Roots: Genesis of the Black Working Class in the American South, 1862–1882*. New York: Oxford University Press, 1986.

L'HEURRUX, Dave. "Black Farmers Awaiting Ruling on Settlement." *The State* [Columbia, S.C.], 14 October 1999, p. B6.

LOW, W. Augustus, and Virgil A. Clift, eds. *Encyclopedia of Black America.* New York: Da Capo Press, 1981.

MITCHELL, H. L. *Roll the Union On: A Pictorial History of the Southern Tenant Farmers' Union*. Chicago: Charles H. Kerr Publishing Company, 1987.

SACHS, Carolyn E. *The Invisible Farmers: Women in Agricultural Production*. Totowa, N.J.: Rowman and Allanheld, 1983.

SCHULTZ, Mark Roman. "A More Satisfying Life of the Farm: Benjamin F. Hubert and the Long Cabin Community." Ph.D. diss., University of Georgia, 1987.

SEALS, R. Grant. "The Formation of Agricultural and Rural Development Policy in the United States with Emphasis on African Americans: The Hatch-George and Smith Lever Acts." *Agricultural History* 65 (spring 1991): 12–34.

SHANNON, Sandra G. *The Dramatic Vision of August Wilson*. Washington, D.C.: Howard University Press, 1995.

SMOTHERS, Ronald. "For Black Farmers, Extinction Seems To Be Near." *New York Times,* 3 August 1992, p. 24.

THOMPSON, Clara Mildred. *Reconstruction in Georgia: Economic, Social, Political, 1865–1872*. New York: Books for Libraries Press, 1971.

WEISBROT, Robert. *Marching toward Freedom, 1957–1965: From the Founding of the Southern Christian Leadership Conference to the Assassination of Malcolm X*. New York: Chelsea Publishers, 1994.

WILDER, Raynicka. "Black Farmers on Verge of Extinction." *New Pittsburgh Courier,* 29 January 1997, p. A5.

WILKINS, Roy, with Tom Matthews. *Standing Fast: The Autobiography of Roy Wilkins*. New York: Viking Press, 1982.

WILLIAMS, Michael W., ed. *The African-American Encyclopedia*. New York: Marshall Cavendish Corporation, 1993.

ZABAWA, Robert. "The Black Farmer and the Land in South Central Alabama, from 1818 to the New Deal: Strategies to Preserve a Scarce Resource." *Human Ecology* 19 (March 1991): 61–81.

ACKNOWLEDGMENTS

Many thanks to everyone who lent their love, support, and guidance to this project. In particular, we thank our mothers — Earlene Gilbert and Connie Eli — as well as Barbara Neely, David Bradley, Leah Williamson, Sonia Malfa, Bob Stern, Theresa Tensuan, Rob Claus, and Amy Smith Bell. A special joint shout-out to Deb Chasman: Thanks for your patience!

We would also like to thank Furthermore for its support of the book, and the following funders for their support of *Homecoming,* the documentary film project: the Independent Television Service, the National Black Programming Consortium, the Soros Documentary Fund, the Waterman Fund of the Philadelphia Foundation, the Funding Exchange/Paul Robeson Fund, the Pennsylvania Humanities Council, and the Mid-Atlantic Arts Foundation.

loathing/inferiority feelings of, 80, 133, 136; stereotyped, 32, 59, 69, 79–80, 108; value of life (white perception of, 151; violence toward, *see* violence, racially related; in World Wars I & II, 71, 108–116, 117. *See also* African-American body politic; slavery

African-American Encyclopedia (Williams, ed.), 111, 151

African-American Odyssey, The (Hines), 29

African Methodist Episcopal (AME) church, 57, 58, 59, 79

Agricultural Adjustment Administration (AAA), 96–97, 98, 101, 102

agriculture: depression in (early 1900s), 32; technology and, 135, 136. *See also* family farm; landownership, black; sharecropping; tenant farmers

Agriculture, U.S. Department of (USDA), 78, 147, 154, 158, 163, 164–167; formation of, 148–149

Alabama Supreme Court, 88

Alliance movement, 37–40, 44, 87, 99, 102. *See also* cooperative groups

Annie Allen (Brooks), 130

apartheid, U.S., 140. *See also* segregation

Armed Forces, U.S., 108–111, 117, 123, 131–132, 139

Army, U.S., 109, 110–111, 139; first black chaplain, 58

Atlanta Compromise address (1895), 53–54, 58

Atlanta Constitution, 125

Atlanta University, 43, 125

atomic bomb, 112

Back to Africa movement, 11, 57–60, 63. *See also* migration from South

bank failures, 77, 79–81

Baptist Church, 145

Before the Mayflower: A History of Black Americans (Bennett), 11, 12, 28, 56, 89, 116–117

Bender, William, 125

Bennett, Lerone, Jr., 11, 27, 28, 56, 89, 116

Bethune, Mary McLeod, 94

Bethune-Cookman College, 94

Black Cabinet (of FDR), 94

Black Economic Development Conference, 154

Black Economic Research Center, 155

income) 95; farmers' alliances and cooperatives in, 39, 40; FDR and, 93; Four Points crossroad, 35–36; Freedmen's Bureau of, 20, 58; Ku Klux Klan in, 37; lynchings in, 135; migration from, 10, 71–73, 78, 121; Native Americans in, 23–24; segregation in, 64, 67; sharecropping in, 29–32, 101; Sherman's march through, 14; slavery in, 78, (post–Civil War) 16, 26; state policies toward blacks, 69–70, 95; and voting rights, 58, 124–126, 130, 146, 153. See also *Way It Was in the South, The: The Black Experience in Georgia* (Grant)

Georgia Merit Farmer, 91

Georgia State Industrial College, 43

Gilbert, Charles Wesley (father), 121

Gilbert, Mrs. Charles (Earlene Mathis, mother), 63, 91–92, 105–106, 121–122, 139. *See also* Mathis family

Glickman, Daniel, 166, 167

Goodman, Andrew, 152–153

Graber, C. Scott, 156

Grange, the, 38, 42, 46

Grant, Donald L., 86, 95–99 *passim,* 109, 113, 124–126 *passim,* 135, 136, 145, 156

Great Depression (1930s), 73, 76–82, 94, 107–108, 109; ends, 114, 115; farm ownership during, 97–98, 119; and party switch, 83–84, 89; tenant farmers during, 85, 96–99; unemployment during, 84, 99, 109; wages during, 75, 76, 101, 112, (NRA and) 95

Green v. County School Board (*"Brown II"*), 134

Greensboro, North Carolina, sit-in, 143

Haiti, consulate appointments to, 83

Hamer, Fannie Lou, 154

Hardin, Clifford, 149

Harding, Vincent, 154

Harlan, John Marshall, 67

Harlan, Louis R., 52, 59

Harlem riot (1943), 112

Harrison, Leon, and Harrison Chapel, 36

Haugebrook, Alice. *See* Mathis, William and Alice

Hayes, Rutherford B., 66

Henderson v. United States, 131

Hines, Darlene Clark, 29

Hitler, Adolf, 108

Homecoming (documentary film), 3–4, 155

Hoover, Herbert, 81–83, 85, 89, 93, 97

Housing Authority, U.S., 111

Houston, Reverend Ulysses L., 19

Hubert, Benjamin Franklin and Zachary Taylor, 43

Hubert brothers (Zach, Floyd, and David), 41–43, 44, 45, 46

inferiority, feelings of, 80, 133, 136

integrationist policies, 10; accommodationism, 53–54, 56–57, 58–59; desegregation, *see* segregation; Du Bois, 51–57, 60; Eisenhower, 132, (Senate opposes) 142; Supreme Court, 131, 132–135; Truman, 116–117, 132

Interior, U.S. Department of the, 148

International Labor Defense, 88

Jackson, Deal, 43

Jackson, Reverend Joseph H., 145

Jacksonville, Florida, sit-in, 141, 143

James, Leroy, Sr., 3

Japanese-Americans, 111–112

Jim Crow laws, 66–67, 68, 71, 123. *See also* segregation

Johnson, Andrew, 19, 21, 27, 29

Johnson, Jack, 67

Johnson, Lyndon B., 147–148, 150–151, 152

Justice Department, U.S., 111, 142

Kennedy, John F., 147, 150

King, Martin Luther, Jr., 75, 121–122, 123, 136, 145, 151; SCLC of, 149–150, 152

Korean War, 131, 132

Ku Klux Klan, 26–27, 37, 66, 126, 147, 153

labor, 49; "Black Codes" regulating, 19–20, 23, 65; cheap, 27, 65, 69, 98, (loss of) 26, 113; Chinese, 70; Executive Order 8802 and FEPC and, 109, 115, 116–117; labor contracts, 20, 28–29; labor unions, 87, 102, 116; migration of, 31, 47, 68, 69, 71–73, 75–76, 118, 119, (and labor shortage) 32, 70, 77, 78, 84, (World War II) 112–113; options increase, 47, 56; Southern recognition of value of, 73; strikes, 87; technology and, 118–119, 136; unemployment, 113, 119, (during Depression) 84, 99, 109; wages, 31, 68, 70, 72, 126, (Depression era) 75, 76, 101, 112, (under NRA)

95, (unpaid) 20, 29, 97, (World War
II) 113. *See also* sharecropping

Land Assistance Fund. *See* Federation
of Southern Cooperatives/Land
Assistance Fund

land grants, 149; promised, denied, *see*
landownership, black

Land Loss Prevention Program, 163

Land Office, U.S., 13

landownership, black: in African-
American culture, 107, 113, (sym-
bolism of farming) 117–118; as civil
right, 129–130; Congress and, 149;
declines, 102–103, 114, 135, 137,
146, 149, 154, 161–165, (property
recovered) 99–101, 154–156; during Depression, 97–98, 119; Du
Bois–Washington debate over, 51–
57; first free black landowners, 36,
37, 41–46 (*see also* family farm); in
Georgia, *see* Georgia; as inheritance,
20, 31, 91, 137, 155, 156–157;
land auctions, 135, 154; land confiscated by Union Army, 16; land
grants promised, denied, 6, 13, 18–
19, 46, 148; in 1910 and 1913, 37,
43, 68; as political issue, 123, 153–
154; power of, 146; as racial issue,
16, 32, 38, 40, 149, 162; Resettlement program, 91, 99, 100, 135;

sharecropping *v.*, *see* sharecropping;
Sherman and, 14–15, 17, 18–19,
21, 46; by slaves, 15, 43; Southern
promotion of, 72; successful, 43,
(elements in) 44–46, 72; suggested
by Thaddeus Stevens (40 acres and a
mule), 12, 17, 46, 148; Supreme
Court decision on homebuying,
107; tax sales and, 154, 155, 156;
tenant farming, *see* tenant farmers;
Tenant Purchase Program, 99;
whites reclaim land, 68; white
supremacists and, 16, 45, 101, 135

Langston University, 43

leadership, black, Du Bois–
Washington debate on, 55–56

Leibowitz, Samuel, 88

Liberia, 99

Liberty County (Georgia), 15

Lincoln, Abraham, 10–11, 19, 58, 92;
Party of, 81–82, 89, 92

living conditions. *See* economic conditions; family farm

Locke, John, 129

Louisiana State University, 131

Low, W. Augustus, 81

Lynch, Reverend James, 16

lynchings, 69, 102; condemned, 72,
(by Communist Party) 86–87; fear
of, 75, 84; government interven-

"crime," 135; membership grows, 116; violence against, 124

National Baptist Convention, 145

National Black Farmers Association (NBFA), 165, 167

National Farmers' Alliance, 38–39, 40, 46

National Industrial Recovery Act (NIRA), 94–95, 96

National Negro Business League, 56

National Race Commission proposal (dismissed), 83

National Recovery Administration (NRA), 95

Native Americans, 23–24

Native Son (Wright), 107

Navy, U.S., 109. *See also* Armed Forces, U.S.

Nazis, the, 110

New Deal, 89, 94–97, 99–102, 108, 114, 147; programs dismantled, 115, 164; Resettlement Admin-istration (RA), 91, 99, 100, 135

New Pittsburgh Courier, 164

New York Times, 154, 162–163

Night Riders, 101, 107. *See also* Ku Klux Klan

Nobel Prize, 130

North Carolina Association of Black Lawyers, 163

North Carolina Black Farmers, 163–164

Office of Equal Opportunity, Compli-ance Branch of, 164

Only Six Million Acres: The Decline of Black-Owned Land in the Rural South (Task Force report), 154

Paige, Ralph, 141, 145, 162, 163

Patent Office, U.S., 148

Patrons of Husbandry. *See* Grange, the

Phillip Primitive Baptist Church, 35

Pigford v. Glickman, 166

Plessy, Homer, 66

Plessy v. Ferguson (1896), 66–67, 132–133

poll taxes. *See* voting rights

population, black: in armed forces, 108, 111; farming, decline in, 102–103, 114, 135, 137, 146, 149, 161–162; migrant, 71, 78, 118; outside South, 143; remaining in South, 78, 143; voting, 107, 125, 146. *See also* migration from South

Postal Service, U.S., 107

Powell, Bartow F., 43–44